About this book

In an increasingly integrated, globalised world with new cross-border threats to health, widening disparities in both health and access to health care, and an unacceptable level of human suffering and premature mortality in developing countries, civil society actors are asking, why is so little progress being made by global health actors?

Like its critically acclaimed predecessor, the second edition of *Global Health Watch* covers a comprehensive range of topics, including access to medicines, mental health, water and sanitation, nutrition, and war and conflict.

Unlike other reports on global health, it also draws attention to the politics of global health and the policies and actions of key actors. *Global Health Watch 2* includes chapters on the United States foreign assistance programme, the Gates Foundation, the World Bank, the World Health Organization and the Global Fund to Fight AIDS, Tuberculosis and Malaria.

Global Health Watch 2 is not only an educational resource for health professionals and activists, it also makes clear the need for global health advocates to engage in lobbying key actors to do better and to do more, whilst resisting those that do harm.

More praise for Global Health Watch 2

'For everyone who remains disappointed by the inability of the many global accounts of health and disease to address the fundamental causes of global ill-health and premature death, this is the alternative. *GHW2* looks fearlessly and truthfully at issues which daily occupy the minds of thinking health professionals: reversing poverty, eliminating inequities, tackling environmental change and dealing directly with the delivery of effective health and social services.... *GHW2* focuses on realisable solutions to each of these problems.'

Hoosen M. 'Jerry' Coovadia, Victor Daitz professor of HIV/AIDS research, University of KwaZulu–Natal, Durban

'An incisive socio-political critique of contemporary global health issues which focuses on determinants rather than diseases, enables the reader to unravel the complexity of global economic governance of health, and helps us understand why appalling health inequities persist across and within nations – a must-read for anyone involved or interested in public health.'

K. Srinath Reddy, president, Public Health Foundation of India

'*Global Health Watch 2* is insightful and provocative. It goes beyond the traditional health sector. It discusses economic, social and political preconditions for improving health for all. It does not shy away from highlighting the relation between the health of poor and marginalised people with the wealth appropriated by richer people, who have access to political power. In this sense, it is a true developmental report. The facts presented are a reason for great concern. They call for action.'

Jan Pronk, professor of theory and practice of international development, Institute of Social Studies, The Hague

Global Health Watch 2

An alternative world health report

People's Health Movement
CAIRO

Medact
LONDON

Global Equity Gauge Alliance
DURBAN

Zed Books
LONDON & NEW YORK

Global Health Watch 2: An Alternative World Health Report was first published in 2008 by Zed Books Ltd, 7 Cynthia Street, London N1 9JF, UK and Room 400, 175 Fifth Avenue, New York, NY 10010, USA

www.zedbooks.co.uk

Designed and typeset by illuminati, Grosmont, www.illuminatibooks.co.uk
Cover designed by Andrew Corbett
Printed and bound in the UK by CPI Antony Rowe, Chippenham, Wiltshire

Distributed in the USA exclusively by Palgrave Macmillan, a division of St Martin's Press, LLC, 175 Fifth Avenue, New York, NY 10010

A catalogue record for this book is available from the British Library
Library of Congress Cataloging in Publication Data available

ISBN   978 1 84813 034 0 Hb
ISBN   978 1 84813 035 7 Pb

Contents

Tables, figures, boxes and images

Acknowledgements

A large number of individuals and organisations have contributed to this report in different ways and to different degrees. Outside of the small secretariat, individuals gave their time for free or, in a few instances, received small honoraria. Most people made contributions to only parts of the *Watch* and cannot therefore be held accountable for the whole volume. The views expressed in this report may not represent the opinions of everyone who has contributed. Ultimately, the *Watch* represents a collective endeavour of individuals and organisations who share a desire to improve the state of global health and to express their solidarity with the need to tackle the social and political injustice that lies behind poor health.

Without the support of funding agencies it would have been impossible to produce this second *Global Health Watch* and we would like to express our grateful thanks to the International Development Research Centre (www.idrc.ca), Research Matters (www.idrc.ca/research-matters), Medicos (www.medico-international.de) and the Swedish International Development Agency (www.sida.se). The views expressed in the *Watch* are not necessarily those of the funding agencies.

The Global Equity Gauge Alliance (www.gega.org.za), Medact (www.medact.org) and the People's Health Movement (www.phmovement.org) contributed their time, resources and expertise to both the development of the *Watch* and the planning and organisation of associated advocacy activities.

The secretariat would like to express their deep gratitude to Tamsine O'Riordan, Julian Hosie and Daniele Och at Zed Books for their efficiency and patience in assisting us in developing this edition of the *Watch*; to Lucy Morton, who project-managed the production; and to cover designer

Andrew Corbett. Thanks also to the Global Equity Gauge Alliance and Health Systems Trust, who housed the secretariat, in particular Ashnie Padarath (editing), Ronel Visser, Farana Khan and Halima Hoosen-Preston. Many people became involved in the organising of launch groups as well as in mobilising civil society around the launch and we appreciate the role they played in helping *GHW2* achieve its objectives. We also wish to thank Hani Serag and Azza Salam from the PHM Global Secretariat, who have supported us so well.

There are many others who have given generously of their time to assist and support the Global Health Watch. Without them the Global Health Watch would not be possible, and we thank you all.

A detailed list of contributors, researchers and peer reviewers, as well as organisations who have contributed to the production of the *Watch*, and photo credits, can be found at the back of the book.

Global Health Watch secretariat and editorial team
Emily Hansson, Bridget Lloyd, David McCoy,
Antoinette Ntuli, Ashnie Padarath, David Sanders

Foreword

Reports on the state of the world's health appear daily in the world's media. UN agencies, NGOs and academic institutions produce vast amounts of data, statistics and analysis. However, what is lacking is a critical and integrated assessment of both the state of global health and the policies and actions taken to reduce global health inequalities and unacceptable levels of ill-health.

Still too often the state of ill-health in many poor countries is framed as a problem of disease, geography, bad luck or poor government. Rarely is it properly framed as a symptom and outcome of political and economic choices, or the current form of globalisation which has created a deep chasm between a minority of 'winners' and a majority of 'losers', whilst simultaneously placing the world at the brink of environmental crisis.

Recent years, however, have seen a rise in interest in 'global health', prompted by the creation of the Millennium Development Goals. Development assistance for health has increased, the number of new global health initiatives has multiplied and the Gates Foundation has massively increased the amount of private financing for global health. But in spite of these developments, why is so little improvement being made?

The People's Health Movement, Medact and the Global Equity Gauge Alliance came together in 2003 to appraise critically the state of global health and to assess the performance and actions of certain key institutions such as the World Health Organization and UNICEF, donor agencies, high-income-country governments, the World Bank, multinational corporations, the International Monetary Fund and the World Trade Organization.

This resulted in *Global Health Watch 2005–2006*, an alternative world health report that highlighted the root causes of poor health and revealed the gap between humanitarian rhetoric and reality. It comprised 22 chapters covering a broad array of subjects on global health and development policy, produced from the contributions of more than 120 individuals and the support of approximately 70 organisations across the world.

GHW 1 was released in July 2005 at the second People's Health Assembly held in Cuenca, Ecuador. More than twenty-two official 'launches' of the report took place worldwide in more than sixteen countries.

A shorter summary and campaigning document *Global Health Action 2005–2006* was also produced and disseminated, and translated and printed in Spanish, French and Arabic. The *Watch* also stimulated the production of a Latin American Health Watch and a UK Health Watch. Two advocacy documents (on WHO and health systems) were developed and distributed at various forums and conferences.

The release of *Global Health Watch 2* coincides with the thirtieth anniversary of the Declaration of Alma Ata. To mark this anniversary, the WHO has released the 2008 *World Health Report* on the revitalisation of PHC. This year also sees the release of the report of the Commission on the Social Determinants of Health. We believe *GHW 2* is important reading to accompany the official world health report.

However, as with *GHW 1*, this report has limitations. Many key issues relevant to health have not been covered. With space constraints, a limited budget and a small secretariat, we were simply unable to cover everything. Some of the data and analyses are also out of date. For example, the crisis around rising food prices occurred after the book was finalised.

Nonetheless, this book covers a range of issues and provides an alternative perspective that is vital to help the world move beyond the currently inadequate approaches and interventions to ensure that all people have their basic and essential health needs met.

We hope that the Watch provides some small contribution to ensuring that politicians, governments, donor agencies, banks and multilateral institutions are kept honest and held accountable.

People's Health Movement
Medact
Global Equity Gauge Alliance

Introduction

Origins

The *Global Health Watch* comes out of one of the largest ever civil society mobilisations in health – the first People's Health Assembly, held in Savar, Bangladesh, in December 2000. Some 1,500 people from 75 nations attended and collectively drew up and endorsed a People's Health Charter. The Charter is a call for action on the root causes of ill-health and the lack of access to essential health care. It set the agenda for the People's Health Movement (PHM) (www.phmovement.org).

The first *Global Health Watch* (*GHW1*) took up the Charter's call for action and brought together health activists, health professionals and academics from around the world to contribute to an alternative world health report. *GHW1* and the Observatorio Latinoamericano de Salud (Latin American Health Watch) were launched at the second People's Health Assembly in Cuenca, Ecuador, in July 2005. Approximately 1,500 people from 83 countries attended this Assembly. In addition, the Assembly saw the birth of the International People's Health University and the global Right to Health Campaign.

Global Health Watch 2 (*GHW2*) has brought together another collection of activists, scientists and practitioners, and applies evidence, intellect and passion to critique both the state of global health and the inadequate global response to poor health and widening disparities. As with *GHW1*, it sets out an explicitly political understanding of the current state of health around the world, highlights poverty as the biggest epidemic the global public health community faces, and emphasises the importance of economic policy as a health issue. And, as before, it notes the impending and potentially cataclysmic effects of climate change. *GHW2* addresses several other underlying determinants of health: access to sanitation facilities, water and food; war and conflict; and the state of primary education.

GHW2 emphasises not just the health needs of poor and vulnerable people, but also their relationship with rich people and the powerful. Improving the situation of the world's poor cannot be achieved through aid or charity alone; profoundly unequal power relationships need to be tackled.

One tool for enabling progressive shifts in the imbalances of power and agency are declarations of human rights that include a right to household food security, essential health care and other provisions necessary for the requirements of human dignity. In today's world it is not just governments that have obligations and duties to fulfil; and neither are obligations and duties limited to fulfilling the rights of people living within national boundaries. Governments, multinational corporations and citizens have duties and obligations to people within and across national boundaries to achieve the universal attainment of human rights.

In light of the evidence that social, political and economic arrangements are failing to reduce adequately the current state of ill-health, poverty and inequity, a stronger mobilisation of civil society committed to the fulfilment of human rights is needed.

What we cover in GHW2

GHW2 has five sections. Section A, 'An Alternative Paradigm for Development', builds on GHW1's analysis of the globalised political economy and its impact on poverty and ill health. It outlines in brief how the current paradigm for development is fatally flawed and ineffective – it does not deliver on poverty reduction; it does not deliver on reducing greenhouse gas emissions; and it does not deliver on health. On the contrary, it is rigged in many ways to do the opposite. But what is significant about Section A is that it puts forward an alternative model of development that combines the twin aims of promoting development where it is needed whilst also addressing climate change, and thinks outside the parameters of mainstream economics.

Section B deals with health sector themes. As with GHW1, there is a strong emphasis on health systems. Chapter B1, 'Health Systems Advocacy', summarises the major arguments about health systems strengthening that were put forward in GHW1, and proposes a nine-point health systems strengthening agenda. The following chapter, B2, covers the limitations and deficiencies of Western models of mental health care, particularly when applied to Southern communities and in humanitarian emergencies where a lack of understanding of the prevailing social mores can result in external assistance being counterproductive and harmful.

Given the increasingly porous nature of national boundaries and the growing number of refugees and asylum-seekers arising from the effects of globalisation, war and climate change, the health of migrants is a critical public health issue. Chapter B3, on migrant health, documents the difficulties and secondary victimisation that migrants and displaced people experience in accessing quality health care, with a focus on their experiences within high-income countries.

Chapter B4 describes the state of health care for prisoners worldwide, and notes the scandalously high proportion of children and people with mental illnesses who have been misdirected to prison. Despite a plethora of international laws and agreements and standards about the treatment of prisoners, wide-scale human rights abuses occur across the globe. The chapter calls for an urgent need to incorporate prison health into public health policy and for the right to health to be recognised in prisons.

The final chapter in this section discusses new mechanisms for financing and incentivising pharmaceutical research and development (R&D). It describes how prize funds offer an alternative method for financing and rewarding the development of effective and affordable medicines, especially for neglected diseases. In addition, the chapter highlights the growing threat of antibiotic resistance. Initiatives to prevent and contain antibiotic resistance must be reframed in a more comprehensive way, and involve the realignment of incentives, the pooling of risks, resources and responses, and a re-engineering of the value chain of R&D.

None of the chapters in Section B deals specifically with HIV/AIDS, nor with TB, malaria or any other disease. Although the mortality and morbidity caused specifically by diseases are significant, the aim of *GHW2* is to examine the underlying determinants of disease, as well as the preconditions required by societies to protect themselves from diseases, and to be treated and cared for when they fall ill. Furthermore, disease-based analyses of global health problems are common and can reinforce the neglect of the social, political and economic solutions to poor health relative to biomedical and technological solutions.

Section C contains chapters related to issues that are 'Beyond Health Care', including carbon trading and climate change, war, food and globalisation, urbanisation, the sanitation and water crisis, oil extraction, humanitarian aid and education. Efforts to depoliticise climate change and restrict international action on reducing carbon emissions within a neoliberal framework are discussed in Chapter C1. It raises questions about the ethical and human rights implications of carbon trading.

Chapter C2, 'Terror, War and Health', notes the terrible human costs of war and conflict and describes the role of health advocates and researchers in monitoring the conduct and documenting the effects of war. It also discusses the definition of terrorism and its interface with health.

Chapter C3, 'Reflections on Globalisation, Trade, Food and Health', examines how the processes driving the integration of global food markets – specifically trade, foreign investment and the growth of transnational food companies – affect our health. It focuses on the growing phenomenon of diet-related illnesses, such as obesity and undernutrition, as well as food safety.

The rate of urbanisation over the past twenty years has been especially high in poor regions, characterised by a massive expansion of informal settlements and slum dwellings. Chapter C4 examines the associated health and environmental problems caused by rapid urbanisation.

The social and health consequences of the lack of water and sanitation, particularly for women and girls, are discussed in Chapter C5. It notes in particular the shameful neglect of sanitation as a public health issue by governments, donors and the international health community as a whole.

In many parts of the world, industry, often designed to support the consumption of the world's rich minority, has detrimental effects on the health of local people in developing countries. The extractive industries in particular have had a poor record of respecting people's rights and protecting the environment. Chapter C6, 'Oil Extraction and Health in the Niger Delta', illustrates this issue, revealing again the fundamentally political nature of development and health.

Chapter C7, 'Humanitarian Aid', considers the concepts and actors involved in humanitarian assistance, in particular the frequently underestimated role of local actors, and the role of the media. The inequalities that underlie disaster response, the commercialisation of humanitarian assistance and the co-option of humanitarian assistance for foreign policy objectives are additional issues discussed.

The final chapter in this section, C8, describes progress towards the attainment of education for all. The value of education as a 'social vaccine' against HIV/AIDS and the gendered nature of the lack of educational opportunities are also presented.

GHW2 is intended to be more than just a report on the state of global health. It is also a report on the performance of key actors related to global health. Section D, 'Holding to Account', includes an important chapter on the Gates Foundation. The Gates Foundation has arguably become *the* major player in the global health arena. The chapter attempts to stimulate a critical discussion about its work and about philanthropy more generally. It also examines the extent of its influence and its lack of accountability.

The chapter on the Gates Foundation is one of a cluster of chapters that reflect upon the global health landscape more generally as well as on other key actors, namely the World Bank, the WHO and the Global Fund to Fight AIDS, TB and Malaria. A reading of all these chapters suggests the existence of a vast, complex and self-serving global health aid industry. It is argued that this industry requires substantial downsizing and rationalisation; that the WHO needs to provide stronger leadership; that greater public accountability is required across the board; and that there needs to be a shift from top-down to bottom-up practices, where those affected by poverty, inequity and poor health have greater say.

Too little is being done by global actors and bilateral donors to get their own houses in order. This undermines low-income countries' ability to provide effective stewardship, and to develop a coherent agenda for the comprehensive development of their health systems. The inadequate global response to the world's health challenges is also a result of poor donor performance. There is still too little development assistance; too much of it is poorly provided; and too much of it is tied to the interests of donor countries. GHW2 questions the value and worth of bilateral donor aid, particularly in the context of a global political economy that maintains economic and political disparities between donor and recipient countries.

Chapter D2.1 describes and discusses the foreign assistance programme of the United States, particularly in relation to health. It describes a set of double standards and internal contradictions and reveals how the US aid machinery is increasingly being shaped to serve the strategic political and economic interests of the United States.

The growing common linkage of global health to global security, which is being driven by the United States and other actors, is a prominent development of the last few years. Chapter D2.3 discusses this issue in greater detail. It describes the potential advantages and disadvantages of such a linkage and calls on the health community to engage in a much more informed and rigorous debate about the issue. There are already strong signs of the HIV/AIDS sector being co-opted to serve foreign policy objectives, and of public health priorities being distorted by an overemphasis on biosecurity and infectious disease control.

It is not just global health institutions and governments that need to be watched. The corporate sector also needs to be watched, as is evident from the shameful behaviour of the oil companies. In Chapter D3.1 we discuss the history and role of commercial companies in promoting infant formula at the expense of breastfeeding. In spite of much progress having been made over the past few decades, the three case studies in this chapter illustrate the need to continue the struggle against unethical corporate practices that contribute to the alarmingly low rates of breastfeeding worldwide and unnecessary infant death and disease. Chapter D3.2 examines the tobacco industry and progress in implementation of the Framework Convention on Tobacco Control.

GHW2 ends with a chapter entitled 'Postscript: Resistance', which describes the ongoing resistance of people around the world against exploitation and subjugation. The struggle for health is a moral imperative, and, as *GHW* shows, is ultimately about unequal political and economic power. Even though it is often the most vulnerable communities that are in the forefront of this struggle, every one of us who is committed to the right to health as a basic human right can make an important contribution. We hope the issues raised and stories told in this *Global Health Watch* will be an inspiration to all those who read it.

A   An alternative paradigm for development

The current dominant model of development, based on market liberalisation and commercial globalisation, has conspicuously failed to deliver Health for All.[1] The rate of health improvement in low- and middle-income countries (LMICs) has slowed dramatically over the past thirty years, while we have been brought to the brink of imminent environmental disaster as a result of climate change. This chapter briefly assesses the performance of the current model against the three critical yardsticks of poverty, health and climate change; proposes basic principles for an alternative model of development; and provides an outline of one such alternative.

The ideas presented here are not definitive. They would require substantial modification for application according to the particular economic, social, geographical, political and cultural circumstances of any individual country. More importantly, this chapter is intended to demonstrate the possibility of visualising a model of development which can deliver more effectively on health and other social objectives, by thinking outside and beyond the parameters of mainstream economics and of historical precedents.

The current model of development

In very general terms, the key components of the currently dominant model of development in LMICs include small or zero budget deficits, tight monetary policies to keep inflation low, competitive exchange rates, the privatisation of state-owned enterprises and public services, the removal of measures to protect LMIC agriculture and industry, deregulation of markets and prices, and a limited role for the state.

This pro-market economic model, often termed neoliberalism, has only come to the fore in the last thirty years. Initially, after World War II, there was a strong consensus on the proactive management of the economy to ensure economic development and full employment, together with social security and universal access to health services and education. The counter-view, championed by Friedrich Hayek, presented the state-ensured collective guarantee of basic social needs as an anathema and equated unregulated markets with freedom. But this was widely seen as the untenable view of an extremist fringe.

However, Hayek's ideas began gradually to penetrate the political establishment, eroding older patrician sensibilities, and academic economics. Vital to this success were a tacit agreement among the proponents of neoliberalism to set aside differences on other issues and promote the central message that free markets provide the best outcomes – in a few key words, – liberalisation, deregulation and privatisation.

When poor economic performance followed the 1973 oil price crisis the neoliberals got their chance. They secured first the Republican nomination in the United States and leadership of the Conservative Party in the United Kingdom (UK) and then election victories in both countries. This led to the era of 'Reaganomics' – the high-water mark of neoliberalism. The US and UK governments included leading proponents of neoliberalism in senior positions, and were able to promote the model globally through the International Monetary Fund (IMF) and the World Bank. Through the course of the 1980s, with the support of the Fund and Bank, neoliberalism became the dominant economic paradigm globally – not least in most LMICs, which had previously followed more interventionist economic models.[2]

During this period, LMICs faced a multitude of major economic shocks, including massive increases in energy prices and interest rates, collapsing prices for commodity exports and the virtual drying up of most forms of external financing. In these circumstances, most LMICs, particularly in sub-Saharan Africa (SSA) and Latin America, had little choice but to accept the policy conditions dictated by the Fund and Bank, which came to be embodied as structural adjustment programmes (SAPs), on which most forms of financing were conditional.

Since the early 1990s, the model has been tempered by greater attention to social issues after the devastating human consequences of SAPs became apparent. Since 1999, adjustment programmes have also been replaced in low-income countries by Poverty Reduction Strategy Papers (PRSPs), which are supposed to be developed through a country-driven process with a high level of engagement by civil society.

In practice, however, PRSPs have been very variable in terms of country ownership and genuine engagement with civil society and have generally resulted in policies little different from SAPs. Attention to social issues has been largely confined to relatively limited 'safety net' programmes and only partial protection of health and education expenditure budgets within an essentially unchanged underlying economic model. The discretion available to national governments has been seriously constrained by macroeconomic parameters set by the IMF, including ceilings on government expenditure. In addition, the values embodied in SAPs have been internalised by low-income-country (LIC) governments and elites, leaving less and less room for alternative approaches.

The policy discretion available to countries has also been constrained by the fact that trade liberalisation policies and the governance of private property rights are now subject to international agreements brokered by the World Trade Organization (WTO) and bilateral trade and investment agreements with rich countries on which LMICs have become increasingly dependent.

While neoliberal policies were promoted to renew economic growth after the slowdown of the 1970s, they have generally failed to deliver on this promise. Economic performance has been disappointing in Latin America, and disastrous in sub-Saharan Africa and those 'transition economies' which have changed their policies towards the neoliberal approach. Those in greatest need have benefited little. The star performers economically, and important drivers of global economic growth, have been East Asian countries, especially China, which have mostly pursued different economic models.

The key challenges of the twenty-first century

Humanity faces three profound challenges:

- eradicating poverty;
- fulfilling the right of all people to good health;
- bringing climate change under control.

All three challenges incorporate problems that are rooted in the global political economy. The coexistence of profound social problems resulting from poverty and an equally extreme environmental crisis associated with excessive *aggregate* consumption can only be explained by a grossly unequal distribution of global resources. This raises fundamental questions about the appropriateness and viability of the model that has dominated economic policy at the global level, based on liberalisation and commercial globalisation.

Poverty

The World Bank estimates that 970 million people were living below the '$1-a-day' poverty line in 2004, and 2,550 million (40 per cent of the world

TABLE A1A   **Changes in global poverty, 1981–2004** (million people)

Poverty line	World				excluding China			
	1981	2004	Change		1981	2004	Change	
($/day)	(m)	(m)	(m)	(%)	(m)	(m)	(m)	(%)
1	1,470	970	−500	−34.0	836	841	5	0.1
2	2,450	2,550	100	4.1	1,576	2,096	520	33.0
2.80	2,640	3,240	600	22.7	1,691	2,649	958	56.6
3.90	2,920	3,810	890	30.5	1,962	3,051	1,090	55.6

TABLE A1B   **Changes in global poverty, 1981–2004** (% of population)

Poverty line ($/day)	World			excluding China		
	1981	2004	Change	1981	2004	Change
1	32.6	15.2	−17.4	23.8	16.6	−7.3
2	54.4	40.0	−14.4	44.9	41.3	−3.6
2.80	58.6	50.9	−7.8	48.2	52.2	4.0
3.90	64.9	59.8	−5.0	55.9	60.1	4.2

Source: Figures for $1 and $2 lines are from Chen and Ravallion 2007; those for $2.80 and $3.90 are from the World Bank's Povcalnet online database.[3]

population) below the '$2-a-day' line (Chen and Ravallion 2007). In addition to serious methodological problems with the Bank's calculations, these lines are essentially arbitrary, and do not reflect what might reasonably be considered a morally acceptable living standard.

Peter Edward (2006) has proposed an 'Ethical Poverty Line', defined as the income level below which further income losses materially shorten life expectancy. He estimates such a line at between $2.80 and $3.90 per person per day. By this definition, some 3.2–3.8 billion people (51–60 per cent of the world's population) live in poverty.[4]

Even using the Bank's calculations, there has been limited progress made in the last twenty-five to thirty years. While the number of people below the '$1-a-day' line fell between 1981 and 2004, this reduction occurred exclusively in China. The number below the '$2-a-day' line actually increased over the same period. The numbers below the 'Ethical

Poverty Line' increased considerably, by 22–30 per cent, resulting in a very limited fall in the proportion of the world's population in poverty by this definition. At this proportional rate of reduction, it would take 209 years to halve poverty based on the $3.90 line, and 116 years based on the $2.80 line. Excluding China, which has only partly conformed to the currently dominant economic model, the picture is considerably worse.

Health

Increases in life expectancy at birth globally averaged 10.4 months per annum (p.a.) in the 1960s, and 4.2 months p.a. in the 1970s, but slowed dramatically after 1982, and have averaged only 1.9 months p.a. since 1987. The slowdown has occurred almost entirely in LMICs, and there have been marked declines in some sub-Saharan and transition countries. As a result, the gap between average life expectancy at birth in low-income countries and in the OECD actually *widened* (by nine months) between 1985 and 2005.

The annual rate of reduction of the under-5 mortality rate for the world as a whole has also slowed progressively from 4.3 per 1,000 live births in the 1960s and 3.0 in the 1970s, to a trough of 0.5 in 1995–2000, partly recovering (to 2.5) only in 2000–2005.

Clearly the HIV/AIDS pandemic has contributed substantially to these trends. However, this is not a wholly exogenous factor, as the impacts of the current economic model on health services, poverty and other social determinants of health have almost certainly contributed to the spread of HIV/AIDS (de Vogli and Birbeck 2005). In this sense, AIDS is at least partly a transmission mechanism from economic policies to health outcomes, rather than purely a confounding variable.

Climate change

It is now generally accepted that a 60 per cent reduction in carbon emissions from their 1990 level is required by 2050 merely to limit the increase in global temperatures to 2°C (which would still result in serious consequences for poverty and health). However, emissions have actually continued to increase, by around 25 per cent, since 1990 (Marland et al. 2006), implying the need for a reduction of 68 per cent (2.6 per cent p.a.) between 2007 and 2050. If global economic growth continues at the post-1990 rate, this would increase global production and consumption by some 500 per cent; this means that carbon emissions *per (real) dollar of production* (carbon intensity) would need to fall by around 95 per cent by 2050.

The current rate of reduction in the carbon intensity of production (1.5 per cent p.a.) comes nowhere close to achieving this. If the current rate of

IMAGE AI   **ExxonMobil gas plant in the village of Finima, Nigeria**

reduction were to continue, global carbon emissions would not fall by 68 per cent by 2050, as required, but would triple. Achieving the necessary reduction in carbon emissions would require an *immediate* quadrupling of the rate of reduction in the carbon intensity of production from 1.5 per cent p.a. to 6 per cent p.a. This represents a huge challenge for humanity.

While there is a considerable level of technological optimism among some decision-makers, it is at best extremely doubtful whether existing and anticipated technologies can deliver the emissions reductions required in the necessary time frame.

Why the current model has failed

The current model of development has failed because of three fundamental flaws. First, it treats economic growth as its primary objective rather than social objectives such as the eradication of poverty and the right to health. The focus on growth arises from a simplification inherent in mainstream economics – the equation of total income with well-being. In a world of extreme inequality this is wholly unrealistic and inappropriate. The benefit to a billionaire of an additional $10 of income is negligible. To the average person living below the '$1-a-day' line, it can be the equivalent of total consumption for six weeks. By focusing on aggregate income and economic growth, mainstream economics illogically treats the benefits to billionaire and pauper as the same.

Faster growth is often argued to be necessary to provide more resources, which can then be allocated according to social needs. However, this requires mechanisms to ensure that resources are indeed allocated according to social needs. Such mechanisms are at best weak in rich countries, generally much weaker in LMICs, and non-existent or dysfunctional at the global level. Moreover, the current approach specifically militates against such resource allocations, by arguing for low tax rates and the avoidance of explicit redistributive measures on the grounds that they impede economic growth.

The argument that explicit redistributive measures would impede economic growth is highly questionable. But even if it were true, it would be both sensible and necessary to define some cut-off point at which reallocation takes precedence over further growth. Otherwise resources would *always* be allocated so as to maximise growth rather than in accordance with social priorities.

The second flaw is the predominant reliance on increasing exports as a source of economic growth, and the requirement for global consumption to grow in order to absorb these extra exports. There are two problems with this. First, there are real environmental limits to total global consumption. Second, the extreme inequality of the global economy means that most of the additional consumption is concentrated among a small relatively wealthy minority of the world's population (whose well-being is increased only slightly as a result), rather than among the poor majority (for whom increased consumption is absolutely essential). Crudely put, the current model requires the rich to get much richer in order for the poor to get even slightly less poor – even though this has a minimal effect on the well-being of the rich, and is destroying the environment on which both rich and poor ultimately depend.

The third flaw is that the current model is based on competition between countries in global markets to secure export markets and to attract foreign investment. This is an extension of the logic of competition between companies within a national market to increase the efficiency of production. But, as in any competition, in order for there to be winners, there must also be losers. Those countries which succeed, such as many of the East Asian countries, embark on a virtuous circle of increasing competitiveness and success. But those which are unable to compete find themselves on a vicious downward spiral of economic failure, compounded by the flight of financial and human capital.

However, unlike an uncompetitive company, a country cannot cease to exist. Neither, in general, can it be taken over by a more successful country. In the absence of such exit mechanisms, the losers risk continuing indefinitely on a downward spiral towards economic and social collapse. The growing number of failed states in sub-Saharan Africa might thus be seen not as an unfortunate accident but as an inevitable consequence of the competitive nature of neoliberalism. Had African countries been more successful, the costs of failure would merely have been shifted to another region.

Prerequisites for a pro-health model

Many critiques of the current development model assume, implicitly or explicitly, that the alternative is a return to one of two previously successful models:

- the *East Asian model*, also based partly on export promotion, but with a much more active and interventionist role of the state; or
- the *import-substituting industrialisation model* characteristic of much of Latin America until the 1970s.

While both were notably more successful than the current model, in terms of economic growth, both share with it a fundamental flaw: they rely primarily on the rich getting richer in order to make the poor less poor, either nationally or globally. In a world of ever-tightening constraints on carbon emissions, the dependence on ever-increasing consumption raises serious questions about their environmental sustainability, or their feasibility (Woodward 2007a). An alternative suited to a carbon-constrained future is needed.

Basic principles for a new alternative

The proposal presented here is based on four underlying principles. The first is that an alternative approach should be *specifically designed* to achieve society's objectives in terms of poverty, health, education and environmental sustainability. The first three of these are encapsulated in the economic and social rights contained in international human rights instruments, while environmental sustainability embodies the rights of future generations.

The second is that the proposed policies, programmes and projects should be designed to achieve these objectives at the local level, with national policies designed to support, promote and facilitate them and global systems designed to foster and accommodate these national policies. This 'bottom-up' orientation is a reversal of the current process in which national policies are driven largely by global economic conditions, within a top-down, one-size-fits-all framework determined primarily by global institutions.

The third principle involves maximising synergies between development, the environment, health and education, taking account of indirect as well as direct social and economic effects. This means addressing the social and environmental determinants of health and providing health-related services as interrelated parts of a holistic framework that includes:

- poverty and economic security;
- food security and nutrition;
- social inclusion;
- peace and personal security;
- availability of time for health-promoting household activities;
- safe living environments and working conditions;
- protection from extreme weather events;
- healthy lifestyles and diets;
- access to education, health services, clean water and sanitation.

Finally, an alternative model should be built upon collaboration rather than competition and on an effective system of global governance, capable of ensuring democratic decision-making in the collective interest, with a long-term time horizon.

If these principles are accepted, what will they look like in terms of actual policies? The next section describes the kinds of policies that would be required at the local and national levels.

Towards a new alternative: local and national policies

Poverty reduction measures

Focusing directly on achieving social and environmental objectives requires an alternative model constructed around measures to support the livelihoods of poor people. These might include:

- microcredit and income-generation schemes;
- labour-intensive public works programmes to develop infrastructure geared to the needs and priorities of poor households;
- public-sector procurement policies designed to maximise opportunities for medium, small and micro-enterprises;
- agricultural extension programmes directed at small farmers;
- social safety nets;
- cash transfer programmes.

Where land ownership is concentrated, reform and redistribution could provide a major boost to poverty reduction and development in rural areas, providing income opportunities for poor households. Improved land rights may also contribute to improvement of informal settlements in urban areas.

Some of these policies (notably microcredit, income generation and social safety nets) are already widely used. However, we propose two key changes. The first is that national economic policies be designed specifically to maximise the extent and effectiveness of such policies. The second is that such policies should be designed to *increase the supply by poor households of goods whose demand will be increased as poverty is reduced*. For example, if poor households buy more vegetables, meat and clothes as their incomes rise, policies should aim to support poor households in producing more of these goods.

This approach has three potentially important benefits. First, since an additional $1 of income provides much greater benefit at the bottom of the income distribution than higher up (and is likely to be less environmentally damaging), focusing on poverty reduction can greatly improve the trade-off between overall well-being and the environmental costs of increased consumption. Further environmental benefits are likely from reducing the financial pressures on poor households to pursue unsustainable productive practices, particularly in agriculture.

Second, the poorest households are likely to spend more of their additional income than the better-off on basic goods and services that can be produced locally by other poor households. As a result, more of the extra spending is likely to *flow among* the poor than 'trickles down' from the better-off in current growth-oriented models.

Third, the approach of reducing the dependency of economic growth on increasing consumption among the better-off has the potential to reduce the disproportionate political influence of the rich, which is a key obstacle to progressive policy change.

Energy management

While there is growing concern about increasing carbon emissions in large and rapidly growing LMICs such as China, India and Brazil, per capita emissions remain far higher in the North, which accounts for some 73 per cent of the current levels of atmospheric carbon *concentration* through its cumulative historical emissions (Raupach et al. 2007). Moreover, a large proportion of Southern emissions are a result of supplying Northern consumption. There is thus an overwhelming case for emissions reduction to take place mainly in the North.

Nonetheless, it will be important to minimise or reverse the increase in carbon emissions associated with additional consumption in the South as a result of poverty reduction. This implies a decisive shift from fossil-fuel-based systems to renewable energy. The need for such a shift is reinforced by the prospect of higher oil prices as existing reserves are depleted faster than viable new sources are discovered.

The logistical problems of providing fossil-fuel-based (or nuclear) technologies in rural areas mean that micro-renewable technologies in particular (wind-driven micro-turbines, micro-hydroelectric generation, solar power etc.) offer a 'win–win' opportunity for poverty reduction, health, development and the environment.

While the cost of installing micro-renewable energy systems is currently a constraint, this could be greatly eased by the application of micro-renewable technologies across all underserved rural areas in LMICs. Establishing a global facility for this purpose, funded from aid or other international resources would have enormous potential for both economies of scale and learning effects to drive down costs. This effect could be further strengthened if rich countries also switched from fossil-fuel generation to renewable energy rather than nuclear power. Equally, even on the current relatively limited scale, the shift towards biofuels based on agricultural crops such as maize has given rise to major increases in the cost of basic foods, with potentially serious consequences for food security.

By creating a very large market in rural areas in LMICs, incentives would be created for producers to develop technologies tailored to these conditions, in terms of both geographical and climatic conditions (maximising efficiency) and social and economic conditions (minimising maintenance requirements).

Public finance, public services and infrastructure

Across much of the developing world, the public sector has been seriously undermined by a combination of policies which have shrunk the role of the state and acute financial constraints. The latter arise from some aspects of the current economic model itself (e.g. reductions in taxes on trade, the corporate sector and incomes), and from some aspects of the global economy (notably the inadequacy of efforts to deal with the debt crisis, serious shortfalls in aid and various forms of tax competition).

These problems have been compounded by continued constraints on administrative capacity for tax collection; the limited success of replacing lost revenue through value-added tax (VAT) (the preferred neoliberal alternative to taxes on incomes and profits), particularly in low-income countries (Baunsgaard and Keen 2005); and questionable macroeconomic policies imposed by the IMF that have constrained public expenditure (IEO 2007).

There is an urgent need to rehabilitate the public sector and public services. Strong, well-resourced and effective governments have been central to the development process in all rich countries and in the most successful

LMICs. There is little reason to think that development elsewhere can succeed without this. This requires strengthening governance structures and promoting democracy and accountability, but in such a way as to take account of local social and cultural contexts. It also requires a considerable increase in administrative capacity, through institutional reform, training and education, and improving salaries and working conditions.

There is also an urgent need in many countries for better maintenance, rehabilitation and further development of physical infrastructure. From a health perspective, water and sanitation are among the highest priorities. Access to water can be assisted by tariff structures which allow free access to water for essential household use, while levying appropriate charges for commercial and luxury use (e.g. swimming pools). Improved access to clean water also reduces the time spent (usually by women or girls) collecting water, thus encouraging girls' education.

Transport infrastructure is critically important, providing multiple benefits in terms of domestic and external trade, travelling time to health facilities and schools, and so on. Communications in LMICs have been revolutionised by mobile telephony. Internet and email access, though still limited, have a similar potential, particularly in rural areas. Efforts to ensure universal coverage of mobile phone and wireless Internet networks and to minimise costs to users should be encouraged. Placing a computer with a reliable Internet connection and mobile phones for communal use in community facilities like schools could widen access considerably.

These measures will require a substantial increase in public resources in most low-income countries. Resources need to be raised in such a way as to minimise both the tax burden on poor households and the burden on generally limited administrative capacity.

Taxes on international trade, corporate profits and income from financial savings are relatively easy to collect. Taxes on financial savings and corporate profits are also much more progressive than consumption taxes such as VAT. Trade taxes could also be made more progressive by excluding essential goods purchased predominantly by poor households, and charging higher rates on luxury goods.

Other means of raising (or saving) public revenues require action at the global level, and are therefore discussed later.

Transforming the corporate sector

During the last twenty-five years, increasing emphasis has been placed on attracting foreign investment rather than stimulating local investment. However, foreign investment has three important disadvantages relative to local investment.

First, the initial inflow of foreign exchange it brings is more than offset over time by a continuing outflow of profits. Keeping cashflow positive over the long term thus requires enough new investment each year to offset the outflow of profits. Since these new inflows add to the stock of foreign-owned investment, when taken to its logical conclusion this implies a progressive transfer of the productive sector (and thus of the profits generated in the economy) into foreign ownership (Woodward 2001).

Second, foreign investment is typically much less labour-intensive than local investment. While foreign investments may appear to create substantial numbers of jobs by virtue of their sheer size, they generally create far fewer than an equivalent amount of local investment.

Third, foreign investment provides much greater opportunities for tax avoidance and evasion through mechanisms such as transfer price manipulation. This undermines the competitive position of local companies by giving foreign investors an artificial financial advantage.

For these reasons, there is a need for a shift of emphasis from foreign to local investment, particularly by small, medium and micro-enterprises. The ground rules for larger companies could be changed to

• ensure power-sharing among a wider range of stakeholders, including consumers, employees and the communities in which they operate;
• maximise their contributions to social and environmental goals.

However, the scope for such changes may be limited at the country level in the absence of international changes, given the increasingly footloose nature of production and the considerable economic and political power of larger corporations.

A case could also be made for placing restrictions on marketing and advertising (beyond the provision of factual information), which are an important driving force behind consumerism and the 'hedonic treadmill' of competitive overconsumption, as well as unhealthy consumption patterns.

The global level: poverty eradication and health for all

In a globalised world, changes made by LMIC governments can only go so far on their own. Changes are also required at the global level. This section describes the supranational policies and actions that form part of the alternative paradigm proposed here.

Global governance and the need for reform

The current system of global governance is seriously lacking in inclusiveness, equality of voice, transparency and accountability – basic preconditions for democracy – reflecting its roots in the colonial era.

The economically weighted voting systems of the IMF and the World Bank give rich countries the majority of the votes (and the US alone a veto on all major policy decisions). The US and European governments choose the heads of the World Bank and the IMF respectively. Together with the vetoes accorded to the US, the UK and France in the United Nations Security Council, this has allowed the developed world effectively to dictate subsequent changes to the system, and to protect their political privileges. In the WTO, while the formal decision-making structures are more democratic, they are of limited relevance as negotiations take place almost entirely through informal processes characterised by lack of transparency and blatant abuse of power (Jawara and Kwa 2004).

The system of global governance has consistently served the commercial and geopolitical interests of the rich countries, often at the expense of the 86 per cent of the world's population who live in the developing world. This is amply demonstrated by the system's repeated failures in dealing with debt and financial crises since the 1980s; WTO agreements which overwhelmingly reflect Northern commercial agendas; and the global imposition of a neoliberal model of economic development.

The system of global economic governance established in 1944 does not meet the needs of the early twenty-first century, or serve the long-term interest of the world's population as a whole. Neither does it reflect contemporary standards of democratic governance. This represents an overwhelming case for fundamental reform.

International finance: crisis prevention and resolution

There is an urgent need to deal with remaining debt problems. The costs of debt crises to development, and their direct and indirect social impacts, have been incalculable. All countries' debts should be reduced to a level at which their servicing (repayment with interest) does not impair their ability to achieve poverty eradication and health and education for all (Mandel 2006a).

In addition, there is a strong case for removing the financial burden resulting from odious debts – debts from unethical lending to undemocratic and/or kleptocratic regimes (e.g. South Africa under apartheid, Indonesia under Suharto and the Mobutu government in Zaire), which had no legitimate right to borrow on behalf of the population. While many of the original loans have now been repaid, the new debts that were incurred to service and repay them continue to impose a major financial burden on many LMICs (Mandel 2006b).

There is also a need to establish a fair and transparent arbitration process (akin to bankruptcy processes at the national level) to deal with future debt crises. This would replace the current system, in which the arbiter is the IMF – both a creditor in its own right and controlled by other creditors (rich-country governments), which in turn have a vested interest in the protection of a third group of creditors (commercial banks). The objective of the process – in marked contrast to the existing system – should be to resolve all future debt crises quickly, effectively and at a minimum cost in terms of social impact.

Changes are also required to ensure that financial crises of the kind which swept 'emerging market' economies in the late 1990s are avoided and resolved more effectively, particularly by reducing the dependency of LMICs on volatile forms of external financial capital. Options include the reintroduction of controls on capital flows, and the introduction of the Spahn tax (a currency transactions tax that is charged at a very high rate in response to extreme movements of the exchange rate) (Spahn 1996). Consideration could also be given to a global intervention fund along the lines of the Chiang Mai Initiative (discussed later) to protect currencies from speculative attack.

International finance: taxation

A system of global taxation needs to be established to provide funding for global institutions and global public goods such as the control of infectious diseases and the development of vaccines. This would help to ensure the independence of international institutions and decision-making against the pressures arising from financial dependency on discretionary funding from rich-country governments.

Funding could also be provided for development – ideally combined with collectivisation of aid, allocated through democratic global institutions. This would help ensure that aid is allocated in accordance with needs and global priorities rather than donors' commercial and geopolitical agendas. It would also help prevent donors from using aid to exercise undue influence. Support for the provision of micro-renewable electricity generation technologies in rural areas would be a high priority for such funding.

Global taxes might include, for example, a currency transactions tax at a very low level on currency exchanges (the Tobin tax), which could be levied through the global clearing system; air passenger or air fuel taxes, on all (or only cross-border) air transport; a levy on trade in carbon emission permits (see below); and taxes on international trade in armaments.

In addition to global taxes, measures are required to relieve global constraints on national taxation. The increasing international mobility of financial capital limits the ability of governments to tax income from financial wealth. This reduces both the amount of revenues and the progressiveness of the tax system. The need to attract foreign investment also puts pressure on countries to reduce corporate taxation rates and provide direct and indirect subsidies to investors, reducing public revenues still further.

These problems are compounded by the proliferation of tax havens, increasingly in major financial centres in the developed world. Such centres act as a magnet for footloose international capital, both constraining tax rates and reducing the tax base by stimulating capital flight. Total assets held through offshore accounts (excluding real estate) have been estimated at US$11,500 billion, resulting in losses of tax revenues estimated at US$255 billion p.a. (TJN 2005).

Further problems arise from the growth of transnational companies, which can minimise the tax they pay by moving their notional base to a country with a more favourable tax regime. Also, around one-third of world trade is between subsidiaries of the same company in different countries (intra-company trade). Because the same company is both the seller and the buyer, it can set an artificially high or low price (transfer price manipulation), as a means of transferring profits to a country with a lower tax rate – often a tax haven. This seriously reduces taxes on the profits of foreign investors, which represent a rapidly growing share of total investment in many LMICs.

Problems of capital flight and constraints on taxing income from financial wealth could be eased by capital controls, and tax competition by strength-ened international coordination of tax rates on financial capital and cor-porate profits. The closure of tax havens and the imposition of minimum tax rates on income from financial capital and corporate profits would also allow public revenues to be increased considerably. Consideration could also be given to allocating taxes on transnational companies' profits according to their value-added in each country where they operate, removing the incentive for transfer price manipulation.

There is a strong case for an international institution with responsibility for tax issues to implement such measures – although it would be essential to ensure effective democratic control and independence from commercial interests.

Enforcing carbon constraints[5]

Ensuring that global carbon emissions fall fast enough to avert catastrophic climate change is essential to any development strategy. This could be achieved through a system of tradable carbon emission permits, issued by a global institution. Fossil fuel and energy companies would need to purchase permits in proportion to the emissions for which they were responsible and would pass on the cost to consumers through pricing. The total supply of permits would be rationed, in line with global emissions targets, and reduced accordingly over time.

Concerns about the distributional effects of carbon trading systems (see Chapter C1) could be resolved by allocating permits on an equal per capita basis. In fact, this would make the system into a powerful tool for redistribution as well as for ensuring compliance with global carbon constraints. No country or individual has a 'right' to a greater share of the world's capacity to absorb carbon than any other. If anything, the per capita entitlements of richer countries should be *lower*, reflecting their far higher emissions in the past. If a proportion of the permits were allocated to governments, this could also provide a very considerable source of public revenues through the sale of these permits.

International trade

International trade rules need to be reoriented to meet social and environmental objectives rather than commercial interests.

Production and export subsidies to large-scale agriculture in LMICs and the dumping of produce in LMIC markets at below-market prices are major obstacles to development and poverty reduction and should be ended. WTO rules should also be revised to allow LMICs to use trade taxes where appropriate, both for revenue-raising purposes and in support of local development, in line with the WTO's stated (though largely ignored) principle of 'special and differential treatment'.

Equally important are measures to reverse the long-term decline in the world prices of tropical agricultural products, which has been exacerbated by the promotion of exports of these goods under neoliberalism. This could be done through a system of coordinated export taxes applied by all producing countries. For many tropical agricultural products, such as coffee, tea and cocoa, demand is not very responsive to price, so that a 1 per cent price increase reduces demand by less than 1 per cent. This means that the proceeds of a universal production tax would be more than the loss of income to producers, so that poorer producers could in principle be compensated, while still generating additional public revenues. Such compensation could usefully be directed to promoting and supporting the production of substitute crops for the domestic market.

Similarly, for countries which export fuels and minerals, both export prices and public revenues could be substantially increased through collective bargaining for extraction rights (including renegotiation of existing agreements). At present, such rights are negotiated bilaterally between individual governments and companies, and contractual terms generally remain secret. Combined with the acute foreign exchange pressure faced by many countries, bilateral negotiations give rise to competition for investment, with the risk of bidding down the terms of agreements, and thereby reducing royalty receipts. The negotiating position of LMICs could thus be strengthened, and the terms available to them improved by establishing a forum for collective negotiation.

From intellectual property to intellectual commons

The global public good of knowledge has effectively been privatised by the WTO's Trade-Related Aspects of Intellectual Property Rights (TRIPS) agreement, and by regional and bilateral agreements between rich countries and LMICs. Proponents of this approach argue that conferring monopoly rights on those who generate new knowledge creates stronger incentives for research and product development. However, this increases the price of new products and technologies, leaving poor people and poor countries out of the market, even where the research activities of rich-country corporations have benefited from substantial public subsidies.

Because the profits generated reflect the ability and willingness of potential buyers to pay, this also skews incentives for research in a number of ways:

- from the urgent needs of the poor to the (often more cosmetic) wants of the rich;
- towards products which provide private rather than public benefits;
- towards technologies which can be embodied in a new product (rather than, for example, health-improving behaviour or nutrition);
- towards curative rather than preventive interventions;
- towards the development of 'copycat' products similar to successful patented products, rather than anything new or innovative;
- against collaboration and information-sharing among researchers.

Even if governments intervene to increase affordability or provide incentives for neglected areas of research, for example by providing funds to purchase the goods required by poor countries, they must offer prices high enough to compete with the increased incentives for research and development of products directed to the wants of the rich. This limits the scope of such intervention and diverts resources away from alternative uses.

It is in any case by no means clear that financial incentives are the most effective means of stimulating research. Many of the most important breakthroughs in medical technology – from anaesthesia, through X-rays and polio vaccine, to oral rehydration therapy – have had little to do with financial incentives.

All this suggests that patents are ineffective, inefficient and probably counterproductive, in terms of stimulating technological innovation in the public good. Alternatives to the current patent-based system of rewarding research and development are discussed in Chapter B5.

First steps towards the future?

The agenda outlined above implies fundamental changes, at every level from the local to the global, and in economic, social, environmental and political dimensions. However, there are signs of a progressive shift in the right direction. There are two major forces behind this process: a renewed energy and independence among some Southern governments; and the growing role of progressive civil society on the global stage.

Recent Southern initiatives

Over the last decade, there have been a number of steps towards developing alternative international structures and national policies, as some Southern governments have become more assertive in their resistance to the current model of development and the global system that underlies it. The first sign of this process was the renaissance of regional trade agreements beginning in the early 1990s, particularly in Latin America and Southeast Asia. This process has seen the expansion of the Association of Southeast Asian Nations (ASEAN), the establishment of Mercosur by Brazil, Argentina, Uruguay and Paraguay, and the resurrection of the Central American Common Market. Existing regional trade arrangements among the LMICs have been strengthened, and there are increasing efforts at collaboration between blocs.

This may be seen as a partial realisation of Samir Amin's argument for the cultivation of regional (South–South) trade, to allow broader involvement in production, with knock-on benefits for local purchasing capacity. Amin (1985) proposes a three-tiered regime of stepped protection, with trade barriers designed to support a degree of national self-sufficiency in the context of regional trade preferences, with participation in global trade as a residual option. In effect, potential losses of efficiency, higher consumer prices and reduction in quality associated with trade barriers are seen as a price worth paying for the promotion of livelihoods, economic diversity and industrial capacity which would arise from retaining more income within developing economies and protection from the competitive pressures that undermine social provision.

However, many regional trading blocs aspire to free trade within the region and WTO rules prevent them from raising trade barriers to other countries. As a result, the only real effect is to lower trade barriers between members of the bloc. To approximate Amin's original vision would require a reversal of this logic and fundamental changes in the multilateral trade system, so that some barriers could be retained within the bloc, with higher barriers between Southern blocs, and still higher barriers to the rest of the world. Ensuring positive effects would also require further consideration of the implications for ecological sustainability of more distributed production; measures to ensure access to advanced technologies (e.g. for renewable energy and pollution control); and a reorientation of values, from the materialism which underpins the current model towards a culture of simple living.

A further important step away from the current model was the Chiang Mai Initiative, agreed by a number of Asian governments in 2000 in response to the IMF's failure to prevent or deal effectively with the region's financial crisis in the late 1990s. It amounts to a regional alternative to the IMF, pooling part of the international reserves of the participating countries to counter speculative attacks on their currencies. It thus provides simultaneously a more effective means of preventing such crises, a more appropriate mechanism for responding to them, and a means of limiting the imposition of inappropriate policy conditions should a crisis occur.

A stronger movement away from neoliberalism is emerging in Latin America, with the advent of several progressive leaders who are breaking away from the neoliberal orthodoxy – notably Hugo Chávez in Venezuela, Evo Morales in Bolivia, and Rafael Correa in Ecuador (Chomsky 2005).

The centrepiece of this movement is the Bolivarian Alternative for the Americas (ALBA), a regional alternative to free trade initiated by Venezuela, following successful efforts to block the US proposal for a Free Trade Area of the Americas (FTAA). ALBA has expanded from two members (Venezuela and Cuba) at its establishment in 2004 to nine, with the addition of Bolivia, Nicaragua, Ecuador, Uruguay, the Dominican Republic, St Kitts and Nevis, and Haiti.

ALBA aims to encourage members to integrate their economies, so as to complement each another rather than to compete. Its objectives are:

- promoting trade and investment between members, based on cooperation and improving people's lives, not making profits;
- cooperation among members to provide free health care and education;
- integration of members' energy sectors to meet their peoples' needs;
- ensuring land redistribution and food security;
- developing and furthering state-owned enterprises;

- developing basic industries to promote economic independence;
- promoting workers', student and social movements;
- ensuring that projects are environmentally friendly.

As well as committing its member states to participatory democracy, ALBA encourages popular participation in its own planning and functioning. In addition to presidential and ministerial councils, its operations are overseen by a third council made up of social movements. Some of the continent's largest social movements, such as the Movement of Rural Landless Workers in Brazil and the International Peasant Movement (Via Campesina), participate, and their ideas around land redistribution, free health care, free education and food security have become part of ALBA's goals.

Examples of ALBA's approach include:

- the exchange of Venezuelan oil worth $1 billion a year for the services of 30,000 Cuban doctors and teachers, allowing Venezuela to staff 11,000 new clinics in poor neighbourhoods (Ali 2006), and new schools and adult literacy centres across the country;
- Cuban donations of medical equipment and supplies, doctors and teachers to Bolivia to help expand its public schools and hospitals;
- a Latin American School of Medicine providing free medical education to students from the region (Janicke 2008);
- five major agricultural projects producing soya, rice, poultry and dairy products, to guarantee food security in Cuba and Venezuela and the provision of free or subsidised food to millions of people in Venezuela;
- Venezuelan and Cuban imports of soya from Bolivia after the US stopped buying them in 2006;
- Venezuelan financial support to Bolivia's state-owned gas sector in exchange for agricultural products (Harris and Azzi 2006);
- the exchange of Venezuelan oil, at discounted prices, for agricultural produce from St Kitts and Nevis, Haiti and the Dominican Republic;
- Venezuelan assistance to Cuba in the construction of a massive aqueduct to improve its water supply;
- mutual assistance agreements between Venezuela and Nicaragua around social programmes, including the provision of housing and education to Nicaragua's 47,000 street children;
- an ALBA fund to improve public schools, health care, and other social services in St Kitts and Nevis, Haiti and the Dominican Republic;
- creation of a Bank of ALBA, run on a democratic basis, with more than $1 billion in capital, making loans to member states without policy

conditions, for infrastructure, health, education, and social and cultural development.

Venezuela, Bolivia and Ecuador are also planning to establish an OPEC-type organisation to help ensure stable and fair prices for gas.

As governments across Latin America have moved away from borrowing from the IMF and the World Bank (Neuber 2007), Venezuela has become the preferred source of loans, lending some $4.5 billion to Argentina, Bolivia and Ecuador since 2005, without policy conditions (McIvor 2007). In 2007, Venezuela, Argentina, Bolivia, Ecuador, Paraguay and Brazil agreed that such lending should be formalised through a Bank of the South (McElhinny 2007), to begin operations in 2008.

Countries will deposit 10 per cent of their foreign currency reserves in the Bank as a start-up fund (Toussaint 2007). Once the Bank is fully operational, member countries will be able both to borrow and to use funds to protect currencies if attacked by speculators, without IMF policy constraints (Toussaint 2006). Most of the countries involved have agreed that the Bank will be run on a one country/one vote basis, unlike the IMF and the World Bank (Zibechi 2007), and to launch a Latin American currency for trade (Ugarteche 2007), to reduce the dominance of the US dollar in the region.

As well as their direct benefits to members, ALBA and the Bank of the South are of great symbolic and political value, demonstrating the feasibility of alternative economic models. Together with the Chiang Mai Initiative, and the reduction of borrowing from the IMF and the World Bank by middle-income countries, they are also putting financial pressure on the Bank and the IMF, highlighting their democratic deficits and lack of legitimacy.

Civil society as a driving force for change

Over the last decade, the role of civil society in influencing economic policies at the global level has increased considerably, strengthened by the development of global networks such as the World Social Forum and the People's Health Movement. Notable successes have included improved mechanisms for debt reduction in low-income countries, blocking the proposed Multilateral Agreement on Investment (MAI), the Doha Ministerial Declaration on Access to Essential Medicines, and blocking WTO agreements unfavourable to the developing world at WTO Ministerial meetings in Seattle and Cancún.

Notable as these successes have been, it is important to recognise their limitations. All have been, in a sense, exercises in damage limitation

– seeking to prevent decisions which would make the situation worse (e.g. MAI and WTO Ministerials), to limit the impact of previous adverse decisions (e.g. TRIPS), or, in the case of debt, to moderate the effects of an adverse side effect of the prevailing model which had already imposed devastating costs for more than a decade.

Where decisions have been blocked, this has often been temporary.

- Failures to reach agreement at WTO Ministerials have only delayed negotiations, without changing the agenda or the undemocratic nature of the negotiation process.
- Having been blocked in the OECD, the MAI proposal resurfaced in a different form, as a proposal for capital account liberalisation in the IMF, and later (when blocked there) in another variant as a proposal for negotiations on an Investment Agreement in the WTO. Even when WTO negotiations on the issue were blocked in the current round of trade negotiations, the issue was only put off until the next round.
- The potential benefits of the Doha Declaration were largely neutralised by the subsequent imposition of burdensome conditions on its provisions, and by the imposition through bilateral trade 'agreements' of standards of intellectual property protection that exceed even those of TRIPS.

On debt, the Heavily Indebted Poor Countries (HIPC) Initiative benefited only some countries needing debt cancellation, set sustainability thresholds too high, was conditional on continued IMF and World Bank programmes similar to structural adjustment, and had long delays built in, so that no countries completed the process in the first five years, and only nine in the following four years (Jubilee Research 2007). Campaigns on debt continue even now.

2005–6 saw an unprecedented global mobilisation of civil society on debt, aid and trade, under the banner of 'Make Poverty History'. While some commitments were made at the Gleneagles G8 Summit, these fell far short of what was demanded, added little to previous commitments made elsewhere, for example EU aid commitments (Jubilee Research 2005), and have been only partly fulfilled.

Nonetheless, civil society has a key role to play as a driver of change. Northern development NGOs have a particular responsibility: the dominance of international decision-making processes by Northern governments means that Northern NGOs, through their influence on their governments, have arguably greater influence in global decisions than do representatives of the South. They have undoubtedly helped to raise the political profile of development issues.

However, to be effective, such campaigns need to be rooted in a much broader social mobilisation, and a radical empowerment of people, particularly in LMICs. If they are to counterbalance the profoundly undemocratic nature of the global governance system, the primary responsibility of Northern development NGOs should be to represent the views and priorities of Southern civil society and to seek reform of international institutions to ensure that Southern countries have influence commensurate with their share of world population in international decisions which affect them.

NGOs have a major role to play in promoting more development-friendly solutions to issues such as debt, intellectual property, tax competition and tax havens, and to bring the corporate sector under effective democratic control. However, the most important priority for civil society activism is arguably the democratic reform of global economic governance. This is both a central cause of the shortcomings in the global economic system and the imposition of the current model of development, and the greatest obstacle to change. Unless and until global governance structures change – fundamentally – civil society efforts on other issues will inevitably remain limited to damage limitation, and at best partially successful.

Global governance reform is also, in some respects, a relatively easy target. The substantive economic issues are many and complex, making the mobilisation of public opinion difficult and stretching the limited advocacy resources of NGOs and CSOs. The principles of democracy, by contrast, are relatively simple, familiar to the general public and generally accepted; and the democratic deficits of the IMF, World Bank and WTO are already receiving increasing media attention.

This provides an invaluable opportunity. The fundamental inconsistency between the democratic principles Northern governments profess domestically, and their defence at the international level of grossly *un*democratic processes dating from the colonial era, makes their position untenable if a sufficient weight of public opinion can be mobilised on the issue.

At the same time, the increasing reluctance of emerging market economies to borrow from the IMF and the World Bank, and the growth of regional alternatives such as the Chiang Mai Initiative and the Bank of the South, undermine their legitimacy, and put the Fund in particular under increasing financial pressure. These developments give the governments of some larger middle-income countries such as China and Brazil a credible 'walk-away' threat, which has the potential to exert considerable pressure on rich-country governments regarding IMF and World Bank governance issues.

However, if this is to lead towards genuinely democratic reform and the empowerment of low-income countries, which are the most marginalised, it will be important to ensure solidarity among Southern governments as a whole (Woodward 2007b). This will also be important in keeping a broad civil society constituency on board.

A key obstacle to global governance reform is the need to secure changes through the very decision-making processes that need to be reformed: as long as Northern governments continue to dominate decisions on governance reform, they will continue to use their dominance to protect their privileges. It is therefore essential to take the process out of these decision-making structures into a separate process akin to the Bretton Woods Conference – but one which reflects current standards of democracy (inclusiveness, equality of voice, transparency and accountability) rather than those of the colonial era.

A major global campaign, across the whole spectrum of civil society, and in close collaboration with LMIC governments, for the establishment of such a process would be a major step towards securing the changes needed to achieve a global economic system for the health of the many rather than the wealth of the few.

Changing lifestyles

Recent years have also seen a growing trend, particularly in the North, in changing lifestyles towards more ethical and sustainable principles. This began with environmental concerns, reflected in increasing interest in recycling in the 1980s, and has been reinforced more recently by increasing energy consciousness, particularly concern about air travel and the carbon costs of long-distance air freighting of foodstuffs.

Development and other social concerns are reflected in growing demand for fair trade goods and other forms of ethical consumerism, while an increasing proportion of savings, pension funds, and so forth, espouse (generally limited) ethical investment principles. The resulting pressures have led growing numbers of companies to take a much more active stance on corporate social responsibility – although this often goes little beyond a public relations exercise.

At the same time, a small but growing number of people are deciding to get off the 'hedonic treadmill' of overconsumption – opting to shift their work–life balance in favour of a higher non-material quality of life rather than working ever-longer hours under ever-greater stress in order to consume more and more, without improving their well-being. As well as positive environmental effects, this is likely to have benefits for their own health. At the same time, the growing participation in environmental and development campaigns, from Jubilee 2000 to Make Poverty History, indicates an increasing trend towards political activism on global issues.

Perhaps the most important of the trends are increasing energy consciousness and reduced consumerism. Living within global carbon constraints while making progress against poverty will require lower and less energy-intensive consumption among the better-off in the North. If this is reflected in a shift in voting patterns – away from personal material gain and towards broader social and environmental objectives – then, coupled with increasing activism, this could also help to shift political dynamics in a positive direction.

Conclusion

This chapter presents a vision of how the world could be run in order to achieve poverty eradication, health for all and education for all, while also ensuring environmental sustainability and bringing climate change under control. But doing so would require genuine political will. This chapter is a starting point for discussion, not a blueprint. But it provides an indication of what might be possible if we are willing to think outside the currently dominant paradigm of economics.

However, the issue of political will is critical. We are in the current situation largely because of politics – specifically, because the global system is effectively run by rich-country governments, which are disproportionately influenced by commercial interests and which have consistently demonstrated their determination both to preserve their power and to use it primarily to advance their own interests.

Any reform of the global system commensurate with the immense challenges we face requires this to change. The proposals outlined here would necessarily imply both financial costs and a loss of control for those who currently have the greatest power – and there is little indication that they will willingly concede either in the near future.

However, if we dismiss the reforms which are so desperately needed as politically infeasible, and focus our efforts exclusively on piecemeal damage limitation within the current paradigm, this will be a self-fulfilling prophecy: a more viable alternative will *remain* politically infeasible. By not pressing for the fundamental reforms which are needed, *as well as* smaller but more immediately achievable changes, we risk legitimising the current global system, and allowing it to become yet more entrenched.

Climate change provides a potentially important political opportunity in this respect. As the impacts are increasingly felt in rich countries, through hurricanes in the US and droughts, floods and heatwaves across Europe, it will become increasingly apparent that the status quo is no longer a viable option. Even in the North, the question is no longer *whether* the system should change, but *how* it must change.

The risk is that the response will be dictated by rich-country governments to protect their own interests at the expense of the remaining 86 per cent of the world. Avoiding this outcome, and ensuring a change which will contribute to meeting the needs of the South, is therefore a key objective.

In order to achieve the necessary changes on the scale required, we need to harness the potential strength of civil society to the greatest possible extent to generate political pressure on those who hold power. This means developing a shared vision, both across national boundaries and across constituencies such as health, development and the environment; and acting together to make that vision a reality. This chapter aims to provide a first small step towards bringing the global health constituency into such a process.

Notes

1. This chapter is based primarily on David Woodward's forthcoming *More with less: Towards a new economics paradigm for poverty eradication in a carbon-constrained world*.
2. The story of how neoliberalism moved from the theoretical margins to the political mainstream is told in Richard Cockett, *Thinking the unthinkable: Think-tanks and the economic counter-revolution, 1931–83*, London: Fontana, 1995.
3. http://iresearch.worldbank.org/PovcalNet/jsp/index.jsp.
4. Based on the World Bank's Povcalnet database, available at http://iresearch.worldbank.org/PovcalNet/jsp/index.jsp.
5. *Editorial comment*: Different perspectives are held on the potential of carbon trading as a means to reduce carbon emissions. Two different positions are reflected within this edition of *Global Health* Watch. For an alternate perspective, see Chapter C1.

References

Ali, T. (2006). *Pirates of the Caribbean: The axis of hope*. London and New York: Verso.

Amin, S. (1985). *Delinking: Towards a polycentric world*. London: Zed Books.

Baunsgaard, T., and M. Keen (2005). Tax revenue and (or?) trade liberalization. Working Paper 05/112, Washington DC: IMF, June.

Chen, S., and M. Ravallion (2007). Absolute poverty measures for the developing world, 1981–2004. Working Paper WPS4211, Development Research Group, Washington DC: World Bank, April.

Chomsky, N. (2005). A dangerous neighbourhood. *Kaleej Times*.

de Vogli, R., and G.L. Birbeck (2005). Potential impact of adjustment policies on vulnerability of women and children to HIV/AIDS in sub-Saharan Africa. *Journal of Health, Population and Nutrition* 23(2), June: 105–20.

Edward, P. (2006). The ethical poverty line: A moral quantification of absolute poverty. *Third World Quarterly* 37(2): 377–93.

Harris, D., and D. Azzi (2006). *ALBA: Venezuela's answer to 'free trade': The Bolivarian alternative for the Americas*. Bangkok: Focus on the Global South.

IEO (Independent Evaluation Office) (2007). *Evaluation report: The IMF and aid to sub-Saharan Africa*. Independent Evaluation Office, Washington DC: IMF.

Janicke, K. (2008). Summit of the Bolivarian Alternative (ALBA) concludes in Venezuela. www.venezuelanalysis.com.

Jawara, F., and A. Kwa (2004). *Behind the scenes at the WTO: The real world of international trade negotiations*. London: Zed Books.

Jubilee Research (2005). The G8 2005: What are the lessons? Jubilee Research at New Economics Foundation, London, 11 July.

Jubilee Research (2007). Jubilee Research database. Jubilee Research at New Economics Foundation, August, Table 1.

Mandel, S. (2006a). Debt relief as if people mattered: A rights-based approach to debt sustainability. London: New Economics Foundation.

Mandel, S. (2006b). Odious lending: Debt relief as if morals mattered. London: New Economics Foundation.

Marland, G., B. Andres and T. Boden (2006). Global CO_2 emissions from fossil-fuel burning, cement manufacture, and gas flaring: 1751–2003. Oak Ridge TN: Carbon Dioxide Information Analysis Center, 30 May.

McElhinny, V. (2007). Banco del Sur: A reflection of the declining IFI relevance in Latin America. www.bisusa.org.

McIvor, P. (2007). Venezuela's Banco del Sur: The end of the IMF in Latin America? http://upsidedownworld.com.

Neuber, H. (2007). Venezuela's withdrawal from the IMF and World Bank. http://milwaukee.indymedia.org.

Raupach, M.R., et al. (2007). Global and regional drivers of accelerating CO_2 emissions. *Proceedings of the National Academy of Sciences* 104(24): 10288–93.

Spahn, P.B. (1996). The Tobin Tax and exchange rate stability. *Finance and Development* 33(2): 24–7.

TJN (Tax Justice Network) (2005). The price of off-shore. Briefing paper, Tax Justice Network (UK), London, March.

Toussaint, E. (2006). Bank of the South, international context and alternatives. www.cadtm.org.

Toussaint, E. (2007). Turning back to the stakes on the Bank of the South. www.cadtm.org.

Ugarteche, O. (2007). Brazil vs Bank of the South. www.Alainet.org/active/19278 &lang=pt.

Woodward, D. (2001). *The next crisis? Direct and equity investment in developing countries*. London: Zed Books.

Woodward, D. (2007a). Economic models: Is there an alternative to neoliberalism?'. Note for the Development and Environment Group, UK, March.

Woodward, D. (2007b). IMF voting reform: Need, opportunity and options. Washington DC: Group of 24, February.

Woodward, D. (forthcoming). More with less: Towards a new economics paradigm for poverty eradication in a carbon-constrained world. London: New Economics Foundation.

Zibechi, R. (2007). Bank of the South: Toward financial autonomy. http://americas.irc-online.org/am/4364.

B I Health systems advocacy

After years of neglect, 'health systems strengthening' in poor countries is receiving some attention. For example, the proposed health agenda for the G8 meeting in July 2008 focuses on health systems (Reich et al. 2008). The GAVI Alliance has invested $500 million for health systems strengthening from 2006 to 2010 (GAVI 2007) and the World Bank's (2007) most recent health strategy strongly emphasises health systems strengthening. Additionally, the World Health Organization's (WHO) 2008 annual report will focus on primary health care and its role in health systems strengthening.

However, it is unclear what is meant by health systems strengthening. But this is important, especially because policies advocated to strengthen health systems may actually end up harming them. It is also important because the way in which health systems are financed and managed also influences the amount and distribution of income of those who produce and provide health care. There are many vested interests at play in discussions about health systems policies.

For example, some health-care practitioners might be keen on policies that will maximise their incomes; drug companies might be keen to maximise expenditure on medicines; and upper income groups may wish to promote health systems that separate them away from the poor. A strong health system may mean different things to different people.

Health systems policies also influence the orientation of health-care provision – for example, determining the mix of biomedical and social interventions, or the extent to which people are viewed as consumers who purchase a commodity versus citizens who receive health care from providers providing a service.

This chapter outlines the factors that undermine health systems, and describes a vision for what makes a 'good' health system.[1]

IMAGE B1.1   **An ill child with diarrhoea arrives by boat and is carried to a health clinic in Matlab, Bangladesh**

Health systems factors

Several factors in low-income countries are often responsible for various negative health systems outcomes, notably: unfair, delayed or unavailable access to health care; inefficient (often unnecessary) health care; medical impoverishment resulting from out-of-pocket payments and a neglect of the underlying social and environmental determinants of ill-health.

In many countries, the resource base of health-care systems is inadequate. Volatile and unreliable health-care funding adds to the problem by making it difficult for countries to make medium- to long-term plans.

Another problem is disharmony. The governance and management of many health-care systems is like an orchestra with musicians playing different tunes without a conductor. The poor coordination of multiple donors and global health initiatives undermines coherent health systems planning, imposes large costs upon ministries of health and health workers who have to liaise with and report to a multitude of stakeholders, and fragments the provision of health care. When inappropriate conditionalities and agendas are imposed by external agencies it can weaken ministries of health.

While vertically organised programmes and selective health-care interventions have arisen partly as a consequence of underfunded and dysfunctional health-care systems, they can also aggravate the problem, cause duplication of systems and services, drain away skilled personnel from the public sector, and prevent integrated, context-based local health planning.

Weak public leadership and management in some countries may reflect the difficulty that ministries of health have in retaining good personnel, as well as the demoralisation that has accompanied the chronic deterioration of public-sector working conditions over the years. It may also reflect other broader deficiencies of governance such as corruption, a weak judiciary, civil conflict or a lack of capacity among civil society institutions to hold governments to account.

The enduring effects of structural adjustment programmes are another cause of dysfunctionality. The commercialised primary care sector, which accounts for the bulk of primary-level expenditure in most low-income countries, grew as a result of cuts in public-sector expenditure, and is largely disorganised and unregulated. As public services deteriorated, cash payments for the purchase of care and medicines became more common, deterring people from accessing health care and entrenching poverty.

More so in middle-income countries, private insurance markets can 'segment out' higher income groups into a separate system of health care, distancing them from the health needs of the poor and the problems of the public system. Although it is argued that the public sector will be able to focus on the poor and ensure access to a basic package of services, often a private system mainly catering for upper income groups will siphon out more resources than it relieves the public sector of workload. It also weakens the social commitment to cross-subsidisation, risk sharing and equitable health care.

The collapse of public-sector services and the increased share of private financing have led to greater market-driven care, and its problems of 'over-servicing'; accentuating a bias towards biomedical interventions at the expense of public health approaches; replacing provider collaboration with provider competition; and deteriorating levels of trust between patients and providers.

Supply-and-demand-driven care also underlies the international brain drain of skilled human resources from poor to rich countries, the diversion of scarce resources in some countries towards a 'health tourism industry' serving economically advantaged patients and contractors from high-income countries. Currently, the medical tourism industry has an estimated turnover of $67 billion, a figure set to rise by 20 per cent a year (Macready 2007). Most of this turnover will be captured by commercial, private providers.[2]

The vision of a 'strong' health-care system

There are no quick-fix solutions. Strengthening health systems requires a multidimensional programme of change and development, guided by a long-term vision. It also requires a set of guiding principles, specifically around:

- progressive health financing;
- pooling health finance to optimise risk-sharing and cross-subsidisation;
- fitting health-care expenditure and utilisation patterns according to need, rather than demand or the ability to pay;
- balancing population-based approaches to health with individualised health care;
- balancing needs-driven and rights-based health provision against commercialisation.

A strong health system should also operate as a social institution that promotes social solidarity, good governance and the right to essential health care.

Ideally, service providers would be adequately paid through a system that delinks their income from the delivery of health care (a critical condition for ethical behaviour and values within health systems), whilst encouraging quality and responsiveness through monitoring and evaluation, competition for non-financial rewards, fostering a culture of excellence and community empowerment.

With these principles in mind, a nine-point health systems development agenda for low-income countries was put forward by Global Health Watch (2006). This chapter now discusses key issues related to this agenda.

I   Comprehensive human resource plans

The nature of the human resources (HR) crisis in low-income health systems is well known (WHO 2006). There are too few health workers. Many of those are, furthermore, demotivated and inadequately trained, supported and supervised. There is also often a maldistribution of health workers, with a high concentration in urban areas. In many countries the public sector struggles to retain skilled staff because of low salaries relative to the private and non-government sector.

One positive development was the creation of the Global Health Workforce Alliance in 2006 and a Global Forum on the Human Resources for Health Crisis, which was held in Kampala in March 2008. But, overall, there has been inadequate progress made in addressing the crisis.

Another less recent but extremely positive initiative was Malawi's six-year Emergency Human Resource Programme (EHRP), supported by the UK

Department for International Development and a grant from the Global Fund (Palmer 2006). The EHRP takes a five-pronged approach:

- improving incentives for recruitment and retention of public-sector and CHAM staff through a 52 per cent salary top-up for eleven professional and technical cadres, coupled with a major initiative to recruit and re-engage qualified Malawian staff;
- expanding domestic training capacity, including doubling the number of nurses and tripling the number of doctors in training;
- using international volunteer doctors and nurse tutors as a short-term measure to fill critical posts while Malawians are being trained;
- providing technical assistance to bolster Ministry of Health capacity in HR planning, management and development;
- establishing robust HR monitoring and evaluation capacity.

In addition, the programme explicitly recognises the importance of improving policies on postings and promotions, training and career development, and incentives for deploying staff to underserved areas (which includes a major effort to improve staff housing).

Sadly, the degree of international support for strengthening and replicating this programme to other countries has been limited. In many countries, effective human resource planning cannot even begin because of a lack of data on the existing number, distribution, location and income of health workers (McCoy et al. 2008). There is a particular lack of data on health workers in the private sector, which makes it difficult for ministries of health to shape the labour market according to sector-wide, priority health needs. Governments, the WHO, the International Labour Organization, research funders and research institutions need to ensure that the data required to produce detailed HR situation analyses are generated. In addition, they need to encourage much greater investment in HR policy research, an aspect of health research that is greatly neglected (Chopra et al. 2008).

Ministries of health, NGOs and donor agencies should also coordinate their HR recruitment and deployment policies rather than competing with each other over scarce staff. Recently, a group of international NGOs developed a code of conduct to discourage NGOs from inadvertently undermining the public sector by, among other things, recruiting its staff.[3]

In the meantime, many responses to the HR crisis have focused on the delegation of tasks to 'lower' and less costly cadres of health worker. Such efforts have shown that well-trained nurses, non-physician clinicians and lay workers can be trained to carry out skilled tasks (Dovlo 2004).

However, a system of fair pay will be important to maintain morale and avoid exploitation.

Interventions to improve the retention, motivation and payment of health workers in the public sector remain mostly neglected, especially for health workers operating in isolated and difficult circumstances. These include enhancing working conditions and the quality of supervision; addressing on-the-job safety and security concerns; and improving management of the payroll.

Despite efforts by the Commonwealth Secretariat to promote voluntary ethical codes of conduct when it comes to high-income countries recruiting health workers from low-income countries, commercial recruitment agencies still operate aggressively in resource-poor countries (Mills et al. 2008). This practice could be stopped if the international community was serious about tackling the crisis.

Finally, for the public sector, there has been insufficient progress made in getting the International Monetary Fund (IMF) and ministries of finance to lift inappropriate ceilings on public-sector wage bills, which prevent some governments from paying public-sector health workers an adequate wage or expanding the public workforce (CGD 2007; Marphatia et al. 2007).

2 *Adequate, sustainable and reliable public financing for the health system*

An adequate human infrastructure for health systems in low-income countries will require increased levels of health expenditure. There are three possible strategies. First, low-income countries can improve health expenditure by increasing their public budgets through more efficient and effective systems, and then allocating a higher proportion of the public budget to health. Second, high-income countries could reach the long-standing target of allocating 0.7 per cent of gross national income (GNI) to development assistance, and commit to reliable transfer of funds for periods of five to ten years. Third, in a globalised world economy, public finance should be generated at the global level, possibly through an international tax authority of some sort that could help reclaim the hundreds of billions of dollars of public revenue lost due to tax avoidance and tax competition (Tax Justice Network 2007). In addition to generating revenue for health and poverty eradication, regulation of global finance and banking could help reduce levels of corruption.

In terms of the first strategy, civil society action to raise the level of domestic public spending on health has been inadequate. Few African countries have reached the Abuja target of allocating 15 per cent of their public budget to health, and in many low-income countries public revenues are a small proportion of gross domestic product (GDP). The effectiveness and accountability of national tax regimes in many low-income countries can and should be strengthened.

So far as the second strategy is concerned, high-income countries have begun to increase volumes of development assistance in recent years. However, it is still a paltry amount that falls far short of the UN target (see D2). Furthermore, much health aid is used poorly, as discussed in later chapters in this book.

So far as the third strategy is concerned, there is still limited political appetite for tackling the problems of capital flight, tax avoidance and tax evasion. The Tax Justice Network campaigns to help low- and middle-income countries reclaim their lost public revenue – they need greater support from the health community, who in turn would benefit from higher levels of health expenditure.

One recent positive development came in 2006 when an international air ticket 'solidarity levy' was established by France, Brazil, Chile, Great Britain and Norway. The money raised is dedicated to projects addressing HIV/AIDS, TB and Malaria and is pooled and administered by a new organisation called UNITAID. By the middle of 2007, thirty-four countries had committed to implementing this levy. UNITAID's expenditure of about US$300 million in 2007 is a relatively small amount of money, but it does represent an innovative new source of global public revenue generation.[4]

3 Harmonised, sector-wide coordination and planning

Effective and coherent health systems development requires effective and coherent health-sector stewardship. In many countries, this doesn't exist for two reasons. First, external development assistance for health is un-coordinated and fragmented. Second, ministries of health are not providing enough effective leadership. Much greater attention needs to be paid to sector-wide funding, budgeting and planning; developing the capacities of ministries of health to provide effective leadership; and enabling civil society organisations to hold both donors and governments to account. These issues are discussed in greater detail in Chapters D1.1 and D1.4.

4 Unhindered access to essential health care

User fees remain an intolerable barrier to essential health care. In many countries, the abolition of user fees in the public sector requires an increase in public health budgets, as discussed earlier. All countries should, as a first step, adopt a target to reduce direct out-of-pocket payments to less than 20 per cent of total health-care expenditure.

Community-based health insurance (CBHI) – also called community-based financing, mutual health organisations, and micro-insurance

IMAGE BI.2   **Women in Sudan attend a birthing ceremony**

programmes for health – is sometimes suggested as a way to mitigate the impact of user fees. The aim of CBHI is to encourage individuals to make prepayments for health care which can be pooled and then used to insure households against the costs of health care. However, the potential of CBHI is limited for several reasons (least of all the fact that poor households would find it difficult to contribute to such a scheme), which are discussed in an accompanying GHW document that can found at www.ghwatch.org/.

Another proposal for raising and organising health finance is social health insurance (SHI), where money is raised directly from the payrolls of employed individuals and then pooled into a health insurance fund. In some countries, SHI only covers those in formal employment, leaving those in informal employment or who are unemployed to be covered by a separate system of public financing. In some countries, SHI schemes receive public subsidies to include those who are unemployed, indigent or working in the informal sector. In many countries, policies to encourage SHI may represent a positive step forward, but there are various pros and cons that need to be carefully weighed. This is discussed in an accompanying GHW document that can found at www.ghwatch.org/.

A number of options are open to countries to remove the harmful and inequitable impacts of user fees. Civil society organisations (CSOs), however, need to study the political, economic and health systems context of each country carefully before adopting a campaigning strategy for health financing that is appropriate and feasible.

5   *Effective health-sector management*

The clear need to improve public-sector governance and management at all levels of the health system in many countries appears to be largely ignored by donors and international health policy experts. As well as improving HR planning and management, other aspects of health management which need to be highlighted include resource management and planning; expenditure monitoring; financial management; information management; essential drugs management; and operational research. These are all aspects of health systems strengthening that civil society organisations need to be monitoring just as carefully as they monitor progress in relation to coverage of disease-based clinical interventions.

In order to force the issue, CSOs in low-income countries could be supported to demand the regular production of national health accounts to describe how health care is financed as well as the pattern of expenditure across geographic areas, socio-economic groups, and between secondary/tertiary hospitals and district health services. This will improve government and donor accountability and strengthen health and management information systems.

However, the current predisposition towards organising health systems as a patchwork of vertical programmes and fragmented projects is distracting attention away from the 'slow-fix' solutions required to tackle deep-rooted deficiencies in health systems management.

6   *Vertical and horizontal alignment*

Although selective and vertical interventions make important contributions to health, the present configuration of multiple funding channels and programmes is hindering the important requirement for integration and coherent health systems development. Rationalisation of the global health aid architecture and sector-wide coordination and management will help improve this situation. But there is a need for a more bottom-up approach and agreement on a common and cross-cutting set of health systems indicators that can be shared by all agencies and programmes. There could also be agreement that certain aspects of a health-care system, such as the supply and distribution system of medicines and laboratory services, should not be duplicated, and certain key components of management, such as information systems, should be aligned.

7   *Public accountability and community involvement*

For public-sector bureaucracies to work effectively, efficiently and fairly, they need to be held accountable internally through rules and codes of conduct, and to communities and the public. Sector-wide budgets and a commitment to public stewardship are insufficient in themselves to get health systems working well – the public sector also needs to be kept honest and accountable. The scope of civil society activities involved in strengthening health-care systems include advocacy, monitoring and participating in planning and decision-making. Civil society can call for streams of funding to support civil society engagement in such activities, either from sector-wide budgets or from external sources.

8   *The district health system*

The district health system (DHS) provides a framework for the integration of policies, programmes and priorities emanating from the centre; for health plans and programmes to be tailored to the needs and characteristics of local populations; and for better community involvement in health. The WHO and others have for many years promoted the rationale of the DHS model. However, implementation has been undermined by the effects of structural adjustment programmes; the persistence of vertical programmes and top-down management cultures; market-based policies; and a reluctance to invest in district-level health management structures with authority, status and skills.

Civil society can advocate for the promotion of the DHS model as an organisational basis for health systems. In countries where non-government providers supply a significant amount of health care, health districts can form the basis for improved collaboration and joint planning with public-sector providers.

9   *A private sector harnessed to serve the public good*

In many countries, a large proportion of health-care provision is carried out by the private sector, much of it by unregulated, small-scale and disorganised private dispensaries, clinics and 'pavement doctors'. This unregulated network of private provision threatens to expand in the current commercial climate favoured by actors such as the Gates Foundation and the World Bank.

Many governments currently lack the capacity to monitor the quality of this health care, let alone improve its quality. This capacity needs to be developed. Meanwhile, civil society can advocate for:

- the completion of in-depth studies of the quality of care provided by the primary-level private sector;
- strategies to integrate the private sector into a structured and accountable framework of standards;

- policy instruments, such as licensing requirements, formal accreditation and price controls, to regulate and improve the quality of care of this sector.

In some countries, further steps need to be taken to regulate organised private insurance markets and to amalgamate them into larger pools of financing, where appropriate. Civil society can call for:

- a review of private insurance markets and private hospitals, and their impact on the public sector;
- laws to promote community rating and prescribed minimum benefits where private insurance schemes exist, and to block payment systems that encourage over-servicing.

Final comment

While it may be easier to advance the goal of 'health for all' through the more straightforward agenda of diseases, it is vital that civil society organisations are able to demystify the set of multiple and technical issues related to health systems in order to campaign on behalf of detailed health systems policies that will promote equity, effectiveness and sustainability in the long run.

Notes

1. For a detailed discussion on health systems, see *Global Health Watch 2005–2006*.
2. See www.ghwatch.org/ for a more detailed description of medical tourism.
3. See http://depts.washington.edu/haiuw/news/newsletters/2007–09.html.
4. See www.unitaid.eu and www.ghwatch.org/ for more details.

References

CGD (Center for Global Development Working Group on IMF Programs and Health Spending) (2007). Does the IMF constrain health spending in poor countries? Evidence and an agenda for action. Washington DC: Center for Global Development. www.cgdev.org/doc/IMF/IMF_Report.pdf.

Chopra, M., S. Munro, J.N. Lavis et al. (2008). Effects of policy options for human resources for health: An analysis of systematic reviews. *The Lancet* 371: 668–74.

Dovlo, D. (2004). Using mid-level cadres as substitutes for internationally mobile health professionals in Africa. A desk review. *Human Resources for Health* 2(7).

GAVI (2007). Experiences of the GAVI alliance health system strengthening investment. The Global Fund's strategic approach to health system strengthening background note 5 for 30–31 July 2007 Consultation. www.who.int/healthsystems/gf23.pdf.

Global Health Watch (2006). A health systems development agenda for developing countries: Time to be clear and visionary. www.ghwatch.org/advocacy.php.

McCoy, D., S. Bennett, S. Witter et al. (2008). Salaries and incomes of health workers in sub-Saharan Africa. *The Lancet* 371: 675–81.

Macready, N. (2007). Developing countries court medical tourists. *The Lancet* 369: 1849–50.

Marphatia, A.A., R. Moussie, A. Ainger and D. Archer (2007). Confronting the contradictions: The IMF, wage bill caps and the case for teachers. Action Aid USA. www.actionaidusa.org/imf_africa.php.

Mills, E.J., W.A. Schabas, J. Volmink et al. (2008). Should active recruitment of health workers from sub-Saharan Africa be viewed as a crime? *The Lancet* 371: 685–8.

Palmer, D. (2006). Tackling Malawi's human resources crisis. *Reproductive Health Matters* 14(27): 27–39.

Reich, M., et al. (2008). Global action on health systems: A proposal for the Tokyo G8 summit. *The Lancet* 371: 865–9.

Tax Justice Network (2007). Closing the floodgates: Collecting tax to pay for development. www.taxjustice.net/cms/upload/pdf/Closing_the_Floodgates_-_1-FEB-2007.pdf.

WHO (2006). *World health report: Working together for health*. Geneva.

WHO (2008). Global Knowledge Base on Transplantation (GKT). www.who.int/transplantation/knowledgebase/en/.

World Bank (1997). Health nutrition and population sector strategy. Washington DC: World Bank. http://web.worldbank.org/wbsite/external/topics/exthealthnutrition andpopulation/0,,contentMDK:20133760~pagePK:210058~piPK:210062~theSitePK: 282511,00.html.

B2 Mental health: culture, language and power

In poor countries, mental illness tends to be grossly neglected by health systems. Diseases tend to get prioritised. This chapter discusses the challenges of caring for people with mental illness and emotional distress. However, emotional distress and mental illness are embedded within and cannot be separated from language, and cultural, social and political context. Placing mental health within these contexts is the essence of this chapter. Those who are mentally ill are also subject to stigma, sometimes feared, and sometimes cared for in inhumane conditions. These crucial issues are not addressed directly but are highlighted in some of the case studies that accompany this chapter on the Global Health Watch website.

Mental health problems are wide-ranging and include depression, schizophrenia, anxiety, stress-related disorders and substance abuse. They may be mild and temporary or chronic and severely disabling and affect all ages. Mental health problems also include organic disorders such as dementia and mental retardation (but not epilepsy, which is sometimes wrongly seen as a mental disorder). Poor mental health can also result in poorer outcomes associated with other diseases such as cancer, HIV/AIDS, diabetes and cardiovascular disease (Prince et al. 2007).

The World Health Organization (WHO 2003) estimated that 13 per cent of the worldwide burden of disease is due to mental health problems, although 31 per cent of countries do not have a specific public budget for mental health (Saxena et al. 2007). In addition, each year nearly a million people take their own lives. Rates are highest in Europe's Baltic States where around 40 people per 100,000 commit suicide annually. However, the incidence of suicide is widely under-reported because suicide is considered a sin in many religions, a taboo in many societies, and a crime in others.

IMAGE B2.1   **Young Brazilian girl suffering from mental illness
is chained to the wall**

Suicide is among the top three causes of death of young people aged 15–35 (WHO 2000) and is one of the leading causes of death of young women in India and China (Wortley 2000).

In spite of the burden of mental illness across the world, 40 per cent of countries have no mental health policies. Thirty-three countries with a combined population of 2 billion invest less than 1 per cent of their total health budget on mental health (WHO 2005a). More than two-thirds of the world's population (68 per cent), the majority of whom are in Africa and South Asia, have access to only 0.04 psychiatrists per 100,000 of the population, although these areas have an extensive network of traditional practitioners (WHO 2005a).

The social and structural determinants of mental ill health

There is a need to improve the availability and quality of mental health-care services worldwide. However, as mental heath is inextricably linked to the cultural and social fabric in which each person lives, improving mental health must also address negative social and economic factors.

A multiplicity of factors can contribute to either increased vulnerability or the development of resilience – that is, the capacity to cope with adversity. Many factors are associated with emotional well-being. These include self-esteem, optimism, a sense of control, and the ability to initiate, develop and sustain mutually satisfying personal relationships. These factors operate at individual, family, community and societal levels.

The dominant model of health care for mental illness focuses on the individual and family, and on providing treatment rather than on prevention and mental health promotion. While treatment is necessary for conditions that have an organic or physical basis, a large proportion of the burden of mental distress is exacerbated by social and economic factors and is preventable. A list of some of the social and structural determinants of mental health is presented below.

Poverty, affluence and inequality

The interrelationships between poverty, affluence, inequality and mental ill health are complex. Poverty can predispose people to mental health problems, but mentally ill people and their families are also likely to move into poverty. Poor mental health can therefore be both a cause and a consequence of poverty. This risk is exacerbated by factors such as insecurity, poor physical health, rapid social change and limited opportunities as a result of less education (Patel and Kleinman 2003).

When people exist in extreme poverty, material progress can increase emotional well-being. However, when material discomfort has been assuaged, extra income becomes much less important than interpersonal relationships.

> When I don't have [any food to bring my family] I borrow, mainly from neighbours and friends. I feel ashamed standing before my children when I have nothing to help feed my family. I'm not well when I'm unemployed. It's terrible. (Patel and Kleinman 2003)

Rich countries have reached a level of development beyond which further rises in living standards fail to reduce social problems or improve well-being or happiness.[1] Indeed, excessive materialism has been described as a cause of social malaise and is sometimes described as 'affluenza' (James 2007).

While levels of income may have an independent effect on levels of mental well-being, recent evidence suggests that the experience of relative poverty and inequality also has a negative effect on both psychological and social well-being (Wilkinson 2005). Inequality has grown dramatically over the last 300 years, both between rich and poor countries and within countries. Cross-country comparisons demonstrate that countries with a wide gap between social classes will be more dysfunctional, violent and have higher rates of mental distress than those with a narrower gap. Further, poor countries with fairer wealth distribution are healthier and happier than richer, more unequal nations (Wilkinson 2005).

Wilkinson (2006) asserts that inequality is the most important explanation of why some affluent societies are 'social failures'. What is important is the scale of difference in social status and divisions within a society. This view is also supported by Richard Layard (2006), a UK economist, who argues that social comparison and status competition in affluent societies are significant factors and that happiness is derived from relative, not absolute, income.

Layard also points to the negative effect of constant competition between individuals and companies for status and material possessions. Advertising colludes with this by encouraging people to feel that possessions can make one feel like a more substantial person in the eyes of others. People also continually adapt to higher income levels so that their idea of a sufficient income grows as their income increases, leaving a large number of people chasing an ever-elusive goal.

Globalisation/industrialisation

Linked to the determinants of material well-being and relative social position are the processes of globalisation and industrialisation. Both have fuelled changes in lifestyle and shaped patterns of inequality within and between countries which have had profound effects. Traditional ways of living have been undermined and devalued as consumerism, materialism and economic growth are promulgated and equated with the concept of 'development'. The speed of change is also such that societies are struggling to adapt. Millions of people, who have been forced to leave the land and their traditional ways of life, are now living in alien urban environments, often with little hope of decent employment and forced to cope with the disintegration of family and community structures.

Globalisation has also contributed to hundreds of millions of people living in increasing poverty. In this sense, the rising tide of suicides and premature mortality in many countries can be viewed not just as 'mental health problems' but also as an understandable consequence of the profound despair experienced as a result of the loss of livelihoods and ways of life. Sengupta (2006) illustrates this despair in his description of how globalisation has affected small-scale farmers in India, who are now subject to unfair competition. Together with the pressure to purchase more expensive genetically modified seeds and susceptibility to monsoons and crop failures, debt and unemployment among Indian small-scale farmers have reached unprecedented levels, and the suicide rate within this group has substantially increased (Patel et al. 2006).

In addition to the movement of people from rural to urban settings, there is increased movement of people internationally. Integration into host countries can be stressful. Forced migration from political violence can magnify the problems, and the mental health of refugees presents ongoing complex needs, some of which are referred to in Chapter B3.

Gender and violence

Gender inequalities are an important social determinant of mental distress. There is a consistent gender difference in risks for common mental disorders in all societies. For example, depression affects twice as many women as men across different countries and settings (Patel and Kleinman 2003). Women's multiple roles as both caregivers and breadwinners, as well as their vulnerability to gender-based sexual violence, are contributory factors. In low-income countries, women also bear the brunt of the adversities associated with poverty, and have less access to school (Wortley 2006).

The relationship between violence and mental health is complex. Domestic violence is ubiquitous and usually directed towards women; political violence creates fear, injury and loss of loved ones and disruption of the social fabric of society. Both are associated with stress and mental disorder. In political violence there may be gender differences in that young men are more likely to take up arms and be casualties, whilst women are left isolated and without means of support.

Children are also deeply affected by political violence and in some cases are even recruited as child soldiers. Mental well-being requires stable caring relationships; violence is the antithesis of this.

Exposure to poverty, inequalities and injustice may contribute to both mental distress and violence, independently of each. Violence may cause mental ill-health, though not all who experience violence develop mental health problems.

In some societies, the mental health system has been used as an instrument of social control and even repression, as was the case in the former Soviet Union. McCulloch's (1995) review of the history of psychiatry in Africa reveals how it was entwined with the ideology of colonialism.

Language, explanatory models and power

Although common biological factors underlie some forms of mental illness across all societies, explanatory models for mental illness and emotional distress are embedded within the assumptions and belief systems of the prevailing culture.

However, those whose language and explanatory models exert greatest power also hold the power to determine and label mental distress. In an increasingly globalised world, it is mainly the materialistic, secular and scientific ideologies of the West that dominate thinking, particularly in international organisations. For example, in 2007 *The Lancet* published a prominent series on global mental health, wherein contributors argue for the universal applicability of Western models. They pay little attention to

---

BOX B2.1   **The importance of language**

In Afghanistan, *mualagh* denotes a feeling of floating in sad uncertainty, like a leaf held aloft only by gusts of wind; in Darfur, *mondahesh* means a sense of shocked surprise; and in East Timor, *hanoin barak* denotes a state of thinking too much. How do these concepts, rooted in local cultural contexts and understandings, relate to Western mental health concepts, if at all?

The problem is not simply one of 'translation'. Every language carries within it all the assumptions used by a society to make sense of the human condition, including inner feelings and emotional distress. These assumptions contain what people *believe* to be 'true' in relation to mental health problems. Just because emotional reactions to distressing circumstances can be found worldwide does not necessarily mean that they *mean* the same thing for people everywhere.

---

the role of traditional healers and make scarce mention of the essential role of language and culture.

The globalisation of Western approaches can sideline the articulation of local understandings of mental distress in indigenous languages and sometimes ignore or pathologise the religious and spiritual dimensions of human experience.

One of the features of Western mental health approaches is an individualistic view of self. Separateness, independence, and the capacity to express one's own views and opinions are both explicitly valued and implicitly assumed. The reductionist neoliberal scientific method favoured by the West tends to reduce phenomena into parts, including how human beings are perceived. Individualism and the scientific approach are coupled with ideologies of consumerism, individual choice and individual fulfilment.

Many non-Western cultures socialise children into a different sense of self where priority is given to connections and interrelationship with others as the basis of psychological well-being. The health of individuals is dependent on, and not separate from, healthy relationships with the wider social, cultural and natural environments – ancestors, the community and the land.

In all societies families and communities are the first line of support when someone experiences emotional distress. How families make sense of what is happening and what they perceive needs to be done cannot be separated from their language, values, assumptions and culture. Socially constructed explanations shape the way people make sense of chaotic and confusing feelings (biochemical cause or evil spell), determine who is socially sanctioned to heal (psychiatrist or shaman), and what people believe will help (Prozac, ECT or rituals to appease the ancestors). The diversity of these assumptions reflects the many ways of making sense of human experience within a multitude of cultural traditions.

Western mental health programmes which focus on the individual have sometimes been inappropriately applied to socio-centric cultures. In societies where recovery for the individual is intimately connected with recovery for the wider community, this can be potentially harmful and undermine communal support systems.

A specific feature of most Western models in mental health is the identification of symptoms, which are then collapsed into a specific diagnosis. This diagnosis is then used to determine 'treatment'. In this model different individuals with similar constellations of symptoms would be likely to receive similar treatment. Cultural, religious and other social factors and unique life histories are considered less relevant to the diagnostic and therapeutic process.

One diagnosis that is the subject of considerable controversy is Post-Traumatic Stress Disorder (PTSD), a term used to describe a severe or prolonged constellation of particular physical and psychological reactions to deeply distressing events. Some of the symptoms of PTSD include intense fear, helplessness, and recurrent, intrusive and distressing recollections of the event; recurrent dreams of the event; acting or feeling as if the traumatic event were recurring; avoiding the place or associations with the trauma; emotional numbing; outbursts of anger; and somatisation (the manifestation of psychological distress through physical symptoms).

After traumatic events such as war, violence and natural disasters, many of the 'symptoms' typical of PTSD tend to be present. However, the significance of those symptoms is dependent upon social, economic, environmental and cultural factors. The ways in which individuals react emotionally to an adverse event are also dependent on past experiences; on the availability of coping strategies and emotional support available from others; on perceptions, understanding and meanings attributed to what is happening; and on perceived capacity to take effective action and plan for the future.

All these variables interact with social, religious and cultural norms in complex ways to determine how someone will react psychologically to trauma *and* how they will recover. The substance of the debate regarding the universal applicability of a diagnosis of PTSD (and associated treatment) is that it does not take these additional factors sufficiently into account.

Many people are resilient and appear able to deal with even quite severe traumatic events, especially if meaningful social structures remain, but there is a danger that Western medico-therapeutic approaches focus on individuals to the exclusion of social factors. These approaches also tend to focus on concepts of forgiveness and acceptance rather than on the need to find a social and moral meaning for the traumatic event. This may include a demand for justice, accountability and punishment of perpetrators, rather than 'acceptance'.

The spread of PTSD as a universal diagnostic category is another reflection of the worldwide influence of the West's medically based way of understanding distress. As Derek Summerfield (2003) comments, 'Western mental health discourse introduces core components of Western culture, including a theory of human nature, a definition of personhood, a sense of time and memory, and a secular source of moral authority. None of this is universal.'

The Western, biomedical approach to mental illness also promotes an approach to 'treatment' that is heavily based on pharmacology. This not only benefits the pharmaceuticals industry, but also creates a privileged position for the medical profession. While psychotropic medication *can* be beneficial for several conditions such as psychoses or bipolar disorders, the increasing use of pharmacological treatments can also undermine other approaches to treatment and care which may be more rooted in local culture.

Mental health in humanitarian aid programmes: a steep learning curve

Ever since the Rwandan genocide and the Bosnian conflict in the early 1990s, health professionals have been grappling with how to address the mental health needs of those affected by humanitarian emergencies. 'Psychosocial' and mental health interventions now draw increasing amounts of donor funding, although vigorous debates about the appropriateness and effectiveness of interventions are ongoing.

Responses from aid agencies following disasters should be underpinned by the principle of supporting and understanding local concepts, perceptions and strategies, which may prove very difficult in practice. Aid workers responding to a disaster may have little local experience or understanding, and pressure from donors may require the implementation of a programme within a short time frame coupled with 'evidence of impact'.

There have been major divisions among Western mental health professionals regarding the severity and prevalence of mental health problems in humanitarian emergencies, particularly in relation to 'trauma'. The debate centres on whether wars, disasters and other humanitarian emergencies generate enormous mental health needs, as is sometimes claimed, and

BOX B2.2 **Fishermen from Sri Lanka**

'We are fishermen and we need space in our houses – not only to live but also to store our fishing equipment. After the tsunami we have been living in this camp, which is 12 kilometres away from the coast and in this place for reconstruction. When the international agency came and started building a housing scheme, we realised that they are building flats, which is not suitable to us. But when we try to explain this to the foreigners who are building this scheme, they looked at us as if we were aliens from another planet. What are we supposed to do?'

'I came to the village the day after the tsunami to look for my children but the guards had already put a fence up. I begged them to let me in but they said it was their land and they would be building a hotel. They held their guns and said that, if I didn't go, I would join those who died in the tsunami. We have lost our families, now we are having our homes stolen too.'

Source: Action Aid International 2006.

whether individual treatment of trauma symptoms or the restoration of the cultural, social and communal fabric should take precedence. The recent synthesis of differing views by WHO (2005b) concludes that there is no consensus regarding the appropriateness of Western-type interventions in non-Western settings.

These issues received particular attention and stimulated worldwide debate in relation to the response to the tsunami in early 2005. After the tsunami many NGOs sought to provide 'mental health assistance', utilising the underlying assumptions of, and believing in, the universality of Western psychological models of distress, including underlying assumptions about the individual nature of trauma. Most were ignorant of local culture and traditions and did not have an understanding of the location of personal identities within a communal society. But was mental health assistance what local communities themselves were seeking? Were their voices heard? How appropriate are mental health interventions if people are losing their access to land, water, natural resources and social services?

Experiences of some mental health interventions have led a number of people to question whether external mental health 'aid' had actually been harmful. In Sri Lanka, the concept of an individual without his/her community does not exist. Positive self-identity is based on harmonious relationships with family and community. A woman is not simply an individual person – her identity is tied to her being a mother, daughter, wife, grandmother and through her work as a farmer or teacher. So, too, for men, children, youth, the elderly and people with disabilities. This identity provides them with a place in the world, including respect and honour. It is in a social setting that those who need help reveal themselves and that the processes which determine how victims become survivors are played out over time.

Inappropriate interventions which afford people only a passive role, for instance awaiting a cure delivered by outside (or inside) 'experts' who depend on Western knowledge, may aggravate feelings of helplessness and vulnerability. Western mental health models involving expertise, training and a new language of medico-therapeutics may contribute to this and devalue local articulations and understandings of distress, undermining some of the local, time-honoured processes that offer protection at a time of crisis.

How are these potentially incompatible approaches to understanding the nature of personhood and identity resolved? Are mental health 'experts' and the trauma industry ready to acknowledge the limited validity of Western psychiatric and psychological formulations, and Western-style counselling, in settings like Sri Lanka?

Despite the limitations of their current form, mental health issues are slowly moving into the mainstream of the humanitarian aid agenda. In 2007 the Inter-Agency Standing Committee (IASC) Task Force on Mental Health and Psychosocial Support published comprehensive guidelines and minimum standards on 'Mental Health and Psychosocial Support in Emergency Settings'. These take a holistic approach, attempting to promote emotional well-being in all areas of aid provision – from sanitation and shelter to psychosocial programmes, psychological self-care for aid workers, and identification and care of the mentally ill.

What needs to be done?

This chapter has highlighted issues of language, culture and power and the importance of context in understanding and responding to mental distress, and also briefly described the main social and structural determinants. This section highlights some conclusions and recommendations.

Advocate for mental health

Caution is required in the application of a scientific ideology which divides human beings into parts rather than seeing people as whole within their own social, political and cultural context. Ancient medical systems such as

Ayurvedic and Chinese medicine took such a holistic view, seeing mind, body and spirit as inseparable. Thus there is the paradox of advocating strongly that mental health and emotional well-being need greater attention in government policies, plans, international NGOs and every aspect of society, but at the same time also advocating for a holistic view of human health. There have been calls for the inclusion of mental health within the framework of the Millennium Development Goals (MDGs), especially because of their influence on policy development and resource allocation decisions, but ideally all MDGs need to incorporate mental health.

At the present time, even when recognising the need for a holistic approach to health, the 'no health without mental health' (Prince et al. 2007) mantra still has to be articulated loud and clear when so much of human economic, social and political activity is inimical to emotional well-being and actively harmful to mental health.

Challenge Western, medico-centric concepts of mental health

Although Western-based mental health care is not homogeneous, a bio-medical and highly individualised strand of Western psychiatry has tended to dominate and influence much of the formal global approach to mental distress. Some aspects of this model and system of practice have a role to play, but the limitations are often minimised. It is particularly important that there is a far more extensive critique of the assumptions underlying Western approaches to mental health care. Such reflection is essential to minimise cultural imperialism and to ensure the necessary degree of respect and care when working in very different cultural contexts.

Above all, there is a requirement for mental health professionals and policymakers to listen, respect and understand how people make sense of emotional distress within their own culture and language. They need to learn and work with the 'untranslatable' (it has been suggested that a worldwide database of indigenous expressions describing experiences of mental distress be developed), and to tailor all therapeutic interventions to the social context.

Promote integration

In spite of enormous cultural differences, certain characteristics of the process of healing appear to be common across different societies. These include:

- an emotionally charged, confiding relationship with a helping person (often with the participation of a group);
- a healing setting;

BOX B2.3   **Traditional healing: Mbarara case study**

Over 90 per cent of mentally ill patients who come to hospital first go to traditional healers (THs). During hospitalisation some patients continue consulting THs while others talk of consulting them after discharge to perform certain rituals or ceremonies. It is a common belief among the majority of our people that witchcraft, sorcery, the evil eye, the breaking of taboo or the neglecting of rituals for ancestral spirits cause mental illness. This explains the reason why THs are consulted.

THs occupy a key position in the community. They see and treat many people with mental problems. They distinguish illnesses according to various physiological systems as in the modern Western system. THs also use psychotherapeutic techniques which include reassurance, suggestion, manipulation of the environment, and ego-strengthening elements such as reciting incantations and the wearing of prescribed amulets. Many THs have described this approach as *siyasa* (psychological manipulation).

The concept of treatment from the TH's point of view often transcends the physical, emotional and psychological to include the social and spiritual parameters. It involves man's relationship with the past, the present and the future and with spirits, especially of ancestors. In addition to psychotherapeutic techniques, herbs are administered. We have identified both good and harmful practices. However, through discussion, good practices have been encouraged. Harmful practices such as starving, tying up patients or cutting the skin of various patients using the same razor blade have been discouraged. THs now recognise the danger of using the same blade on different people and have willingly accepted change. While THs can treat various kinds of psychological problems, they do not have the means of treating severe mental disorders. Traditional and scientific approaches must therefore be seen as complementary.

Source: Case study submitted by Elias Byaruhanga (Uganda).

- a rationale, conceptual scheme or even a myth that provides a plausible, culturally appropriate explanation for the patient's symptoms and prescribes a ritual or procedure for resolving them;
- a ritual or procedure that requires the active participation of both patient and healer, and that is believed by both to be the means of restoring the patient's health (Frank and Frank 1991).

Many traditional approaches to healing are effective because they are embedded within local social and cultural structures, but, as with all

mental health care, they are by no means perfect. Western psychiatry, traditional healing and systems of self-caring have both benefits and limitations.
However, a greater appreciation of the strengths of indigenous or traditional
healing practices and their underlying cultural assumptions could help lead
to a more appropriate integration of and synergy between different systems
and models of care. The case study in Box B2.3 illustrates the successful
integration of traditional and Western approaches to mental health care.

Generating such joint working has significant implications for the training of all mental health professionals. The capacity to integrate different
cultural perspectives needs to be at the core of the curriculum for the
training of formal mental health professionals in both Western and low-
income countries. This would enable them confidently to work across and
between different cultures and languages, rather than being trained in
the application of Western approaches. Even today, the training of mental
health personnel in low-income countries can still be based on a Western
curriculum that ignores the local language and cultural context, and some
who train in Western countries even become ashamed of their own culture.
Those with knowledge of indigenous language, practices and beliefs should
be seen as exceptionally valuable resources and should not have to abandon
that understanding when they begin professional training.

Promote a holistic approach to mental health

Improving psychological and emotional well-being should be made a
primary aim of public policy not just within the health sector, but also in
the education, housing, employment, trade and justice sectors.

The elimination of poverty, a reduction in social and economic disparities, respect for women, the acknowledgement, understanding and acceptance of cultural diversity and language must all be essential components
in national and global health plans. Although mental health is gradually
receiving more attention, a holistic approach to well-being and the inclusion
of mental health as a cross-cutting feature of national health plans and
poverty reduction strategies remains elusive.

Research

There is a need for greater dissemination of research on the effects of
culture, language and social structure on mental illness. This must be accompanied by a commitment to extend further and develop an appropriate
evidence base. Western research methods themselves are a product of a
specific 'scientific' way of understanding phenomena and can be ill-suited
to capturing the emotional, spiritual and existential dimensions of human
existence and challenges brought about by globalisation, economic reforms

and political processes. There is much to be learned from other disciplines, particularly anthropology.

There is also a need for more detailed and thoughtful analysis of the policies and programmes of the key global and international health institutions such as the WHO and the World Bank. To what extent do they promote a holistic and culturally appropriate model of mental health care? If funding for mental health programmes is expanding, how exactly is this extra money being used?

There is no doubt that great progress has been made in bringing mental health issues into the mainstream, and that this presents increasing opportunities for funding, programmes and developing of services. The experience of emotional distress is part of being human, and a concern for mental health is one of the commonalities that unites all people and all societies. However, mental illness, emotional distress and psychological well-being are expressed through a myriad languages and cultural and social contexts. We have the knowledge and understanding to rise to the challenge of recognising the commonalities we share while still being able to safeguard our own uniqueness as human beings. Will our social and political systems allow us to turn that understanding into a reality?

Notes

1. For more information, see www.happyplanetindex.org.

References

Action Aid International (2006). *Tsunami response: A human rights assessment.* www.actionaid. org.uk/_content/documents/tsunami_HR01.pdf.

Frank, J.D., and J.B. Frank (1991). *Persuasion and healing.* Baltimore MD: Baltimore University Press.

James, O. (2007). *Affluenza.* London: Vermillion.

Layard, R. (2006). *Happiness: Lessons from a new science.* London: Penguin.

McCulloch, J. (1995). *Colonial Psychiatry and the African Mind.* Cambridge: Cambridge University Press.

Patel, V., and A. Kleinman (2003). Poverty and mental disorders in developing countries. *Bulletin of the World Health Organization* 81(8): 609–15.

Patel, V., B. Saraceno and A. Kleinman (2006). Beyond evidence: The moral case for international mental health. *American Journal of Psychiatry* 163(8), August.

Prince, M., et al. (2007). No health without mental health. *The Lancet* 370: 859–77.

Saxena, S., et al. (2007). Resources for mental health: Scarcity, in equity and inefficiency. *The Lancet* 370: 878–89.

Sengupta, S. (2006). On India's farms, a plague of suicides. *New York Times*, 19 September.

Summerfield, D. (2004). Cross cultural perspectives on the medicalization of human suffering. In G. Rosen (ed.), *Posttraumatic stress disorder: Issues and controversies.* London: John Wiley.

WHO (World Health Organization) (2000). *Preventing suicide: A resource for primary health care workers.* WHO/MNH/MBD/00.4. Geneva. www.who.int/mental_health/media/en/59.pdf.

WHO (2003). *Investing in mental health.* Geneva.

WHO (2005a). *Mental health atlas.* Geneva. www.who.int/mental_health/evidence/atlas/.

WHO (2005b). Mental and social health during and after acute emergencies: An emerging consensus? *Bulletin of the World Health Organization* 83(1): 71–6.

Wilkinson, R.G. (2005). *The impact of inequality: How to make sick societies healthier.* London and New York: Routledge.

Wilkinson, R.G. (2006). The impact of equality: Empirical evidence. *Renewal* 14(1): 20–26.

Wortley, H. (2006). *Depression a leading contributor to global burden of disease.* Washington DC: Population Reference Bureau. www.prb.org.

B 3   **Access to health care for migrants and asylum-seekers**

Migrants, refugees and displaced people

In a world where one in thirty-five of us are migrants, migration has been described as 'one of the defining issues of the 21st century'. The International Organisation for Migration estimates that the number of international migrants increased from 76 million to 191 million between 1960 and 2005. Of the 191 million people living outside their country of birth in 2005, 8.7 million were refugees and 773,000 asylum-seekers. By the end of 2006, there were approximately 9.9 million refugees worldwide, an increase of 14 per cent from late 2005 (UNHCR 2007a). There were also 24.4 million 'internally displaced persons' who had been forced to flee their homes but not crossed national borders (IDMC 2007). Many of the internally displaced persons live in 'refugee camps', mostly in low- and middle-income countries (IDMC 2007). While the unmet health needs of the millions of people living in makeshift camps across the world are a public health challenge, this chapter mainly draws attention to the plight of migrants, refugees and asylum-seekers.

Migration has tended to be seen as either *forced* or *voluntary*. 'Forced migration' includes movement of people displaced by conflict, political or religious persecution, natural or environmental disasters, famine, chemical or nuclear accidents or 'development projects'. 'Voluntary migration' has been used to describe those who migrate of their own accord, for instance to find work. For example, in the Middle East, a large number of foreign contract workers from Asia and Africa have fulfilled the demand for unskilled workers. In other instances, workers migrate for shorter-term, seasonal work. However, there is growing recognition that it is difficult to distinguish between forced and voluntary migration.

BOX B3.1 **Some definitions**

Refugees are defined by the 1951 Convention Relating to the Status of Refugees as people who 'owing to well-founded fear of being persecuted for reasons of race, religion, nationality, membership of a particular social group or political opinion' are outside the country of their nationality and who are unable to or, owing to fear, unwilling 'to avail (themselves) of the protection of that country'. Asylum-seekers are people who have fled to another country where they have applied for state protection by claiming refugee status, but have not received a final decision on their application.

Contrary to the impression given by Western media, developing countries host 70 per cent of the global refugee population. Africa hosts 25 per cent of all refugees, Europe 18 per cent, North and South America 10 per cent, and Asia/Pacific 9 per cent. Pakistan hosts the greatest number of refugees with over a million. Iran and the United States host the next highest numbers of refugees, respectively. Most refugees in 2006 came from Afghanistan (21 per cent of all refugees). Iraqi refugees quintupled in 2006, with Sudan following behind (UNHCR 2007a). Tanzania has the highest number of refugees in relation its economic capacity: between 2001 and 2005 it hosted 868 refugees for each US dollar of gross domestic product (GDP) per capita. This compares to 21 refugees per GDP$1/capita in Germany, the highest ranking industrialised country (UNHCR 2007b).

In developed countries, public attention and debate are often focused on people who have entered a country without authorisation or who have overstayed their authorised entry. They are variously labelled as 'irregular', 'undocumented', 'illegal' or 'unauthorised' migrants. There are an estimated 30 to 40 million such migrants worldwide, of which 4.5 to 8 million are thought to be in Europe and an estimated 10.3 million in the United States (European Commission 2007; IOM 2007). Another group of people, mostly women and children, who can also be classified as migrants are the estimated 2.5 million victims of 'human trafficking'.

Migration, health and rights

People who migrate tend to be stronger and healthier than the populations they leave behind. Despite this 'healthy migrant' effect, migrants, especially 'forced migrants', face considerable threats to their health and barriers to receiving health care. Not only do many flee from hazardous situations,

BOX B3.2   **Stuck, ignored and isolated in transit**

'Fatima', a young Nigerian woman who found herself stuck in Morocco, gave birth to a baby in a forest near Oujda. Because her baby suffered an infection of the umbilical cord, she sought medical help from an NGO and was referred to the hospital. She was then transferred to a penitentiary centre and detained for five days, after which she and her baby were taken to the Algerian border in the desert and abandoned with the prospect of a perilous journey across no-man's land.

'Edwin' was trying to migrate to the United States from Guatemala by travelling on the infamous train known as 'the Beast', which travels through Mexico. Dizzy from fatigue and hindered by the crush of migrants, he fell off the train and lost his left leg. Edwin was lucky enough to be cared for by nurse and human rights activist Olga Sanchez. Although Mexican laws recognise the right of migrants to health care, most Central American migrants are unaware of these rights or are too afraid to contact services.

Sources: MSF 1997; Miller Llana 2007.

but they are exposed to risks during their migration journey; these include exposure to physical danger, violence, extreme temperatures and lack of access to food. Furthermore, as border control policies become tighter, migration routes become more risky. In 2006, for example, 7,000 people were estimated to have died making the dangerous crossing to the Canary Islands from the African coast (EU 2007).

The tightening of border controls in developed countries has also resulted in many migrants being stuck in low- and middle-income 'transit countries'. For example, North Africa is a transit area for people trying to reach Europe. Many transit countries, however, do not have the resources to respond to the needs or to protect the rights of this vulnerable population (see Box B3.2).

Migrants also face health-related problems after being settled in their host country. Poor mental health is commonly due to social isolation, poverty, loss of status and hostility from the local population. For those already suffering from distress caused by persecution, torture and violence, these exacerbating factors can result in serious mental illness and suicide. Migrants are also often overexposed to poor living conditions and more likely to be involved in jobs that are 'dirty, difficult and dangerous' (IPPR 2006) and that lack basic occupational safeguards and workers' rights (EC 2007).

BOX B3.3 **Access to health care for 'internal migrants' in China**

In China, the migration of 150–200 million people from rural areas into cities has been called the 'world's largest ever peacetime flow of migration' (Tuñón 2006). Many of these internal migrants end up in hazardous occupations and poor housing, often in overcrowded factory dormitories. Many are officially registered as 'temporary residents'. These temporary residents are also known as 'floating citizens' and have restricted entitlements to local health care. They are often ineligible for urban health insurance schemes and unable to afford private insurance or health-care fees (Amnesty International 2007). Thus, when Cha Guoqun left his village to do work in the city of Hangzhou and ended up with a leg injury that got infected, the doctor at the local state hospital gave him two options: either pay 1,000 yuan (US$120) a day for treatment (the equivalent of his entire monthly income), or have his leg amputated. Cha got lucky. He received subsidised treatment from a charity hospital, and was able to save his leg. As he said, 'I was lucky this time, but, on the whole, medical treatment is too expensive for people like me.'

Source: Amnesty International 2007.

Finally, migrants tend to experience poorer access to health care compared to the rest of the population. National health systems often discriminate against migrants and asylum-seekers in spite of several international treaties and commitments protecting their rights. The most vulnerable group are 'unauthorised' or 'undocumented' migrants. In Europe, the prevailing official attitude has been to treat them as though they are 'rightless', without basic legal protection or avenues to claim their entitlements (Human Rights Watch 2002; Jesuit Refugee Service 2001).

Access to health care in Europe

Asylum-seekers

A recent study of the legal situation in the twenty-five European Union (EU) countries found some restrictions on the access of asylum-seekers to health care in ten of them (Norredam et al. 2006), in spite of their being 'documented' migrants. The same study found that in five countries pregnant asylum-seekers were allowed access to emergency care only and that the entitlements of children were restricted in seven countries.

In Germany, for example, asylum-seekers do not have the same rights as citizens until they have lived in the country for three years (Médecins

---

BOX B3.4   **Migrants' rights**

Article 25 of the Universal Declaration of Human Rights states that *everyone* has the right to a standard of living adequate for the health and well-being of himself and of his family, including medical care and necessary social services.

The 'right of everyone to the enjoyment of the highest attainable standard of physical and mental health' is also laid down in the International Covenant on Economic, Social and Cultural Rights (ICESCR). The 156 countries that have ratified the Covenant must 'refrain from denying or limiting equal access for all persons' to preventive, curative and palliative health services, including 'asylum-seekers and illegal immigrants'.

The 1951 Convention Relating to the Status of Refugees states that 'refugees shall be accorded the same treatment' as nationals in relation to maternity, sickness, disability and old age.

The 2003 International Convention on the Protection of the Rights of All Migrant Workers and Members of their Families has set out the rights of migrant workers to health care (although it fails to address their rights to preventive measures and early treatment).

---

du Monde 2007). In Sweden, asylum-seeking children have the same access to health care as other children, but asylum-seeking adults do not have the same access as other adults (Hunt 2007).

Undocumented migrants

Relatively little is known about the access to health care of 'undocumented migrants'. However, in 2007 findings from a Médecins du Monde survey of 835 'undocumented migrants' in seven European countries were published. Although they are not a representative sample of undocumented migrants, the findings illustrate some of the problems faced in accessing health care. Some of these findings were:

* Although 78 per cent of the informants had in theory some right to access health care, only 24 per cent had any real access to it.
* As many as 32 per cent of those who had legal entitlement to health care were not aware of that right.
* More than two-thirds of the chronic health problems identified were untreated.
* Some 47 per cent of those with at least one health problem had suffered a delay in treatment.

IMAGE B3.1   **Undocumented migrant seeking care from Médecins du Monde UK's Project, London**

The survey also revealed major differences between countries. Both Belgium and France have special schemes to ensure some free medical care for 'undocumented migrants'. However, because of poor awareness of these rights and complex administrative procedures, these health-care entitlements are often unrealised.

In Spain, the law recognises 'the right to health protection and assistance for medical care for all Spanish citizens and foreign nationals residing on Spanish soil'. Undocumented migrants must register with the local municipality to obtain a health-care card. Although this does not require legal residence, the law allows the police to access local registers, thus deterring many undocumented migrants from registering. Migrants who do not have a health-care card are only able to access emergency treatment, except for children and pregnant women, who are entitled to the same health care as Spanish citizens.

Under Greek law, undocumented migrants have no right to health-care cover, with a few exceptions – emergencies including maternity care and treatment of certain infectious diseases.

In the United Kingdom, various reports have documented the poor access to health care for refused asylum-seekers and undocumented migrants. They point to a particular problem with access to maternity care for pregnant women (Refugee Council 2006; Médecins du Monde UK 2007). Of the

---

BOX B3.5   **Aisha and Jacob**

Aisha and her husband Jacob fled to the UK after they had been threatened because of their inter-faith marriage. Their claim for asylum was refused. They were not allowed to work and were surviving on £35 in vouchers and support with accommodation. Then Aisha became pregnant. 'Four months into the pregnancy the overseas visitors officer started telling us that they would stop access to the hospital ... when we questioned her on where my wife should deliver her baby she said we can deliver it at home.'

Source: Médecins du Monde UK 2007.

---

women attending Médecins du Monde UK's clinic in London in 2006, 23 per cent were pregnant women needing access to primary care, antenatal care or termination of pregnancy. Over half had not had any prior antenatal care, and of these 40 per cent were more than twenty weeks pregnant.

Regarding Sweden, Paul Hunt, UN Special Rapporteur on the right to the highest attainable standard of health, commented that when 'examined through the prism of the right to health, some health policies are a genuine cause for concern' (Hunt 2007). Undocumented migrants have no right to publicly funded health care, including emergency treatment, and have to pay for care received. Thus many tend not to seek health care at all or delay seeking care.

A common feature across Europe is the lack of awareness among migrants, refugees and asylum-seekers about their entitlements. Another is that claims to these entitlements are often blocked by administrative barriers. The fear of being reported to immigration authorities also deters 'undocumented migrants' from seeking health care, especially when there are real or perceived links between health professionals and immigration officials. In Germany, for example, since 2005, health administrators are required to report the presence of undocumented migrants to immigration officials. Another important issue is that there are few well-developed plans to address the diverse and complex health requirements of migrants. There are few measures designed to overcome cultural and language barriers, for example.

Detention centres

Many asylum-seekers, refused asylum-seekers and undocumented migrants are held in detention centres. Some are waiting for their claim to be processed. Others await deportation. There has been a lot of criticism of the arbitrary nature of detention. In the UK, immigration detention has been criticised as being 'protracted, inappropriate, disproportionate and unlawful' (Amnesty International 2005). In Europe, there were 218 detention facilities for migrants and asylum-seekers in twenty-three different countries at the end of 2007. As of June 2005, there were 885 persons in immigration detention centres in Australia (Phillips and Millbank 2005).

Virtually all asylum-seekers apprehended at US borders are subjected to lengthy detention regardless of their circumstances. Examples include:

- a Burmese woman, a member of a religious and ethnic minority group, detained for nearly two years in a Texas immigration jail, even though she would clearly face torture and persecution if returned to Burma;
- a pastor who fled Liberia after criticising the use and abuse of child soldiers was detained for three months in a New Jersey immigration jail;
- a young human rights worker from Cameroon, who had been arrested, jailed and tortured on three occasions, was detained for sixteen months at New York and New Jersey immigration jails before being granted asylum and released.

Studies in many countries point to unmet health needs and inadequate health care in centres. Research in the UK, Australia and the US has also shown the detrimental impact of detention on the mental health of an already traumatised population (Cutler and Ceneda 2004; PHR 2003).

In the UK, the management of detention or removal centres is often contracted out to private companies, and health-care services are further subcontracted. An inquiry by the Chief Inspector of Prisons into the case of a Ugandan asylum-seeker 'who was reduced to a state of mental collapse' at Yarl's Wood removal centre, criticised the inadequate mental health care provisions, unclear management arrangements and weak clinical governance. Further concerns have been expressed in the UK about the detention of pregnant and breastfeeding women, contrary to UNHCR guidelines, and the inadequate provision of pre- and postnatal care; and about the detention of people with serious health problems, including mental illness, in spite of guidelines that such people, including torture survivors, should not normally be detained.

According to Human Rights First (2007), asylum-seekers in the US are detained in conditions that are inappropriate, often for months and sometimes years. The US Commission on International Religious Freedom reported the following findings from visits to nineteen detention centres:

- widespread use of segregation, isolation or solitary confinement for disciplinary reasons;

BOX B3.6 **Not a criminal but held in detention**

In his South Asian country, HN was forced into hiding to avoid arrest because of his political activities. Fearing for the safety of his family, he fled to the US. There, he endured three and a half years of detention, with extended periods of solitary confinement. 'I was sick in my mind, had nightmares, stomach pain, and couldn't sleep. Always I was thinking someone's going to kill me. I don't know why they kept me to a small room with no people there. I felt like I was dying. I cannot breathe there.' After repeated requests over several months, HN saw a psychiatrist, although no translation was provided. HN finally won asylum (PHR 2003).

- significant limitations on privacy;
- use of physical restraints in eighteen facilities;
- lack of staff training focused on the special needs and concerns of asylum-seekers, particularly the victims of torture or trauma.

Detained asylum-seekers suffer extremely high levels of anxiety, depression and post-traumatic stress. In a US study, 86 per cent of the interviewed asylum-seekers suffered significant depression, 77 per cent suffered anxiety and 50 per cent suffered from Post-Traumatic Stress Disorder (PTSD). They also suffer verbal abuse by immigration inspectors at US airports, as well as verbal abuse and other mistreatment at the hands of officers staffing detention facilities (PHR 2003).

Migrating for health care; deportation because of ill health

Within this context of increased migration, some commentators have expressed concern about people migrating with the specific purpose of obtaining health treatment which is not available in their country of origin. There is, however, little evidence of this so-called 'health tourism'. The UK government admitted in testimony to the Parliamentary Health Select Committee that it did not have any such evidence. According to the Committee (2005), the evidence 'suggests that HIV+ migrants do not access NHS services until their disease is very advanced, usually many months or even years after their arrival in the UK, which would not be the expected behaviour of a cynical "health tourist" who had come to this country solely to access free services.'

There have also been examples of governments using illness as a reason for restricting migration or leading to deportation. For twenty years, the US has had a 'policy of inadmissibility' which prohibits non-US citizens with HIV from entry into the country. This policy is contrary to WHO/UNAIDS guidance. In 1998 the United Arab Emirates carried out a screening programme and deported all the migrant workers who tested positive for HIV/AIDS (WHO 2003).

Discussion

Without even covering the plight of refugees, migrants and 'internally displaced persons' in low-income countries in any detail, this chapter paints a bleak picture of access to health care for migrants and asylum-seekers.

The issues raised in this chapter cannot be discussed without placing them in the context of a hostile global political economy for hundreds of millions of people. The World Commission on the Social Dimensions of Globalisation (2004) described the 'deep-seated and persistent imbalances in the current workings of the global economy' as being 'ethically unacceptable and politically unsustainable', explaining how 'the rules of world trade today often favour the rich and powerful'.

Hundreds of millions of people, mainly in low- and middle-income countries, have been socially and economically disenfranchised by a brutal and predatory system of global capitalism. The governments of many poor countries are increasingly unable to manage their economies and fulfil their duties and obligations. Added to this is the tolerance of corruption and oppression within low- and middle-income countries by world powers when it suits them. It is no surprise that millions of people are prepared to risk death to escape their countries for a better life.

Under these conditions it is fitting that all migrants, including temporary migrants, refugees, asylum-seekers and 'illegal' or 'undocumented' migrants, are accorded clear rights and entitlements to health care. In fact, all nations that have signed the ICESCR have a legal obligation to ensure that proper health care is accessible to all. However, countries do not always comply with this obligation.

In this increasingly globalised world, there is a need to rework the definition of citizenship so that it includes a more robust set of social and health rights for all global citizens, irrespective of their nationality, country of residence or immigration status.

As a starting point, the discrimination and persecution of migrants from poor countries who have successfully reached the shores of wealthy countries must be stopped. Exaggerated press stories about the negative impact of migrants must be countered with a more reasoned and honest account of the nature of the global political economy and the underlying causes of migration.

More countries should follow the Spanish example of incorporating into national law the rights of migrants to health care, irrespective of their status. Governments should also actively inform potential beneficiaries of their rights to health care and how to access it, and remove any administrative obstacles to health care. Health workers must resist measures that compromise their independence by ensuring clear boundaries between health services and immigration law.

While there are strong moral reasons for providing access to health care for all groups of migrants, it also makes public health sense. Not only does it help with the control of communicable diseases; easier access to health care will allow treatment to be provided earlier, thus avoiding the costly provision of emergency care or expensive treatment of diseases in an advanced stage.

There are encouraging examples of civil society defending the rights of 'undocumented migrants' to health care. In Europe, the Platform for International Cooperation on Undocumented Migrants (PICUM) has found that health professionals 'are reluctant to accept national government pressure to preclude vulnerable migrants' from health services (Flynn and Duvell 2007). And in recent years several countries have seen hundreds of thousands of people peacefully demonstrating in defence of migrants' rights.

There are also examples of regional or local governments adopting positive initiatives. In Belgium, some Flemish mayors have said that they will refuse to sign deportation orders. A municipal council in Switzerland passed a resolution to ensure that undocumented migrants have access to services. And in the US, several cities have declared themselves 'sanctuary cities' which seek to provide services and protection to all residents, regardless of their status, and to prevent city employees from cooperating with immigration enforcement.

References

Amnesty International (2005). *UK: Seeking asylum is not a crime: Detention of people who have sought asylum*. London.

Amnesty International (2007). *Internal migrants: Discrimination and abuse. The human cost of an economic miracle*. London.

Cutler, S., and S. Ceneda (2004). *They took me away: Women's experiences of immigration detention in the UK*. London: BID/Asylum Aid.

EC (European Commission) (2007). *Improving quality and productivity at work: Community strategy 2007–2012 on health and safety at work*. COM (2007) 62.

EU (European Union) (2007). *The future development of EU migration policy*. Speech by Franco Frattini, European Commissioner responsible for justice, freedom and security, 3 July.

Flynn, D., and F. Duvell (2007). *Undocumented migrants: Symptom, not the problem. A*

PICUM policy brief. Brussels: Platform for International Cooperation on Undocumented Migrants.

Health Select Committee (2005). *New developments in sexual health and HIV/AIDS policy.* House of Commons. HC252-1-2005.

Human Rights First (2007). *Background briefing note: The detention of asylum seekers in the United States: Arbitrary under the ICCPR.* New York.

Human Rights Watch (2002). The human rights dimension of EU Immigration policy: Lessons from Member States. HRW statement on the occasion of the Academy of European Law Conference, Trier, 25–26 April. www.hrw.org/backgrounder/eca/eu-immigration.pdf.

Hunt, P. (2007). *Implementation of General Assembly Resolution 60/251 of 15 March 2006 entitled Human Rights Council.* Report of the Special Rapporteur on the right of everyone to the enjoyment of the highest attainable standard of physical and mental health, Paul Hunt. Addendum, Mission to Sweden. A/HRC/4/28/Add 2.

IDMC (2007). *Internal Displacement: Global overview of trends and developments in 2006.* Geneva: Internal Displacement Monitoring Centre.

IOM (International Organization for Migration) (2007). Global estimates and trends. www.iom.ch/jahia/Jahia/pid/254.

IPPR (Institute for Public Policy Research) (2006). *Irregular migration in the UK. An IPPR factfile.* London: IPPR.

Jesuit Refugee Service (2001). *Irregular migration in Europe: New empirical studies.* Brussels: Jesuit Refugee Service.

Médecins du Monde (2007). *European survey on undocumented migrants' access to health care.* Médecins du Monde. European Observatory on Access to Healthcare. Paris.

Médecins du Monde UK (2007). *Project: London report 2006.* London.

Médecins Sans Frontières (n.d.). *Violence and immigration: Report on illegal sub-Saharan immigrants (ISSs) in Morocco.* London.

Médecins Sans Frontières (1997). *Refugee health: An approach to emergency situations.* London: Macmillan.

Miller, L.S. (2007). Olga Sanchez's refuge of hope in the South. *Christian Science Monitor,* 31 July.

Norredam, M., A. Mygind and A. Krasnik (2006). Access to health care for asylum-seekers in the European Union: A comparative study of country policies. *European Journal of Public Health* 16(3): 285–9.

Phillips, J., and A. Millbank (2005). *The detention and removal of asylum-seekers.* E-brief on Parliamentary Library, Parliament of Australia, Canberra.

PHR (Physicians for Human Rights) and Bellevue/NYU Program for Survivors of Torture (2003). *From persecution to prison: The health consequences of dentention for asylum-seekers.* Boston and New York.

Refugee Council (2006). First do no harm: Denying health care to people whose asylum claims have failed. London: Refugee Council and Oxfam.

Tuñón, M. (2006). *Internal labour migration in China: Features and responses.* Beijing: ILO Office, April.

UNHCR (United Nations High Commission of Refugees) (2007a). *2006 global trends: Refugees, asylum-seekers, returnees, internally displaced and stateless persons.* Geneva.

UNHCR (2007b). *UNHCR Statistical Yearbook 2005. Trends in displacement, protection and solutions.* Geneva. April.

World Commission on the Social Dimensions of Globalisation (2004). *A fair globalisation: Creating opportunities for all.* Geneva: ILO.

WHO (World Health Organization) (2003). *International migration, health and human rights.* Health and human rights publication series. Geneva.

B4 Prisoners

More than thirty years ago, a young black medical student named Steven Bantu Biko spearheaded the formation of the Black Consciousness movement in South Africa, an important contribution to the eventual downfall of apartheid. In the years that followed, he was kept under surveillance by South Africa's security police, subjected to repeated interrogations and detention, and banned from making public speeches. On 12 September 1977 Biko died of a severe head injury in Pretoria Central Prison following an interrogation during which he was beaten, chained to a window grille and left to lie in his own urine. Biko was one of more than seventy detainees in South Africa who died in detention between 1960 and 1990. In 1997 South Africa's Truth and Reconciliation Commission heard how two doctors serving Pretoria Prison at the time had failed to render adequate medical assistance to Biko following the assault he had been subjected to. The dereliction of duty of these doctors had been raised in 1978. At the time, however, the Medical Association of South Africa defended the prison doctors, demonstrating the apathy and complicity of the medical profession towards the systematic abuse and killing of many prisoners. Torture and death form the extreme end of a spectrum of public health problems that concern people who are imprisoned or held in detention.

This chapter discusses the health-care needs and living conditions of prisoners and detainees deprived of their freedom by the state, and for whom the state is thus responsible. Although the words 'prison' and 'jail' are often used interchangeably in many countries, 'jail' often refers to a place used to hold persons awaiting trial or serving sentences of less than one year, whereas prisons are usually used to hold those serving longer sentences. 'Detention centre', on the other hand, describes a facility used

TABLE B4.1   **Prison population rate**

Country	prisoners/100,000 population
United States	738
Russia	611
St Kitts & Nevis	547
US Virgin Islands	521
Turkmenistan	489
Belize	487
Cuba	487
Palau	478
British Virgin Islands	464
Bermuda	463
Bahamas	462
Iceland	40
Nigeria	30
India	30
Nepal	26
Mauritiana	26
Central African Republic	24
Congo	22
Faroe Islands	15

Source: Wamsley 2007.

to confine persons detained without charge or awaiting trial, those facing immigration issues, refugees and minors. Where the word 'penal institution' is used in the context of this chapter, it refers to both prisons and jails.

At the end of 2006 over 9 million people were being held in penal institutions worldwide. The United States incarcerates the greatest number of people (2.19 million in 2006), nearly a quarter of the world's prison population. This is followed by China (1.55 million) and Russia (0.87 million) (Wamsley 2007).

Many prisoners around the world are victims of unsafe convictions, imperfect judicial systems and poor living conditions in prisons. The majority come from the poorest and most marginalised sections of society with limited or no access to health care. Shockingly, a large number of those held in prisons and detention facilities are children. A significant proportion of prisoners suffer from mental illnesses, making prisons the new 'mental asylums' of our time (Fellner 2007). Ritual humiliation and sexual abuse by prison guards and other prisoners pose further threats to a prisoner's physical and mental well-being.

Prisons and health

Information on the state of prison health around the world is incomplete and largely inadequate. In 1993, Human Rights Watch (HRW) conducted a major review of prison conditions worldwide and found that the great majority of prisoners were 'confined in conditions of filth and corruption, without adequate food or medical care, with little or nothing to do, and in circumstances in which violence from other inmates, their keepers or both is a constant threat'. HRW also noted that incidences of cruelty frequently occur because 'prisons, by their nature, are out of sight; and because prisoners, by definition, are outcasts'.

Eight years later, another international review noted that living conditions in prisons 'have certainly not improved uniformly in the past decade, and in many countries, overcrowding has made these conditions even worse' (Van Zyl Smit and Dunkel 2001).

In 2007, a prison health brief found that 'the prevalence of disease, malnutrition, mental illness and general ill health among the global prison population provides overwhelming and incontrovertible evidence that prisons are bad for your health. For many, imprisonment is marked by the deterioration in health and well-being – in some cases it is tantamount to a death sentence' (Penal Reform International 2007).

Prison health in the context of public health and policy

In many countries, prison health care falls under the remit of the Ministry of Justice rather than the Ministry of Health, often resulting in the exclusion of prison health from wider public health policy development. This is particularly short-sighted as the majority of prisoners will eventually re-enter the civilian population and custodial personnel, health staff, visitors, delivery personnel, repairmen and lawyers act as 'bridge populations' between prisoners and the outside world (Reyes 2007).

Communicable diseases: HIV and tuberculosis

The prevalence of HIV and other sexually transmitted infections (STIs) tends to be higher among prison populations compared to the general population (UN Office on Drugs and Crime et al. 2006). In South Africa,

---

BOX B4.1 **The campaign to gain access to anti-retroviral treatment (ART) in South African prisons**

In August 2005, a South African NGO, the AIDS Law Project (ALP), became aware of the plight of HIV-positive prisoners at Westville Prison who were being denied access to ART. The ALP initiated legal proceedings on behalf of the prisoners and in June 2006 the High Court ruled that the South African government should ensure that all HIV-positive prisoners are assessed for treatment. However, by August 2006, prisoners with AIDS had still not received treatment, forcing the courts to order the government to provide ART to sick prisoners with immediate effect. This and the ensuing media coverage eventually forced the government to make a vital policy shift.

Source: Hassim 2006.

HIV prevalence in prison is twice that in the general population (Goyer 2003). In Central Asia, one-third of people living with HIV are in prison; in Krygstan this figure is as high as 56 per cent (Walcher 2005). High rates of HIV prevalence in prison settings are due to an over-representation of three high-risk groups: intravenous drug users, commercial sex workers, and men who have sex with men (WHO 2007). In spite of this, HIV/STI programmes in prisons have not been implemented in many countries (see Box B4.1).

In many countries, tuberculosis (TB) is a leading cause of mortality in prisons, where the rate of infection may be 100 times higher than the rest of the population (Reyes 2007). In the Ukraine in 2003, about 30 per cent of TB patients resided within the penitentiary service, with the disease accounting for about 40 per cent of all prison mortality. In Russia in 2002, 42 per cent of all known TB cases were estimated to be prisoners (Prison Healthcare Project n.d.). Between 10,000 and 30,000 of prisoners released each year in Russia are believed to have active TB.

However, with sufficient political will and appropriate policies, progress can be made. In Azerbaijan, the treatment of about 7,000 prisoners with TB reduced mortality rates from 14 per cent in 1995 to 3 per cent in 2004. In Georgia, TB treatment programmes resulted in prevalence falling from 6.5 per cent in 1998 to 0.6 per cent in 2005 (ICRC 2006).

In cases of prisoners on antiretrovirals (ARVs), there is often no cohesive follow-up or support system upon release from prison. In countries where health care is largely privatised, prisoners struggle to keep up with their

IMAGE B4.1   **Overcrowded remand cell in Malawi**

treatment regimens, even if they were compliant in prison. This not only impacts on the health of ex-prisoners and their ability to seek and maintain employment (helping break the cycle of reincarceration), but also fuels wider disease transmission and the development of drug resistance, particularly multi-drug-resistant TB.

Sanitation and living conditions

Many prisons are overcrowded and unfit for habitation. In 2006, the UN Office on Drugs and Crime found that 'overcrowding, violence, inadequate natural lighting and ventilation, and lack of protection from extreme climatic conditions are common in many prisons of the world', often combined with 'inadequate means for personal hygiene, inadequate nutrition, lack of access to clean drinking water, and inadequate medical services'.

On average, prisons in Europe run at 130 per cent of official capacity. In the US, prisons are at 107 per cent capacity. Prisons in Bangladesh currently hold 288 per cent of their official capacity. However, the country with the highest level of prison overcrowding is Kenya: 337 per cent of official capacity (Penal Reform International 2007).

According to the European Committee for the Prevention of Torture, cells intended for single occupancy should be about 7 square metres.

However, in May 2006, Georgia's Tbisli Prison No. 5 held 3,559 prisoners in a facility originally designed for 1,800 prisoners, resulting in 1 square metre or less per prisoner (HRW 2006a). One cell was found to contain 75 prisoners with only 25 beds, non-private toilet facilities and piles of uncollected refuse.

The excessive use of pre-trial detention and slow, bureaucratic criminal justice systems are major contributing factors to prison overcrowding. In India, for example, seven out of ten people held in penal institutions are pre-trial detainees, while in Nigeria over 25,000 prisoners are awaiting trial (Penal Reform International 2007).

Mental health issues

The criminalisation and incarceration of people with mental illness is a human rights issue in need of urgent attention. People with mental illnesses often end up being 'misdirected towards prison rather than appropriate mental health care or support services' (Commission on Human Rights 2005).

A systematic review of surveys from twelve different countries estimated the prevalence of psychiatric disorders in a total population of 22,790 prisoners. It found that among male prisoners included in the review, 3.7 per cent had a psychotic illness, 10 per cent major depression and 65 per cent a personality disorder. Among women prisoners surveyed, 4 per cent had a psychotic illness, 12 per cent major depression and 42 per cent a personality disorder (Fazel and Danesh 2002).

Prisons in the US are now host to three times more adults with serious mental health disorders than the general population. In 2005, it was estimated that around 50 per cent of prison inmates were suffering from a mental health problem – over 1 million men and women. Many have ended up in prison because 'community mental health systems are in a shambles – fragmented, under-funded and unable to serve the poor, the homeless and those who are substance-addicted as well as mentally ill' (Fellner 2007). Furthermore, around a half of prisoners with mental health problems were imprisoned for non-violent offences.

Prison mental health services are frequently lacking in funding, resources and adequately trained medical personnel. In many areas of the world, prison mental health services are non-existent, with prison staff often receiving little or no training in managing prisoners with mental health problems. Common practices such as solitary confinement only serve to further fuel mental illness.

BOX B4.2   **Human rights abuses at Guantánamo Bay**

Since January 2002, more than 750 individuals of some 45 nationalities have been detained at the US's offshore prison camp at Guantánamo Bay, Cuba. Among the detainees were children as young as 13. Amnesty International (2007) has found that 'their dignity, humanity and fundamental rights have been denied', including the right to due legal process. Five years since the start of the 'war on terror', hundreds of individuals remain in detention without having been formally charged or brought to trial.

In 2005, in spite of having condemned the practice of binding and shackling of prisoners' limbs in China, Eritrea, Iraq, Israel, Libya and Pakistan, the US government allowed the use of 'stress positions' and the shackling of prisoners in painful positions for extended periods of time in Afghanistan. The US also condemned forced nudity when used by regimes in North Korea, Egypt, Syria and Turkey but used it as a tactic in detention camps in Afghanistan and Iraq. Solitary confinement and isolation in China, Jordan, Pakistan, Tunisia, Jordan, Iran, North Korea and pre-war Iraq had also been condemned, but later approved for use by the US military (Malinowski 2005). The CIA is also believed to have used 'water-boarding', a tactic that simulates drowning, during interrogation sessions. The UN Working Group (UN Economic and Social Council 2006) on the situation of detainees at Guantánamo Bay found that although thirty days was the maximum time permissible for detainees to be held in isolation, detainees were put back in isolation after very short breaks, resulting in quasi-isolation for up to eighteen months.

Torture and abuse

In 1984 the UN Convention Against Torture was adopted by the United Nations General Assembly. To date, over 140 countries have ratified it. In spite of this, in 1998 the UN Special Rapporteur on Torture reported that 'systematic torture was still being practised in over 70 countries' (BBC News 1998). According to HRW, the US, China, Iran, Egypt, North Korea, Pakistan, Brazil, Libya, Burma, Zimbabwe and Tunisia are among the worst offenders (HRW 2005). In 2006, the Medical Foundation for the Care of Torture Victims (a UK-based NGO) received 2,145 new referrals from 86 different countries. The top ten countries that produced the most referrals were Iran (235), DRC (193), Eritrea (150), Turkey (142), Somalia (118), Cameroon (104), Afghanistan (101), Sri Lanka (80), Sudan (80) and Iraq (74).

Judicial caning

Judicial caning continues to be used as a form of punishment in a number of countries including Malaysia, Singapore, Brunei and Hong Kong. In 2007, Malaysia came under criticism following the release of a video showing a naked and screaming prisoner strapped to a wooden frame whilst being beaten with a rattan stick by a prison guard (CNN 2007). Amnesty International and various other human rights advocates have spoken out against this form of cruel and degrading punishment on a number of occasions, to no avail.

The complicity of medical professionals in torture and abuse

The complicity of medical professionals in the conduct of torture includes disclosing confidential medical details to those committing torture; providing clinical support for the initiation and continuation of torture; or simply remaining silent about such abuse.

In his book which details how physicians at Abu Ghraib and Guantánamo Bay prisons violated codes of good medical practice, Stephen Miles (2006) concludes that 'the US military medical system failed to protect detainees' human rights, sometimes collaborated with interrogators or abusive guards, and failed to properly report injuries or deaths caused by beatings.' This also involved delays in issuing and falsifying death certificates. Doctors are also known to have broken detainee hunger strikes through forced feeding via the insertion of nasogastric tubes (Rose 2006).

Evidence of medical complicity from other countries also exists. Amnesty International (2001) has reported the widespread use of torture and cruel treatment within Brazilian prisons and places of detention. In some instances, doctors examining torture victims were alleged to have omitted documenting evidence of torture in medical case notes and failed to carry out thorough medical examinations, including examining prisoners fully clothed. Under the regime of Saddam Hussein in Iraq, doctors are known to have been involved in torture (for example, amputating ears of dissidents), although in many instances doctors are thought to have been forced to act under extreme duress (Reis et al. 2004).

HRW (2004) has produced a report highlighting the persecution and torture of men who have sex with men in Egypt. Between 2001 and 2004, at least 179 men were charged with the 'crime' of homosexuality. Many were forced to undergo cruel and degrading physical examinations in order to 'prove' their sexual orientation, which included the use of rectal sonograms and manometry. Although doctors claim to have obtained consent prior to these examinations, HRW found documentation of this in only one of the hundred case notes it examined.

Counterculture

Turkey is one example of a country where the practice of torture is being overturned (Worden 2005). There have been multiple accounts of students, intellectuals and government critics being subjected to brutal torture. However, when Turkey ratified the European Torture Convention in 1998, it was forced to open itself up to greater international scrutiny. This included granting the European Committee for the Prevention of Torture access to police stations for unscheduled visits. In 2003, immunicado detention was officially abolished. The medical profession and other civil society groups within Turkey began speaking out against torture, and evidence on the practising of torture was presented to parliament. Since 2000 there have been no further recorded deaths in police custody. In 2005, HRW reported a reduction in the number and severity of torture cases.

Children

According to the United Nations Children's Fund (UNICEF) (2006) there are over 1 million children held in detention worldwide, the majority of whom are held for minor offences or petty crimes such as truancy, vagrancy, begging or alcohol use. Many of these offences are 'status' dependent, meaning that such actions would fail to be a 'crime' if carried out by adults. Many legal systems do not take into account a child's age when handing out sentences.

Child detention: some examples

HRW has reported that an estimated 400 children between the ages of 13 and 18 are incarcerated in state prisons in Burundi, three-quarters of whom are held under pre-trial detention. Many of the children had been awaiting trial for months, and in some cases years. Many were also being held in communal holding cells and police lock-ups, awaiting transfer to state prison facilities. In some cases children were tortured to obtain confessions and most of the children had no access to legal counsel (HRW 2007). Lack of space, poor sanitation facilities, along with inadequate bedding, food and water, are daily threats to the well-being of these children. Whilst in prison children receive no education. In breach of international law, children and adult prisoners are in contact for much of the day, making child prisoners in Burundi vulnerable to physical and sexual abuse.

Vietnam is a country that routinely and arbitrarily detains street children. Children are held in state 'rehabilitation' centres for periods of time ranging from two weeks to six months. Serious abuses of street children held at the Dong Dau and Ba Vi 'social protection centres' on the outskirts of Hanoi have been documented. Children were confined to their cells for twenty-three hours a day in filthy, overcrowded conditions with only a bucket available for use as a toilet. Lights were kept on both day and night. There was no access to medical or psychological treatment and frequent beatings and verbal abuse by prison staff were also reported (HRW 2006b).

Children and the death penalty

Despite clear prohibitions in international law against the use of the death penalty for juvenile offenders, child executions still exist in some parts of the world. Amnesty International (2006) has documented a total of fifty-three child executions in eight countries since January 1990. Offending countries include Iran, Nigeria, Saudi Arabia, the Democratic Republic of Congo, Yemen, China, Pakistan and the US. Iran and the US accounted for more executions than all other countries combined. Twenty-one executions took place in Iran and nineteen in the US. In 2005, the US Supreme Court finally found the execution of child offenders to be unconstitutional.

Response of the international community

While prisoner health remains by and large a neglected public health domain, a number of important initiatives have been undertaken by various organisations to address some of these critical issues. These include efforts to improve data collection and monitoring; advocacy for more effective and just penal systems; and the development of guidelines and instruments to improve prison health programmes. However, many of these initiatives are in urgent need of funding, as well as greater attention and support from the health community at the levels of both policymaking and implementation. A brief overview of some of these initiatives and the organisations leading them is available from the GHW website at: www.ghwatch.org.

Recommendations

Governments

GHW reiterates the call to governments worldwide to incorporate prison health into public health policy; for prison health to fall under the jurisdiction of ministries of health; and for the right to health to be recognised in prisons. Firm political commitment is needed to combat the spread of infectious disease, particularly TB, HIV and hepatitis C. Mental health-care provision and substance dependency management are two other areas that require urgent attention and that could help to break the revolving-door syndrome of reoffending and reincarceration. Urgent steps must be taken to improve basic sanitation, living conditions and treatment of prisoners. Robust mechanisms for monitoring prison conditions are required that allow rapid action to be taken when incidences of abuse and injustice are uncovered.

WHO and the United Nations

Efforts made by the World Health Organization (WHO) and the UN in advancing health in prisons in Europe (particularly eastern Europe) are encouraging. However, this needs to be extended, particularly to countries in Africa and Asia. Initiatives such as the WHO Prison Health Database need to be promoted and supported to ensure progress and sustainability. Other initiatives such as the UN Special Rapporteur to African Prisons require increased funding and support to enable them to widen their scope of activities and influence.

National medical associations

National medical associations need to lobby governments to make prison health a public health priority and encourage continual professional development and conduct among prison doctors. They need to support doctors within their own countries to speak out against incidences of abuse, neglect and torture. Disciplinary action should also be taken whenever members are found to violate ethical codes of conduct.

Non-governmental organisations

Much of the research into prison conditions and health has thus far been conducted by non-governmental organisations (NGOs). Whilst their contribution has been vital, greater government, UN funding and private philanthropy are needed to ensure that a systematic, comprehensive and coordinated review of prison conditions takes place at least every five years. Whilst the Health in Prison Project has made good progress in Eastern Europe and Asia in particular, little information is available on prison conditions in China, South America and Southeast Asia.

In summary, prison health is a major public health issue in need of urgent and immediate attention. Overcrowding, unsanitary living conditions, the dangers of transmittable and highly infectious diseases, poor mental health services, torture, abuse and the scandal of child imprisonment continue to plague prison services worldwide. We need to remember that prisoners are sent to prison as punishment, not for punishment. Dying from TB, dysentery, malnutrition or from a beating by prison officials should never form part of a prisoner's sentence.

References

Amnesty International (2001). Fighting impunity in Brazil: Challenges and opportunities for physicians. London. www.amnesty.org/en/library/asset/AMR19/026/2001/en/dom-AMR190262001en.pdf.

Amnesty International (2006). Death penalty statistics 2006. ACT 50/012/2007. London. www.amnestyusa.org/document.php?id=ENGACT500122007&lang=e.

Amnesty International (2007). *USA – close Guantánamo – symbol of injustice.* AMR 51/001/2007. London.

BBC News (1998). Torture systematic in over 70 countries. 2 April. http://news.bbc.co.uk/1/hi/world/73154.stm.

CNN (2007). Naked prison caning video draws fury. 3 August. www.cnn.com/2007/WORLD/asiapcf/08/03/naked.caning.reut/.

Commission on Human Rights (2005). *Report of the Special Rapporteur on the right of everyone to the enjoyment of the highest attainable standard of physical and mental health.* Geneva.

Fazel, S., and J. Danesh (2002). Serious mental disorder among 23000 prisoners: Systematic review of 62 surveys. *The Lancet* 359: 545–50.

Fellner, J. (2007). Cruel and sadly usual: Prisons should not be mental wards. *Boston Herald*, 26 March.

Goyer. K.C. (2003). HIV/AIDS in prisons: Problems, policies and potential. *Monograph* 79, February.

Hassim, A. (2006). The '5 star' prison hotel? The right of access to ARV treatment for HIV positive prisoners in South Africa. *International Journal of Prisoner Health* 2(3): 157–71.

HRW (Human Rights Watch) (1993). *Global report on prisons.* New York.

HRW (2004). *In a time of torture: The Assault on justice in Egypt's crackdown on homosexual conduct.* New York.

HRW (2005). *Torture: A human rights perspective.* New York: New Press.

HRW (2006a). Undue punishment: Abuses against prisoners in Georgia. *HRW Report*, 18(8)D September. www.hrw.org/reports/2006/georgia0906/georgia0906webwcover.pdf.

HRW (2006b). Children of the dust: Abuse of street children in Hanoi. *HRW Report.* 18(14)C, November. http://hrw.org/reports/2006/vietnam1106/vietnam1106webwcover.pdf.

HRW (2007). Paying the price: Violations of the rights of children in detention in Burundi. *HRW Report* 19(4)A, March. www.hrw.org/reports/2007/burundi0307/.

ICRC (International Committee of the Red Cross) (2006). Tuberculosis in prisons: A forgotten killer. Press release, 22 March. Switzerland.

Malinowski, T. (2005). Banned state department practices. In K. Roth, M. Worden and A Berstein (eds), *Torture: A human rights perspective.* New York: New Press.

Miles, S.H. (2006). *Oath betrayed: Torture, medical complicity and the war on terror.* New York: Random House.

Penal Reform International (2007). Penal reform briefing no. 2: Health in prisons. www.penalreform.org/resources/brf-02-2007-health-in-prisons-en.pdf.

Prison Healthcare Project (n.d.). *Improving prison healthcare in Eastern Europe and Central Asia: Fighting tuberculosis.* International Centre for Prison Studies, King's College London.

Reis, C., et al. (2004). Physician participation in human rights abuses in southern Iraq. *JAMA* 291: 1480–86.

Reyes, H. (2007). Pitfalls in TB management in prison, revisited. *International Journal of Prisoner Health* 3(1), March: 43–67.

Rose, D. (2006). The scandal of force-fed prisoners. *Observer*, 8 January.

UN Economic and Social Council (2006). Situation of detainees at Guantánamo

86   The health-care sector

Bay. Report of the chairperson of the Working Group on Arbitrary Detention. E/CN.4/2006/120.

UNICEF (2006). *The state of the world's children 2006: Excluded and invisible.* New York.

UN Office on Drugs and Crime, WHO and UNAIDS (2006). *HIV/AIDS prevention, care, treatment and support in prison settings: A framework for an effective national response.* New York: UN Office on Drugs and Crime, WHO and UNAIDS.

Van Zyl Smit, D., and F. Dunkel (2001). *Imprisonment today and tomorrow: International perspectives on prisoners' rights and prison conditions.* Leiden: Brill.

Walcher, G. (2005). Prisons as regional drivers of HIV/AIDS and tuberculosis in some Central Asian countries: A matter of 'least eligibility'? *International Journal of Prisoner Health* 1(204): 103–15.

Wamsley, R. (2007). *World Prison Population List.* London: Home Office.

Worden, M. (2005). Torture spoken here: Ending global torture. In K. Roth and M. Worden (eds), *Torture: A Human Rights Perspective.* New York: New Press.

WHO (2007). *Health in prisons. A WHO guide to the essentials in prison health.* Geneva.

B5 Medicine

There are major problems with the way medicines are developed, marketed, priced, prescribed and consumed across the world. Three underlying factors deserve particular attention: a patent-driven system for pharmaceutical innovation; the predominance of profit-seeking actors within the sector; and the failure of public institutions to correct market failures and protect the public good.

These three factors were described in some detail in the first *Global Health Watch*. This chapter builds on that analysis by focusing on two policy issues:

- New mechanisms for financing and giving incentive for pharmaceutical research and development (R&D).
- The growing threat of antibiotic resistance.

The Innovation + Access (I+A) movement has brought the first issue to the discussions of the World Health Organization's Intergovernmental Working Group on Public Health, Innovation and Intellectual Property. An emerging coalition, Action on Antibiotic Resistance (ReAct), has begun to raise the profile of the second issue. The discussion of each flags serious challenges to improved innovation and affordable access to essential medicines. By no means though does this chapter discuss all the responsible factors. Other concerns which plague health-care systems include poor quality clinical care, ineffectual drug supply and distribution systems, and the lack of infrastructure required to ensure an effective cold chain.

A better system of pharmaceutical R&D

Problems with the current system

The public sector provides for extensive funding of research, training of the scientific workforce, and paying for the procurement of pharmaceuticals. Taking into account tax credits, the public sector provides 60 per cent of the funding for global health R&D (GFHR 2006). Yet the priorities of pharmaceutical R&D are largely shaped by the granting of patents to private corporations.

In the hands of profit-seeking drug firms, the time-limited market exclusivity conferred by patents shapes not only the process of scientific discovery and medical innovation, but also their approach to pricing and marketing.

Consistently one of the most profitable sectors, the pharmaceuticals industry is under pressure to maintain high returns. Not surprisingly, this translates into prioritising classes of drugs which are likely to generate large streams of revenue with low levels of R&D investment, rather than prioritising medicines of high public health priority. As a result, 'me too' drugs for chronic diseases take priority over novel treatments for acute illnesses. The improvement of a 'me too' drug may only be marginal over existing therapies, but a consumer buying a chronic-disease drug for years returns far more revenues than a short antibiotic course.

Tropical diseases remain neglected while lifestyle medications receive priority in the R&D pipeline. Though tropical diseases may impose a far greater burden of disease, these neglected diseases often afflict resource-poor markets from which patents can extract little in the way of profits. Under the current system of financing pharmaceutical R&D, public health and private-sector priorities have become misaligned.

The wish to generate high revenue streams also incentivises pharmaceutical companies to spend large amounts on advertising, marketing and influencing the prescribing behaviour of doctors, to downplay considerations of safety, and to set prices to maximise revenue rather than access.

Finally, and equally troubling, R&D productivity has fallen over the past decade: industry R&D expenditures have gone up 147 per cent from 1993 to 2004 while the approval of new chemical entities by the US Food and Drug Administration dropped from a peak of 53 new molecular entities in 1996 to 18 in 2007 (GAO 2006; Jordan 2008). To maintain this R&D premium, the International Federation of Pharmaceutical Manufacturers & Associations (IFPMA) reports that the industry spent $51 billion in 2005, which amounts to less than 9 per cent of global sales (IFPMA 2006; IMS Health 2005). Most of the R&D premium is recouped in the industrialised

IMAGE B5.1   **A vendor sells pharmaceuticals at a street market in Senegal**

world. The pharmaceuticals market of the developing world, by value, amounts to only 8.8 per cent (WHO 2004a). What type of R&D, though, does this system buy?

Existing strategies for overcoming financial barriers to access

A variety of strategies are used to overcome the barriers to access caused by the high price of medicines. These include promotion of the use of differential pricing schemes (tailoring the price of medicines to the differential purchasing power of different countries); voluntary licences (where patent holders voluntarily award a licence to a manufacturer to produce a patented medicine at a lower price); and corporate social responsibility approaches such as making drug donations or selling medicines at a discount.

Public strategies include governments issuing compulsory licences to get around the monopoly pricing of patented drugs. Another has been to allocate more public and donor money to purchase medicines on behalf of poor people. Various public–private partnerships have also been developed, often involving public finance, United Nations agencies, private companies and non-profit, non–governmental organisations (NGOs), to develop new and affordable medicines and other health technologies. Partnerships, as well as the use of Advance Market Commitments (AMCs), have also been encouraged as a strategy for addressing the gaps in R&D for neglected diseases.

Finally, poor people also implement their own strategies. These include diverting household income from food to medicines, taking children out of school, and selling off what little assets they have. They may also resort to purchasing cheaper medicines on the informal market, exposing themselves to fraud and harm.

But the strategies described above, even collectively, do not provide an adequate or equitable response to the problem of inaccessible medicines. And none of them addresses the fundamental problems of a system based on patents and profit-seeking behaviour.

A new system for financing and rewarding pharmaceutical R&D

Over the last few years, efforts have been made by various academics and civil society groups to develop a strategy that would overcome the flaws in the current system. In 2003, the WHO's Commission on Intellectual Property, Innovation and Public Health (CIPIH) was established to review existing medical R&D efforts and intellectual property regimes, and to consider other incentive and funding mechanisms for stimulating R&D.

However, at the time of its establishment, the US government and the pharmaceuticals industry lobbied to prevent the CIPIH from considering any amendments to existing international legal or trade instruments, or to consider suggestions that had been made for an international R&D treaty. As a result, a diverse group of NGOs, academics and health experts decided to formulate and draft the outline of a possible R&D treaty. In February 2005, 162 individuals petitioned the WHO Executive Board and the CIPIH to formally evaluate the draft treaty.[1]

The treaty was based on the idea that governments should spend a certain proportion of national income on medical R&D and that there would be maximum sharing of any knowledge and technology that would emerge from this public investment. The treaty became an issue of great debate within the CIPIH. When the Commission published its final report in April 2006,[2] it noted the need for sustainable sources of finance into R&D for neglected diseases and said that the proposed international R&D treaty provided some new ideas that deserved further discussion.

Meanwhile, Kenya and Brazil had been leading a process to introduce a resolution to the World Health Assembly (WHA) on the creation of a 'Global Framework on Essential Health Research and Development'. In spite of attempts to have this blocked, resolution WHA 59.24 was adopted in

May 2006 incorporating several recommendations made by the CIPIH and by Kenya and Brazil. It also called for the establishment of the Intergovernmental Working Group on Public Health, Innovation and Intellectual Property (PHI/IGWG).

PHI/IGWG was tasked with drawing up a global strategy and plan of action to secure, inter alia, an enhanced and sustainable basis for needs-driven, essential health R&D. Its first meeting took place in December 2006. In February 2006, Bangladesh and Bolivia submitted papers to PHI/IGWG calling for consideration of new methods of stimulating medical R&D in which incentives for stimulating innovation are separated from the prices of medicines, such as the use of prizes.

What's the big idea about prize funds?

The proposal that 'prize funds' be used as an alternative method for financing and rewarding successful investments in R&D has been addressed in detail by, among others, the NGO and think-tank Knowledge Ecology International (KEI).[3]

Prize funds are basically a way of providing an alternative reward to innovators – one that is not linked to the sale and price of the product. Instead, innovators would be rewarded on the basis of the contribution they make to improving health outcomes. Clearly, an important requirement of prize funds is the generation of finance for the fund and a system to adjudicate the value of the innovation or invention.

Prize funds could, however, exist together with patents. But patents would be used to make a claim against a monetary prize, rather than an exclusive right to make, market or use an invention. By divorcing the incentive for innovation from the product's price to consumers, outputs of the R&D could be placed in the public domain immediately, so that competition among manufacturers and suppliers would lead to low prices and more efficient medical innovation. It would also promote rational drug use and reduce spending on unimportant 'me too' products that do not improve health outcomes and curb spending on marketing.

The idea of prize mechanisms to stimulate R&D will require effort and political will. But there are some starting points. For example, a proposed US Medical Innovation Prize Fund would reward successful drug developers with monetary prizes, not a temporary monopoly. Each new successful drug would qualify for prize money, the amount of which would depend upon the overall size of the fund and evidence of the incremental impact of the new product on health outcomes. While every new product would be a 'winner', they would also compete against each other for a share of the total prize fund.

Another proposal involves the special case for medicines that rely on money from donors. The suggestion is that donors would set aside a fixed proportion (e.g. 10 per cent) of their existing budget for drug purchases to finance a prize fund. However, prizes would only be available to patent owners who agree to license their patents to a shared patent pool. Manufacturers could then compete to produce generic versions of the medicines in the patent pool. The patent owners would be rewarded according to the positive impact of their inventions on health outcomes in developing countries.

A precedent for the use of prize funds is the 2005 Grainger Challenge, which involved prizes of up to US$1 million for the development of cheap filtration devices for removing arsenic from well water. Over seventy entries were submitted. The winning entry, announced in 2007, is now being used to provide safe drinking water to hundreds of thousands of people. Less successful was the 1994 US$1 million Rockefeller Prize for developing a low-cost diagnostic test for gonorrhea or chlamydia. The prize expired in 1999 without a winner.

Prize mechanisms are not a magic-bullet solution to the inequities and inefficiencies of the pharmaceuticals sector. Neither do they address the low levels of technical capacity in low- and middle-income countries. Unless such capacity is developed, it will mainly be established pharmaceuticals companies that are able to compete for the prize funds. Prize mechanisms therefore need to be seen as part of a larger set of systems and incentives that includes direct or indirect government funding of basic research, non-profit product development partnerships (PDPs) and technology transfer agreements. What prize funds offer uniquely is an alternative to the marketing monopoly as an incentive for private investment.

Meeting the challenge of antibiotic resistance: public good and collective action[4]

Antibiotic resistance represents another illustration of the current failings of the pharmaceuticals sector as well as a neglected public health priority in its own right. Although the intensity of antibiotic use is greatest in industrialised countries, the burden of infectious disease falls disproportionately on developing countries where national strategies to contain antibiotic resistance are often absent and where there is a general lack of access to reserve antibacterials (Fasehun 1999; WHO 2004b).

Antibiotic resistance recognises no geographic boundaries. Last year, global media tracked the story of a plane passenger who purportedly had multi-drug-resistant tuberculosis (MDR-TB), but who had managed to trek across Europe and Canada on his return to the United States while untreated and infectious (CNN 2007).

Less widely reported is the fact that XDR-TB (extensively drug-resistant tuberculosis) has been identified in every region of the world, most frequently in the former Soviet Union and in Asia (WHO 2006). During the 1990s, a resistant strain of *Streptococcus pneumoniae* spread worldwide from Spain (Smith and Coast 2002).

Within countries, antibiotic resistance is no longer a problem primarily found in hospital wards, but has extended into the community. Increasingly, transmission of community-acquired, multi-drug resistant infections is occurring in developing countries (Okeke et al. 2005).

Strategies to counter resistance can be divided between those that conserve the effectiveness of antibiotics and those that replenish the supply of new drugs. To conserve the effectiveness of antibiotics, steps can be taken to reduce infections in the first place, delay the emergence of resistance, and slow its spread. To replenish the supply of new antimicrobials, the R&D pipeline for new drugs, or, better still, new classes or mechanisms of antibiotic therapy, needs to be primed with new drug candidates and financed.

Ensuring the effectiveness of antibiotics involves tackling both underuse and overuse. Underuse stems from problems of therapeutic, financial and structural access. The lack of therapeutic access refers to the failure of the R&D pipeline to produce appropriate drugs or drug combinations. The lack of financial access arises from unaffordable prices, and can result in patients truncating a full treatment course, thereby facilitating the emergence of resistance. Finally, limited resources might prompt procurement agencies to opt for less costly therapy at the expense of more appropriate therapy. An example from a related area is the use of quinine therapy or artemisinin monotherapy when, in fact, artemisinin combination therapy would work most effectively in the face of growing malarial resistance.

Problems of structural access can take various forms. Antibiotic overuse also hastens the emergence of resistance. Overuse might take the form of using an antibiotic when not necessary or using an overly broad-spectrum antibiotic for a narrow clinical indication. Various reasons contribute to overuse (Elamin 2003). Typically, overuse mitigates risks perceived by the health provider – risks of missing a treatable diagnosis, losing a patient in follow-up, or incurring the costs of return visits. Health providers may opt for presumptive therapy when rapid diagnostics are not available, handing out prescriptions to meet patient expectations and substituting antibiotic treatment for clinic visit time (Schartz 1997). As resistance grows, so might the perceived need for broad-spectrum antibiotics in a vicious feedback loop.

Together, underuse and overuse of antibiotics are rampant. WHO (2004b) estimates that 'more than half of medicines are prescribed, dispensed or sold inappropriately' and 'half of all patients fail to take [medicines] correctly'. As much as 20–50 per cent of antibiotic prescriptions in community settings and 25–45 per cent of antibiotic prescriptions in hospital settings may be unnecessary (Hooton 2001). Irrational drug prescribing has been noted for decades but still receives cursory policy attention.

Antibiotic resistance both removes therapeutic options and imposes significant economic costs. Treatment alternatives may no longer work, or their effective market life may be shortened. The impact, however, extends to other life-prolonging and life-saving technologies reliant on the complementary use of antibiotics. Antibiotic resistance places many advances of modern medicine, ranging from organ transplants to cancer chemotherapy, in jeopardy. Measuring the economic toll of antibiotic resistance is methodologically complex, but significant by any measure. Indeed, estimates of the costs to the US alone range from $350 million to $65 billion (Foster 2007; Laxminarayan et al. 2007).

Conserving the effectiveness of antibiotics

The preservation of effective antibiotic therapy is a typical public good (Smith and Coast 2003). The two defining characteristics of a public good are non-rivalry (where consumption by one person does not limit or diminish access to the good by the next person) and non-exclusivity (where access to the good cannot be restricted, and therefore is available to everyone). Examining each dimension provides insight into the problem of containing antibiotic resistance.

In so far as the benefits of new antibiotics are beyond the financial reach of those in developing countries, the benefits are excludable. In so far as the benefits extend beyond the individual's consumption, the lower risk of communicable disease is community-wide and thereby non-exclusive. Like vaccines, the use of antibiotics can reduce the spread of contagion. Unlike vaccines, no herd immunity results, and any public benefit is mostly local and transitory.

The containment of antibiotic resistance, however, can be both non-excludable and non-rival. This leaves open the possibility of a *tragedy of the commons*, which arises when the gains for individuals impose costs on the community collectively (Hardin 1968). Antibiotic resistance pits the micro-motives of particular stakeholders against those of the entire community. This tension plays out at multiple levels between physician and patient, hospitals and health insurers, and drug companies and health insurers.

In the face of diagnostic uncertainty, the physician minimises risks to the individual patient and reaches for presumptive therapy. To order a further diagnostic test would likely involve more money and greater delay. A timely start to treatment may improve the likelihood of clinical success. Imprecise diagnostics contribute to the use of broader-spectrum antibiotics. That uncertainty in clinical decision-making also extends to variations in the prescribed duration of antibiotic therapy.

If vaccines were available, the physician would not face this dilemma and the need for antibiotics would be reshaped. For example, pneumococcal conjugate vaccine prevents 35 antibiotic prescriptions per 100 children, with savings estimated at 1.4 million antibiotic prescriptions in the United States each year by reducing the incidence of otitis media (Fireman et al. 2003). Importantly, a study in South Africa demonstrated that the carriage of antibiotic-resistant strains may decline after vaccination (Mbelle et al. 1999).

The financial incentives facing hospitals may provide no incentive for tackling antibiotic resistance if all they see are beds filled for longer hospital stays and corresponding payments. Infection control measures such as hand hygiene are investments that no single insurer would make if they imposed higher operating costs and encouraged freeriding by other insurers. Among hospitals serving the same catchment area, there may be little incentive to undertake aggressive infection control measures.

In the Netherlands, a strict containment approach to methicillin-resistant *Staphylococcus aureus* (MRSA) has kept prevalence below 0.5 per cent in contrast to higher rates of 1.6 per cent to 62.4 per cent in neighbouring Belgium (Verhoef et al. 1999). Not only were patients infected with MRSA isolated, but all health-care workers in contact with that patient also are swabbed regularly. In fact, all patients from outside the Netherlands undergo quarantine for forty-eight hours or until three successive tests come back negative for MRSA. Although this policy cost €2.8 million, it was estimated to be half the anticipated cost that might have otherwise resulted from MRSA and related infections (Vriens et al. 2002).

At the market level, there is a trade-off between the rapid scaling up of antibiotic use and the emergence of resistance. Rapid scaling up might ramp up pharmaceutical revenues, but rapid emergence of resistance might shorten the period that an antibiotic remains effective. Modelling suggests that antibiotics marketed aggressively at the outset of entry into the health system return lower revenues than those gradually introduced to reduce the emergence of antibiotic resistance (Power 2006). However, the reality is that there are many existing antibiotics in the marketplace, and with competition within a therapeutic class there is little incentive for any single manufacturer to exercise restraint in marketing the use of an antibiotic.

Replenishing the supply of antibiotics

Between the 1930s and 1970s, over a dozen new classes of antibiotics entered the marketplace. However, in the last four decades, only two new classes have surfaced (IDSA 2004). Only thirty-one anti-infective drugs are currently under development among the top fifteen multinational pharmaceuticals companies (Spellberg et al. 2004). Among these, only five are antibacterials (comprising only 1.6 per cent of the publicly disclosed pipelines of these companies), none of which appears to have a novel mechanism of action. Adding the seven largest biotechnology companies to this analysis did not improve the outlook.

A more in-depth analysis of the entire industry in 2005 provides a clearer picture. White (2005) found seventy drug candidates in the pipeline, thirteen of which were in five new classes of antibiotics. Of the forty-four candidates whose bacterial targets were known, most were for Gram-positive bacteria. Additionally, all the drug candidates for new classes of drugs – where targets were disclosed – targeted only Gram-positive and respiratory-tract bacteria. There were no new class candidates for Gram-negative bacteria.

Companies set R&D priorities according to the net present value and a measure of expected revenue for R&D investment. Antibiotics have a low net present value compared to many other types of therapy (Projan 2003; Projan and Shlaes 2004), due in part to shorter treatment length compared to chronic therapies, high therapeutic competition, the restriction of use of new antibiotics to resistant infections, and decreased value due to the emergence of resistance (Charles and Grayson 2004).

Mobilising for solutions

Combating antibiotic resistance has generated lengthy lists of proposed policy interventions (Laxminarayan et al. 2007; WHO 2005; Smith and Coast 2003). While more research may be needed to develop new and effective antibiotics, action plans can build on the ample evidence base for prevention and containment. More importantly, mobilising for change involves strategic choices. These choices should prioritise pathways that:

- make data actionable;
- reframe antibiotic resistance as a cross-cutting concern;
- realign incentives by pooling risks, resources and response;
- re-engineer the value chain of R&D for new diagnostics, drugs and vaccines.

To make data actionable, one has to motivate its collection. Access to over-the-counter drugs, unnecessary presumptive treatment and weak regulatory systems hinder efforts to bolster rational use of antibiotics.

Though some parts of the world track antibiotic resistance patterns (e.g. the European Antibiotic Resistance Surveillance System), most regions do not have effective surveillance systems in place. Improved data collection is also important for mobilising action and monitoring efforts to improve clinical practice. At the country level, such steps may help spur and revitalise rational prescribing programmes, use of essential drug lists, and other activities by ministries of health.

In the US, for example, the Institute for Healthcare Improvement launched the 100,000 Lives Campaign to reduce preventable deaths in US hospitals. The campaign targeted six best-practice interventions, including the prevention of infections at central line and surgical sites. By setting quantifiable goals and targets, and developing a methodology for counting the number of lives saved, the Campaign and more than 3,000 participating hospitals were able to achieve remarkable success. Building on this, the '5 Million Lives Campaign' is now under way to prevent 5 million incidents of iatrogenic harm in the US.[5]

The example demonstrates how making antibiotic resistance a cross-cutting concern may give it greater traction. Through a campaign aimed at improving patient safety in the hospital, infection control measures might be implemented, which in turn makes the environment less conducive to the development of antibiotic resistance. Extending the approach further, the World Alliance for Patient Safety has set its sights on campaigning to combat antibiotic resistance, building upon the stepping stones of previous efforts to improve hand hygiene and safe surgery.

Antibiotic resistance is an issue that cuts across AIDS, tuberculosis and malaria programmes. Lessons learned about surveillance and syndromic management, for example, might apply across these programmes. By coordinating these efforts, the WHO might develop synergy among these vertical disease programmes and lead by example on these issues.

Another strategic approach involves the pooling of health financing and health risks in order to improve the rational use of drugs. For example, a competitive health insurance market creates weak incentives for insurance companies to motivate infection control in local hospitals. But if the patients going to hospitals belong to the same health insurance pool, then the individual health insurance company internalises these costs and has a stronger incentive to act. By apportioning costs that otherwise might fall as an externality on others, policies that pool resources among these stakeholders share the burden of supplying a public good.

Finally, what about R&D for new antibiotics and complementary technologies like diagnostics and vaccines? There are multiple points along the value chain of R&D that would benefit from re-engineering. Various groups have called for applying a range of financial incentives to encourage drug manufacturers to develop new antibacterial drugs (Laxminarayan et al. 2007; IDSA 2004; Spellberg et al. 2007). In addition to changing the nature of financing and incentives, there is a need to rethink the opportunity costs, economies of scale and profit expectations.

For example, by working with manufacturers in emerging economies, academia has the potential to change the value chain of drug R&D more fundamentally. Sunil Shaunak and his colleagues at Imperial College in London recognised that the treatment for hepatitis C was too expensive for widespread use in the developing world. When they modified pegylated interferon to make it last longer and work better in tropical climates, they created a company, PolyTherics, to handle the new product and then licensed the drug directly to a company in India to conduct the clinical trials and to make the product available at a target $3/dose, much lower than the current $200/dose. The deal does not generate as much revenue for PolyTherics on a per unit basis, but it does illustrate a model of partnership between academia and developing-country drug manufacturers that enables more affordable access in poor countries.

Firm size and cost of operations appear to be important as well. Manufacturers with lower overhead costs might be more willing to serve markets where the profit margin is tighter. Where the big drug companies may not find markets attractive, universities or smaller companies in developing countries may step in. For example, after losing money on the tuberculosis drug Seromycin, Eli Lilly transferred rights on the drug to Purdue University. Purdue believes that its lower overheads and smaller capacity will allow it to manufacture this drug without suffering losses, and this will make Purdue the only supplier of Seromycin in North America (Purdue 2007).

The R&D of new diagnostics also requires attention. The basic technique for diagnosing TB has evolved little in over a hundred years and remains complicated and costly. Simplifying and streamlining the process would mark a significant advance. For other infectious diseases like malaria, paediatric diagnostics alone could prevent approximately 400 million inappropriate treatments every year (Global Health Diagnostics Forum 2006). Point-of-care diagnostics for bacterial infections could help reduce the clinical uncertainty that results in unnecessary, presumptive treatment of patients with antibiotics and improve care. Rapid diagnostics for the detection of bacterial pathogens in food also could reframe how policymakers handle food safety and trade. Importantly, moving from the detection of antibiotic residues in food to the finding of antibiotic-resistant plasmids in poultry and livestock products could bolster efforts to limit the inappropriate use of antibiotics in animals.

Conclusion

The victims of antibiotic resistance are too often faceless. As with other public goods, combating antibiotic resistance will require effective governmental, civil society and private-sector efforts. Policy interventions have to change the rules of the game. Surveillance has to be redesigned to create actionable, follow-on steps. The issue of antibiotic resistance has to be reframed to be a problem of more than just the community focused on infectious diseases. Pooling can help realign incentives and enlist key stakeholders to contribute to the public good of preventing and stemming the emergence of antibiotic resistance. Re-engineering the R&D and delivery of antibiotics offers some creative pathways forward. The challenge of antibiotic resistance has the form of a repeated game, but only through the spirit of public-sector collective action will humankind go the distance and ensure a future with effective antibiotics.

Taking concerted action, ReAct, a coalition to combat antibiotic resistance, has emerged to tackle this challenge. The coalition's vision is that current and future generations of people around the globe should have access to effective treatment of bacterial infections as part of their right to health.

Notes

1. See www.cptech.org/workingdrafts/rndsignonletter.html.
2. See www.who.int/intellectualproperty/report/en/index.html.
3. See www.keionline.org for more information.
4. This discussion of antibiotic resistance draws upon an abbreviated version of A. So and C. Manz, Meeting the challenge of antimicrobial resistance: Public good and collective action, www.react-group.org.
5. See www.ihi.org/IHI/Programs/Campaign for more information on the campaign.

References

Charles, P., and L. Grayson (2004). The dearth of new antibiotic development: Why we should be worried and what we can do about it. *Med Jour Australia* 181(10): 549–53.

CNN (2007). Border security scrutinized after TB patient slips in. 1 June. CNN.com.

De Francisco, A., and S. Matlin (eds) (2006). *Monitoring financial flows for health research 2006: The changing landscape of health research for development*. Geneva: Global Forum for Health Research. www.globalforumhealth.org/filesupld/monitoring_financial_flows_06/Financial%20Flows%202006.pdf.

Elamin, E. (2003). Deadweight loss of bacterial resistance due to overtreatment. *Health Econ* 12: 125–38.

Fasehun, F. (1999). The antibacterial paradox: Essential drugs, effectiveness, and cost. *Bull World Health Organ* 77(3): 211–16.

Fireman, B., et al. (2003). Impact of the pneumococcal conjugate vaccine on otitis media. *Ped Infect Dis Jour* 22(1): 10–16.

Foster, S. (2007). The economic burden of antibiotic resistance. Presentation at Alliance for Prudent Use of Antibiotics World Congress. Boston MA.

Global Health Diagnostics Forum (2006). The right tools can save lives. *Nature* 444: 681.

Hardin, G. (1968). The tragedy of the commons. *Science* 162: 1243–8.

Hooton, T. (2001). Antimicrobial resistance: A plan of action for community practice. *Amer Fam Physician.* 63(6): 1087–96.

IDSA (Infectious Disease Society of America) (2004). *Bad bugs, no drugs: As antibiotic discovery stagnates … a public health crisis brews.* Alexandria VA. www.idsociety.org/WorkArea/showcontent.aspx?id=5554.

IFPMA (International Federation of Pharmaceutical Manufacturers and Associations) (2006). Statement on IGWG agenda item 2.3: 'Elements of the global strategy and plan of action'.

IMS Health (2005). New products and markets fuel growth in 2005. www.imshealth.com/web/content/0,3148,64576068_63872702_70260998_77974518,00.html.

Jordan, G.E. (2008). Where have all the new drugs gone: Industry's medicine cabinet running empty on compounds. *The Star Ledger,* 9 January.

Laxminarayan, R., et al. (2007). *Extending the cure: Policy responses to the growing threat of antibiotic resistance.* Washington DC: Resources for the Future. www.extendingthecure.org/downloads/ETC_FULL.pdf.

Mbelle, N., et al. (1999). Immunogenicity and impact on nasopharyngeal carriage of a nonavalent pneumococcal conjugate vaccine. *Jour Infect Dis* 180: 1171–6.

Okeke, I.N., et al. (2005). Antibiotic resistance in developing countries. Part I: recent trends and current status. *Lancet Infect Dis* 5: 481–93.

Power, E. (2006). Impact of antibiotic restrictions: The pharmaceutical perspective. *Clin Microbiol Infect* 12(5): 25–34.

Projan, S. (2003). Why is Big Pharma getting out of antibacterial drug discovery? *Curr Opin Micro* 6: 427–30.

Projan, S., and D.M. Shlaes (2004). Antibacterial drug discovery: Is it all downhill from here? *Clin Microbiol Infect* 10(4): 18–22.

Purdue University (2007). Purdue takes on North American battle against multi-drug-resistant tuberculosis. Press release. 11 December. http://news.uns.purdue.edu/x/2007b/071211HornettChao.html.

Schartz, B. (1997). Preventing the emergence of antimicrobial resistance: A call for action by clinicians, public health officials, and patients. *JAMA* 278: 944–5.

Smith, R., and J. Coast (2002). Antibiotic resistance: A global response. *Bull World Health Organ* 80(2): 126–33.

Smith, R.D., and J. Coast (2003). Antimicrobial drug resistance. In R. Smith et al. (eds), *Global public goods for health: Health, economic and public health perspectives.* New York: Oxford University Press.

Spellberg, B., et al. (2004). Trends in antimicrobial development: Trends for the future. *Clin Infect Dis* 38: 1279–86.

Spellberg, B., et al. (2007). Societal costs versus savings from wild-card patent extension legislation to spur critically needed antibiotic development. *Infection* 35: 167–74.

US Government Accountability Office (GAO) (2006). *New drug development: Science, business, regulatory, and intellectual property issues cited as hampering drug development efforts.* GAO-07-49. www.gao.gov/new.items/d0749.pdf.

Verhoef, J., et al. (1999). A Dutch approach to methicillin-resistant *Staphylococcus aureus.* *Eur J Clin Microbiol Infect Dis* 18: 461–6.

Vriens, M., et al. (2002). Costs associated with a strict policy to eradicate methicillin-resistant Staphylococcus aureus in a Dutch university medical center: A 10-year survey. *Eur J Clin Microbiol Infect Dis* 21: 782–6.

White, T. (2005). Inventory of new antibacterials under development. Paper given at EU Intergovernmental Conference, 'Antibiotic resistance: Action to promote new technologies', Birmingham.

WHO (World Health Organization) (2004a). *The world medicines situation*. Geneva. WHO/EDM/PAR/2004.5.

WHO (2004b). *Medicines strategy 2004–2007*. Geneva.

WHO (2005). Resolution WHA58.27: Improving the containment of antibiotic resistance. May. Geneva. www.who.int/gb/ebwha/pdf_files/WHA58/WHA58_27-en.pdf.

WHO (2006). Emergence of XDR-TB. Press release. Geneva. www.who.int/mediacentre/news/notes/2006/np23/en/index.html.

C I **Carbon trading and climate change**

Small fluctuations in the earth's climate and temperature are nothing new. Throughout history our ancestors endured droughts, floods and famine. To survive, they invented new ways to farm and to hunt, to make their dwellings and to clothe themselves; they migrated across the globe, and they fought each other.

The climatic fluctuations they faced were relatively small. The earth's climate and temperature have been remarkably constant for millennia, with an average temperature of around 15°C – about 33°C warmer than it would have been without a natural greenhouse effect produced by water vapour in the atmosphere. The total amount of heat and light energy absorbed from the sun almost exactly equals the heat energy that radiates out into space – *almost*, because a small amount is captured by plants and oceanic algae for photosynthesis. Photosynthesis converts solar energy, CO_2 and water to energy-dense carbon containing organic molecules, releasing oxygen.

Over millennia the atmosphere was cleared of CO_2 while massive amounts of solar energy accumulated under the earth's surface and the depths of the oceans in carbon reservoirs of oil, coal and gas. This gave us a life-sustaining atmosphere consisting mainly of nitrogen, oxygen and water vapour.

As the atmosphere supports life, so life sustains the atmosphere. It does so through the carbon cycle – a natural carbon-recycling system powered by photosynthesis. Carbon enters the atmosphere from an above-ground pool of biomass in the ocean, soil and plants through respiration, the decay of dead plants and animals, and combustion. It is recycled by photosynthesis. This natural system can recycle a limited amount of carbon between the atmosphere and superficial biomass, but it has no effective way of returning it to the subterranean reservoirs.

IMAGE C1.1
**Dry river bed,
Namibia**

Until just over two centuries ago the carbon cycle was in balance. But when we discovered that we could unleash the solar energy stored over millennia as coal, gas and oil in carbon reservoirs and use it to drive machines, the amount and the rate at which carbon entered the atmosphere began to increase. This was the start of the Industrial Revolution. It made mechanical work on a massive scale possible. The combustion of fossil fuels pumps between 5 and 6 gigatons per year into the atmosphere. This exceeds the recycling capacity of the carbon cycle by more than 1.6 billion tons per year. At this rate many times more fossil carbon will be added to the atmosphere over this century than since the industrial era began.

The fundamental cause of today's climate change is that we have reversed the overall direction of carbon flow that brought the earth to life and keeps it alive. If it continues, the atmosphere will look more and more like it did before life appeared. It threatens nothing less than planetary death.

How climate change affects health

Climate change is already having profound effects on health. As it continues, this will escalate. People who live in poor countries (those least responsible for producing climate change) will bear a far larger burden than citizens of rich countries whose wasteful lifestyles are the major cause (GHW 2005). Inequality in social and economic development, education, the accessibility and quality of health care, public health initiatives and infrastructure and so on will also be critically important in determining the impact of climate change. Again, it is poor people who will suffer the most.

Increasing temperatures result in an increased number of deaths from heat-related causes. For example, the European summer of 2003 average temperatures were 3.5°C above normal. Between 22,000 and 45,000 people died from heat-related causes. It was the hottest summer ever recorded, with maximal temperatures beyond the range of normal variability. This was not completely unpredictable: climate modelling had shown that the risk of a heatwave of this size had more than doubled as a result of human-induced climate change (Patz et al. 2005).

Apart from the direct heat-related causes of death, climate change can affect human health in many ways. Below are some of the direct and indirect health-related consequences of climate change (GHW 2005):

- Droughts or increased rainfall will damage agricultural systems, thereby threatening the food supply of millions.
- Many people may have to leave their homes as a result of environmental damage or rising sea levels, increasing poverty and dependence on international aid. The Intergovernmental Panel on Climate Change predicts that warming oceans could contribute to increasingly severe hurricanes and cyclones with stronger winds and heavier rains. While it is not possible to attribute specific events to climate change, the events in New Orleans after Hurricane Katrina and the aftermath of Cyclone Nargis in Burma, where tens of thousands were killed and hundreds of thousands made homeless, show the kind of devastation that can be expected.
- Deaths will increase as a result of extreme temperature changes – both hot and cold. Children and the elderly will be particularly vulnerable. A rise in heat-related deaths in hot countries will be larger than any fall in cold-related deaths in cold countries (McMichael et al. 2006).
- Infectious diseases will increase, especially those transmitted by mosquitoes. Diseases such as malaria and dengue fever will increase in their current regions and may spread to nations which currently do not have such illnesses.

- Polluted water supplies will heighten the risk of diarrhoeal diseases including typhoid. Malnutrition will increase in poor communities; along with causing mortality, it may also damage child growth and development.
- Rodent-borne diseases may also increase as a warmer climate allows them to seek habitats in new areas. This increases the risk of illnesses such as Lyme disease and tick-borne diseases.

It is believed that at current trends there will be an increase of 2°C by 2050 (GHW 2005). This could result in:

- 220 million more people at risk from malaria;
- 12 million more at risk from hunger as a result of failing crops;
- 2,240 million more people at risk from water shortages, particularly in developing nations.

Meeting the challenge of climate change

Though climate change is the most serious threat we have faced throughout human history, very few leaders are prepared to tackle the problem at its roots. Despite the flourishing denialist industry, the main problem is not denial but rather that powerful countries and groups are seeking to turn the crisis to their own advantage. They have steadily entrenched their power over the past two decades.

In *Carbon Trading: A Critical Conversation on Climate Change, Privatization and Power*, Larry Lohmann, of the Corner House,[1] argues that a new enclosure movement has formed around three interlinked and mutually reinforcing strategies aimed at depoliticising the climate change debate and trapping 'official international action ... within a US-style framework of neoliberal policy'. The three strategies are the knowledge fix, the technological fix, and the market fix (Lohmann 2006).

The *knowledge fix* aims to reshape or suppress public understanding of the problem so that reaction to it presents less of a political threat to corporations. Here is how it works.

By the mid-1980s, mounting evidence of rising atmospheric CO_2 levels and concern among climatologists about global warning led to a series of landmark conferences for scientists (e.g. Villach, Austria, in 1985) and policymakers (e.g. Bellagio, Italy, in 1987). At the Villach conference climatologists warned of a rise in global temperature 'greater than any in man's history' in the first half of the twenty-first century, and of the prospect of rising sea levels. Faced with this clear warning the US government moved to shift the scientific climate change debate away from independent academics towards government-linked science bureaucracies. These include the Intergovernmental Panel on Climate Change (IPCC), established in 1988 to look at the science and consequences of global warming (Lohmann 2006).

Lohmann describes clearly how these bureaucracies are subject to US and corporate influence, and increasingly to that of other Northern governments. This is not to say that the IPCC is *directly* controlled by these forces; the ways in which power influences science are complex and subtle. They can best be understood if we first accept that scientific agendas reflect specific political and economic contexts. The questions scientists ask, the way they seek the answers, and the way they communicate their findings to policymakers and the public reflect the prevailing political and economic milieu and the dominant mindset. They are influenced by competition for, and sources of, funding; the power of the corporate-owned media; culture; and so on.

In a world dominated by neoliberalism, the scientific research agenda is biased towards seeking technological or market-related solutions. And, since scientific bodies like the IPCC require consensus before issuing reports, the language in their reports avoids contentious issues and reflects the lowest common denominator. To free climate science from neoliberal domination we must accept that science is unavoidably heavily politicised and, rather than plead for 'objective science', oppose the neoliberal project globally in all its manifestations.

Public understanding of climate change is also influenced by a host of think-tanks, corporate-backed NGOs, and business groupings linked to the oil, energy, transport and other related industries whose aim is to spread disinformation and to perpetuate the idea that anthropogenic climate change is controversial. This includes the still flourishing denialism industry, which George Monbiot describes very well in *Heat,* his excellent book on global warming (Monbiot 2006).

As with science, the mass media approach to climate change also tends to follow the neoliberal paradigm, focusing almost exclusively and uncritically on technical magic bullets and carbon trading. This includes Nobel prizewinner Al Gore's film *An Inconvenient Truth,* which, though very informative about climate issues, seeks solutions in carbon trading, tree planting and other technical approaches.

The *technological fix* is based on the notion that the solution to climate change lies in new technology that will allow continued exploitation of fossil fuels and continuing profit for the oil and motor corporations. Examples include giant mirrors in space to reflect solar energy; spraying the stratosphere with fine metallic particles to reflect sunlight (Edward Teller, the father of the hydrogen bomb, argued that such unilateral action to dim the sky would be cheaper than seeking 'international consensus on ... reductions in fossil fuel-based energy production'); massive tree plantations – perhaps using genetically modified trees – to mop up CO_2; bio-fuels; injecting CO_2 into the deep ocean; and seeding the oceans with iron filings to encourage the growth of CO_2-absorbing plankton.

The US National Science Foundation is discussing 'creating a biological film over the ocean's surface to divert hurricanes', and scientists convened by the George W. Bush White House have proposed a fleet of giant ocean-going turbines to throw up salt spray into the clouds to increase their reflectivity (Lohmann 2006).

While such technical approaches will give corporations exciting and lucrative business opportunities, their unintended ecologic results do not seem to merit much attention; nor does the more fundamental idea of cutting down on energy expenditure as a means of reducing fossil fuel extraction and emissions.

The *market fix* is the third leg of the global strategy to depoliticise climate change while simultaneously creating new opportunities for corporate profit-making. Following the idea of marketable pollution rights, proposed by the Canadian economist John Dales in the 1960s to control water pollution (Erion 2005), the market fix for climate change developed in the wake of the 1987 Montreal Protocol that established pollution trading as a means to control substances that damage the ozone layer. This was followed by a system of emissions trading introduced by the United States government in 1990 that set targets for reducing sulphur dioxide emissions that were causing acid rain.

In 1992 the United Nations Framework Convention on Climate Change (UNFCC) was presented for ratification with the stated aim of achieving 'stabilization of greenhouse gas concentrations in the atmosphere'. Though it did not set specific targets, it provided for subsequent updates. The most important update is the 1997 Kyoto Protocol (Kyoto), which aims to bind industrialised countries to a 5.2 per cent reduction in greenhouse gas emissions from 1990 by 2012.[2]

Pushed by the US, pollution trading came to form the core of Kyoto (no doubt pleasing bankers and companies who hoped to profit from the lucrative trade in carbon). Carbon trading allows countries or corporations to balance their CO_2 emissions by buying 'carbon credits' from others who emit less than their own target maximums. This allows major polluters to avoid the modest cuts required under Kyoto.

Article 17 of the Protocol establishes a system of 'Emissions Trading' where Annex 1 countries[3] can trade emission credits among themselves.

The next type of carbon trading, 'Joint Implementation', allows Annex 1 countries to invest in other Annex 1 countries to help them reduce emissions. The investing country gets the credits.

In practice, neither Emissions Trading nor Joint Implementation has played a significant role in the global carbon market. The main area of carbon trading falls under Article 12, the 'Clean Development Mechanism' (CDM). The CDM allows countries to avoid emission cuts at home by investing in UN-approved greenhouse-gas-saving projects such as wind farms, methane capture, biofuels and so on, in poor countries.

The CDM has two broad objectives. First, it has to help Annex 1 countries meet their emission reduction commitments. Second, it must help poor countries to achieve sustainable development. Both these goals raise controversial issues. A complex bureaucratic set of processes and structures have been set up to assess these questions.

To qualify for the CDM a project has to show that its emissions reductions are *additional* to those that would have happened if the project did not exist. If so, it qualifies for certified emissions reductions (CERs). These ingenious so-called 'clean development mechanisms' prevent any possible shortage of quotas; their supply can be increased as necessary. The UN does not charge for CERs, and investors can either use them to meet their Kyoto commitments or sell them on the market like state-allocated quotas. Writing in *Le Monde Diplomatique*, Aurélien Bernier (2008) describes how the creation of CERs actually *increases* the amount of carbon currency circulating on the global market. The price of carbon credits have plummeted to well below that required to reduce emissions or to give polluters any idea of their real cost.

Furthermore, in addition to the controversy surrounding CERs, the CDM does not have a universal definition of what sustainable development means; nor can it hold projects accountable in meeting this criterion.

Carbon trading and human rights

Greenhouse gas trading as set out in Kyoto establishes 'property rights' in the earth's carbon-cycling capacity (Lohmann 2006). This notion of 'rights' needs careful scrutiny.

The 1948 Universal Declaration of Human Rights sees human rights as inalienable and indivisible. All of us possess them in equal measure by simple virtue of the fact that we are human. Since fixed carbon is fundamental to all life, each one of us has a just claim to a fair and equal share of the earth's carbon cycling capacity – our human rights must include the rights to use and emit a certain amount of carbon.

IMAGE CI.2   **Busy street in Cairo**

But how big is our fair share? If we want a stable and healthy planet for ourselves, and our grandchildren, then the total amount of all our emissions cannot exceed the amount that the earth can recycle. To meet this requirement, a drastic cut   of the order of at least 60 per cent – in global greenhouse gas emissions is an absolute requirement. To calculate our fair share of emissions we must first cut current global emissions by 60 per cent and then divide the remainder by the earth's total population. This is the idea behind *Contraction and Convergence*, which is well described by Monbiot (2006).

If I claim more than my fair share, then one of two things must follow. Either others must make do with less than their fair share, or CO_2 must accumulate in the atmosphere and climate change will accelerate. To claim as a 'right' any use of carbon that exceeds my fair share is a fundamental contradiction of the principles of human rights.

In poor countries, most people do not have the means to access their fair share. Rich people, on the other hand, consume vastly in excess of theirs. The carbon market assigns a uniform price to the 'luxury emissions' of the First World and the 'survival emissions' of the Third World (Narain and Agarwal 2006). Carbon trading amounts to the privatisation of the world's capacity to maintain a life-sustaining climate. Thus the 'rights' granted by Kyoto have been appropriated by the rich and powerful, and in particular by those who, historically, have been the worst polluters. Again, this is the very antithesis of any notion of human rights.

Instead of cutting the extraction of fossil fuels, the practical results of current carbon-trading policies actually *promote* fossil fuel burning. Other current solutions such as tree plantations and biofuels often drive people out of their traditional living grounds, destroy biodiversity, and lead to increased food prices as people are forced to compete with motor cars for the products of land use. Not surprisingly, this system sets up political conflicts and blocks effective climate action.

The way forward?

Fundamentally, we can only combat climate change and secure a liveable world for our children and grandchildren if we leave sequestered carbon – coal, oil and gas – under the earth's surface in the reservoirs nature created. There is no doubt that this is a daunting task.

Possible ways forward are easier to see if we remember that the knowledge fix, the technology fix and the market fix are pushed by a small group of people and neoliberal institutions.

Lohmann (2006) suggests that a good way to start would be a package of approaches already making headway in Northern countries where steep cuts in fossil fuels are high on the agenda. The package includes:

• Large-scale public works programmes to help reorganise infrastructure away from dependency on fossil fuel by, for example, revamping transport systems, decentralising electricity supply and developing solar and wind power.
• Phasing out subsidies aimed at promoting fossil fuel and car use, airport expansion, deforestation, the military, while scaling up subsidies for solar and wind energy, more energy-efficient housing, better insulation, and other genuinely green technologies that do not affect local communities adversely (as forest planting and gas extraction projects from landfill sites tend to do).
• Regulations that set strict standards for buildings, transport and land use planning.
• Phasing in taxes on carbon use and the use of materials like throwaway metal, water, wood and plastics.
• Use of the courts to apply human rights law to, say, greenhouse gas polluters.

These strategies should be backed and monitored by popular movements and held to account against clear short- and long-term targets. Where appropriate, they should be controlled by local communities. Vulnerable and marginalised groups must be included in all their diversity.

As in struggles around health, the fundamental problems of climate change are more political than technical. Ultimately, we cannot deal with climate crisis without all the painstaking work that goes into democratic mobilisation and political organisation and struggle. This involves building alliances around the many issues closely or loosely relevant to climate change that affect people in many different ways. As Lohmann (2006) says, 'the fight against global warming has to be part of the larger fight for a more just, democratic and equal world.'

Notes

1. The Corner House publishes regular briefing papers on a range of topics. It supports democratic and community movements for environmental and social justice. www. thecornerhouse.org.uk.
2. *Editorial comment*: Different perspectives are held on the potential of carbon trading as a means to reduce carbon emissions. Two positions are reflected within this edition of *Global Health Watch*. For an alternate perspective, please see Section A.
3. Annex I countries are those countries that have agreed to binding targets under Kyoto. They have to submit annual greenhouse gas inventories. Countries that have no such obligations (i.e. poor countries) but who may participate in the CDM are known as 'non-Annex I countries'.

References

Bernier, A. (2008). Corporates hunt for profits as the climate change crisis builds. *Le Monde Diplomatique*, January.

Erion, G. (2005). Low hanging fruit always rots first: Observations from South Africa's crony carbon market. Center for Civil Society, University of KwaZulu-Natal, Durban. October.

GHW (2005). *Global Health Watch 2005–2006: An alternative world health report*. London: Zed Books for People's Health Movement, Medact and Global Equity Gauge Alliance.

IPCC (Intergovernmental Panel on Climate Change) (2007). *Climate change 2007: The physical science basis*. Contribution of Working Group I to the Fourth Assessment Report of the Intergovernmental Panel on Climate Change. New York: Cambridge University Press.

Lohmann, L. (2006). Carbon trading: A critical conversation on climate change, privatisation and power. *Development Dialogue* 48. Dag Hammarskjöld Foundation and Corner House. September.

McMichael, A.J., R.E. Woodruff and S. Hales (2006). Climate change and human health: Present and future risks. *The Lancet* 367: 859–69.

Monbiot, G. (2006). *Heat: How to stop the planet burning*. London: Allen Lane.

Narain, S., and A. Agarwal (2006). *Global warming in an unequal world*. New Delhi: Centre for Science and Environment.

NASA (2008). The carbon cycle. http://earthobservatory.nasa.gov/Library/Carbon Cycle/carbon_cycle4.html.

Patz, J.A., et al. (2005). Impact of regional climate change on human health. *Nature* 438, 17 November: 310–17.

C2 Terror, war and health

The role of the public health community in responding to the health impacts of war and conflict has become increasingly important in the context of the changing nature of war and conflict. Rarely do armies wear distinctive uniforms and fight across clearly drawn battle lines. Modern wars and conflict are characterised by aerial bombardment, guerrilla tactics and acts of 'terrorism', substantially changing the nature of the primary victims of war (Levy and Sidel 2008). Since World War II, civilians, especially women and children, have constituted the majority of deaths in wars.

While the global health community may have limited power to curb the aggression and belligerence of political and military leaders seeking out war and conflict, it can promote informed and open public debate about the causes of war and conflict by providing timely and credible information on the expected and actual health consequences of conflict. The health community also has an important role in preventing and treating injury and disease, as well as monitoring the impact and the conduct of war within the legal framework set out by the Geneva Conventions and other instruments of international law.

Terrorism and war: defining the boundaries

At a global level, 'terrorism' is an ill-defined yet widely used term. Numerous definitions are contained within international law and national legislation. Coming up with an internationally accepted definition is still a work in progress. Although people may often have no trouble in recognising 'terrorism' when they see it, a common definition and understanding of terrorism is much harder than might be first supposed. One of the complica-

---

BOX C2.1 **The risk of war**

The greater the wealth of a nation, the lower its chances of having a civil war. A country with a gross domestic product (GDP) per capita of US$250 has a 15 per cent probability of a war in the next five years, and this probability reduces by approximately half for a country with a GDP per capita of $600. Countries with per capita GDP of more than US$5,000 have less than a 1 per cent probability of having a civil war. Other factors that raise the risk of armed conflict include poor health, low status of women, large gaps between the rich and the poor, weak civil society, a lack of democracy, limited education, unemployment and access to small arms and light weapons (SIPRI 2006; deSoysa and Neumayer 2005).

---

tions about the definition of terrorism is that some institutions exclude it as a phenomenon during war because terrorism during war is best classified as a war crime. However, this contention is complicated by the existence of a definition and the prohibition of terrorism within the laws of war.

At the core of most definitions is the notion that terrorism involves targeting civilians with the intention of creating fear and terror in the population. Some definitions go on to say that terrorism must also be planned so as to achieve a change in the policies or practices of governments.

Attacks by nation-states are rarely termed 'terrorism' even when they use tactics that deliberately target civilians. Examples of terrorism perpetrated by nation-states include the Nazi bombing of Guernica during the Spanish Civil War; the bombing of cities in Europe during World War II; the nuclear destruction of Hiroshima and Nagasaki; and the carpet-bombing of Vietnam. Other examples of state terror have occurred in almost every recent war.

By contrast, when non-state groups or individuals use violence to accomplish their ends, these acts are often labelled 'terrorism' whether or not they deliberately harm civilians. Indeed, US law defines 'terrorism' as 'premeditated, politically motivated violence perpetrated against non-combatant targets by sub-national groups or clandestine agents' (CULS 2006). This definition excludes acts committed by nation-states. It also excludes the threat of violence as a means of terrorism. Furthermore, economic exploitation is often backed by the implied or explicit threat of superior force. The threat may often be unacknowledged, even by its victims, who may be led to believe they are less worthy, less hard-working, or less capable, and hence deserve exploitation. The implicit or explicit

TABLE C2.I   **Framework for defining terrorism**

What does it include?	Politically motivated violence (physical or psychological), or the threat of violence, especially against civilians, with the intent to instil fear and cause damage to health
Who might the perpetrators be?	State or non-state organisations or individuals
Where might such acts take place?	Within or across national boundaries
When can it occur?	During war, peace, or periods of internal or civil conflict

threat of use of force can be as unjust as the actual use of that force and may account for more total damage to health than implemented acts of military aggression. Economic sanctions and blockades intended to produce destabilisation may also be viewed as a weapon of war; current examples of this include Gaza and Cuba.

This chapter advocates a definition of the term 'terrorism' that is comprehensive and that is not based on a distinction between state and non-state actors, nor whether the scenario is characterised as war or peace. Rather, we define terrorism as 'politically motivated violence, or the threat of violence, especially against civilians, with the intent to instil fear, whether conducted by nation-states, individuals or sub-national groups'.

As is often noted, one person's 'terrorist' is another person's 'freedom fighter'. Thus the political context and the causal pathway leading to an act of terrorism are salient issues. While attacks on unarmed civilians can never be justified, it is argued that violence committed in resistance to oppression, subjugation or attack is not the same as violence conducted as an act of aggression or offence.[1] However, while it is important to understand the root causes of violence, others argue that making a distinction between different causes of violence is unhelpful and ultimately self-defeating.

War, terrorism and the state

Preoccupation with preparation for wars is sometimes known as 'militarism', particularly when it is excessive or disproportionate to a perceived threat, or when it is accompanied by acts of aggression. It may lead to the subversion of efforts to promote human welfare. This preoccupation can also lead to 'pre-emptive war' (responding to an allegedly imminent attack) and to 'preventive war' (responding to an attack that is feared some time in the future).

Militarism is a problem worldwide but is especially important in developing countries that spend substantially more on military expenditures than on health. In 1990, Ethiopia spent $16 per capita for military expenditures and only $1 per capita for health, and Sudan spent $25 per capita for military expenditures and only $1 per capita for health (Foege 2000). Militarism can also affect the social environment by encouraging violence as a means of settling disputes and infringing upon civil rights and liberties.

The actions of governments in the recent violent history of Latin America are especially worth considering in this discussion of terrorism. In Chile, for example, the military dictatorship that followed the assassination of President Salvador Allende led to a reign of terror over the population that included the arrest, torture and execution of thousands of people (Klein 2007).

In other countries, a 'low-intensity conflict' (LIC) was experienced in which small-scale, guerrilla-style methods were applied to avoid full military engagement. Although described as 'low intensity', its sustained use inflicted overwhelming damage in some countries (Braveman et al. 2000). For civilians, who are often targeted, the conflict is anything but low in intensity.

In El Salvador during the 1970s, when Catholic priests and peasants took action to improve their living and working conditions, the country's landowners responded violently with 'death squads'. This was followed by a military coup in 1979 that led to hundreds of unarmed unionists, moderate political opposition leaders and priests being killed and mutilated. Subsequently an armed revolutionary organisation was formed to oppose the illegitimate military government, led by the Farabundo Martí National Liberation Front (FMLN). Twelve years of civil war followed until a peace accord was signed in 1992.

During this time nearly 1.5 per cent of the Salvadorian population (70,000 people) were killed by government forces and allied death squads. Life expectancy fell to 50.7 years in the period 1980–85. Government documents confirm that civilian assassination campaigns were planned with the full knowledge of the US administrations at the time. Torture was an unofficial but systematic policy of the government, reportedly with the assistance of US military advisers.

Parts of the country were subjected to a campaign of terror which included starving civilians and subjecting them to air attacks, including with napalm. In 1980 a group of at 600 unarmed civilians, mostly women and children, were killed by the military while fleeing to Honduras. In 1981, 7,000 people were massacred while fleeing to Honduras. About a million Salvadorans (20 per cent of the population) fled the country as refugees; another 500,000 were displaced within the country.

Events in Guatemala present another example of state-sanctioned terrorism. In 1954, the elected government of Jacobo Arbenz was overthrown by a CIA-directed coup, following his attempt to nationalise the unused land of the multinational United Fruit Company, so that it could be used for domestic food production. Over the next few decades resistance to the military government was brutally repressed. Health-care workers who served the poor were among those targeted. From 1980 to 1985, over 137 violations of medical neutrality were documented by the Guatemala Health Rights Support Project. Health workers were shot, 'disappeared', or driven into exile. Tens of thousands of peasants were driven from their villages and subsistence farms, especially by the government's 'scorched earth' strategy. Many fled to the remote jungles and mountains, further restricting opportunities for subsistence living and access to health care. By 1989, 71 per cent of rural Guatemalans lived in extreme poverty (Braveman et al. 2000).

Meanwhile a wealthy elite from within and outside the country gained control of the economy. While basic grain production failed to keep up with population growth, land was used to grow cash crops for export. Much of the US government's 'Food For Peace' programme, which provided basic grains to Guatemala, was used to generate cash income for the government instead of meeting the needs of the population.

Sadly, there are many other examples of state or state-sanctioned terrorism from across the world: these include events currently taking place in Darfur and Chechnya.

Based on the limited definition of 'terrorism' used by the United States, the US National Counterterrorism Center reported that, during 2006, there were 14,352 terrorist attacks worldwide, which resulted in 20,573 deaths (13,340 in Iraq), with an additional 36,214 people wounded. There were nearly 300 incidents that resulted in ten or more deaths, 90 per cent of which were in the Near East and South Asia. Armed attacks and bombings caused 77 per cent of the fatalities (NCTC 2007).

Acts of violence perpetrated by individuals and non-state groups include the chemical attacks in subways in Japan in 1995 which led to twelve deaths and approximately 5,000 injuries, and the 11 September 2001 attacks which led to almost 3,000 deaths, including those of firefighters and rescue workers who rushed to the scene.

The health and social consequences of the 'War on Terror'

Terrorism and perceived threats of terrorism can have long-lasting social, political and economic consequences: widespread fear, curtailment of civil liberties and the promotion of a dysfunctional climate of fear. Some governments have also used 'terror' as a pretext for suppressing democracy and legitimate political opposition.

The United States' response to the 11 September attacks is a case in point. Health-related consequences within the US have included interference with training of health personnel, diversion of resources needed for public health and medical care, and erection of barriers to health services. For example, billions of dollars have been spent on emergency preparedness and response capabilities for potential terrorist attacks. While some of these huge allocations of money have improved public health capabilities, they have also diverted attention and resources away from other more pressing public health problems (V.W. Sidel 2004).

There have been many examples of dysfunctional 'preparedness'. For example, a campaign of mass smallpox vaccination was announced by President Bush, despite there not having been any cases of smallpox anywhere since 1981. The focus was on 500,000 military personnel, 500,000 health workers, and up to 10 million emergency responders. Many public health workers expressed concerns about the risks associated with smallpox vaccination and the cost of implementing the programme. Even when it was implemented on a much smaller scale than originally planned, it resulted in at least 145 serious adverse events and 3 deaths (CDC, MMWR 2003) as well as the neglect of other urgent public health problems (Cohen et al. 2004).

In another example, the US Department of Defense (DoD) ordered all US service members to be immunised against anthrax. Reports of adverse reactions and doubts about the effectiveness of the vaccine against inhalation anthrax led a number of service members to refuse, resulting in their demotion, dismissal or court martial. In response to a class-action lawsuit, an injunction was issued against further administration of the vaccine. When the injunction was lifted in 2005, the court ordered that the immunisations be voluntary rather than compulsory. Subsequently, a total of 1.1 million service members have been immunised at a cost of hundreds of millions of dollars.

Another consequence of US 'preparedness' programmes and their political use has been widespread fear through constant reference to current levels of 'terrorism risk' (dramatised by use of five colour codes) and the frequent mobilisation of the emergency services and National Guard. This has enabled the government to gain congressional approval for additional major funding for counterterrorism programmes (M. Sidel 2004; Siegel 2005), not to mention fuelling discrimination against people who 'look like terrorists' (MacFarquhar 2006).

Civil liberties have also taken a pounding. The Homeland Security Act of 2003 has undermined the system of checks and balances that limits the power of any one branch of government, and has greatly concentrated power in the executive branch and the presidency. Federal actions of doubtful legality include the taping of telephone conversations between people in the US and in other countries by the National Security Agency (NSA) and the request by the NSA to telephone companies to provide records of billions of domestic telephone calls. Further breaches of civil liberties can be seen in an agreement with the European Union to provide thirty-four categories of personal information to US authorities about airline passengers on flights to the US.

For the first time since the Civil War, the US has been designated as a military theatre of operations. This represents a radical change in the role of the DoD and an erosion of the principle that the US military *not* be used for domestic law enforcement.

Finally, international human rights conventions have been violated. There has been torture and other forms of maltreatment of detainees in Iraq and Afghanistan; within the US military base in Guantánamo Bay; and in prisons in Central and Eastern Europe operated by the Central Intelligence Agency (CIA). In addition, the US has participated in acts of 'extraordinary rendition' in which detainees have been transferred to countries with poor human rights records, where they are likely to have been tortured or maltreated (Scheinin 2007).

Measuring and describing war and conflict

The past few years have seen a growing public health movement aimed at ensuring a more complete assessment of the impact of war on human health. Ugalde and colleagues (2000) argue that the long-term and indirect effects of environmental damage and the destruction of schools, electricity networks and sewerage systems must be measured. Most of the 3.8 million civilian deaths that occurred in the DRC, for example, were not directly due to warfare, but to malnutrition, infectious disease, and other indirect effects (Roberts and Muganda 2008).

Others have highlighted the importance of measuring the long-term effects on mental health (Murthy and Lakshminarayana 2006) and the consequences of the damage done to social and family structures and the breakdown of communal ties. And there are costs associated with transgressions in the conduct of war – the more often the Geneva Conventions are flouted, the more likely it is that civilians will suffer in future wars and conflict. But the belligerents involved a war may not want a full and proper assessment of its impact, nor any monitoring of the conduct of war. This section provides two case studies demonstrating the importance of sound research and the role of academic and non-government organisations in describing the impact and conduct of war.

Counting the dead in Iraq

It is now accepted that the invasion and occupation of Iraq have been a humanitarian disaster. However, what was not readily apparent was the full extent to which the population in Iraq has been brutalised, at least not until a group of researchers from Johns Hopkins University in the US and the Al-Mustansiriya University of Iraq decided to estimate the excess mortality caused by the war.

The first piece of research was published in 2004. It consisted of a survey of 33 randomly selected clusters of thirty households across Iraq that was designed to determine the excess mortality during the 17·8 months after the 2003 invasion (Roberts et al. 2004). The study estimated an excess mortality of 98,000 people (95 per cent CI: 8,000–194,000), over half of which were reported to have been from violent causes. There was widespread vilification of these findings from many quarters.

Between May and July 2006 a second and larger survey concluded that mortality had more than doubled from a pre-invasion rate of 5·5 per 1,000 people per year to 13·3 per 1,000 people per year in the 40 months post-invasion. It was estimated that as of July 2006, there had been 654,965 (CI: 392,979–942,636) excess Iraqi deaths as a consequence of the war.

The research also found that mortality rates from violent causes had increased every year post-invasion. Gunfire accounted for about half of all violent deaths. Deaths from air strikes were less commonly reported in 2006 compared to 2003–04, but deaths from car explosions had increased. Deaths and injuries from violent causes were concentrated in adolescent to middle-aged men, some of whom would have been active combatants. By contrast, before the invasion in 2003, virtually all deaths in Iraq were from non-violent causes.

The estimates were immediately denounced by the coalition forces, Iraq Body Count as well as other researchers and individuals amidst accusations of bad science and irresponsible medical journalism. Certainly there were methodological limitations to both surveys; however, these were carefully explained in the published papers, and conclusions drawn on the basis of conventional scientific practice. A number of potential biases could have over- or under-estimated the number of deaths. In fact, according to the UK's Ministry of Defence's chief scientific adviser, the second survey's study design was described as being 'robust' and close to 'best practice', given the difficulties of data collection and verification in the present circumstances in Iraq (Bennett-Jones 2007). Significantly, it was based on primary data

---

BOX C2.2 **Health and health care in Iraq**

Since 2003, the country's health sector has been in a downward spiral. Supplies of water and electricity are limited, as are medical personnel, equipment and essential drugs. Half of Iraq's 24,000 doctors have left. As many as 185 Iraqi university professors have been assassinated. The Ministry of Health is reported to have lost more than 720 physicians to death or injury (DFI 2007).

Many Iraqis now experience poorer access to water and electricity. The country's water and sanitation system, once the most advanced in the region, is now damaged and broken. Child malnutrition rates have jumped from 19 per cent to 28 per cent since the invasion (NCC/Oxfam 2007).

A recent United Nations Assistance Mission for Iraq report estimated that 54 per cent of Iraqis were living on less than US$1 a day and almost half of all children were malnourished (UNAMI 2007).[2]

---

collected from households, a method that is superior to data collected from passive surveillance measures, which are usually incomplete, even in stable circumstances.

Apart from the tragedy of the death and destruction in Iraq, what is revealing about these studies is the criticism and denial they engendered from the scientific and media establishment because the findings were inconvenient and uncomfortable. It is to the credit of the researchers and *The Lancet* journal that these detractors were confronted head-on in order to defend both science and the right of the public to crucial information. The continued importance of academic attention to the Iraq War is highlighted by ongoing disagreements about the measurement of deaths and casualties.[3]

Others have also played an important role in highlighting the bias inherent within the mainstream Western media when it comes to reporting on the conduct and impact of war and conflict. In the same way that it has been considered necessary to establish an 'alternative world health report', it has been vitally important to establish a 'watch' on the mainstream global media. One such initiative is Media Lens, which has not just monitored and revealed cases of biased and false reporting on the war in Iraq, but has also acted as a conscience for journalists who want to report accurately and honestly.

The conduct of war in Lebanon

The people of the Middle East have suffered decades of violence. This has included wars and conflict between Israel and Lebanon that have gone on since the 1960s. In July and August 2006 this conflict broke out again, and ended with Israel launching a 33-day attack on Lebanon, coupled with an air, sea and road blockade that lasted until 7 September.

A feature of the war was the overwhelming force with which Israel attacked Lebanon. Israeli warplanes launched some 7,000 bomb and missile strikes, supplemented by numerous artillery attacks and naval bombardment. Tens of thousands of homes were destroyed or damaged. More than 1,200 people were killed, a third of whom were children under 13 years. Thousands were injured. Over a million people were displaced (Haidar and Issa 2007).

The impact on civilian infrastructure and the environment was catastrophic. Schools, clinics, hospitals, roads and bridges were destroyed or damaged. Power plants, factories and fuel stations were also attacked. A massive oil spill affected 130 km of coastline. The burning of more than 45,000 tons of heavy fuel released noxious chemicals into the atmosphere for weeks (Haidar and Issa 2007).

Hezbollah attacks against Israel also caused death and damage, but on a smaller scale. Its rocket attacks resulted in the deaths of 43 Israeli civilians and 12 Israeli soldiers, as well as the injury of hundreds of Israeli civilians.

The scale of the impact of the war on Lebanese civilians and the apparent disregard for the Geneva Conventions called for independent verification of what had taken place. Israel contended that the high civilian fatality rate was due to Hezbollah's practice of hiding its combatants and equipment among civilians. In September 2007, Human Rights Watch published a report of its research and investigation into the conduct of the war (HRW 2007).

According to HRW, the primary reason for the high civilian death toll was Israel's frequent failure to abide by a fundamental obligation of the laws of war: the duty to distinguish between military targets, which can be legitimately attacked, and civilians, who cannot be subject to attack. HRW found that in the vast majority of air strikes that it investigated, there was no evidence of Hezbollah military presence, weaponry, or any other military objective that would have justified the strike. Throughout the conflict, warplanes targeted civilian vehicles and homes. Israeli officials also stated that they considered Hezbollah's extensive political, social and welfare branches to be part of an integrated terror organisation. Civilian institutions such as schools, welfare agencies, banks, shops and health facilities were therefore targeted.

According to HRW, Hezbollah did at times fire rockets from within populated areas, allow its combatants to mix with the civilian population, and store weapons in populated civilian areas. However, such violations were not widespread.

Israel also made extensive use of cluster munitions, particularly during the last three days of the conflict when a settlement was imminent. The way cluster bombs were used and the reliance on antiquated munitions have left about 1 million hazardous unexploded submunitions in southern Lebanon. As of 20 June 2007, the explosion of cluster munitions since the ceasefire had killed twenty-four civilians and injured many more.

The purpose of this case study is to highlight the need for methodologically sound and independent investigations into the conduct of war. Such investigations are required in many other parts of the world where international laws are being transgressed. They not only place on record the suffering of civilian populations, but they also bolster the work of international judicial bodies in holding governments to account for violations of international law and crimes against humanity. They are important for preventing further atrocities from occurring in the future and are thus an important public health intervention.

Retrospective documentation: Srebrenica

Epidemiologists and statisticians are not the only health scientists with a role to play in accurately monitoring the conduct and effects of war and terrorism. For example, a six-member international forensic scientific team, coordinated and sponsored by the Boston-based Physicians for Human Rights, conducted investigations into the mass graves in the Srebrenica region in Bosnia and Herzegovina, which then provided evidence to the International Criminal Tribunal for the former Yugoslavia.

Conclusion

There are several examples of the health community acting against weapons proliferation, in terms of both weapons of mass destruction and small arms and light weapons. Other efforts led by health workers have included the successful campaign to force the publishing company of *The Lancet*, Reed Elsevier, to divest from its long-standing business of hosting and organising arms fairs.

Beyond restricting the availability of weapons, action must be taken to alleviate the causes of terrorism, including poverty, illiteracy and gender inequality; as well as the practice of religious fundamentalists of all persuasions of encouraging, justifying or glorifying aggression and violence.

It is worth noting the response of the Lebanese people during the war with Israel. In spite of a history of sectarian divides, the homes of people living in relatively safe areas were opened to receive the flood of internally displaced persons from the South. Eyewitness accounts report numerous examples of spontaneous solidarity between people with religious, political and class differences (Shearer 2006).

In addition to material support, there were many examples of psychosocial support provided to children and families having to cope with displacement, bereavement and ongoing fear (Shearer 2006; Haddad 2006). Part of this response was due to the existence of a network of NGOs with long experience in providing humanitarian relief. Within days of the first attacks, coalitions of NGOs and independent volunteers had been formed, armed not only with practical experience but also with a local knowledge and sensitivity to people's needs and values. The existence of such resilience in the face of war has been described as a 'social vaccine' which protected Lebanon from descending into chaos and collapse.

Standard public health principles and implementation measures can also be applied to help address the problems described in this chapter. These include:

- surveillance, research and documentation;
- education and awareness awareness-raising;
- advocacy;
- implementation of programmes aimed at both prevention and the provision of acute and long-term care.

Those who wish to resist exploitation and oppression often face a dilemma. Should they advocate violent acts, which the powerful define as 'terrorism', or should they advocate non-violent methods? Mohandas Gandhi in India, Nelson Mandela in South Africa, and Martin Luther King in the United States have all argued eloquently that non-violence may be more powerful than violence in resisting oppression. In his speech accepting the 1964 Nobel Peace Prize, King said:

> This award . . . is a profound recognition that nonviolence is the answer to the crucial political and moral question of our time – the need for man to overcome oppression and violence without resorting to violence and oppression. Civilisation and violence are antithetical concepts. Negroes of the United States, following the people of India, have demonstrated that nonviolence is not sterile passivity, but a powerful moral force which makes for social transformation. Sooner or later all the people of the world will have to discover a way to live together in peace.

Notes

1. *Editorial comment*: In the formulation of this chapter we have endeavoured to be particularly sensitive to the strong antipathy held by some to the use of the term 'terrorism', which since 9/11 has been increasingly misused, and often in a discriminatory way.
2. For a more comprehensive and up-to-date summary of the state of health and health care in Iraq, see the 2008 Medact report: Rehabilitation under fire: Health care in Iraq 2003–7. Available at: www.casualty-monitor.org/2008/01/rehabilitation-under-fire-health-care.html.
3. For an overview of this issue, see the casualty monitor website: www.casualty-monitor.org/.

References

Bennett-Jones, O. (2007). Iraq 'deaths' survey was robust. http://news.bbc.co.uk/1/hi/uk_politics/6495753.stm.

Braveman, P., et al. (2000). Public health and war in Central America. In B.S. Levy and V.W. Sidel (eds), *War and public health*. Washington DC: American Public Health Association.

CDC, MMWR (2003). Update: Adverse events following civilian smallpox vaccination: United States, 2003. *MMWR* 53(5): 106–7.

Cohen, H.W., R.M. Gould and V.W. Sidel (2004). The pitfalls of bioterrorism preparedness: The anthrax and smallpox experiences. *American Journal of Public Health* 94: 1667–71.

CULS (Cornell University Law School) (2006). *Annual country reports on terrorism*. US Code, Title 22, Section 2656f(d).

Desoysa, I., and E. Neumayer (2005). Resources wealth and the risk of civil war onset: Results from a new data set of natural resources 1970–1999. Presented to the European Consortium for Political Research Conference, Budapest, September.

DFI (Doctors for Iraq) (2007). *Health Check* 1, Summer.

Foege, W.H. (2000). Arms and health: A global perspective. In B.S. Levy and V.W. Sidel (eds), *War and public health*. Washington DC: American Public Health Association.

Haddad, M. (2006). Turning relied into self-reliance. Speech at the 12th Congress on Poverty and Health, Berlin, December.

Haidar, M., and G. Issa (2007). The July 2006 Israeli war on Lebanon: Its impact and the lessons learned. Presentation at the 2nd World Social Forum on Health, Nairobi, January.

HRW (2007). Why they died: Civilian casualties in Lebanon during the 2006 war. *Human Rights Watch* 19(5)E. http://hrw.org/reports/2007/lebanon0907/lebanon-0907webwcover.pdf.

Klein, N. (2007). *The shock doctrine*. New York: Metropolitan Books.

Levy, B.S., and V.W. Sidel (eds) (2008). *War and public health*, 2nd edn. New York: Oxford University Press.

MacFarquhar, N. (2006). Terror fears hamper U.S. Muslims' travel. *New York Times*, 1 June.

Murthy, R.S., and R. Lakshminarayana (2006). Mental health consequences of war: A brief review of research findings. *World Psychiatry* 5(1), February: 25–30.

NCC (NGO Coordination Committee in Iraq) and Oxfam (2007). *Rising to the humanitarian challenge in Iraq*. Oxfam Briefing Paper 105, July. www.oxfam.org/files/Rising%20to%20the%20humanitarian%20challenge%20in%20Iraq.pdf.

NCTC (National Counterterrorism Center) (2007). *Report on terrorist incidents – 2006*. 30 April. http://wits.nctc.gov/reports/crot2006nctcannexfinal.pdf.

Roberts, L., et al. (2004). Mortality before and after the 2003 invasion of Iraq: Cluster sample survey. *The Lancet* 364: 1857–64.

Roberts, L., and C.L. Muganda (2008). War in the Democratic Republic of Congo. In B.S. Levy and V.W. Sidel (eds), *War and public health*, 2nd edn. New York: Oxford University Press.

Scheinin, M. (2007). *Report of the Special Rapporteur on the promotion and protection of human rights and fundamental freedoms while countering terrorism.* New York: Human Rights Council of the United Nations General Assembly. http://daccessdds.un.org/doc/UNDOC/GEN/G07/149/48/PDF/G0714948.pdf?OpenElement.

Shearer, D. (2006). Lebanon, a unique example of humanitarian solidarity. *Daily Star*, 26 September.

Sidel, M. (2004). *More secure, less free? Antiterrorism policy and civil liberties after September 11.* Ann Arbor: University of Michigan Press.

Sidel, V.W. (2004). Bioshield, biosword. *Gene Watch* 17(5/6): 3–7, 20.

Siegel, M. (2005). *False alarm: The truth about the epidemic of fear.* New York: Wiley.

SIPRI (Stockholm International Peace Research Institute) (2006). *SIPRI yearbook 2006: Armaments, disarmament and international security.* Oxford: Oxford University Press.

Ugalde, A., et al. (2000). Conflict and health: The health costs of war: Can they be measured? Lessons from El Salvador. *BMJ* 321(7254), July: 169–72.

UNAMI (United Nations Assistance Mission for Iraq). (2007). Humanitarian briefing on the crisis in Iraq. www.uniraq.org/documents/UN-Iraq%20Humanitarian%20Briefing%20Fact%20Sheet%20May%2007.pdf.

C3   **Reflections on globalisation, trade, food and health**

In 2006, the Food and Agricultural Organization of the United Nations (FAO) reported that, despite declining rates of child undernutrition in many developing countries, the number of undernourished people in the world remained 'stubbornly high'. In 2001–03 there were an estimated 854 million undernourished people worldwide (FAO 2006). Since 1990–92 the undernourished population in developing countries has declined by only 3 million people. By contrast, the undernourished population fell by 37 million in the 1970s and by 100 million in the 1980s. Just a year earlier, the World Health Organization (WHO) noted the growing burden of chronic diseases caused in part by unhealthy diets and excessive energy intake. In 2005, 22 million children worldwide were overweight. The WHO predicts that by 2015 some 2.3 billion adults will be overweight and more than 700 million obese.

The WHO has also declared foodborne disease an urgent threat to health. According to the 2007 *World Health Report*, 'although the safety of food has dramatically improved overall, progress is uneven and foodborne outbreaks from microbial contamination, chemicals and toxins are common in many countries.' The extent to which foodborne diseases affect health in developing countries is not fully known, but it is clear that contaminated food affects millions of adults and children every year.

While these global public health problems take on different forms, they are all linked to the production and consumption of food. And while what we eat is ultimately affected by what we do or do not place in our own mouths, there are far larger forces at work. One of these is 'globalisation', a process promoted as a solution to world food problems.

IMAGE C3 1
How will rising food prices affect nutrition of consumers and producers?

The promise of globalisation

Back in the 1970s, state-led intervention in the food and agriculture sector was, according to the theories of neoclassical economics, falling short. In Europe and North America, subsidies were leading to surpluses, so damaging the international market for agricultural products from developing countries. In developing countries, government procurement of agricultural outputs by state marketing boards (to stabilise prices) and the use of trade barriers (to protect domestic food production) were creating 'inefficiencies' by reducing incentives for productivity growth and raising prices. At the same time, because agriculture was seen primarily as fuel for industrial growth rather than as a source of economic growth and development itself, 'discriminatory' policies such as low food prices and land taxes were applied to agricultural producers (Hawkes 2006a). Moreover, millions of people were experiencing food insecurity and undernutrition.

The solution, it was purported, was to reduce or remove state involve-ment, encourage privatisation and liberalise the agricultural sector. This would shift the sector away from national or regional systems of food self-sufficiency towards a global model. Privatisation, more open trade and export-led growth would lower the costs of production and consumer food prices, prevent fluctuations in food supply and increase farmers' incomes. The net result supposedly would be a food system more responsive to market demands, and more capable of producing food and ultimately leading to greater food security (Babinard and Pinstrup-Andersen 2001). It would also produce a greater and better variety of foods, thus improving diets. Meanwhile, international agreements on food standards would help countries upgrade their national food safety systems and result in better health protection and improved confidence in exported food products on world markets.

That was the promise of globalisation. And the idea prevailed.

In low- or middle-income countries (LMICs), it started with the struc-tural adjustment programmes of the World Bank and the International Monetary Fund (IMF). Countries experiencing balance-of-payments prob-lems were loaned money on condition that they introduce reforms, notably the liberalisation of trade, investment and the financial sector, and the deregulation and privatisation of nationalised industries. Throughout the 1970s and 1980s, many countries opened up their markets by dismantling state food marketing monopolies, reducing subsidies on agricultural inputs (e.g. on fertilisers) and lowering barriers to trade and investment. The globalisation of food and agriculture had begun.

The pace of change speeded up when free-trade agreements became the focus of policy development in agriculture. In 1994, food and agriculture were for the first time included in a multilateral trade agreement, the Agreement on Agriculture. The Agreement pledged countries to open their markets by reducing tariffs, non-tariff barriers, export subsidies and domestic agricultural support.

The 1995 Agreement on the Application of Sanitary and Phytosanitary Measures (SPS) further reduced trade barriers by encouraging countries to adopt the same or equivalent food safety standards. The Technical Barriers to Trade Agreement obliged countries to ensure that national regulations, voluntary standards and conformity assessment procedures – including those affecting food – would not create unnecessary obstacles to trade.

As markets opened up and the role of governments shrank, private property rights were strengthened. The Agreement on Trade-Related Aspects of Intellectual Property Rights (TRIPS) expanded the scope of private property rights on food products, including patents on seeds, and copyright on certain food identities with a geographical basis (for example, champagne) was similarly strengthened.

The dual-track process of liberalisation and strengthened private property rights that handed increasing power to the corporate food industry was also pursued through regional and bilateral agreements. Regional trade agreements were signed at a rate of fifteen per year in the 1990s (FAO 2004). The result of these reforms on the volume of trade was dramatic.[1]

World agricultural trade increased from US$243 billion in 1980–81 to US$467 billion in 2000–01, representing an annual rate of increase of 4.9 per cent in the 1980s, and 3.4 per cent in the 1990s (Ataman Aksoy 2005). For an average developing country, food import bills as a share of gross domestic product (GDP) more than doubled between 1974 and 2004 (FAO 2004). The share of agricultural production that was exported was also increased, from 19 per cent in 1971 to 40 per cent in 2003 (FAOSTAT 2005).

Importantly, the pattern of food trade also changed:

- Food imports into developing countries increased far faster than into developed countries. While gross food imports into developed countries grew by 45 per cent between 1970 and 2001, they grew by 115 per cent into developing countries (FAO 2004).
- There was a large increase in the exports of certain high-value foods from developing to developed countries. Non-traditional agricultural exports, such as fruits, vegetables and flowers, have grown. The amount of fruit and vegetable imported by developed countries increased from 41.1 to 119.2 million tonnes between 1980 and 2003 (FAOSTAT 2005). For fish, developing countries now account for about 50 per cent of world export values, up from 37 per cent in 1976 (Allain 2007).
- There has been a significant variation in the rate of trade between different foodstuffs. The amount of trade in cereals declined relative to higher-value products such as seafood, fruits and vegetables. Whereas cereals once dominated international food trade, they now comprise less than 50 per cent of total agricultural imports by developing countries (FAO 2004). The amount of trade in processed foodstuffs also increased far more rapidly than raw agricultural commodities, largely as a result of increased exports from developed countries (Rae and Josling 2003).

Liberalisation and the growth of TNCs

An important process of trade liberalisation has been the growth of foreign direct investment (FDI) – a long-term investment made by individual, government or enterprise in one country into an enterprise in another.

BOX C3.I   **How trade liberalisation has encouraged the growth of transnational food corporations**

- FDI into the food industry was the key process by which TNCs formed and grew by enabling companies to buy, sell and invest in other companies in other countries.
- The commercialisation and privatisation of state food monopolies (pushed heavily by the World Bank) also opened up opportunities for investment by the private sector.
- FDI into the service sector, the streamlining of dispute settlement mechanisms, as well as stronger and broader intellectual property rights, created a better business climate and increased access to capital and technology, which further encouraged investment by TNCs.
- More liberalised cross-border trade and FDI facilitated 'global vertical integration'. This describes the process of TNCs buying and contracting companies and services involved in all aspects of the production, processing, distribution and sale of a particular food, thereby bringing the entire food supply chain under its control.
- Greater liberalisation of cross-border trade also facilitated 'global sourcing', which is when a company searches for inputs, production sites and outputs where costs are lower and regulatory, political and social regimes favourable. Both vertical integration and global sourcing enable TNCs to cut costs and create safeguards against the uncertainty of commodity production and product sales – thus stimulating further growth of TNCs.

There were a total of 232 international agreements containing investment provisions as of 2005, and the number of bilateral investment treaties rose from 181 to 2,495 between 1980 and 2005 (UNCTAD 2000, 2006). FDI is particularly important to food because it enables companies (usually in North America, Europe and Japan) to buy foreign affiliates in other countries, thus leading to the formation of transnational corporations (TNCs). FDI in the food processing and retailing industries has been key to the growth of transnational food corporations, alongside a range of other trade-related policies and incentives (Box C3.1).

The growth of transnational food corporations has been one of the most transformative processes of food globalisation. These corporations have affected the whole food supply chain: the seeds that are planted in the fields, the fertilisers and pesticides applied to the foods, the production, processing and manufacturing of these foods, and the way they are sold and marketed to consumers. TNCs are now leading traders of food.

The FDI that enabled TNCs to grow and function occurred in three waves, all of which continue today. The first major phase of FDI in the food supply chain occurred in the 1960s–70s when agribusinesses invested abroad in trading and processing raw commodities (e.g. cereals, oilseeds) for export. Most of these mainly US-based agribusinesses, such as Cargill, Con Agra and Archer Daniels Midland (ADM), then continued to expand into different processing activities, foods and geographical regions.

Take the case of Cargill, now present in sixty-six countries. One of its earliest expansions was into Argentina, where it invested in grain trading and animal feed in the 1960s. The company is now the largest Argentine agrifood exporter and the second largest Argentine exporter overall, dealing not just with grains but with oilseeds, poultry, peanuts, olive oil and beef (Cargill 2007). Cargill entered China in the early 1970s and currently sells grains, oilseeds, sugar, fruit juices, meats and other commodities and operates twenty-five companies and joint ventures. The company continues to expand, now affecting much of the food eaten by much of the world. As they once famously commented: 'We are the flour in your bread, the wheat in your noodles, the salt on your fries. We are the corn in your tortillas, the chocolate in your dessert, the sweetener in your soft drink. We are the oil in your salad dressing and the beef, pork or chicken you eat for dinner.'

The second wave of FDI, in the 1980s, was into the manufacturing of highly processed foods – for example, snacks, baked goods, dairy products, soft drinks (Hawkes 2005). Largely through the purchase of foreign affiliates, FDI from US-based food manufacturers alone grew from US$9 billion in 1980 to US$39.2 billion in 2000 (Bolling and Somwaru 2001). The result was successful: sales from foreign affiliates increased from US$39.2 billion to US$150 billion in the same period, and TNCs from both the US and Europe became market leaders in their core brands – such as Lay's potato chips and Nestlé ice cream.

Beginning in the 1990s, FDI penetrated supermarkets. FDI from US-based supermarket chains grew to nearly US$13 billion in 1999, up from around US$4 billion in 1990 (Harris et al. 2002). Leading retailers are now larger than leading food manufacturers in terms of sales (Table C3.1). In Latin America, it is estimated that supermarkets increased their share of the retail market from 10–20 per cent to 50–60 per cent between 1990 and 2000. In China, the supermarket sector is growing at a rate of 30–40 per cent sales growth per year (Hu et al. 2004) The food retail market is becoming more concentrated everywhere through the process of mergers and acquisitions. In 2004, Wal-Mart was estimated to have 6.1 per cent of the global grocery market, with the French company Carrefour at 2.3 per cent. As a result, more people are buying more food in supermarkets relative to smaller

TABLE C3.1   **World's largest packaged food manufacturers and food retailers, by sales** (US$ billion)

	Food manufacturers	Packaged food sales, 2005
1.	Nestlé (Switzerland)	50.3
2.	Kraft (US)	39.2
3.	Unilever (UK/Netherlands)	37.0
4.	PepsiCo (US)	26.8
5.	Danone (France)	21.1
	Food retailers	Total sales, 2006
1.	Wal-Mart Stores (US)	312.4
2.	Carrefour (France)	92.6
3.	Tesco (UK)	69.6
4.	Metro Group (Germany)	69.3
5.	Kroger (US)	60.6

Sources: Hendrickson and Heffernan 2007; Euromonitor 2007.

stores, and supermarkets have emerged as dominant players in the food system (Murphy 2006; Vorley 2003). The increase in the value of food sales through supermarkets, especially in developing countries, is also enabling transnational supermarket chains to maintain and grow their profit margins, so further increasing their power in the global food supply chain.

Importantly, the degree of 'transnationalisation' of the world's largest food manufacturers and retailers has grown significantly since the early 1990s. Between 1990 and 2001, the foreign sales of food-related TNCs within the world's largest 100 TNCs rose from US$88.8 billion to US$234.1, with total foreign assets rising from US$34.0 billion to US$ 257.7 billion. The foreign assets of Nestlé increased from US$28.7 billion in 1992 to US$65.4 billion in 2003 (UNCTAD 2006; Hawkes 2005). The degree of transnationalisation of food-related TNCs is also high relative to other TNCs (UNCTAD 2006, 1995).

Food, globalisation and health

What of the promise of globalisation to improve food-related health? Has it increased food availability, lowered food prices for consumers and boosted the incomes of the rural poor? Has it led to better food safety? Is there now more and better food available at lower prices?

The effect of trade liberalisation on food availability, prices and agricultural incomes has been uneven and context-specific. Trade liberalisation has both increased and decreased food availability, depending on the balance between production, imports and exports. In the most comprehensive assessment of the national impact of trade reform on food security to date, the FAO found enormous differences in the effects on food availability between countries. While in China, per capita supplies of the principal nutrients grew significantly in the post-reform period, rates of change were very modest in Malawi, and in Tanzania they declined (FAO 2006).

The effect on food prices has been equally complex and dependent on the nature of trade reform, the domestic context, and the roles of the private and public sectors. Furthermore, the effect has varied between prices paid to agricultural producers for their products (farm-gate prices) and those paid by consumers (food retail prices). Thus, when lower food prices may have benefited poor consumers (because food was cheaper), they would have had the opposite effect on agricultural households (because they received a lower price for their products). For agricultural households, then, 'trade reform can be damaging to food security in the short to medium term if it is introduced without a policy package designed to offset the negative effects of liberalization' (FAO 2006).

And have food consumers benefited from lower retail prices? Again, the outcome has proved context-specific and by no means certain because lower farm-gate prices may have simply benefited the processors, manufacturers and retailers who purchase the raw commodities, rather than being passed on to consumers. There are surprisingly few data on this issue. What is clear is that despite trade reforms, food prices are now increasing as a result of rising demand from India and China, climate change and diversion of food for biofuels.

Has any of this affected undernutrition? Food availability is one factor in explaining the prevalence of undernutrition. It is estimated that increased food supplies have resulted in significant reductions in malnutrition since the 1970s despite population increases over the period (Smith and Haddad 2001). And retail food prices are critical to consumers who spend a high proportion of their income on food. An important question for the coming years will be how rising food prices will affect nutrition among both food consumers and producers. Concerns are being raised that rising food prices will place the poor at greater risk of malnutrition. But there are also positive implications if poor agricultural households receive higher prices for their products. The balance of effects on producers and consumers remains to be seen.

Moreover, it is important to note that in developing countries the majority of moderate and severe cases of underweight among children below 2 years are primarily caused by inappropriate weaning practices and a high vulnerability to infectious diseases. These primary causes are in turn affected by maternal education, access to health care, sanitation and water. Thus, how trade liberalisation affects these underlying determinants is as important as its effects on the food supply, if not more.

One of the infectious diseases most associated with malnutrition among infants is diarrhoea. And this can often stem from unsafe food. How has the promise of globalisation fared here?

Globalisation is often regarded as a danger to food safety since traded food can introduce new hazards and spread contaminated food more widely. But this is largely a developed-country concern owing to increasing imports of perishable foods from developing countries. There have been some highly publicised cases such as the *Cyclospora*-related illness from Guatemalan raspberries in the US in 1996 (Unnevehr 2003). Although serious when they do occur, such cases remain fairly infrequent and tend to deflect attention away from the far more serious problem of foodborne disease in developing countries.

Most developing countries have weak food regulation systems. The need to adhere to the SPS Agreement presented an opportunity for countries to upgrade their national food safety programmes with some assistance from international and bilateral agencies. In theory, this would improve consumer protection. But the theory has yet to be translated into a reduced burden of foodborne disease for the world's most vulnerable. Rather than focusing on food consumed by the poorest sectors of society, the process of improving standards has focused on where the profit lies for TNCs: foods for export to developed countries as well as foods sold in supermarkets in developing countries. The process is driven by regulations set by developed countries and transnational supermarkets. In developed countries, the range of food safety regulations is wider than ever despite the SPS Agreement (Josling et al. 2004). And globally, more stringent standards have been set by transnational supermarket chains.

Take the case of Kenyan fish exports to Europe. Although there are domestic standards in Kenya, the European Union imposes stricter hygiene and phytosanitary standards on imported fish. As a result of the costs incurred, the final product has become more expensive for the domestic market and little effort has gone into setting and enforcing domestic safety standards. Thus, 'the costs of producing high-quality fish for export largely fall to local communities, while they also bear the cost of consuming unwholesome fish' (Abila 2003).

TABLE C3.2 **Domestic availability and import quantity of vegetable oils, 1980 and 2003**

		1980	2003	% change
Domestic availability	developed countries	20.6	37.9	84.0
(million tonnes)	developing countries	20.8	65.1	213.0
Import quantity	developed countries	7.1	21.2	198.6
(million tonnes)	developing countries	6.0	28.6	376.7
Calories available	developed countries	310.9	421.7	35.6
(per capita/day)	developing countries	132.6	239.1	80.3
Imports (as % of	developed countries	34.5	55.9	62.3
domestic supply)	developing countries	28.8	43.9	52.3

Source: FAOSTAT 2005.

Much of the emphasis on standards has not even been on safety, but on 'quality'. Take the case of the transnational supermarkets operating in Latin America. The main standards imposed by these supermarkets relate to size and appearance, not safety. One study found that just two countries, Brazil and Costa Rica, imposed and enforced food safety standards for fresh produce, whereas supermarkets in all countries imposed quality standards on producers (Berdegue et al. 2003). The privatisation of food safety and quality standards has favoured the relatively small set of more commercialised suppliers to supermarkets. The smaller producers with less capital to meet the standards set by the supermarkets have found themselves relegated to waning and unprofitable markets, again, compromising their income.

Has, then, globalisation fulfilled its promise of bringing greater food variety and choice at lower prices? Processes of globalisation have indeed been able to deliver this in urban areas, as well as in rural areas with access to transportation networks and electricity. But with it has come a new health epidemic: obesity and diet-related chronic diseases because trade liberalisation has increased the availability and lowered the prices of high-calorie, nutrient-poor foods.

Take the case of vegetable oils. Over the past twenty-five years, leading vegetable oil producers – Argentina, Brazil, the United States, Indonesia and Malaysia – implemented policies to facilitate exports. With a more favourable investment environment, TNCs such as Bunge, Cargill and ADM increased their processing capacities through acquisitions and expansions. In Brazil, by the end of the 1990s, the five largest TNCs owned about 60 per cent of total crushing capacity (Schnepf et al. 2001). In China, the majority of soya beans are now processed in facilities subject to foreign investment.

At the same time, key importing countries like India and China have reduced import barriers (Hawkes 2006b). As a result, vegetable oil exports and imports have soared (Table C3.2). And as imports increased, vegetable oil prices fell, driven by lower costs of production in exporting countries (FAO 2004). The result has been a greater consumption of vegetable oils. Between 1989/91 and 2000/02, calories available from soya oil per person per day increased from 27 to 78 in China, and 11 to 48 in India (Hawkes 2006b). And overall, between 1982/84 and 2000/02, vegetable oils contributed more than any other food group to the increase of calorie availability worldwide. Vegetable oils can thus clearly be implicated in rising dietary fat intakes worldwide. The hydrogenation of vegetable oils for use in processed foods has also led to the increase in consumption of the heart-deadly trans-fats.

The market for highly processed foods has also been profoundly affected by trade agreements. Consider the case of Mexico (Hawkes 2006b). The North American Free Trade Agreement (NAFTA), signed by Mexico, the US and Canada in 1994, contained key provisions designed to facilitate foreign investment. A consequence of these more liberal investment rules was a rapid acceleration of FDI from the US. In 1993, US FDI into the Mexican food processing industry was US$210 million. Five years after NAFTA, the US invested US$5.3 billion in the Mexican food industry, nearly three-quarters of which was in the production of processed foods. FDI clearly stimulated the growth of the processed foods market in Mexico.

Between 1995 and 2003, sales of processed foods (e.g. soft drinks, snacks, baked goods and dairy products) expanded by 5–10 per cent per year. In 1999, processed foods contributed 46 per cent of the total energy intake of children aged between 1 and 4, including a disproportionately large amount of saturated fat (Oria and Sawyer 2007). At the same time, obesity and diabetes have risen to epidemic proportions: the prevalence of overweight/obesity increased from 33 per cent in 1988 to 62.5 per cent in 2004, and over 8 per cent of Mexicans now have diabetes, which the WHO estimates costs the country US$15 billion a year.

Mexico's example is typical: annual sales growth of processed foods has been far higher in developing countries than in developed countries (Table C3.3). Sales of processed products, now criticised in Western markets for their ill-health affects, are now soaring in developing countries. Between 1997 and 2002, average annual sales growth of carbonated soft drinks was 1.4 per cent in the United States, compared with 8.8 per cent in China,

TABLE C3.3   **Growth in retail sales of packaged foods, 1996–2002**

Country group	Per capita retail sales of packaged foods, 2002 ($)	Retail growth of packaged foods 1996–2002 (%)	Per capita growth of packaged foods (%)
High income	979	3.2	2.5
Upper middle income	298	8.1	6.7
Lower middle income	143	28.8	28.1
Low income	63	12.9	11.9

Source: Euromonitor 2007.

7.9 per cent in India, 7.8 per cent in Indonesia and 6.2 per cent in South Africa (Gehlhar and Regmi 2005).

Food: a public health priority

It is easy to argue about the technical outcomes of globalisation policies and processes on food-related health. Food availability goes up and down. Prices change this way and that way. Food becomes more or less safe. Incomes rise for some and fall for others. Regulations and standards have uneven effects. Though it is possible to see positive and negative in all these machinations, something is fairly clear: globalisation has not lived up to its promise. Thus far, it has failed to create a food market that provides healthy and safe food for all. Too many people are still suffering from undernutrition; foodborne disease is only becoming a more serious problem; the burden of obesity and diet-related chronic diseases is ever greater.

There are two possible ways forward. One is to make globalisation work better. This is the approach taken by the multilateral institutions, which recommend programmes to help farmers access international export markets and supermarkets, capacity-building for food safety regulation, and safety nets for the poor (though they tend to be silent on the issue of obesity). A second is to fight food globalisation. Groups of farmers and landless peoples the world over are, for example, pursuing the concept of 'food sovereignty' – that is, the 'right of peoples to define their own food, agriculture, livestock and fisheries systems' – in contrast to having food largely subject to international market forces. Whatever way, given how integral food is to our health, the health community needs to act. Healthy food production and consumption should be a global public health priority.

Note

1. As agricultural trade has increased, so has the volume of agricultural production, notably of the higher value products, which have also experienced the fastest rates of increase of trade. Indeed, between 1982 and 2002, the highest annual percentage rate of increase was for vegetables (4.2%) and oilcrops (3.8%), followed by meat (2.8%), fruit (2.4%), and fish (2.4%), with the lowest rate for cereals (1.1%).

References

Abila, R.O. (2003). Case study: Kenyan fish exports. In L. Unnevehr (ed.), *Food safety in food security and food trade.* 2020 Vision Focus 10. Washington DC: IFPRI.

Allain, M. (2007). *Trading away our oceans: Why trade liberalization of fisheries must be abandoned.* Amsterdam: Greenpeace International.

Ataman Aksoy, M. (2005). The evolution of agricultural trade flows. In M. Ataman Aksoy and J.C. Beghin (eds), *Global agricultural trade and developing countries.* Washington DC: World Bank.

Babinard, J., and P. Pinstrup-Andersen (2001). Nutrition. In E. Diaz-Bonilla and S. Robinson (eds), *Shaping globalisation for poverty alleviation and food security.* Washington DC: International Food Policy Research Institute.

Berdegue, J.A., et al. (2003). Supermarkets and quality and safety standards for produce in Latin America. In L. Unnevehr (ed.), *Food safety in food security and food trade.* 2020 Vision Focus 10. Washington DC: IFPRI.

Bolling, C., and A. Somwaru (2001). US food companies access foreign markets though direct investment. *Food Review* 24: 23–8.

Cargill (2007). *Argentina.* www.cargill.com/worldwide/argentina.htm.

Euromonitor (2007). www.euromonitor.com.

FAO (Food and Agricultural Organization of the United Nations) (2004). *The state of agricultural commodity markets 2004.* Rome.

FAO (2006). *The state of food insecurity in the world 2006.* Rome.

FAOSTAT (2005). FAOSTAT. http://faostat fao org/default aspx.

Gehlhar, M., and A. Regmi (2005). Factors shaping global food markets. In A. Regmi and M. Gehlhar (eds), *New directions in global food markets.* Agriculure Information Bulletin 294. Washington DC: United States Department of Agriculture.

Harris, J.M., et al. (2002). *The US food marketing system, 2002.* Washington DC: USDA.

Hawkes, C. (2005). The role of foreign direct investment in the nutrition transition. *Public Health Nutrition* 8(4): 357–65.

Hawkes, C. (2006a). Agricultural and food policy for cardiovascular health in Latin America. *Prevention and Control* 2: 137–47.

Hawkes, C. (2006b). Uneven dietary development: Linking the policies and processes of globalisation with the nutrition transition, obesity and diet-related chronic diseases. *Globalisation and Health* 2(1), March: 4.

Hendrickson, M., and W. Heffernan (2007). *Concentration of agricultural markets.* April. National Farmers Union. www.nfu.org/wp-content/2007-heffernanreport.pdf.

Hu, D., et al. (2004). The emergence of supermarkets with Chinese characteristics: Challenges and opportunities for China's agricultural development. *Development Policy Review* 22(5): 557–86.

Josling, T., D. Roberts and D. Orden (2004). *Food regulation and trade.* Washington DC: Institute for International Economics.

Murphy, S. (2006). *Concentrated market power and agricultural trade.* ECOFAIR Trade Dialogue. Discussion Paper No. 1, August. Berlin: Heinrich Böll Stiftung; Aachen:

Misereor; Wuppertal: Wuppertal Institute for Climate, Environment and Energy. www.ecofair-trade.org/pics/en/EcoFair_Trade_Paper_No1_Murphy_new.pdf.

Oria, M., and K. Sawyer (2007). *Joint U.S.–Mexico workshop on preventing obesity in children and youth of Mexican origin: Summary report.* Washington DC: National Academies Press.

Rae, A., and T. Josling (2003). Processed food trade and developing countries: Protection and trade liberalization. *Food Policy* 28: 147–66.

Schnepf, R.D., E. Dohlman and C. Bolling (2001). *Agriculture in Brazil and Argentina: Developments and prospects for major field crops.* Washington DC: USDA.

Smith, L., and L. Haddad (2001). How important is improving food availability for reducing child malnutrition in developing countries? *Agricultural Economics* 26: 191–204.

UNCTAD (United Nations Conference on Trade and Development) (1995). *World Investment Report 1995.* Geneva.

UNCTAD (2000). *World Investment Report 2000.* Geneva.

UNCTAD (2006). *World Investment Report 2006.* Geneva.

Unnevehr, L.J. (2003). *Food safety in food security and food trade.* 2020 Vision Focus 10. Washington DC: IFPRI.

Vorley, B. (2003). *Food, inc. Corporate concentration from farm to consumer.* London: IIED.

WHO (2006). Obesity and overweight. WHO Fact Sheet no. 311. Geneva.

WHO (2007). *The world health report 2007: Global public health security in the 21st century. A safer future.* Geneva.

C4   Urbanisation

More than half of the world's population now live in urban areas. At the end of the nineteenth century less than 3 per cent of the world's population lived in towns and cities (Weber 2007), and in 1950 Africa and Asia were still almost wholly rural. The pace of urbanisation in the past twenty years has been especially high in the poor regions of the world where the growth of informal settlements has brought with it attendant problems of environmental health (UN Habitat 2006). These informal settlements, generally called 'slums'[1] in UN literature, are characterised by poverty and precarious living and working conditions (Kjellstrom et al. 2007). In a context of intensely competitive demand for land in cities, the residents of these settlements often have little or no claim on city or national governments.

Three associated trends are worth noting. First, the cities of developing countries will absorb 95 per cent of all urban growth over the next two decades, and by 2030 will be home to almost 4 billion people, or 80 per cent of the world's urban population. Second is the increased urban–urban migration and the reclassification of many rural areas to urban,[2] both of which contribute to the urbanisation in Africa, Asia and Latin America. Third is the seemingly contradictory trend of, on the one hand, the increasing number of 'metacities' and 'megacities', with conurbations of over 20 and 10 million people respectively, and, on the other hand, the population growth of medium-sized cities, of fewer than 500,000 inhabitants.[3] Already more than half of the world's urban population live in cities of fewer than 500,000 inhabitants and almost one-fifth live in cities of between 1 and 5 million inhabitants (UN Habitat 2006).

The above trends are significant in understanding the phenomenon of urbanisation, even though countries employ different definitions of 'urban'

IMAGE C4.1 **Rio**

which may also change over time (Satterthwaite 2006; Vlahov et al. 2007). Many question the very concept of a rural–urban divide, noting that 'village communities' exist within cities and that urban societies exist in rural areas (Pacione 2005; Pahl 1965).

This chapter examines the associated health and environmental problems caused by the rapid growth of cities and the challenges of rapid urbanisation, including urban poverty and the attendant growing inequities now seen within as well as between many cities of the world.

Understanding the nature and context of urbanisation

The current nature of urbanisation can only be understood within the macro-political and social contexts of individual countries and overall global trends. For example, what are *the process and causes* of urbanisation, particularly with reference to the political economy and the impact of capitalism on rural areas?

First, the most important driving factor of global urbanisation is natural population growth in existing urban settings. However, rural-to-urban migration is an important factor in some contexts. As described in Chapter

C3, agricultural sector policies in Asia and Africa which have reinforced colonial patterns of agricultural production and stimulated the growth of export-oriented crops at the expense of food crops have dramatically increased rural poverty. This process also takes place in Latin America, in particular in Brazil. Moreover, in Asian countries the Green Revolution plays a role. Deforestation, mining and hydroelectric projects have also contributed to landlessness and the forced displacement of millions of people, leading to even deeper levels of rural poverty. Consequently, people have been pushed from rural areas and pulled into cities, in search of better sources of livelihood.

The poverty of recent migrants is aggravated by the losses of subsistence farming opportunities and the supportive kinship ties that exist in rural areas. Migrants are particularly affected by social and economic exclusion and often have no access to health care, education or decision-making.

Changes brought about by economic globalisation include the weakened ability of governments and nation-states either to influence or to control the external forces that impact on local economic and health develop-ment. Many cities are drawn into the dominant chain of global economic activity and have become focal points for foreign direct investment, while productive capacity is often restricted to a limited number of cities. 'Global' cities such as Bangalore and Johannesburg combine rapid economic growth – which benefits an affluent minority – with rapid urbanisation of poverty, environmental degradation and a weakened social fabric.

An accompanying change is the accelerated *informalisation* of the urban economy, coupled with *de-industrialisation* (UN Habitat 2004), leading to increasing underemployment (ILO 2005).[4]

These social and economic changes affect workers, but also impact on the governance of cities, as public authorities are unable to obtain the revenues required to provide public services. Also worth noting is the weakening of national and local public institutions, relative to the arrival of powerful multinational, external private-sector companies, following the advent of neoliberal policies in the 1980s and 1990s.

Other new challenges posed to the global community are the effects of migration and industrialisation, notably due to climate change and several aspects of environmental degradation. Security analysts fear that the tidal wave of forced migration will not only fuel existing conflicts, but create new ones in some of the poorest and most deprived parts of the world. Furthermore, as noted in Chapter B3, most of these refugees will become internally displaced peoples who will end up in the informal settlements and 'slums' of cities and remain largely invisible to the people of the rich world.

The health implications of urbanisation

In a context of limited financial resources and weak institutional capacity, urban services and infrastructure development have not kept pace with urban population growth in many cities of developing countries. Public institutions have failed to anticipate, adapt and manage urbanisation and its impact on population health, and an increasing proportion of people are expected to be without adequate housing, water supply, drainage and sanitation facilities (see Chapter C5). Furthermore, information systems in many least developed countries often do not capture the living conditions, environment and health status of populations living in unplanned and informal urban settlements and these remain outside official government records.

Disaggregated data reveal urban informal settlements as areas of concentrated disadvantage. When data are not disaggregated and one standard is applied across urban and rural divides, the peculiar situation and needs of the urban poor are hidden. But where disaggregated data exist, they reveal startlingly high intra-urban inequalities related to socio-economic status and living conditions. One study of twenty-three countries highlighted that inequalities are generally greater within urban areas when compared with rural areas, except in countries where rural economies are structured around plantation agriculture (Mitlin 2003).

Urban dwellers who live in these settlements contend with three groups of factors which combine to keep them perpetually at health risk. First are the direct effects of poverty: low income, limited education and unequal access to food. Second are man-made conditions of the living environment: poor housing, overcrowding, pollution and increased exposure to infectious diseases. In informal settlements, the ratio of population to water and sanitation facilities, if available, is quite high. Even the minimum standard of one standing tap to 200 persons proves highly inadequate. Third are social and psychological problems due to the lack of social support systems, urban violence and the impact of social exclusion.

The urbanisation and feminisation of poverty have a direct bearing on the progress and well-being of women and girls. An additional concern is meeting the challenges of physical and psychological development faced by adolescent boys and girls in informal settlements (see Box C4.1). These manifest in unwanted pregnancies, sexually transmitted diseases, illegal and unsafe abortion, sexual exploitation, early marriages, malnutrition, drugs, substance abuse, violence and trauma. Youth violence is one of the most severe public health problems in many cities of the world and it could be an even more important burden of health in the future. In Cali, Colombia,

---

BOX C4.1   **Health risk of street children**

Tanzania is one of the countries with the highest number of urban street children. According to recent estimates there are 3,000 street children in Dar es Salaam. Most come from rural areas and have either left or been abandoned by their families. Living on or off the street is a survival strategy for children orphaned by AIDS when their family or community cannot support them. A study into the effects of street life on children's health showed that the unhealthy urban environment has a major impact (Lugalla and Mbwambo 1999). While boys can find some casual work in the informal sector, girls often end up as commercial sex workers and face a much greater risk of becoming HIV-infected. In Mwanza, 80 per cent of the street girls had suffered an STI at least once, compared with 30 per cent of the boys (Rajani and Kudrati 1996; Williams 2007).

---

homicide rates of up to 200 per 100,000 inhabitants have been recorded in the most deprived neighbourhoods (Rodriguez 2006).

Climate change is expected to affect, in particular, cities in developing countries; within those settings, the urban poor are most at risk (Campbell-Landrum and Corvalan 2007).

A critical review of the Healthy Cities initiative

Addressing the health needs and increasing health inequities of urban populations in the context of economic globalisation, persistent and high unemployment, economic stagnation, climate change and weak national and local public institutions demands a radical reorientation of public health systems, policies and processes. Fundamentally, there is a need to break out of the common single-sector approach and the patterns of narrow focus of single-issue programmes[5] that are designed in isolation of the local context and without proactive efforts to engage with and to develop capacity of community-based organisations, particularly those living in poor and in-formal settlements, in empowering initiatives. There is a need for a systemic approach to build effective public policies that improve living conditions and the environment and reduce health inequities.

The Healthy Cities and Municipalities Movement (HCMM) was initiated by the World Health Organization (WHO) in Europe in 1987, and subsequently taken up in other regions, and in others developed differently without its explicit identification as a 'healthy setting or healthy city'.

The HCMM was an important development because of its focus on the role of political leaders, intersectoral collaboration and participatory governance in policymaking and programme development, rather than a response that decontextualises health and medicalises its response. Indeed, it has been used in many countries as a platform for legitimising and supporting community-based civil society initiatives, often in collaboration with local governments and health systems (Perez Montiel and Barten 1999). Also explicit was recognition of the need to challenge power relations between public-sector providers and the people they serve. The HCMM was not conceived of only to improve health; it also aimed to tackle the power imbalance between the public and government; between people and bureaucrats; and between the poor and professionals. The HCMM also placed emphasis on equity and social justice.

The collective experiences of HCMM have provided valuable lessons, both positive and negative. Among the strengths have been the value of an area-based approach to population health rather than the traditional vertical, issue and disease-based approach; the recognition that shared ownership across official institutions and community-based organisations has to be actively developed, with capacity-building required by both communities and the professionals engaged in the initiatives; and that successful initiatives were sustained by a strong social vision by community members (Baum et al. 2006; Mendez and Akerman 2002). Also important was the recognition that health cuts across different policy sectors, which led to the development of mutually beneficial links with other global initiatives focusing on the improvement of the environment and quality of life in cities. These include Local Agenda 21, Habitat and the Initiative Local Facility for Urban Environment (LIFE). Among the many benefits of the collaborations has been the heightened profile in health within these initiatives, along with the strengthened urban planning and environmental profile of the HCMM.

The constraints and inherent contradictions, however, have meant that despite the progressive rhetoric and frameworks, the HCMM as a whole has been unable to achieve its intended radical agenda. Instead of power-sharing, the traditional power imbalance between the sectors have been maintained (Mendez and Akerman 2002; Ziglio et al. 2000), with the authorities dominating the priorities, the processes and the extent of engagement (Stern and Green 2005). This has been manifest in several ways. Technical solutions have replaced the ideal of addressing fundamental contextual and power-related issues, and flexible and innovative local partnerships have been stifled by hierarchical and vertically structured bureaucracies (Harpham and Boateng 1997; Pickin et al. 2002).

Control over civil society organisations (CSOs) by national governments and/or donors has also predominated in some countries, with priorities and funding favouring selective, vertical programmes that focus on single issues rather than 'bottom up' participatory and intersectoral initiatives and comprehensive approaches at all levels. In addition, in many instances CSOs have become delivery agents for donor-funded programmes, causing the energy for social and political mobilisation to be dissipated, directed towards competing for funds or controlled by the donors.

Perhaps the starkest contradictions are the attempts to develop HCMM initiatives within a context of neoliberal reforms, such as privatisation and outsourcing in many cities. On the one hand, HCMM was promoting social development and community participation, while on the other policies were promoting the market and converting 'community members' into 'individual consumers'. Also contradictory is the local HCMM focus on equity, at a time when globalisation is making it increasingly difficult for local actors to address many of the fundamental driving forces of poverty and inequality. Many of the HCMMs have been developed in a context of structural adjustment programmes (SAPS) and, in many cases, political upheaval and the near collapse of public health systems.

The HCMM has nevertheless been an important landmark. The framework provided by the HCMM, along with its principles now echoed in the Commission on Social Determinants of Health, provide an opportunity and a challenge for progressive civil society to build on the rhetoric to strengthen their role, relevance and impact.

Governance and health issues in cities: water and sanitation

The tensions and contradictions inherent in the HCMM become clearer as we examine the provision of safe water and sanitation for the poorest and most vulnerable people living in cities of developing countries.[6]

Inadequate supply of drinking water and sanitation at the household level remains the most critical and widespread water-related problem in low-income urban settlements. Despite this, financial allocations to the water sector as a whole are shrinking. Unreliable coverage data and limited transparency in governance further inhibit effective planning for utilities by governments and communities.

The low priority and low level of resources accorded to sanitation are further exacerbated by poor coordination, unclear roles and responsibilities, and conflicting policy, legal and regulatory frameworks. For instance, sanitation is the responsibility of several government departments, which operate conflicting policies and regulatory regimes. Because targets are

---

BOX C4.2 **People-centred drinking water and sanitation services in Venezuela**

The desire to re-establish citizen involvement in the management of water services led the Venezuelan water sector to discuss and debate the communal management of Hidrocapital, the water company of the capital, Caracas. Following on from this, the authorities adopted the development of 'Water Technical Roundtables' and 'Water Communal Councils', designed to harness the knowledge and skills of the community to help solve the problems of the water sector. They facilitated 'community mapping' which harnessed the knowledge of community members about the location of the various installations of the water service network; the diagnosis of problems; and the formulation of repair and maintenance plans.

Water Communal Councils provide a platform for communities, Water Technical Roundtables, representatives of the Hidrocapital and elected local government officials to exchange information, discuss and debate. They are open to all citizens and meet at a regular time and in a well-known place. They help to prioritise needs on the basis of inputs from all sections of society; organise a work programme agenda to which both the water company and the community commit; and exert social control over the public company.

Within five years, there has been a transformation of the water and sanitation sector, not least of which is the public water companies meeting with citizens, and the increasing number of communities that are managing their own water resources.

Source: Rodríguez 2005.

---

often set at the aggregate level, issues of exclusion and inequity and of sustainability and long-term functionality are not addressed.

Revamping the operations of public utilities is critical to fulfilling the water and sanitation Millennium Development Goals (MDGs), especially for the urban impoverished population. Public utilities currently provide as much as 95 per cent of coverage for up to 35–45 per cent of urban residents served by a piped network supply. Even during the height of the privatisation era in the 1990s, private-sector investment in water and sanitation was only 5 per cent of all private investments in infrastructure.[7] According to the World Development Movement, only 1 per cent of promised private sector investment in water globally since 1990 was targeted at sub-Saharan Africa.

However, public utilities have not taken the measures to improve and extend provision in urban areas. Governments, international finance institutions and donors must now move away from debating the pros and cons of privatisation towards determining how public-sector utilities can turn around their performance, promote 'public–public partnerships' and help utilities in developing countries improve services through peer support and collaboration (see Box C4.2).

The recognition of non-state providers (NSPs) or small-scale service providers (SSSPs), including community-managed systems, as the dominant providers for the poor in slums and peri-urban settlements is also pertinent. NSPs serve between 30 and 60 per cent of urban residents through a variety of formal and informal arrangements. However, the sector currently lacks the governance and regulation required to secure the necessary standards of water cleanliness at affordable prices.

Participatory governance

Participatory governance is an important tool of development, which is gaining an increasing acceptance in all sectors. In some policy contexts community involvement in water and sanitation and alliances between government and civil society organisations are contributing to achieving best practices and sustainability. Examples of best practices abound globally.

Partnership and resource mobilisation

Several donors have shown commitment to the concept of public–private 'partnerships'. In line with this concept, the UN outlined the concept of Water Operators Partnerships (WOP). UN-HABITAT's Water and Sanitation Trust Fund uses 'partnership' as the key strategy for leveraging more funds and expertise for the water and sanitation sector. With modest sums, the agency is partnering with development banks and other international finance institutions to leverage more funds in grants and these are being followed up with increased investment loans. Through such partnerships, a synergy is built to ensure sustainability.

The role of civil society in water governance

Many past efforts to sustain improved water and sanitation services in urban centres have failed as supportive capacity-building was not clearly thought out in the planning design stages of the systems, in local or regional institutions. The resultant lack of human resources and capacity to operate and maintain the existing systems is one of several reasons that has led to the poor performance in the water and sanitation services in urban areas, especially in the slums.

BOX C4.3 **Partnership for pro-equity water supply and sanitation, Madhya Pradesh**

'The Slums Environmental Sanitation Initiative (SESI) was set up as a pilot project in October 2005 and was to be executed in four project cities in a tri-partite partnership model.' The project brought together resources and expertise from the UN-HABITAT, WaterAid India and its local non-governmental organisation (NGO) partners and the four municipal corporations of Bhopal, Gwalior, Jabalpur and Indore for the benefit of 20,000 households, with each city identifying poverty pockets of 5,000 households which lack water and sanitation infrastructure. The project creates awareness among the people about the use of sanitation facilities in informal settlements.

Based on a situational analysis, the SESI projects are being implemented in these areas. The local partner NGOs play pivotal roles in mobilisation of the residents to form Community Water Supply and Sanitation Committees (CWASC), some of which are now registered as legal entities. The Community toilet has separate toilets for men and women, disabled and the elderly. There are also child-friendly toilets for boys and girls as well as bathing facilities for men and women.

Already, sixteen poverty pockets within the participating four cities have become the first open defecation-free 'slums' in India. Recently, the government of Madhya Pradesh State has drafted the State Sanitation Policy.

Source: Water for Asian Cities 2007.

Also there are many dynamic NGOs and community-based organisations at the local level that have developed and sustained innovative initiatives, but there are few linkages with city-level government, meaning that good practices are seldom replicated or properly evaluated with respect to their impact on local government systems. UN-Water for Cities programmes add value to the services delivery sector by developing the capacities of civil society organisations through technical cooperation and demonstration of community-oriented water supply and sanitation. These investments enhance the possibility for an acceptable degree of ownership, which to a good extent ensures a higher rate of return on investments by international finance institutions (IFIs) and assures sustainability and a credible level of output from facilities.

Recommended policy responses for reducing inequities[8]

- *Political commitment* is critical to addressing urban health inequities. This includes ensuring that all enjoy the right to the city and that health equity initiatives target and engage those most in need.
- *A systems approach* which acknowledges the relationship between urban and rural development and the influence of supra-local factors and need for action on local, national and global determinants is required.
- *Effective or healthy governance.* It is impossible to address the social determinants of health inequities in isolation from the broader remit of management of national development, or from the wider macro-policy level environment of decision-making.
- *Develop capacities of CSOs* for meaningful participation at all levels.
- *Develop a local knowledge base* that captures the reality of informal settlements.
- *Strengthen relevant existing initiatives* and processes.
- *Equip local government* with sufficient means and resources. Decentralisation has been recommended as a tool to strengthen local authorities for more effective service delivery, but the devolution of functional responsibilities has presented local governments with a major challenge, compounded by adverse economic and political conditions. Municipalities need to be strengthened to achieve a match between their newly acquired responsibilities to provide services and to fund capital improvements, and a higher degree of control over their revenue sources.

There is clearly an important role for public health advocates to play at the interface between essential services, urban planners, water and sanitation providers and education. There is also a need to develop the capacities of community-based, civil society organisations and local governments to ensure effective public policies that address social exclusion and reduce urban health inequities.

Conclusion

The complexity and magnitude of the problems of the urban social and physical environment posed by the current trends of urbanisation, migration, climate change, conflict and uneven development are immense. Although the MDGs have acknowledged the need to reduce urban poverty, the implications of the urban context for policy and for the achievement of all MDGs are not sufficiently understood. The renewed interest in Primary Health Care (PHC) and the WHO Commission on the Social Determinants of Health provide a new opportunity.

It is clear that improvements in health and health equity demand not only changes in the physical and social environment of cities, but also approaches that take into account wider socio-economic and contextual factors. The creation of more and better employment and social protection is a crucial challenge. Health systems have an important role to play, particularly at primary care level, where the interaction with communities is facilitated and the linkage between health and living conditions cannot be neglected. Disaggregated information on the (potential) health impact of policies and decisions taken by other sectors and governance levels is important. Comprehensive PHC can play an important role in developing the capacities of civil society and community-based organisations in order to ensure meaningful participation, to influence policymaking processes and to guarantee the right to the city for all.

While it is important to acknowledge how bottom-up participatory processes can contribute to sustainable health plans and healthy urban settings, there is also a need for local actors to address the supra-local and global factors that impact on cities and the distribution of power and resources. Duhl (1984), in his seminal paper on 'Healthy Cities', argued for the need to conceive of the city as *a whole*. Barten et al. (2006), in their recent analysis of the need to address social determinants of health to reduce urban health inequity, argue that it is necessary not only to conceive of the urban setting as a whole, but also to take a *national and global perspective* on the social, economic and political determinants of urban health inequity.

Notes

1. The identification of an area as a 'slum' contributes to stigma and discrimination against its residents. Also, the labelling of 'slums' excludes even more deprived areas.
2. Reclassification can be due to increased population or the redefinition of an urban area. Several countries face this dilemma following population growth or political pressures.
3. It is almost impossible to determine the cut-off for a city as different criteria are applied by countries. These classifications are therefore more for illustration than the rule.
4. This is a situation where qualified labour engages in less lucrative or less skilled jobs (such as petty trading) following a retrenchment or lack of job opportunities.
5. These focus mainly on effects instead of addressing the political, social, economic and environmental determinants.
6. For a detailed discussion on the social and health consequences of water and sanitation shortages, see Chapter C5. Also see *Global Health Watch 2005–2006* for a discussion on the privatisation of water and sanitation.
7. *International Herald Tribune*, www.iht.com/articles/2006/03/20/news/water.php.
8. Taking into account the impact of climate change.

152   **Beyond health care**

References

Barten, F., et al. (2006). *Integrated approaches to address the social determinants of health for reducing health inequity*. Background paper for the Knowledge Network on Urban Settings of the WHO CDSH. Kobe: WHO Kobe Centre.

Baum, F., et al. (2006). What makes for sustainable Healthy Cities initiatives? A review of the evidence from Noarlunga, Australia after 18 years. *Health Promotion International* 21: 259–65.

Campbell-Landrum, D., and C. Corvalan (2007). Climate change and developing country cities: Implications for environmental health and equity. *Journal of Urban Health* 84(3): 109–17.

Duhl, L. (1984). Healthy cities. Paper presented at Healthy Toronto 2000 (Proceedings). Department of Public Health, Toronto.

Harpham, T., and K.A. Boateng (1997). Urban governance in relation to the operation of urban services in developing countries. *Habitat International* 21: 65–74.

ILO (International Labour Organization) (2005). *Global employment trends*. Geneva.

Kjellstrom, T., et al. (2007). Urban environmental health hazards and health equity. *Journal of Urban Health* 84(3): 86–97.

Lugalla, J., and J. Mbwambo (1999). Street children and street life in urban Tanzania: The culture of surviving and its implications for children's health. *Int. J Urban & Regional Research* 23(2): 329.

Mendez, R., and M. Akerman (2002). Healthy cities in Brazil. In V.T. Naerssen and F. Barten (eds), *Healthy cities in developing countries: Lessons to be learned*. Saarbrücken: Verlag für Entwicklungspolitik.

Mitlin, D. (2003). Understanding urban poverty: What the Poverty Reduction Strategy Papers tell us. Working Paper 13. International Institute for Environment and Development. London.

Pacione, M. (2005). Concepts and theory in urban geography. In M. Pacione (ed.), *Urban geography: A global perspective*. New York: Routledge.

Pahl, R. (1965). *Urbs in rure*. London: Weidenfeld.

Perez Montiel, R., and F. Barten (1999). Urban governance and health development in Leon, Nicaragua. *Environment and Urbanization* 11(1): 11–26.

Pickin, C., et al. (2002). Developing a model to enhance the capacity of statutory organisations to engage with lay communities. *Journal of Health Services* 7: 34–42.

Rajani, R., and M. Kudrati (1996). The varieties of sexual experience of the street children of Mwanza, Tanzania. In S. Zeidenstein and K. Moore (eds), *Learning about sexuality: A practical beginning*, New York: Population International Women's Health Coalition.

Rodriguez, C. (2006). *Reduccion de la violencia juvenil en barrios de bajo-ingreso en Cali, Colombia*. Cali: FUNDAPS.

Rodríguez, S.A. (2005). The Venezuelan experience in the struggle for people-centred drinking water and sanitation services. In B. Balanyá et al. (eds), *Reclaiming public water: Achievements, struggles and visions from around the world*. Amsterdam: Transnational Institute and Corporate Europe Observatory.

Satterthwaite, D. (2006). *Outside the large cities: The demographic importance of small urban centres and large villages in Africa, Asia and Latin America*. Human Settlements Discussion Paper. London: International Institute for Environment and Development.

Stern, R., and J. Green (2005). Boundary workers and the management of frustration: A case study of two Healthy City partnerships. *Health Promotion International* 20: 269–76.

UN Habitat (2004). *State of the world's cities 2004/2005. Globalization and urban culture*. London: Earthscan.

UN Habitat (2006). *State of the World's Cities 2006/7*. London: Earthscan.

Vlahov, D., et al. (2007). Urban as a determinant of health. *Journal of Urban Health* 84(1): 16–26.

Water for Asian Cities (2007). *Regional newsletter* 3(6), November–December.

Weber, A. (2007). *The growth of cities in the nineteenth century.* New York: Macmillan.

Williams, S. (2007). Street children and their health. Rotation Health Care in Developing Countries, Sumve Designated District Hospital, Tanzania. Unpublished report. Nijmegen: UMCN Radboud University of Nijmegen.

Ziglio, E., S. Hagard and J. Griffiths (2000). Health promotion developments in Europe: achievements and challenges. *Health Promotion International* 15(2): 143–53.

C5 The sanitation and water crisis

One of the greatest public health crises in the developing world is largely being overlooked by donors and developing-country governments alike. In the developed world, the greatest advances in increasing life expectancy and reducing infant mortality rates came as a result of public investments in clean water and sanitation. But the potential these two sectors hold for advancing public health in developing countries today is being overlooked by donors who favour investments in curative approaches to health.

While the water and sanitation sectors remain largely sidelined by governments, it is the poor, on the rare occasions when they are asked, who repeatedly put water and sanitation as their highest priorities. So, the paradox is that while donors and recipient governments continue to marginalise the sector, the evidence in the form of international commitments to the Millennium Development Goals (MDGs) and the preferences of the poor points to the need for a much greater effort on the part of the official development community. This chapter shows the scale of the main challenges involved in the water and sanitation sectors and points to some of the strategies needed to turn around what is, arguably, the biggest driver of infant mortality in the developing world.

The scale of the problem

The key starting point to understanding the scale and nature of the sanitation and water crisis is grappling with the available data sources. The main global sector survey report is provided in the biannual Joint Monitoring Programme (JMP) survey (JMP 2006).

BOX C5.1   **The MDGs**[1]

At the United Nations' Millennium Summit at the turn of the century, heads of government signed up to the goal of halving the numbers of people living in poverty and a series of other Millennium Development Goals, including providing access to the core essential services – primary education, primary health care and access to safe water.

The seventh MDG is to ensure environmental sustainability. One of the specified targets linked to this goal is 'to reduce by half the proportion of people without sustainable access to safe drinking water and sanitation'.

Access to water

According to the JMP's 2006 figures, the world is 'on track' to meet the MDG target for water supply coverage. However, while this represents some progress, there are three major concerns.

First, the JMP warns that the improvement trend is deteriorating. Table C5.1 shows current and projected rates of progress. On current trajectories, the current rate of progress is expected to slow and the world will end up missing the 2015 MDG target. And, even if progress *is* accelerated sufficiently to reach the target, nearly 800 million people will still be 'unserved' and will daily face life-and-death choices in where and how they source their drinking and domestic water supply.

Second, the figures shown above obscure the presence of huge regional disparities. While the most populous countries are on track, most of sub-Saharan Africa (SSA) is lagging well behind. While coverage in SSA has improved from 49 per cent to 56 per cent, on the basis of the current trajectory, the report speculates, the continent will not achieve its MDG goal until as late as 2076.

TABLE C5.1   **Global water coverage and MDG 7**

	1990 (actual)	2004 (actual)	2015 (projected)	2015 (target)
Served (million)	4,092	5,320	6,300	6,425
Unserved (million)	1,187	1,069	919	794
Unserved (%)	22.5	16.7	12.7	11.0

Source: JMP 2006.

IMAGE C5.1
Young girl carrying water

Third, the JMP analysis is almost certainly an overestimate of access to (where this is taken to be synonymous with *usage* of) safe domestic water. The JMP definition of access is 'the availability of at least 20 litres per person per day from an 'improved' source within one kilometre of the user's dwelling'. An 'improved source' is 'one that is likely to provide 'safe' water, such as a household connection or a borehole', and 'be within a reasonably convenient distance from the home, to ensure that sufficient water can be used'.[2] So, at the extreme, a household accessing its water from a borehole 1 kilometre distant from the home is defined as 'having access to safe water'.

The tyrannies of physical distance, the lack of controlling standards and the sheer weight of water hauling suggest the need for some serious qualifications around claims of the numbers of people gaining access to safe water. Not all improved sources yield safe water (as defined in WHO standards) and, even if they do, water which is safe at the point of source may be contaminated in transit so it is not safe at the point of consumption. The labour and time involved in carrying large volumes of water large distances result, unsurprisingly, in smaller volumes of water *actually* being hauled than instances where the locations are closer to the source. Many people are simply unable to walk these sorts of distances and carry the weight of water for their own, and their dependants' needs. With reducing consumption per capita comes a decreasing ability to meet minimum requirements for health and hygiene.

Thus official descriptions of reported availability do not necessarily equate to access. Access is not the same as consumption. It is the pattern and content of *consumption* that is the critical determinant of health and hygiene.

The highest price

The world's poorest people:
5000 children die every day because of a lack of safe, clean water.

Tanzania's poor:
£4 per m³
(from street water vendors in the slums of Dar es Salaam).

Kenya's poor:
£3.60 per m³
(for the poorest families in Kiberia, Africa's largest slum, who buy their water from street vendors).

UK:
81p per m³
(based on Southern Water's prices for water meters).

USA:
34p per m³

FIGURE C5.1   **The price of water**

Source: WaterAid 200/.

So, the figures for people who do not *consume* safe water are higher than those for people who do not have *access*, as presented in the JMP.

However, irrespective of the selectivity of data and the accuracy of the nature of the water crisis they represent, the critical driver behind the crisis is the central problem of inequality in the distribution, entitlement and allocation of supply. Most human consumption of fresh water is taken up first by agriculture, then by industry. Other key issues regarding water sources come in the form of rapid urbanisation and the cost of extracting ground water. While there are new large uncertainties on the horizon – particularly the hydrological unpredictabilities associated with climate change – the central problem across rural and urban areas is that while there are sufficient volumes of water for domestic consumption, the issue is one of how that supply is managed and distributed (and therefore limited) for the domestic consumption of the poor. In addition, climate change is anticipated, in some geographical areas, to become a further limiting factor.

Equity in the distribution of access to water

The maxim is that the poorer you are, the more you pay. If you live in an urban slum, you will pay up to ten, or even twenty, times as much as the people who have yard connections in an adjacent residential area. And

even that will pale into insignificance when set against the amount paid
by people in the rich countries of the North. Slum dwellers of Lagos pay
some forty times the amount paid by someone in a downtown New York
apartment – and this does not even take into account income disparities.

Access to sanitation

Is sanitation an outcome or a driver of underdevelopment? While the
situation with regard to water is grim and acts as a continuing driver of
underdevelopment and avoidable disease, the situation when it comes to
sanitation is nothing less than scandalous.

Starting from an even lower rate of coverage than is the case with
water supply, the required rate of improvement was always going to be
higher for sanitation. But, as Table C5.2 shows, more than 40 per cent of
the world's population (about 2.6 billion people) did not have access to
'improved sanitation' in 2004, and it is predicted that the world will miss
the MDG sanitation target by over half a billion people. In some locations,
particularly in some of the mega-cities, the rate of coverage is actually
slipping, as populations soar and the increasing and large-scale pattern of
rural to urban migratory flows is leading, in some cities, to the 'slumisation'
of the majority of human habitats. And, even more so than with water, the
JMP data represent an overestimation of coverage. Measurement is carried
out by extrapolation from surveys in which people are asked what type of
latrine/facility they use. The data-gathering methods can lead to skewed
and inaccurate results where people can be embarrassed to admit to open
defecation, or to the use of non-sanitary methods of disposing of faeces.

The grim reality millions of people is a depressing and undignified life of
having to live in a smelly world full of untreated shit. In many areas, people
are reduced to defecating in plastic bags and throwing their faeces ('flying
latrines') into ditches; they may defecate in fields and behind bushes, or in
flimsy structures from which their faeces fall into ponds or lakes ('hanging

TABLE C5.2   **Global sanitation coverage and MDG 7**

	1990 (actual)	2004 (actual)	2015 (projected)	2015 (target)
Served (million)	2,569	3,777	4,829	5,414
Unserved (million)	2,710	2,612	2,390	1,805
Unserved (%)	51.3	40.9	33.1	25.0

Source: JMP 2006.

IMAGE C5.2   **Child collecting water in Indonesia**

latrines') and contaminate sources of drinking water. Children walk over faeces-ridden fields barefoot to schools.

While it is possible to describe at length the social and economic inconveniences associated with inadequate basic sanitation, the fact that tends to be overlooked by much of the donor community is that it is a huge silent killer in the developing world and most of its victims are children.

It is a paradox of the aid system that while the developed world and some of the East Asian tigers saw investments in sanitation as critical to achieving huge public health gains, it is arguably one of the most sidelined of all development sectors and it is being overlooked with widespread lethal results.

The underestimated social and health consequences

The World Bank has identified hygiene promotion as the most cost-effective of all interventions to control high-burden diseases in the developing world, with sanitation promotion close behind (Laxminarayan, Chow and Shahid-Salles 2006). Additionally, in a recent poll conducted by the *British Medical Journal*, the provision of 'clean water and sewage disposal' was voted the greatest advance in medicine in the last 150 years, outscoring antibiotics, vaccines, anaesthesia and the discovery of the structure of DNA.

BOX C5.2   **The slums of Tiruchiripalli**

Due to lack of drainage facilities, water stagnation was common. More-over lack of toilets or lack of toilet use where this facility existed led to open defecation being practised by the entire slum community. It was common to see entire areas polluted by human faeces. As both sexes used the same spot, women and men had different times for defecation, leading to problems for women. Women thus practised defecation either in the early morning or at night while men and children used the same spot at any time during the day.

Source: Damodaran 2005.

The *direct* health consequences of poor hygiene and sanitation are generally well known. It is estimated that nearly 5,000 children die *every day* from the effects of diarrhoeal illnesses, 90 per cent of which are attributable to poor hygiene, sanitation and unsafe water (UNICEF 2006). Improved hygiene, particularly handwashing with soap, could also halve the incidence of acute respiratory infections, a leading cause of childhood death worldwide, by interrupting the route of infection from contaminated hands (Luby et al. 2005). In countries with high infant mortality rates, the lack of access to clean water and sanitation kills more children than pneumonia, malaria and HIV and AIDS combined. Half of the world's hospital beds are occupied by people suffering from waterborne diseases. Hygiene and sanitation also help to control many non-fatal diseases which afflict young children, such as intestinal parasites, blinding trachoma and impetigo. Finally, improved hygiene and sanitation have important positive impacts on the quality of life enjoyed by children, including the benefit of being part of a household with a greater chance of escaping poverty.

Poor access to water and sanitation also has a wide range of *indirect* health effects. In rural areas, women and girls have to walk often long distances to waterholes or rivers to scoop up to 20 litres of water into a container and carry it back to their homes, maybe twice or three times a day. In northern Ghana girls spend up to five hours a day fetching water. On average, a sub-Saharan African woman living in a rural area will spend more than two hours a day fetching and hauling water. In cities, women may have to wait for hours at a standpipe or buy water from an unregulated vendor at extortionate prices.

The lack of access to a private latrine also carries a number of often unrecognised problems, as depicted by the description in Box C5.2 from the slums of Tiruchiripalli in India. In addition to the pain and health risks

FIGURE C5.2   **Effects of poor sanitation on school absenteeism**

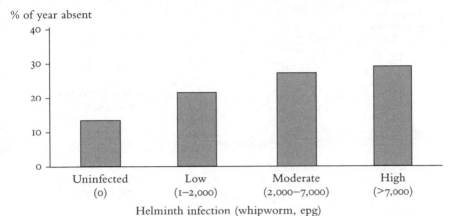

Source: Nokes and Bundy 1993.

of having to control bodily functions, and the indignity associated with open defecation, women are vulnerable to sexual and other violent abuse when going out at night to defecate.

Poor access to water and sanitation also has important knock-on effects in terms of the attainment of educational goals, particularly for girls (DFID 2007). Girls stay away from school because it is seen as their job to fetch water. Also, they are kept away from school for want of sanitation facilities when menstruating. Intestinal worms, spread by poor sanitation, also inhibit cognitive development, and illnesses due to poor hygiene and sanitation prevent children from attending school. The United Nations Children's Fund (UNICEF) (1999) found that improved school sanitation boosted girls' school attendance by 11 per cent in Bangladesh – a degree of impact that is likely to be as significant as major educational reform. A WaterAid Tanzania (2002) study found that school attendance rose by 12 per cent when safe water was made available fifteen minutes rather than one hour away from children's homes. Additionally, children queuing for inadequate communal toilets at school or near home miss out on classwork or homework. And, in some instances, teachers have been found to resist being posted to communities which lack adequate sanitation.

The WHO has estimated that the world could gain an additional 443 million school days every year, currently lost annually due to diarrhoeal disease, with universal access to safe water and sanitation (UNDP 2006). However, schools are the ideal institutions to spread habits of hygiene and use of sanitation; a school without sanitation can miss this opportunity for a generation.

FIGURE C5.3   **Effects of poor sanitation on school performance**

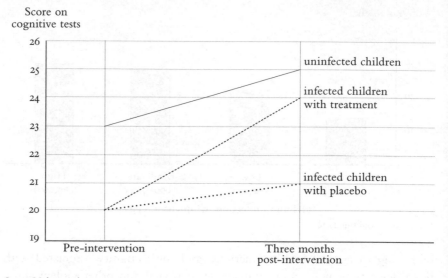

Score on
cognitive tests

Source: Nokes et al. 1991.

Sanitation and hygiene are also important for achieving MDG 6 in relation to HIV/AIDS, malaria and other diseases. Access to clean water is an important requirement for antiretroviral and tuberculosis (TB) treatment adherence. And poor sanitation facilities, especially in many slum areas, cause flooded pit latrines and blocked drains, which can act as a breeding ground for malaria-transmitting mosquitoes (Stephens 1995).

There are also effects on maternal health and survival. The need to walk long distances to a convenient defecation site or to wait until nightfall is particularly onerous. Women's holding on until nightfall or walking long distances to secluded defecation sites can lead to urinary infections and present other health risks, particularly during pregnancy.

The official response

In spite of the recognition that clean water and environmental hygiene are crucial building blocks in the process of health improvement, the response of governments, donors and international agencies has been poor.

While the sanitation and water crisis present technological challenges, they are far from insurmountable. And while the cost of meeting reasonable targets is not insubstantial, the amounts required are small compared with European spending on luxuries such as perfumes or pet food. While

BOX C5.3   **What the poor say**

On the few occasions when poor people are actually asked to prioritise their needs, safe water comes in the top three. Research shows that people are fully aware of the cost of poor water supply, in terms of sickness, energy, time and money. However, research shows that people are often less aware and/or more constrained to speak about the importance of improved sanitation. This is because there is less appreciation of the link between sanitation/hygiene and health outcomes, and because social taboos associated with defecation and menstruation limit the extent to which information and education are effective.

In much the same way that stigma around HIV/AIDS has had to be challenged, stigma and taboos associated with defecation and menstruation need to be confronted. Experience shows that demand needs to be stimulated before more appropriate hygiene behaviours are adopted and there is significant uptake of latrines – this demand stimulation cannot take place where these taboos and stigmas remain.

prolonged and extensive advocacy has helped to improve official recognition, it has not necessarily translated into greater budget allocation. The reason for this abysmal state of affairs is a lack of political will to confront the crisis.

Research into the status of water and/or sanitation in a selection of developing-country Poverty Reduction Strategies Papers (PRSPs) found a disturbing lack of alignment between what poor people themselves prioritise and what their governments do in response:

> While most PRSPs mention water, sanitation and water resource problems in the discursive parts of the strategies devoted to analysis of poverty issues, this was not and is not being reflected in the crucial section of the strategy where action plans and budget allocations are presented. This is an important issue because PRSPs now account for a significant proportion of ODA. (Foxwood and Green 2004)

The Cameroon PRSP reported that 60 per cent of people identified the lack of water as a cause of their poverty. In Malawi, 88 per cent of Village Development Committees put water in their top three priorities. In Zambia, water emerged as the top priority in all the poverty consultations in 1994, 1996 and 1999. But in each of these countries, the priority ascribed to water and sanitation by people was not reflected in the final national development plans.

FIGURE C5.4   **Aid to the water supply and sanitation sectors compared with overall aid, 1999–2004**

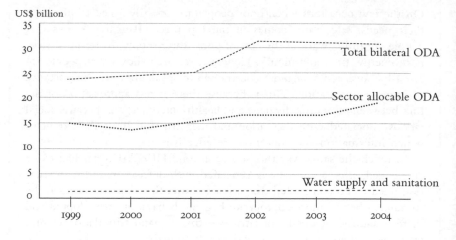

US$ billion

Source: WaterAid 2007. Data from DAC European countries.

And what of the donors? Figure C5.4 shows the rising level of overseas development assistance (ODA) from European countries, both as a total and as allocated to specific sectors. ODA for water and sanitation has remained largely static and a low percentage of the total – in the context of rising ODA, allocations to the water and sanitation sector have actually *declined* as a proportion.

Additionally, much of the aid that is directed to water and sanitation does not flow to where it is needed: of the top ten recipients of aid for water and sanitation, only three are low-income countries and only one of those is in sub-Saharan Africa, the region most off-track to meet the water and sanitation MDGs.

So, while people in developing countries see the lack of access to safe water as a critical problem, and while professionals recognise water and particularly sanitation as vital to public health and broader development efforts, national governments and donors tend to have a policy blind spot. Clearly there is paradox, an accountability crisis, at the heart of official development efforts.

In pushing for accelerated progress towards achieving internationally agreed upon development goals, it is necessary to guard against a situation where official efforts lead to a targeting of the easiest-to-reach populations – this would almost certainly result in the poorest and most vulnerable being marginalised even further.

There is a case for achieving the MDG target by focusing our efforts on where conditions are most propitious and the greatest numbers of un-served are to be found. But this would ignore the moral dimension of those whose need is greatest. The challenge, therefore, is to meet the water and sanitation MDG targets with equity i.e. without leaving the poorest nations, regions or communities behind. (WaterAid 2006)

While the MDGs are a useful device to draw attention to the gravity and depth of poverty across the world, focusing on them could create two serious and unwanted problems:

- the 2015 MDG target becomes the end product and not a stepping stone on the way to universal and equitable access;
- if the MDG targets are not reached, the world will look away and forget about water and sanitation.

WaterAid's paper marking the halfway point in the MDG timescale notes:

There is a genuine risk that the human development-related Millennium Development Goals will not be met if international donors continue to pursue single issue 'global causes' instead of building an aid system that will respond to the complex needs of poor communities. Progress in health and education is dependent on access to affordable sanitation and safe water. And yet both donors and developing-country governments have failed to recognise the interrelationship between health, education, water and sanitation. Global aid spending on health and education has nearly doubled since 1990 while the share allocated to water and sanitation has contracted. (WaterAid 2007)

Sanitation is particularly poorly served. The JMP found that spending on sanitation was as little as one-eighth that of spending on water, while the Global Water Partnership estimated in 2000 that only $1 billion was spent in developing countries on sanitation compared with $13 billion on water.

If donor funds for water and sanitation do reach low-income countries, they are often misdirected. Sanitation in particular is underprioritised locally and by international donors. Many countries do not have a co-ordinating institution responsible for sanitation and there is rarely a national budget dedicated to sanitation. For example, WaterAid (2006) examined the fourteen countries in which it works and only one was found to have coordinated planning and reporting systems for sanitation including a dedicated sanitation budget. Even though more than twice as many people lack sanitation as safe drinking water, spending on sanitation is only a fraction of the spending on water.

Often donor funds will be directed to projects that benefit the relatively well-off through favouring relatively high-cost-per-capita, high-technology schemes. For example, the Melamchi project in Nepal was projected to cost $312 per capita and is to be directed at the middle-class parts of Kathmandu – the cost of a rural water point is typically $10 per capita in that country (WaterAid 2006).

In Tanzania, donors are mainly funding *piped* water supply schemes in rural areas which generally serve the better-off sections of the population and utilise technologies that are at least ten times more expensive than low-cost ones such as boreholes and wells. So for every additional household connected to such a piped water scheme, ten poorer households are denied access to a (cheaper) protected water source (de Waal 2003).

With sanitation, there is an emerging consensus that in order to accelerate progress communities need to be motivated to understand the benefits of improved sanitation *and* hygienic behaviours. It is accepted that the mere provision of latrines does not automatically result in the desired change in behaviour. Instead there is too often a waste of resources, when latrine provision is not accompanied by a concerted attempt to change attitudes and behaviour. In addition, the subsidy involved in supply-driven approaches is often captured by the relatively affluent, or latrines are built by the poor for the wrong reasons, and then not used properly, or at all.

Sanitation

The 2006 *Human Development Report* (HDR) identified six barriers to improving sanitation.

The first is the lack of acceptable and appropriate policy at a national level, even in some countries where good progress is being made with water supply. The key issue is the lack of institutional responsibility, alongside a lack of dedicated sanitation finance and capacity in municipalities.

The second barrier is that the poor themselves place a low premium on sanitation. The benefits of sanitation are dependent upon a range of factors, many of which are beyond the influence of households, including, for example, at a local level, where individuals in households with good hygiene and sanitation practices are victims of the insanitary practices of others, and at a wider level, where sewage is often partially treated (or not treated at all) prior to discharge into watercourses.

Third, people tend not to see the health benefits of sanitation. It is important to recognize that latrine uptake is dependent on issues of pride, dignity and safety. In a number of programmes approaches are now being used that successfully change understanding and behaviour, on the basis of an improved understanding of the health benefits.

The decision to install a sanitary facility, usually a latrine, is made at household level – probably by the (usually male) head of household. If that household is poor, then the cost of even low-cost technology may be well beyond them. So the fourth barrier emerges: 'why should I build a house for shit', as a Zambian woman was quoted as asking in recent WaterAid research into drivers of sustainable sanitation, 'when I can't afford a roof on the house where I sleep?'

The fifth barrier is that in many locations there simply isn't the necessary supply of technology of the right sort and at the right price to allow local people to choose something to suit their cultural and financial requirements. People have been motivated to create their own low-cost designs in some locations, whereas in most others such levels of motivation have not been generated, and/or materials that allow low-cost designs are simply not available.

Finally, sanitation demand is low because it is women who bear most of the disease burden. So the lack of perceived demand for sanitation is often a function of the disempowerment of women. It is women's voices that are suppressed, not raised or not heard. The personal experience of women is disproportionately harsh in relation to sanitation, from school through to adult life, through exposure to indignity, shame, lack of privacy, illness and violence. In some communities taboos prevent women from using the same latrines as men or even from using them at all. Empowering women may therefore be one of the necessary conditions of accelerating progress.

The way forward

First, donors and national governments need to act on the evidence that is before them: that sanitation, water and hygiene promotion are not additions to development efforts; they underpin the successful achievement of all the MDGs.

Second, ODA and national planning systems need to be responsive to the domestic demands of the poor and to evidence of the most critical areas of deprivation.

As sanitation, water and hygiene form a critical part of development plans, it follows that sector-led development approaches are inappropriate. There is a pressing need for all sectors to coordinate policies.

The 2006 HDR identified the critical determinant to overcoming the water and sanitation crisis as a lack of political will. Good governance in both water and sanitation sectors is critical. The HDR highlighted the fundamental problem of weak, incapable and inadequately accountable governments. It is vital that water be seen as a public good that needs to be subject to some form of public and democratic control/regulation; also that within the sector there has to be a mix of different kinds of actors involved in the provision and management of water resources and services.

Over 90 per cent of water supply is provided through public agencies. The key to equitable, affordable and efficient service delivery, and thereby accelerated pro-poor targeting of service delivery, in the vast majority of cases, lies in supporting public-sector reform. This is happening in most countries, but at far too slow a pace; it is held back too often, again, by a lack of political will.

The key to ensuring that governments, donors and service delivery agencies all play their role is increased accountability. Those acting in the water and sanitation sectors are generally not accountable to those they are supposed to serve. The results lead to woefully inadequate service levels; in absent services to the poor; in inequitable tariff differentials between the rich, connected and the poor, who get their water from unregulated vendors; and in weakly managed and inappropriate privatisations of utilities.

A way forward in all instances is to support local efforts to create institutionalised structures for local people to demand and maintain accountability, and for similar efforts at regional, national and even the global level. In other words, structures of accountability and platforms for dialogue between communities and those charged with serving them need to be created. Examples of such engagement come from across the globe: Red Vida, the Friends of the Right to Water, the Pan African Water Network, UNDP's Community Water Initiative, WaterAid's Citizens Action work and the Water Dialogues. There are many, many more.

In March 2007 the members of a coalition of Southern and Northern NGOs and individuals called End Water Poverty launched their campaign. At the time of writing, the coalition had more than half a million members. It is grounded in the belief that access to sanitation and safe water is a most basic human right and that, above all, it is the duty of governments to ensure that these rights are met with affordable, sustainable and equitable services.

Notes

1. See www.un.org/millenniumgoals/ for further details.
2. www.wssinfo.org/en/122_definitions.html.

References

Damodaran, S. (2005). *India's first 100 per cent sanitised slum in Tiruchiripalli.* Tiruchiripalli: Gramalaya.

de Waal, D. (2003). What sort of rural water supply infrastructure should Tanzania invest in? In *Poverty and Human Development Report 2003.* Dar es Salaam: Government of the United Republic of Tanzania.

DFID Sanitation Reference Group (2007). *Water is life, sanitation is dignity.* Sanitation Policy Background Paper. London: Department for International Development. www.dfid. gov.uk/consultations/past-consultations/water-sanitation-background.pdf.

Foxwood, N., and J. Green (2004). *Making every drop count.* Teddington: Tearfund.

JMP (2006). *Meeting the MDG drinking water and sanitation target: The urban and rural challenge of the decade.* Geneva: WHO/UNICEF.

Laxminarayan, R., J. Chow and S.A. Shahid-Salles (2006). Intervention cost-effectiveness: overview of main messages. In *Disease control priorities in developing countries.* New York: Oxford University Press.

Luby, S.P., et al. (2005). Effect of handwashing on child health: A randomised controlled trial. *The Lancet* 366(9481): 225–33.

Nokes, C., and D.A.P. Bundy (1993). Compliance and absenteeism in school children: Implications for helminth control. *Transactions of the Royal Society of Tropical Medicine and Hygiene* 87: 148–52.

Nokes, C., et al. (1991). Geohelminth infection and academic assessment in Jamaican children. *Transactions of the Royal Society of Tropical Medicine and Hygiene* 85: 272–3.

Stephens, C. (1995). The urban environment, poverty and health in developing countries. *Health Policy and Planning* 10(2): 109–21.

UNDP (2006). *Human Development Report 2006. Beyond scarcity: Power, poverty and the global water crisis.* New York.

UNICEF (1999). *Sanitation and hygiene: A right for every child.* New York.

UNICEF (2006). *Children and water, sanitation and hygiene: The evidence.* Issue note for the UNDP 2006 *Human Development Report.* New York.

WaterAid (2002). *Water and sanitation in Tanzania: Poverty monitoring for the sector using HBS, the DHS and the population censuses.* WaterAid Tanzania with Eastern Africa Statistical Training Centre and National Bureau of Statistics. Dar es Salaam: WaterAid Tanzania. www.wateraid.org/documents/population_census_study.pdf.

WaterAid (2006). *Getting the off track on target.* Background paper for the UNDP 2006 *Human Development Report.*

WaterAid (2007). *'Global cause' and effect: How the aid system is undermining the Millennium Development Goals.* London.

C6   Oil extraction and health in the Niger Delta

Brief overview of oil-exporting developing countries

Industrial nations tend to be large consumers of oil and oil products, but minor producers. Most OECD (Organization for Economic Cooperation and Development) nations depend on the Organization of Petroleum Exporting Countries (OPEC) for oil supplies (Karl 1997). The majority of oil reserves are located in the Middle East. The largest non-Middle Eastern oil-exporting countries include Venezuela, Nigeria, Indonesia, Libya, Algeria, Ecuador and Gabon. New technologies and rising prices have increased the volume of offshore oil extraction, resulting in areas such as the Gulf of Guinea off Africa emerging as a major global hydrocarbon supplier.

However, Bergesen and Haugland (2000) show that natural resource endowment has not been positively correlated with economic development and social progress. Paradoxically, countries rich in natural resources have performed poorly when compared to countries that have possessed fewer natural resources. Resource-rich countries are more likely to experience higher levels of conflict (Collier and Hoeffler 1999; Peluso and Watts 2001). A substantial body of research suggests that despite the considerable wealth tied to oil extraction, oil-exporting low-income countries suffer from economic deterioration and political turmoil (Hodges 2003; Karl 1997; Watts 2005).

Karl's in-depth analysis of 'petro-states', which covers a diverse range of countries and regime types, including Venezuela, Iran, Nigeria, Algeria and Indonesia, reveals that they all fall prey to troubling development paths despite their resource wealth (1997). Countries such as Angola, the DRC, Ecuador, Gabon, Iran, Iraq, Libya, Peru, and Trinidad and Tobago experience entrenched poverty, environmental degradation and stark health disparities in the context of great resource wealth, leading economists to frame the term 'resource curse' (Sachs and Warner 1995; Gary and Karl 2003). What follows is a description of this 'resource curse' in Nigeria using a 'health lens'. It demonstrates the political nature of development and how a complex web of actors including transnational oil companies, military personnel and government officials conspire to keep millions of Nigerians unhealthy in spite of Nigeria's rich oilfields.

The 'new' gulf

Africa is currently experiencing a large oil boom, while the continent delivers approximately 10 per cent of world oil output and holds 9.3 per cent of known reserves (Zalik and Watts 2006). It has been conservatively estimated that sub-Saharan African governments will receive over $200 billion in oil revenues over the next decade (Gary and Karl 2003). Among the twelve major African oil-producing states, Nigeria combined with Algeria, Libya and Angola account for 85 per cent of the continent's output (Ghazvinian 2007). With a population approaching 140 million citizens, Nigeria is not only the most populous country in Africa, it is also a major supplier of petroleum to US and European markets. Human rights concerns and conflicts in other areas have led to the offshore region of the Gulf of Guinea in West Africa being identified as the *new Gulf*. The Gulf of Guinea region could receive $40 billion in investment by 2012 according to the petroleum industry, and the National Intelligence Council has stated that the significance of West Africa to US energy supplies may rise from 16 per cent to 25 per cent by 2015 (Zalik and Watts 2006).

Lubeck et al. draw our attention to the increased US military involvement in and around the Gulf of Guinea and 'greater American-Nigerian cooperation in managing security in the Gulf of Guinea' (2007: 10). During the next two decades, it is expected to become even more critical, along with other oil-producing countries in the West African 'Oil Triangle'. Civilian functions previously organised under the State Department's health, water and education agencies are now increasingly managed under the Trans-Sahara Counter Terrorism Initiative (TSCTI) and the US military (Lubeck et al. 2007). US officials affirm that the TSCTI strategy resembles 'ring fencing' in order to protect Nigeria, Africa's largest oil producer (Wallis 2007). The introduction to the 2005 Council on Foreign Relations document entitled 'More than Humanitarianism: A Strategic U.S. Approach Toward Africa', stated that 'By the end of the decade sub-Saharan Africa is likely to become as important as a source of U.S. energy imports as the Middle East' (Foster 2006). Zalik and Watts observe that this US report's focus is on 'Sub-Saharan

---

BOX C6.1   **Overview of the Niger Delta**

The Niger Delta incorporates nine states in the country: Akwa Ibom, Cross River, Rivers, Edo, Delta, Bayelsa, Imo, Abia and Ondo. The Delta and Rivers states are the dominant oil producers, producing approximately 75 per cent of Nigeria's petroleum (World Bank 1995).

The people of the Delta are predominantly fishermen and farmers who depend on the ecosystem for survival. The region is made up of four main ecological zones, harboring a high diversity of flora and fauna: coastal barrier islands, mangroves, fresh water swamp forests, and lowland forests. The Delta is one of the world's largest wetlands and has the largest mangrove forest in Africa.

Africa as a key source in US oil imports, the growing role of China in the African oil and gas industry and, of course, Africa as the new frontier in the fight against *terror* and revolutionary Islam' (Zalik and Watts 2006). However, Lubeck et al. insist that the only way to secure areas including the Delta region is to improve health, education and living standards, guarantee democratic elections, resolve resource conflicts, and include residents as stakeholders who will benefit from oil revenues (2007).

The Niger Delta makes Nigeria the largest oil producer in Africa and the eleventh largest producer of crude oil in the world. The Delta's oil has the potential to create wealth and opportunities for the Nigerian population. Instead, it has entrenched poverty and led to high levels of conflict, repression, corruption and environmental degradation (Watts 2004). Such an intense contradiction has been framed as a 'paradox of plenty' (Karl 1997).

> The problem, in a nutshell, is that for fifty years, foreign oil companies have conducted some of the world's most sophisticated exploration and production operations, using millions of dollars' worth of imported ultramodern equipment, against a backdrop of Stone Age squalor. They have extracted hundreds of millions of barrels of oil, which have sold on the international market for hundreds of billions of dollars, but the people of the Niger Delta have seen virtually none of the benefits. (Ghazvinian 2007)

The oil extraction industry

The search for crude oil began in 1908 when the German firm Nigerian Bitumen Corporation began exploration in Western Nigeria. However, it was not until 1956 and after investing over $30 million that Shell struck oil in commercial quantities.

IMAGE C6.1   **In the village of Kpean, Nigeria, an oil wellhead that had been leaking for weeks has caught fire**

The political economy of oil in Nigeria involves the complex interaction of the state, military and transnational oil companies (TNOCs). The federal government owns Nigeria's oil resources and exerts a statutory monopoly over all mineral exploitation. The state sets the rules for the operation of a series of joint ventures with TNOCs, which are granted territorial concessions. By the 1990s, Shell controlled over 60 per cent of Nigeria's known oil reserves and currently remains the biggest TNOC operator, controlling over 50 per cent of the oil wealth in Nigeria (Okanta and Douglas 2003). Other major players include Chevron, ExxonMobil and Nigeria Agip Oil Company.

The state security apparatuses, working with the private security forces of the companies, also play an important role. TNOCs have exploited oil resources for decades while several authoritarian military regimes have shielded them from litigation and liability for ensuing environmental damage and human rights violations. The systematic neglect underlying the Niger Delta problem has been described as a 'matrix of concentric circles of payoffs and rewards built on blackmail and violence' (Ibeanu 2002), involving actors from within and without the country.

According to one recent assessment of the situation,

Ten years after the execution of human rights campaigner Ken Saro-Wiwa and eight of his colleagues by the Nigerian government, the issues of human rights and environmental devastation in the oil-producing Niger Delta remain unresolved. Despite the return to civilian rule in 1999 and pledges by oil companies to implement voluntary corporate responsibility standards, new reports by Environmental Rights Action and Amnesty International document only limited action to correct abuses and deliver benefits to the residents of the oil producing areas. (Africa Focus Bulletin 2005)

Nigeria currently produces over 2 billion gallons of oil a day, valued at approximately $40 billion a year (Watts 2007). Nigeria is the world's eighth largest exporter of crude oil (US EIA 2007; Falola and Genova 2005). Petrodollars account for 83 per cent of federal government revenue and about 40 per cent of GDP (Watts 2005). Some 85 per cent of the oil monies are accrued by 1 per cent of the population, with 70 per cent of wealth held in private hands abroad (Watts 2007), while 70 per cent of the people of the Niger Delta live below the poverty line and the majority of Nigeria's oil and gas is consumed in developed countries.

Nnimo Bassey, executive director of Environmental Rights Action/ Friends of the Earth Nigeria, has captured the twin interests of international capital and the domestic rentier economy:

As the world continues to hunger for hydrocarbons, so the oil giants conveniently maintain a stranglehold on the Niger Delta in indifference to the cries of the people. As the IMF, World Bank and the Paris Club scheme on even more ingenious ways to skim off whatever funds trickle into our national treasury, so the fangs of rigs of the oil internationals sink defiantly into the heartlands and offshore of the oil coasts. (ERA/FoEN 2005)

Environmental and social consequences of oil extraction in the Delta

Nigeria ranks 158th out of 177 nations on the Human Development Index, and 91 per cent of Nigerians live on less than $2 a day (UNDP 2006; UNAIDS 2006). Over 3.5 million people live with HIV and average life expectancy is 45 years. Nigeria's health system is under-resourced, with government expenditure on health being only US$13 per capita (1.4 per cent of per capita gross national income).

In the Delta, various stages of oil exploration and extraction cause tremendous environmental and social damage. These include seismic surveys, drilling, road and pipeline construction, river dredging and gas flaring. Long-standing pollution also results from pipeline leaks and oil spills, waste dumping and blowouts, all exacerbated by the neglect of proper maintenance and management.

Local communities eking out subsistence through fishing, cassava processing, palm oil processing, orchard tending and non-timber forest product gathering have experienced a devastating change in their lives. Deforestation, air and water pollution, desertification and loss of arable land have contributed to high rates of disease and physical, mental and social ill-health (US EIA 2007).

Oil spills, either from pipelines (which often cut directly through villages) or from blowouts at wellheads, are a major cause of pollution and ill health. There have been over 6,000 oil spills totalling over 4 million barrels between 1976 and 1996. Many pipeline leakages might have been avoided if the pipelines were buried below ground as in other countries and if ageing or damaged sections were repaired. Ageing and poorly maintained infrastructure also contributes to pipeline fires and explosions, which claim hundreds of lives annually. In 2006, over 400 people died in two pipeline explosions in Lagos, where leaking pipelines were left unremedied and crowds of impoverished residents desperately scooped up buckets of fuel, to sell or for personal use (Associated Press 2006).

In June 2001, an oil spill occurred in the rural town of Ogbodo. A study found that after a delay in clean-up efforts of at least three months, 15 km of soil along the Calabar river had been severely affected. High levels of oil and grease, laden with hydrocarbons, had damaged the soil, aquatic resources and the biodiversity of the area. Health impacts included respiratory and gastro-intestinal diseases, as well as mental distress (ERA/FoEN 2005).

All across the Delta, the water and soil have been poisoned with hydrocarbons, heavy metals and other substances (ERA/FoEN 2005). Thousands of toxin-containing waste pits are suspected of being linked to rising cancer rates, while waterborne illnesses such as cholera, typhoid and diarrhoeal diseases from unsafe drinking water present challenges for local communities. The power supply and stagnation of water have created breeding grounds for various waterborne diseases; and stagnant water in oil boreholes provides ideal habitats for disease-spreading mosquitoes.

All too often, oil spills are blamed on local sabotage. One spill in Rumueke that was claimed to be 'a result of sabotage' by Shell was later confirmed to have been caused by a leak in a pipeline. Numerous petitions from communities have been ignored (ERA/FOEN 2005; Amnesty International 2005).

The inactions of the TNOCs amount to a wilful neglect of the environment and local communities. In spite of the branding of oil companies as 'green corporate citizens', this neglect continues (in the Delta and elsewhere). The clean-up methods initiated by oil firms remain unsatisfactory. A traditional scoop-and-burn method consists of scooping up oil onto water or land surfaces and then dumping it into open pits where it is burnt. Such fires set forests and rivers ablaze, and damage farmlands and communal property.

Another cause of ill health and environmental destruction is gas flaring. An estimated 2.5 billion cubic foot of gas is burnt on a daily basis (Osuoka and Roderick 2005). Soot, laden with harmful chemicals, drifts to the ground, adversely affecting soil fertility. Acid rain reduces the life of the corrugated iron sheets used for roofing from twenty to five years. Many of the 250 or so toxic chemicals in the fumes and soot of the gas flares and produced in the burning of oil spills have been linked to respiratory disease and cancer. Flares from nearby oil plants have caused an epidemic of bronchitis in adults as well as asthma and blurred vision in children (Piller et al. 2007). Medical staff report treating patients with many ailments and illnesses they believe are related to the products of the gas flares, including bronchial, chest, rheumatic and eye problems (Quist-Arcon 2007). Gas flares and their soot contain toxic by-products such as benzene, mercury and chromium, which contribute to lowering the immunity of community members, in particular children, making them more susceptible to diseases such as polio and measles (Piller et al. 2007).

Flaring also represents a significant economic loss – estimated at US$2.5 billion per annum (Osuoka and Roderick 2005). Cruelly, most Nigerian households suffer from chronic energy shortages while gas is burned virtually next door. Experts say that eliminating global flaring would curb more carbon dioxide emissions than all the projects currently registered under the Kyoto Protocol's Clean Development Mechanism (Quist-Arcon 2007). Although 2004 was originally set as the year by which non-operational gas flaring would end, the government has informed the UN that it has reset the date to 2010.

Negative health impacts have also occurred through social processes. Oil firms mainly employ expatriates, migrant contract workers (often from the host country) and only a minority of local workers from the communities. The first two categories usually receive better pay and benefits. Where foreign nationals and local labourers exist alongside one another, exclusionary dynamics similar to those under apartheid often exist, with luxurious secure compounds housing foreign oil workers (Watts 2005). High alcohol use and disrespectful behaviour towards the local community aggravate the situation further (Essential Action and Global Exchange 2000).

Oil workers and the high concentration of military and private security officers have created a market for commercial sex and account for the high incidence of violence, abuse and sexually transmitted infections including HIV/AIDS (Izugbara and Otutubikey 2005). Traditional gender roles and a lack of formal employment opportunities contribute to sex work serving as a survival strategy for women living near oil compounds and installations where many male field-based oil workers reside (Faleyimu et al. 2000).

Community and economic development efforts have been sorely lacking, while many development projects result in contracts being awarded or even bribes given without delivering any tangible benefits to the community (HRW 2007). Perceived inequalities in terms of the distribution of corporate benefits in various guises have resulted in violent responses (Cesarz et al. 2003).

Conflict

Not surprisingly, conflict and violence have been a defining feature of the Niger Delta. Protest by local communities has often resulted in brutal repression. The murder of Ken Saro-Wiwa and others, and the massacre of citizens in Odi in Bayelsa in 1999, in which the army killed 2,500 civilians, typifies the oppression in the region (Odey 2005). Amnesty International (2004) reports over 1,000 oil-related deaths in the Niger Delta in 2003 alone.

Internecine war and conflict between ethnic groups in the Delta pre-dated the discovery of oil. However, the nature of these conflicts has been altered by the oil economy. Notably, TNOCs have exacerbated violence in the area through land-use payments, environmental damage, price inflation and corruption.

Small arms and light weapons proliferation has accompanied the rise in the number of private security firms as well as community militia groups. The weapons have also been used for criminal purposes, for intimidation and violence during elections or campaigns, and during inter-communal disputes (Vines 2005). A HRW (2004) profile of violence in Rivers State featured the manipulation and militarisation of youths by local politicians and predatory oil firms.

Okanta and Watts carefully analyse how petrocapitalism as tied to an oil complex (an institutional configuration of firms, state apparatuses and oil communities) has contributed to territorial and indigenous rights disputes and exacerbated conflict related to perceptions of ethnic difference in Nigeria (Watts 2005, 2007; Okanta and Douglas 2003). Colonialism and the subsequent discovery of oil ruptured earlier forms of community, systems of ethnic identity, the functioning of local state governance, and

IMAGE C6.2   **Armed militants make a show of arms in support of their fallen comrades deep in the swamps of the Niger Delta**

territorial understandings. Watts (2007) posits that ethnic youth movements in contemporary Nigeria are a significant political development that has recently involved an upsurge in violence directed at oil firm employees – from kidnapping to armed militia attacks on security forces to vandalism aimed at disrupting oil operations. The restive youth problem results from large numbers of unemployed men who are 'incredibly alienated and angry at the consequences of this catastrophically failed oil development' and 'are either fighting among themselves or fighting local chiefs, local elites, for a cut of the oil money' (Bergman 2007).

Health care in the Delta

Repressive military rule, corruption and the theft of public funds have resulted in substandard public services, including a barely functioning public health-care system (Hargreaves 2002). Low-quality public health services, high user fees, shortages of drugs, equipment and personnel, combined with persistent high unemployment and poverty rates, contribute to a crisis of confidence and affordability in terms of health-care access and status in the Niger Delta (Chukwuani 2006).

Current donor-driven vertical disease-control initiatives have been criticised for setting targets driven by international agendas that adversely

IMAGE C6.3 **Oil pipelines and woman with company umbrella in Okrika**

affect the development of local health systems. The state of health care in Nigeria has been worsened by many Nigerian doctors emigrating to North America and Europe.

Nigeria is only one of ten countries where 50 per cent of the population is unvaccinated (Schimmer and Ihekweazu 2006). A burgeoning epidemic of HIV/AIDS leaves over 3.5 million infected and without access to the most basic care (UNAIDS 2006). Yellow fever remains a constant threat. Nigeria is listed eighth on the World Health Organization (WHO) list of countries with excessive tuberculosis mortality, and also has a major measles problem with an estimated 96,000 deaths per year. The Delta is a malaria endemic region. Until the WHO Roll Back Malaria campaign started in April 2000, there had been no defined malaria control programme. Epidemics are swift, frequent, and inevitably lead to high case-fatality rates, most often among children.

Médecins Sans Frontières (MSF) operates a surgical programme in Port Harcourt. Over 25 per cent of emergencies treated in May 2006 were for violence-related injuries (MSF 2006). In August 2007, Port Harcourt and surrounding Delta communities experienced weeks of violence, resulting in the deaths of dozens of people.

Most Nigerians have lost faith in government-run services, turning to various private providers including traditional healers, private pharmacists and an array of charlatans who operate on a fee-for-service basis (Hargreaves 2002). A chronic shortage of essential drugs results in the purchase of substandard and counterfeit drugs from private pharmacists and street vendors with little or no regulation.

There is only one doctor for every 150,000 residents in the oil-plentiful Bayelsa, Rivers and Delta states (Zalik and Watts 2006). A 2007 HRW report on visits to primary health-care centres in five local government areas in the Delta found that all but a few lacked basic medicines, water and electricity. Some were housed in structures nearing the point of collapse, while many had been abandoned by demoralised staff (HRW 2007).

In November 2005, MSF had to end a malaria project in Bayelsa because local authorities were unwilling to improve health facilities and staffing. When funds are allocated to improve the provision of health care, as is the case with many development efforts in the Niger Delta, the money is often diverted to other purposes or channelled into 'projects' that are never executed.

Combating the resource curse

Will Nigeria's petrodollars help reduce poverty and improve health, or will conflict, oppression and environmental destruction be the experience of local communities?

Nigeria has taken small but important steps in the right direction. For the first time in the country's history, one civilian government has handed over power to another. Corruption remains rampant, but there is no shortage of Nigerians desperate to rid the country of its reputation.

The positive steps taken by Nigeria can be greatly supported by improved efforts from the international community to clean up the act of the TNOCs and the international banking system in facilitating corruption. Perhaps some of the millions of dollars that go missing or are spent on ineffective development programmes would be better spent on developing the capacity of civil society to monitor and campaign for a clean-up of the oil industry, or to support the legal action of communities claiming damages for the harm caused by the industry.

Transparency initiatives are currently inadequate. Publish What You Pay, which largely focuses on oil-producing companies, and the Extractive Industries Transparency Initiative (EITI) both fail to examine the components inside the cost base, which may include bribes, commissions and mispricing, missing oil or misstated oil volumes (Shaxson 2005).

In 2003 the UN Norms for Business were introduced to strengthen the 1948 Universal Declaration of Human Rights, which requires transnational corporations and other business enterprises to respect responsibilities and norms contained in UN treaties and other international instruments (UN 2003). However, not all states are parties to the treaties and enforcement mechanisms are sorely lacking.

The Voluntary Principles on Security and Human Rights (VPs) are a voluntary code of conduct for the extractive industry. However, the Principles are unaccompanied by a monitoring or compliance mechanism and many oil firm representatives or community stakeholders are unaware of their existence (Zalik 2004). The voluntary nature of these codes allows for broad discrepancies in implementation (Seidman 2003). Zalik suggests that, ultimately, security for global capital serves as their primary function.

Other approaches include taking legal action. There has been a worldwide increase in the number of lawsuits against oil companies for human rights violations and environmental destruction (Gary and Karl 2003). The Center for Constitutional Rights is involved in a class action lawsuit charging Chevron/Texaco Corporation with human rights violations in the Niger Delta. Three other lawsuits involve Royal Dutch Petroleum Company and Shell Transport and Trading Company for human rights abuses against the Ogoni people in the Delta. Elsewhere, legal action is being pursued against Chevron Texaco in Ecuador, Unocal in Burma, ExxonMobil in Indonesia and Occidental in Colombia.

Amnesty International and other organisations have also encouraged shareholder campaigns (Amnesty International 2007). Most publicly traded companies have a 'one share, one vote' policy, which allows any shareholder to make proposals at annual meetings or to become a signatory to a petition. Using such opportunities can attract media attention, allow interaction with management and the board of directors, and shame companies into taking appropriate action. One successful campaign helped pressure copper and gold producer Freeport–McMoRan to address indigenous and environmental rights in Indonesia (Friends of the Earth 2000). Another example is the Expose Exxon Campaign aimed at countering ExxonMobil's efforts to block action on global warming, drill in the Arctic Refuge, and encourage the overconsumption of oil.

Needed are further resources and support for independent environmental impact assessments (EIA) of the Niger Delta; credible, independent judicial mechanisms to adjudicate compensation claims, ensuring that the credibility of environmental assessments are not influenced by funding from or association with government and energy firms; and efforts made towards the transparent distribution of compensation to communities. Moreover, company environmental impact assessment studies should be transparent and accessible to community groups, which should be consulted before proceeding with infrastructure or development projects. Recent efforts to extend impact assessment processes to include social and health issues are positive steps forward, but capacity and regulatory related challenges must be addressed in relation to the government as well as the oil firms (Birley 2007).

Finally, also important are the development of and support for local grass-roots leadership and civil society organisations using a range of strategies in their claims for economic, social and cultural rights. The importance of holding official conduct up to scrutiny and generating local public outrage, while drawing on surrogate publics worldwide, has been stressed.

Conclusion

The purpose of this chapter is to make the link between the process of oil extraction and a variety of health, social and environmental outcomes. As with other chapters in *Global Health Watch 2*, it illustrates the fundamentally political nature of health and thereby highlights the requirement for political therapies and solutions. Health organisations, whether based within the UN system or within civil society, have a difficult challenge in combining political and social action with traditional clinical or public health programmes. But to neglect the former is to neglect the root causes of ill-health of millions of people. The oil extractive sector is one arena within which there is a compelling case for greater public health action around the politics of ill-health. A set of concrete recommendations related to this chapter can be found on the GHW website.

References

Africa Focus Bulletin (2005). Nigeria: Delta oil and human rights. 13 November. www. africafocus.org/docs05/nig0511.php.

Amnesty International (2004). *Human rights and oil in Nigeria.* http://asiapacific.amnesty. org/library/Index/ENGAFR440232004?open&of=ENG-NGA.

Amnesty International (2005). *Nigeria ten years on: Injustice and violence haunt the oil delta.* www.amnesty.org/en/report/info/AFR44/022/2005.

Amnesty International (2007). *Taking stock of corporate behavior: Using shareholder activism to defend and promote human rights.* www.amnestyusa.org/business/shareholder.html.

Associated Press (2006). More than 30 killed in Nigeria fuel pipeline fires. *International Herald Tribune,* 26 December. www.iht.com/articles/ap/2007/12/26/africa/AF-GEN-Nigeria-Pipeline-Fire.php.

Bergesen, H., and T. Haugland (2000). The puzzle of petro-states: A comparative study of Azerbaijan and Angola. Unpublished paper cited in Hodges 2003.

Bergman, B. (2007). Taking a bullet for research. *Berkeleyan,* 6 December. www.berkeley. edu/news/berkeleyan/2007/12/06_watts.shtml.

Birley, M.H. (2007). A fault analysis for health impact assessment: Procurement, competence, expectations, and jurisdictions. *Impact Assessment and Project Appraisal* 25(4): 281–9.

Cesarz, E., S. Morrison and J. Cooke (2003). Alienation and militancy in Nigeria's Niger Delta. *CSIS Notes*, May. www.csis.org/africa/sarah.htm.

Chukwuani, C.M., et al. (2006). A baseline survey of the primary health care system in southeastern Nigeria. *Health Policy* 77: 182–201.

Collier, P., and A. Hoeffler (2000). Justice-seeking and loot-seeking in civil war. Paper for Conference on Economic Agendas in Civil Wars, London, 26–27 April.

ERA/FoEN (Environmental Rights Action/Friends of the Earth) (2005). *The Shell Report: Continuing abuses in Nigeria 10 years after Ken Saro-Wiwa*. Benin City: ERA/FoEN.

Essential Action and Global Exchange (2000). *Oil for nothing: Multinational corporations, environmental destruction, death and impunity in the Niger Delta*. www.essentialaction. org/shell/report/index.html.

Faleyimu, B.L., et al. (2000). Facilitators of sexual networking at oil locations in Nigeria: Implications for women in the shadow of AIDS. Abstract. International Conference on AIDS, 9–14 July.

Falola, T., and A. Genova (2005). *The politics of the global oil industry: An introduction*. New York: Praeger/Greenwood.

Foster, J.B. (2006). A warning to Africa: The new U.S. imperial grand strategy. *Monthly Review*, June. www.monthlyreview.org/0606jbf.html.

Friends of the Earth (2000). *Shareholder activity as a tool for corporate transparency and democracy*. www.foe.org/international/shareholder/toolsfordemocracy.html.

Gary, I., and T.L. Karl (2003). *Bottom of the barrel: Africa's oil boom and the poor*. Washington DC: Catholic Relief Services.

Ghazvinian, J. (2007). The curse of oil. *Virginia Quarterly Review*. www.vqronline. org/printmedia.php/prmMediaID/9388.

Hargreaves, S. (2002). Time to right the wrongs: Improving basic health care in Nigeria. *The Lancet* 359: 2030–35.

Hodges, T. (2003). *Angola: Anatomy of an oil state*. Indiana: Indiana University Press.

HRW (Human Rights Watch) (2004). *Violence in Nigeria's oil rich Rivers State in 2004: The emergence of armed groups in Rivers State*. New York.

HRW (2007). *Chop fine: The human rights impact of local government corruption and mismanagement in Rivers State, Nigeria*. New York.

Ibeanu, O. (2002). Janus unbounded: Petrobusiness and petropolitics in the Niger Delta. *Review of African Political Economy* 29(91): 163–7.

Izugbara, C., and C. Otutubikey (2005). Ashawo suppose shine her eyes: Female sex workers and sex work risks in Nigeria. *Health, Risk and Society* 7(2): 141–59.

Karl, T.L. (1997). *The paradox of plenty: Oil booms and petro-states*. Berkeley: University of California Press.

Lubeck, P., et al. (2007). *Convergent interests: U.S. energy security and the 'securing' of Nigerian democracy*. Washington DC: Center for International Policy report, February.

MSF (Médecins Sans Frontières) (2006). MSF activity report on Nigeria. www.doctorswithoutborders.org/news/nigeria.cfm.

Odey, J.O. (2005). *Democracy and the ripples of executive rascality*. Enugu: Snaap Press.

Okanta, I., and O. Douglas (2003). *Where vultures feast: Shell, human rights, and oil*. London and New York: Verso.

Osuoka, A., and P. Roderick (2005). *Gas flaring in Nigeria: A human rights, environmental and economic monstrosity*. Amsterdam: Friends of the Earth International Climate Justice Programme.

Peluso, N., and M. Watts (2001). *Violent environments*. New York: Cornell University Press.

Piller, C., et al. (2007). Dark cloud over good works of Gates Foundation: The world's largest philanthropy pours money into investments that are hurting many of the people its grants aim to help. *Los Angeles Times*, 7 January.

Quist-Arcon, O. (2007). Gas flaring disrupts life in oil-producing delta. National Public Radio morning edition, 24 July. www.npr.org/templates/story/story.php?storyId=12175714.

Sachs, J., and A.M. Warner (1995). *Natural resource abundance and economic growth*. Development Discussion Paper no. 517a. Cambridge MA: Harvard Institute for International Development.

Schimmer, B., and Chikwe Ihekweazu (2006). Polio eradication and measles immunisation in Nigeria. *Lancet Infectious Diseases* 6: 63–5.

Seidman, G. (2003). Monitoring multinationals: Lessons from the anti-apartheid era. *Politics and Society* 31(3): 381–406.

Shah, S. (2004). *Crude: The story of oil*. London: Seven Stories Press.

Shaxson, N. (2005). New approaches to volatility: Dealing with the resource curse in Sub-Saharan Africa. *International Affairs* 81(2): 341–60.

UNAIDS Joint United Nations Programme on HIV/AIDS (2006). *Report on the global AIDS epidemic*. www.unaids.org/en/KnowledgeCentre/HIVData/GlobalReport/2006/.

UNDP (United Nations Development Programme) (2006). *Niger Delta Human Development Report*. Abuja.

United Nations (2003). Norms on the responsibilities of transnational corporations and other business enterprises with regard to human rights. U.N. Doc. E/CN.4/Sub.2/2003/12/Rev.2. www1.umn.edu/humanrts/links/norms-Aug2003.html.

US EIA (United States Energy Information Administration) (2007). *Country Analysis Brief: Nigeria*. www.eia.doe.gov/emeu/cabs/Nigeria/pdf.

Vines, A. (2005). Combating light weapons proliferation in West Africa. *International Affairs* 81(2): 341–60.

Wallis, D. (2007). Oil profits boost east Africa exploration. Reuters. http://uk.reuters.com/articlePrint?articleId=UKL1921930120070222.

Watts, M. (2004). Resource curse? Governmentality, oil and power in the Niger Delta, Nigeria. *Geopolitics* 9(1): 50–81.

Watts, M. (2005). Righteous oil? Human rights, the oil complex and corporate social responsibility. *Annual Review of Environment and Resources* 30: 373–407.

Watts, M. (2007). Crisis in Nigeria: Oil curse. *Counterpunch*, 2 January. www.counterpunch.org/watts01022007.html.

World Bank (1995). *Defining an environmental strategy for the Niger Delta*. Washington DC: World Bank.

Zalik, A. (2004). The peace of the graveyard: The voluntary principles of security and human rights in the Niger Delta. In L. Assassi, K. Van der Pijl and D. Wigan (eds), *Global regulation: Managing crises after the imperial turn*. London: Palgrave.

Zalik, A., and M. Watts (2006). Imperial oil: Petroleum politics in the Nigerian Delta and the new scramble for Africa. *International Socialist Review*, April.

C7 Humanitarian aid

Much of humanitarian assistance is about health: preventing death and restoring well-being after a disaster. However, if humanitarian assistance is to live up to its name, the political context of emergency aid needs to be understood.

This chapter has two sections. The first considers the concepts and actors involved in humanitarian assistance, in particular the frequently underestimated role of local actors, and the role of the media. The inequalities that underlie disaster response is another theme of this section. It concludes with examples of the use of the rights-based approach to improve the quality of humanitarian assistance. The second section is about the commercialisation of humanitarian assistance and the co-option of humanitarian assistance for foreign policy objectives.

Concepts and actors

> One country's emergency may end up being better than a normal day in another. (Cheechi 2005)

Humanitarianism includes the belief that a human life has the same value wherever an individual is born: 'There should be the same attention to northern Uganda as to northern Iraq, the same attention to the Congo as there was to Kosovo.' However, when Jan Egeland, then UN Under-Secretary General for Humanitarian Affairs, said this in 2005, he continued, 'that is not the case today'. Which situations are called emergencies and the degree of humanitarian response they receive vary according to who is affected, where, and how they relate to global politics.

TABLE C7.1   **Rustaq earthquake in Afghanistan and Northridge earthquake in Los Angeles**

Indicator	Rustaq, February 1998	Northridge, January 1994
People dead	2,323	57 (33–73)
People injured	818	9,000 (8,000–12,000)
Houses destroyed	8,094	
Buildings and structures damaged		112,000 (8,000–12,000)
Livestock killed	6,715	
Production losses		$220,300,000
People dead	High number of deaths	Low number of deaths due to quality of construction, general infrastructure and disaster preparedness
People injured	Injuries very likely under-reported: untreated unless serious and only if facilities available	All injuries registered at treatment centres and for insurance purposes
Houses destroyed	Uninhabitable houses registered	
Buildings and structures damaged		All damaged structures recorded
Livestock killed	Not monetised	
Production losses		Monetised

Source: Bolin 1998; Longford 1998.

A disaster has been defined as 'a situation or event which overwhelms local capacity, necessitating a request to a national or international level for external assistance' (CRED 2008). The term 'complex humanitarian emergency' attempts to capture the political and social upheaval, the deterioration in all aspects of living conditions, and the indeterminate length of some emergencies.

The most common indicator used to define an 'acute emergency' is a doubling of the Crude Mortality Rate (CMR). If the baseline CMR is not known, a CMR greater than 1 death per 10,000 people per day is considered to be an emergency (Sphere Project 2004a). This means that a country with a high 'normal' CMR has a much higher threshold for a disaster to be considered an emergency than a country with a lower initial CMR. Poorer countries with a high baseline CMR therefore have greater difficulty having their disasters defined as acute emergencies, whilst also tending to have fewer resources with which to respond.

The data in Table C7.1 are from the Rustaq earthquake in Afghanistan and the Northridge earthquake in Los Angeles in the United States. Both were caused by a similar level of shock. These figures – including what information is and is not available – illustrate the hugely unequal circumstances of the people behind the statistics of the two disasters.

Natural or man-made and implications for accountability

The Centre for Research on the Epidemiology of Disasters (CRED) lists the following as 'natural' disasters: drought, earthquake, epidemic, extreme temperature, flood, insect infestation, slides, volcano, wave/surge, wildfires and wind storm.

There is much debate about the word 'natural' with its implications of inevitability. Scientists concluded in 2006 that the rise in frequency of hurricanes cannot be explained by natural variability. Despite this, a reluctance to accept the underlying causes of natural disasters persists because of concerns about responsibility and liability. This could particularly be the case with extreme weather caused by climate change, as richer countries produce close to 80 per cent of carbon emissions, while Asia and Africa are home to 62 per cent of 'natural' disasters and 74 per cent of the resulting economic damage (Hoyois et al. 2007).

Is it or isn't it, and does it matter?

The definition of an emergency has several important implications:

- Apart from the International Committee of the Red Cross (ICRC) and certain United Nations agencies with particular mandates, humanitarian actors have to be invited to provide humanitarian assistance by a national government. This is normally done by a government declaring an emergency and signalling a need for international help.
- Once there is a declared emergency, donor funds can be disbursed more quickly than otherwise is the case.
- The declaration of an emergency can also spur organisations to deliver assistance without the consent of a country's government. This can be done for purely humanitarian purposes, but can also be done to justify external interference in a country for strategic and foreign policy purposes.

Who responds and who is seen to respond: the role of local actors

Most definitions of 'disaster' refer to the need for 'outside' assistance. In fact much disaster relief, particularly in the early stages, is provided locally.

After the Rustaq earthquake in north-east Afghanistan it was found that the response of survivors, neighbours, local government and the local military was swift and effective and that many presumed dead were actually with friends and relatives in neighbouring villages (Longford 1998). In Indonesia after the tsunami, 91 per cent of rescue services in the first 48 hours were provided by private individuals (Fritz Institute 2005). Despite this, there is a lack of investment in local and regional preparedness for responding to disasters. Instead, considerable resources are invested in, for example, search-and-rescue teams coming from countries outside the affected region.

The day after the Pakistan earthquake in October 2005, a reporter wrote: 'I've literally seen hundreds of people being pulled from the wreckage of Balakot' (BBC News 2005). Two days or so later, the 38-member UK Fire Search and Rescue Team arrived (with 37 personnel from other UK agencies) and were 'involved in 14 rescues' (FRS Online 2006). It has to be asked if some of the considerable resources involved in this would not have been better spent on improving local or regional disaster preparedness.

Perceptions and the media

Over the last twenty years there has been improvement in the way the media cover disasters: local actors are more frequently interviewed, and local responses receive more attention. However, coverage is still short-term, puts too much emphasis on the influence of international aid, and is sometimes politically biased. All too often in the Western media, a stereotypical and unbalanced picture of 'givers and receivers' is projected.

Hurricane Katrina was one of the most extensively analysed disasters with regard to its media coverage. Although this was a disaster that occurred in the rich North, it amply demonstrates the way in which disasters can be distorted along racial and political lines. One study found that 'minorities are disproportionately shown in a passive or "victim" role and are rarely shown in positions of expertise' (Vick and Perkins n.d.), Another noted that the media 'overestimated crime and panic (amongst the largely black population) and underestimated acts of kindness' (Tierny et al. 2006), while a third report described how misreporting could have 'delayed the arrival of relief teams and volunteers who feared for their safety' (Starks 2006).

Relief and development: difficulties with the divide

The short time frames within which donor funding for emergencies has to be spent have implications for making the transition from an 'emergency response' to the more long-term requirements for reconstruction and development.

For example, after the 2000 floods in Mozambique, donors were keen to support the rehabilitation of health centres: an essential activity, and one with a clearly demonstrable outcome within a reasonably short and predictable time frame. However, infrastructure such as roads had not yet been reconstructed and in some cases construction materials had to be flown in at great expense. With more flexibility it would have been possible to prioritise road-building while health services continued to be delivered out of temporary structures, and to carry out the rehabilitation of health facilities when materials could have been brought in by road. This would have been more cost-effective.

For health workers trying to ensure a continued service supply, the 'end' of an emergency may present particular challenges: 'If during the war you have access to health care and all of a sudden that disappears when peace comes, you start to wonder if only conflict is worthwhile' (Walter Gwenigale, Liberian minister of health, quoted in *Independent*, 24 May 2007).

The conflict in Liberia lasted fourteen years, ending in 2003, during which time an estimated 80 per cent of health care was supported by non-governmental organisations (NGOs). Yet there was no replacement or phasing-out strategy for the departing 'emergency' organisations, and by 2007 maternal mortality and life expectancy rates were still worse than during many emergencies. In general, those organisations which try to continue working in countries in the medium term after emergencies have problems accessing funds.

Prevention and disaster preparedness

Disaster prevention and preparedness should be an integral follow-on from any emergency. However, being a preventive measure that necessitates long-term commitment, it is nearly always insufficiently funded – with the tsunami being a welcome exception, as there have been considerable investments in preparing for future tsunamis.

Food security indicators can act as an early warning of potential disaster, and over the last twenty-five years have received more attention from the UN and the humanitarian community. However, more is needed. The opinion of senior nutritionists with regard to the Ethiopian emergency in 2003 was that 'the current crisis is partly caused by structural food insecurity and should have been countered by long-term development planning rather than emergency aid' (Institute for International Studies 2003).

The need for disaster preparedness has been urgently underlined by climate change. Taking this into account, some civil society organisations are promoting disaster risk reduction methods which integrate continual preparation for disasters into 'regular' development programmes.

IMAGE C7.1 **Woman in India carrying water in area where citizens were relocated following a natural disaster**

Addressing vulnerabilities through long-term prevention and preparedness programmes involves a degree of wealth redistribution which may challenge the status quo, as it did in El Salvador following Hurricane Mitch (Wisner 2001). This needs to be anticipated and absorbed into the strategy of disaster preparedness programmes.

Attempts to achieve minimum standards: the rights-based approach

During the first half of the 1990s there was increasing discussion about the right to receive humanitarian assistance of a certain quality. One of the outcomes was the Sphere Project for Minimum Standards in Humanitarian Assistance, which through a consultative process produced standards and associated indicators in four technical areas: water, sanitation and hygiene promotion; food security, nutrition and food aid; shelter settlements and non-food items; and health services (Sphere Project 2004b).

While a few organisations considered the standards potentially restrictive, many adopted them and now conduct voluntary self-monitoring of their implementation. Another aim of the Sphere Project was to shift underlying attitudes away from 'charity' towards a duty to provide assistance. Despite these efforts, those receiving assistance are in many instances still treated as a less powerful 'partner'.

While the Sphere Project concentrates on minimum standards for interventions, humanitarian assistance can also be used as an integral part of directly empowering civil society to demand their rights. One year after the Gujarat earthquake in 2001 local organisations, supported by the international NGO ActionAid, protested that many people had not received the compensation they were owed from the district government. These organisations not only provided humanitarian assistance but actively engaged with disadvantaged local groups to raise awareness of their rights and break down communal barriers.

Geographical and political priorities: size and quality of response

Most humanitarian organisations make great efforts to respond according to need in disasters: this is the basis for the core principle of impartiality. Individual programmes often achieve this within a contained population, but when the global picture is considered the humanitarian response is far from impartial.

In 1998 Julius Nyerere pointed out that a country was more likely to be a priority for humanitarian assistance if it had the potential to create a refugee problem for donor countries. For example, while $166 per capita was spent on humanitarian assistance in the former republic of Yugoslavia, only $2 per capita was spent in Eritrea (WHO 2008).

The war in Iraq demonstrates the way in which humanitarian assistance is distorted. As of July 2007, approximately 4 million Iraqis – either refugees or internally displaced persons – were receiving inadequate general rations and poor shelter. The insufficient response in 2007 reflects the nature of changing political priorities. In 2003, the planned swift and generous response would potentially have won local hearts and minds; in 2007 the refugees and displaced only serve as a reminder of how badly things have gone wrong for the US and its allies.

Changing political priorities can also mean that the pledges made in the immediate aftermath of an emergency are not delivered. Of the $9 billion pledged to Central America following Hurricane Mitch in 1998, only 50 per cent had been delivered by the end of 2004. A year after the Bam earthquake in Iran in 2004, only 12 per cent of the promised $1 billion had been delivered (Mansilla 2005).

On the other hand, donations from the public and non-governmental bodies are often underestimated as they may not be captured in standard calculations. Humanitarian resources received from the public globally almost certainly exceed those from official sources. Funds from diaspora groups, Islamic agencies and Islamic government-to-government funding are thought to be particularly prone to underestimation, as is the investment in time and resources involved in the response of the disaster survivors themselves.

Despite the considerable effort made by those working in humanitarian assistance to keep their work impartial, the type and degree of response are still influenced by the foreign policy objectives and national interests of the contributing nations. One clear illustration of this is the recent history of food aid.

Food aid: for whose benefit?

The United States has historically provided large amounts of food aid for humanitarian programmes. As discussed in Chapter D2.1, the US has used food aid to subsidise its domestic agricultural industry.

For those at the receiving end, food aid can result in unfamiliar food of dubious quality being supplied late, and sometimes with damaging effects on fragile, local markets. Food aid provided in Ethiopia in 2002, for example, flooded the market and undermined local farmers still further.

Attempts to provide genetically modified (GM) crops in recent years (at the same time that some European countries were refusing GM products) is another illustration of inappropriate food aid. One concern of governments receiving the food aid was that farmers would save some of the GM crops for the next planting season. But as GM seed does not propagate itself, this could mean that no seed would be produced for the next harvest and that national control of the seed stock would be severely damaged. In August 2002, when President Mwanawasa of Zambia refused to accept imports of GM maize as food aid, it led to claims that he was 'refusing to feed GM grain to the starving'. The Zambian government cited their concerns about future seed stocks, and offered to accept the food if it was milled, eliminating the possibility of GM crop planting. However, the US government refused to donate cash for milling or local purchase, unlike the UK government, which supported the purchase of local and regional grain.

Highjacking humanitarianism – intervention and invasion

Humanitarian assistance has always often been used to further the foreign policy objectives or national interests of donor countries. In the case of the UN agencies, funding reflects the priorities of donor member states.

Humanitarian space has been defined as 'a space of freedom in which we are free to evaluate needs, free to monitor the distribution and use of relief goods, and free to have a dialogue with the people' (Wagner 2005). This space has been challenged in recent years. Security concerns in Iraq and Afghanistan were high on the agenda of the 160 NGOs that met at a meeting in Washington DC in May 2004. At the same time NGO staff were avoiding using agency T-shirts and painting over logos on their vehicles to decrease the risk to staff through perceived association with the countries of military actors in the conflicts. There was 'a lot of concern in the humanitarian community about whether the definitions of humanitarianism are changing', potentially making aggressive acts more acceptable to the public, and easier to justify to an electorate or political opposition.

The bombing of Kosovo saw the first use of the term 'humanitarian bombing'. In fact the bombing, which was justified on the grounds of humanitarianism, was also the cause of a humanitarian disaster. Events in Afghanistan and Iraq have also shown how wars undertaken supposedly to liberate people from tyrannies have been conducted in ways that have decreased the safety, security, health and well-being of the population.

However, a study carried out in 2007 indicates that for the people of Iraq the underlying principles of humanitarianism had not changed: 'Although humanitarian principles are in general warmly embraced in Iraq, we also heard with consistency that humanitarian action that falls short of the ideal is recognized as such and is prone to rejection' (Hansen 2007). Association with the invading military forces, and a blurring of military 'hearts and minds' activities and humanitarian action, have diminished humanitarian space. This reduces access to assistance, and puts both humanitarian actors and those they are trying to help at greater risk. According to Mark Malloch-Brown, former UN Deputy Secretary-General: 'I have watched the work I used to do get steadily more dangerous as it is seen as serving Western interests rather than universal values.'

Humanitarian space reflects an understanding by all sides in a conflict of the right of those affected to receive humanitarian aid. It implies that armed forces will take the necessary steps to allow humanitarian activities to take place. It needs an understanding of the risks for civilians, including those providing assistance, of any association with military actors.

In the north and east of Sri Lanka, assistance was able to be provided during a very volatile and violent period (1987–90) by establishing clear and agreed travelling procedures between humanitarian actors, the Indian Peace Keeping Force (IPKF), the Sri Lankan army and airforce, and the Liberation Tigers of Tamil Ealam.

The influence of 'new' actors: the military and private business

Over the last fifteen years the military have played an increased role in humanitarian assistance, with straplines such as 'a force for good in the world' and recruitment that emphasises the 'humanitarian' aspects of the

job. The Defence Medical Corps – or equivalent – of most armies traditionally had the responsibility of ensuring the health of the armed forces. While
there have always been instances when the military has treated civilians, this
has previously been done in an ad hoc manner. Their present role implies
a more formalised function in treating civilians.

Actions related to civilian health have often been carried out by the
military in the name of winning the 'hearts and minds' of the local population; it 'gives the military commander a 'carrot' to complement his 'stick' in
gaining compliance'. 'Hearts and minds' activities have more recently been
called Quick Impact Projects (QIPs). If it can be claimed that armed forces
are routinely supplying humanitarian assistance, then claims that military
interventions are 'humanitarian' can be strengthened. Given their need
to win hearts and minds in the short term, the medium- to longer-term
implications of these projects are likely to be ignored.

For non-military humanitarian actors, an expanded role for the military
can also mean a loss of perceived impartiality, with consequences for the
security of humanitarian workers as well as those they try to assist.

Humanitarian aid has become increasingly project-oriented, with an
emphasis on demonstrable impact, in all but the very acute stage of emergencies. This can restrict responsiveness to changing local contexts, impose
impractical time frames and limit flexible strategic planning. While impact
assessment is important, it can also lead to perverse incentives if inappropriately applied, and to humanitarian actors doing what they will be able
to measure, rather than doing what is more appropriate and sustainable.

In 1996, WorldAid 96, a major global expo and conference on emergency
relief, was held in Switzerland. It attracted many NGOs, but also 274 companies. Products from landmine flailers to water purifiers were on display.
Discussion at the event showed considerable confusion as to its purpose:
was it to market the items that humanitarian agencies could purchase, or
was it suggesting that private companies could better provide humanitarian
services? The private delivery of humanitarian assistance raises concerns
about profit maximisation and the lack of market regulation in the context
of vulnerable 'consumers'.

It has been claimed that private companies are more efficient than the
voluntary sector, although the evidence does not support this. The United
States Agency for International Development (USAID) awarded Abt Associates – a Massachusetts-based consulting firm – a contract for US$43
million to improve the health sector and distribute medical supplies in
Iraq. According to a USAID audit, 'medical kits intended for 600 clinics
contained damaged or useless equipment', and USAID eventually cancelled
the contract.

BOX C7.1   **The Humanitarian Response Index**[1]

The Humanitarian Response Index (HRI) is a recently developed tool for measuring the performance of donors in relation to the widely accepted Principles and Good Practice of Humanitarian Donorship.

In light of the poor practices described in this chapter, it is hoped that the Index will catalyse more equitable and ethical practices by the donor community, as well as improve the efficiency and quality of humanitarian action.

The tool uses 25 quantitative and 32 qualitative indicators to measure donor performance in terms of five pillars of humanitarian assistance: responding to humanitarian needs, integrating relief and development, working with humanitarian partners, implementing international guiding principles, and promoting learning and accountability.

According to the Index, which was published for the first time in 2007, Sweden, Norway, Denmark and Netherlands were the best performers among the 23 donors that were assessed. Portugal, Italy and Greece fared the worst. The US is 16th on the list of 23. Canada, whose humanitarian assistance is discussed in Chapter D2.2, is in 7th place. But Cuba, which mounted a humanitarian response to the earthquake in Pakistan, is not included in the HRI.

The 2004 Indian Ocean tsunami brought about increased involvement of private companies in humanitarian relief for no immediate profit motive, for example through the donation of goods. However, the motivation behind this engagement appears to be driven, at least in part, by a desire to build a positive brand and to 'insure' against potential future political crises, and by the chance to gather business intelligence (Binder and Witte 2007).

These are clearly different from humanitarian motivations, as represented by the humanitarian charter of the Sphere Project or the code of conduct for the International Red Cross and Red Crescent Movement and NGOs in disaster relief. Nevertheless the international human resource director of one large humanitarian NGO has been reported as saying that they were 'openly inviting applicants from the business world and the public sector because their skills are transferable'.

The role of civil society

Civil society has a vital role to play in preserving humanitarian space, whether it is receiving assistance, providing assistance or monitoring events. What should be done will depend on the particular context. However, some key issues can be highlighted:

- ensuring that local actors are recognised and supported during emergencies, particularly in relation to defining needs and priorities and developing strategies;
- advocating for changes to reduce the inequalities that underpin vulnerability to disasters;
- supporting the further use of the Sphere Project's minimum standards for the implementation of humanitarian interventions;
- using the Humanitarian Response Index to campaign for better donor practice (see Box C7.1);
- campaigning for international humanitarian law to be respected in all disaster situations.

Note

1. For more information on the HRI, see www.daraint.org/web_en/hri.html.

References

BBC News (2005). Reporter's Log, S Asia earthquake. Andrew North Blalkot, Pakistan, 8/9 October, 14.15 GMT. http://news.bbc.co.uk/1/hi/world/south_asia/4325640.stm.

Binder, A., and J. Witte (2007). *Business engagement in humanitarian relief: key trends and policy implications.* HPG background paper. London: Global Public Policy Institute and Overseas Development Institute.

Bolin, R., and L. Stanford (1998). The Northridge earthquake: Community-based approaches to unmet recovery needs. *Disasters* 22(1): 21–38.

CRED (Centre for Research on the Epidemiology of Disaster) (2008). www.em-dat. net/disasters/profiles.php.

Cheechi, F. (2005). Background paper prepared for the WHO workshop Tracking Health Performance and Humanitarian Outcomes, 1–2 December, Geneva: IASC/WHO.

Fritz Institute (2005). *Recipient perceptions of aid effectiveness: Rescue, relief and rehabilitation in tsunami affected Indonesia, India and Sri Lanka.* San Francisco: Fritz Institute. www.fritzinstitute.org.

FRS Online (2006). Eight days in Pakistan: UK search and rescue teams save lives. www.frsonline.fire.gov.uk.

Hansen, G. (2007). *Taking sides or saving lives: Existential choices for the humanitarian enterprise in Iraq.* Briefing paper. Feinstein International Centre. Medford: Tufts University.

Hoyois, P., et al. (2007). *Annual Disaster Statistical Review.* Numbers and Trends 5.1. CRED and University of Louvain.

Institute for International Studies (2003). Aid policy and practice. In *Food Security and Emergencies.* Copenhagen: Institute for International Studies.

Longford, S. (1998). *Study of the UN system-wide response to the earthquake in Rustaq, North Eastern Afghanistan, 4th Feb 1998.* Geneva: UN OCHA.

Mansilla, E. (2005). Smoke and mirrors: Deficiencies in disaster funding. *British Medical Journal* 330: 247–50.

Sphere Project (2004a). *Health services: Prioritising services.* Health systems and infrastructure guidance Note 3. Geneva.

Sphere Project (2004b). *Humanitarian charter and minimum standards in disaster response.* Geneva.

Starks, T. (2006). Katrina panel indicts response. *CQ weekly*, 64, 00488. CQ Public Affairs Collection.

Tierny, K., et al. (2006). Metaphors matter: Disaster myths, media frames and their consequences in Hurricane Katrina. *Annals of the American Academy of Political Science* 604: 57–81.

Vick, J., and D. Perkins (n.d.). 'Came hell and high water': the intersection of Hurricane Katrina, the news media and poverty. Centre for Community Studies, Peabody College, Vanderbilt University.

Wagner, J. (2005). An IHL/ICRC perspective on 'humanitarian space'. *Humanitarian Exchange* 32. Humanitarian Practice Network. London: Overseas Development Institute.

WHO (2008). *Health Action in Crises*. Analyzing Disrupted Health Services – Manual Module 3: Country Background: Humanitarian Aid. www.who.int/hac/techguidance/tools/disrupted_sectors/module_03/en/index4.html.

Wisner, B. (2001). Risk and the neoliberal state: Why post-Mitch lessons didn't reduce El Salvador's earthquake losses. *Disasters* 25(3): 251–68.

C8 Education

At the turn of the millennium, leaders of rich and poor countries together committed themselves to a set of Education For All (EFA) goals aimed at guaranteeing every child and adult the chance to transform their lives through education. Two of the EFA targets were incorporated into the Millennium Development Goals (MDGs): completion of primary schooling for all children, and elimination of gender inequality at all levels of education.

Within two years, the Education for All – Fast Track Initiative (FTI) was launched with the aim of ensuring that good education plans were backed by 'more, better, faster' aid. Since then, the numbers of children enrolling in school has been rising at an unprecedented rate: 37 million more children were brought into the schooling system between 2000 and 2005, and the gender gap is slowly closing (FTI Secretariat 2006).

Most progress is being made where the challenges are greatest – in sub-Saharan Africa (SSA) and West and South Asia. But while this progress is encouraging, challenges endure. In SSA, only 63 per cent of children finish primary school; pupil : teacher ratios have skyrocketed, reaching over 65 : 1 in countries such as Mozambique, Malawi and Burundi (UNESCO 2006). This chapter lays out an agenda for shared concern and joint action for the education and health constituencies.[1]

Mutual benefits, common agendas

There are a number of commonalities in the struggles to secure rights to education and health. The following section examines some key issues facing the movements championing these rights. It calls for an organised

IMAGE C8.1   **Schoolgirl in Mozambique**

and politicised response by civil society actors to promote and support citizens' claim-making.

Public goods need state action

Historical evidence shows that large-scale gains in health and education have been made when the state takes responsibility for providing essential services (PSI 2005). No rich country achieved universal schooling without an organised programme of action led by government, backed with public resources, which was designed to reach the entire population. In various breakthrough periods Botswana, Zimbabwe, Mauritius, Sri Lanka, South Korea, Malaysia, Barbados, Costa Rica, Cuba and Kerala all achieved primary school enrolments close to 100 per cent for girls and boys, decades before other developing countries. Significantly, child deaths were simultaneously reduced (Mehrotra and Jolly 1997).

As attention turns to regions and countries where improvements in education and health remain elusive, international debates have focused increasingly on the role of the non-state sector to resolve the crisis in provision. There are calls from some quarters – especially the World Economic Forum and the World Bank – to further liberalise the sectors and create 'global industries' in education and health. A growing body of research notes that private and other non-state providers have mushroomed in response to state failure, and argues that this private provision is more 'pro-poor' due to the presumed greater accountability and responsiveness

IMAGE C8.2   **Students in Sri Lanka**

of providers to client demand (Tooley 2001). The proliferation of private and community-run schools in Zambia and Pakistan is cited as a product of the poor 'voting with their feet', seeking better and more accessible services because the state has let them down.

Donor governments and international institutions have promulgated multi-stakeholder provision as the magic bullet that will enable countries to achieve the MDGs. The 2004 *World Development Report* proposed market and private-sector solutions, and privatisation remains a condition of multilateral lending to the poorest countries.

The reality is that the increased presence of private actors is an ideologically driven trend that serves the material interests of some better than others. Recent studies reveal that non-state solutions are not a universal panacea, do not work, and are not what people want (Oxfam 2006). Privately provided services are often too expensive for poor people and the profit motive skews provision away from the poorest and most disadvantaged. The so-called promotion of 'community participation' in education has been top-down, with limited consultation with communities about the ways in which they may (or may not) wish to participate (Rose 2003). The outcome has been to shift state responsibility for the provision of services on to communities.

The charging of fees – in both the private and public spheres – is still alarmingly prevalent. In education, although an increasing number of countries are abolishing tuition fees, with positive effects on enrolment

FIGURE C8.1   **The value of teachers' salaries has fallen dramatically over the last twenty-five years**

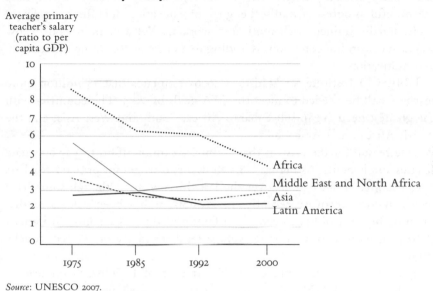

Source: UNESCO 2007.

rates, fees are expanding for other costs. One study (Tomasevski 2006) identified seventeen different types of fees facing a child in school and found that charges were present in over ninety countries worldwide. Many governments which pronounce education to be 'free' charge for textbooks, uniforms, transport, school equipment, heating or building maintenance. The report cites numerous countries where poor people have to pay unacceptable proportions of their incomes to educate their children, and where children are forced to work to pay the cost of their primary education.

User fees are among the most socially retrogressive policy measures that can be implemented by governments, and a major cause of inequitable access. They force families into debt; into making painful choices between boys or girls going to school; or into seeing their children go hungry to pay for medical care for another family member. In the more extreme cases, poor people are excluded altogether. Women and girls bear the brunt of the impact. In contrast, when Uganda made schooling free for up to four children in every household, primary school enrolments nearly doubled between 1990 and 2000 and gender gaps in education were virtually eliminated (Oxfam 2006).

Workers are the cornerstone

One factor crucially determines a country's ability to make speedy and meaningful progress towards the goal of education for all: a supply of professionally trained, well-motivated workers. Yet a combination of low wages and working conditions is leading to a crisis of recruitment, retention and motivation.

UNESCO Institute for Statistics (2006) estimates that 18 million more teachers will be needed to meet the EFA goals by 2015. The countries with the greatest need are in sub-Saharan Africa, South and West Asia, and the North African and Arab states.

One reason for the crisis is that countries cannot afford to pay adequate salaries and benefits. As Figure C8.1 shows, real wages for primary teachers have declined in all regions over the last thirty years, although some have seen a modest recovery recently. In Zambia, it has been calculated that the monthly cost of basic needs for a family of six was 1.4 million kwacha (US$410), more than twice the average teacher's salary of 660,000 kwacha ($191).

The situation is exacerbated by the impact of HIV/AIDS on teacher mortality rates (UNESCO 2006). Experts estimated between 1,100 and 3,000 teacher deaths as a result of AIDS in each of Kenya, Tanzania, Zambia and Mozambique in 2005.

Another cause of shortages is out-migration of teachers to countries such as the US, Canada, the UK and France. In some cases, rich countries have been actively recruiting teachers from countries such as Guyana. This has led directly to the adoption by ministers of education of the Commonwealth Teacher Recruitment Protocol, a voluntary code which complements the 2003 Commonwealth Code of Practice for the International Recruitment of Health Workers.

Paying up: rich and poor country governments must meet their commitments

A fee-free, public system staffed by motivated professionals implies a substantial cost for governments. Following years of cuts and constraints to public spending on education, there are some modestly encouraging trends. The most recent EFA Global Monitoring Report (UNESCO 2007) showed that about two-thirds of countries raised public spending on education as a share of gross national product between 1999 and 2004. The share of education in total government expenditure increased in about three-quarters of countries with data. Through the Education for All – Fast Track Initiative, some thirty-two low-income countries have met the stringent tests of political commitment and sound planning to become eligible for better and faster aid.

BOX C8.I **Migration of teachers in Guyana**

'They come back every year, and every time they come, we lose dozens of teachers', complains Avril Crawford, President of the Guyana Teachers' Union (GTU). 'They' are the British recruiters on their annual visit to Guyana to meet teachers who replied to their advertisements for applicants to teach in Britain. 'Recruitment agencies from the United States and the Bahamas are now flocking in, too. Even Botswana looks for teachers here', exclaims Avril Crawford. The Bahamas and Bermuda are the Caribbean countries that headhunt most from their neighbours. Guyana is one of the few Latin American English-speaking countries. Its teachers are highly trained, but working conditions are poor, making them more open to attractive offers from elsewhere. The highest monthly salary that a Guyanese teacher could earn is €400, which even a novice teacher in the Bahamas would spurn.

Source: Education International 2005.

However, some countries with large education challenges still do not spend anything like the sums needed to guarantee education for all citizens. Pakistan, for example, spends less than 3 per cent of its gross national product (GNP) on education. In these contexts, sustained public pressure is needed to call governments to account for their commitments.

However, the burden should not be borne by poor countries alone. Financing basic education became a mutual responsibility of poor and rich nations when 186 leaders signed a 'global compact' on education which noted that the 'international community acknowledges that many countries currently lack the resources to achieve education for all within an acceptable timeframe ... We affirm that no country seriously committed to education for all with be thwarted in their achievement of his goal by a lack of resources.'

Regrettably, commitments have not been matched by action at the scale required. The total external financing requirement for achieving the EFA goals is estimated to be $16 billion per year (DFID 2005). Aid to basic education rose steadily between 2000 and 2004, when it reached a high of $4.4 billion – still far short of the total needed. However, shockingly, it actually fell in 2005 (the latest year for which data were available).

The Global Campaign for Education (GCE) has measured each donor country's contribution to education financing and has concluded that the G7 countries are in large part responsible for the scarcity of funds. If they

BOX C8.2   **Promises to keep: how the Nine is Mine campaign is holding the Indian government accountable**

Launched by more than 4,500 children in Delhi, India, in October 2006, the 'Nine is Mine' campaign is a participatory children's advocacy initiative calling for 9 per cent of gross domestic product (GDP) to be committed to health and education. This initiative of children, schools and civil society organisations across fifteen states of India is being led by Wada Na Todo Abhiyan (WNTA) and aims to put children at the centre of an advocacy effort.

January 2007: 20 children lead the Nine is Mine delegation to meet the prime minister of India at his residence. The meeting culminated with the presentation of a giant Nine is Mine postcard representing over 200,000 signatures and a giant white band representing the Global Call to Action Against Poverty.

gave their 'fair share' contribution, this would provide an additional \$5 billion each year, enabling some 60 million more children to go to school. The amount is the equivalent of five weeks' spending on the EU Common Agricultural Policy or the cost of four US Stealth bombers (GCE 2007).

Furthermore, the aid that is provided is not targeted to the poorest countries or to those with the greatest challenges. Less than 20 per cent of aid to education is available for a list of countries defined as conflict-affected and fragile (Save the Children 2007). Far too little aid is actually spent on the core running costs of education – books, teacher salaries and classrooms. Donors persist in ensuring that aid benefits the originating countries through tying and technical cooperation. Oxfam found that in 2004, less than 8 per cent of aid was directed into government plans and budgets (Oxfam 2007).

These problems are compounded by the International Monetary Fund (IMF). By its own account, targets on low inflation and fiscal deficit have led to the adoption of public-sector wage bill ceilings in at least seventeen countries in Asia, Central America and sub-Saharan Africa (Fedelino et al. 2006). A study of three countries by ActionAid International (2005) found that these caps had devastating impacts on the availability and quality of education. Mozambique, for example, has over half a million children out of school and pupil:teacher ratios of 74:1, yet recent attempts to boost the teaching staff by 12,000 (only 10 per cent of the total needed to provide universal schooling by 2015) were cut back due to the wage bill ceiling. The Center For Global Development (2007) highlighted similar issues in the health sector and concluded that IMF wage ceilings 'sit uneasily with the designation of priority poverty-reducing expenditures' and recommended that they be dropped in all but a few extreme circumstances.

The trials of conflict and fragility: where the state is weakest

War and conflict cause damage to every aspect of society. Education structures are often targeted during civil unrest. In Liberia, 80 per cent of schools were destroyed during the civil war. As a result, conflict-affected countries have some of the highest out-of-school populations. Save the Children (2006) estimates 43 million children to be out of school in thirty conflict-affected countries. In DRC alone 5 million primary school children are out of school. In Darfur, only one in every three children is in primary school.

The longer a conflict continues, the harder it is to fund and administer education systems. Holding national exams, paying teachers, and getting materials to school become increasingly difficult. Yet the benefit of school and education is what can bring the hope for peace and development. Schools not only bring life-saving skills, but offer a place of routine and play; somewhere to escape violence, and to reunite friends and families during times of trauma.

Despite the acute needs of conflict-affected countries, they receive up to 50 per cent less education aid than other low-income countries. Sierra Leone recently developed a new education plan to realise the universal primary education goal by 2015. Over a hundred schools have been built, over a million textbooks have been purchased, and teachers and school management committees are being trained. Liberia is in a similar situation, but both countries are awaiting the full amount of financing needed to enable them to put their education plans fully into place.

Stemming the tide? Education and HIV/AIDS

The misconceptions and stigma attached to HIV/AIDS often penetrate school walls. Orphaned children may be discriminated against by their classmates and teachers. HIV-positive teachers risk facing discrimination if they disclose their status. Sexual violence within schools, between classmates or between teachers and pupils, puts students at risk of HIV infection. Many schools fail to provide adequate HIV/AIDS training to teachers, or an age-appropriate HIV/AIDS curriculum, because of moral arguments about sex education. The restriction of USAID funding to 'abstinence until marriage' programmes has left many young people without access to condoms, and lacking information about safer sex (HRW 2005).

Quality education, preferably gender-equitable in nature, is, however, increasingly recognised as a 'social vaccine' against HIV and AIDS (Hargreaves and Boler 2006). Research has shown that educating girls is one of the best ways to tackle the HIV epidemic. However, education systems have varied greatly in their response. In Asia and Latin America, HIV/AIDS has largely been regarded as a responsibility of the department of health. In Africa, ministries of education have set up HIV/AIDS units but these are frequently under-resourced. Their lack of engagement with civil society, teachers and ministries of health has led to HIV/AIDS curricula being ignored, unvalued or misunderstood by teachers (Boler and Jellema 2005).

But where schools are safe and non-discriminatory places of learning, where teachers are trained to impart life skills and provide accurate knowledge, where there is sensitivity to the needs of orphans and vulnerable children, and when governments protect HIV-positive teachers and provide them with access to treatment, education can be the most effective of all public health interventions responding to the HIV/AIDS epidemic.

Gender inequality

In situations where governments face multiple challenges in the provision of education and health, girls and women nearly always fare the worst. Moreover, when girls get to schools, they are often not equipped to benefit them. A lack of toilets, for example, poses a particular problem for adolescent girls during menstruation. Research (Migwi 2007) in Kenya found that girls often missed school one week in every month due to their menstrual cycle.

However, quality and gender-equitable education is crucial for tackling the inequalities that women and girls face. It enables them to take care of their own reproductive health, protect themselves from HIV, and raise healthier children, who are then also more likely to go to school. It further assists them to ensure their own economic security and that of their community and society (ActionAid 2006).

For these reasons the rights of women and girls have been prioritised in international commitments. Of all the MDGs, only one was set with an early date of 2005 – getting an equal number of girls and boys into primary school. The goal, however, was missed by ninety countries, and, shockingly, went unmentioned at the UN+5 summit. Urgent steps must now be taken to ensure girls get to school, and to ensure they receive the quality of education needed to empower them.

Recommendations

This chapter suggests a shared change agenda for the education and health communities. Joint action will help achieve mutually reinforcing goals.

Campaign when it counts

Health and education campaigners should unite around key political milestones such as election campaigns or budget cycles. During these times, there are real opportunities to engage the public's interest and influence the political agenda. We may pressurise political parties or individuals competing for public office to include commitments to eliminate user fees and increase public spending on health and education. Pre-budget planning is a critical time to push for improved allocations to health and education, with special attention on the rights of marginalised and excluded populations. Monitoring the implementation of policy and budget commitments at the local level also needs to be strengthened.

Keep the focus on rights

Campaigners should put the rights of citizens at the centre of their efforts. This may include pursuing advocacy through the justice system, calling for constitutional provisions and testing the state's commitment to them in the courts if necessary.

Put workers in the forefront of demands, and the campaigning movement

Building a professional and accountable public-sector workforce should be a priority demand for both the health and education sectors. Forging alliances between the trade-union movement and grassroots campaigners can bring benefits.

Think local, national and global

Many of the pressures facing the health and education movements are influenced by global agendas and events. The quantity and quality of aid, the poaching of workers, macroeconomic policy conditions are all examples of issues that have national effects but are driven by global institutions. Conversely, the international arena offers opportunities to elicit new commitments and hold governments and agencies to account, especially in the media. Campaigning organisations should continue to build worldwide popular movements calling for accountability from national governments and international institutions.

Join hands and reach out

This chapter makes a clear case for greater collaboration between education and health activists. The links identified between gender, HIV and education also point to a need to foster alliances with the international women's movement and HIV campaigners. Transparency advocates are also increasingly aware that they need to make links to communities and

208 **Beyond health care**

activists campaigning for better public service provision. In order to avoid competing for political space and scarce resources, it is essential to be open to new forms of cooperation and joint working.

Note

1. Evidence of the many direct and indirect links to health was presented in *Global Health Watch 1* and is available on the GHW website. A longer version of this chapter is also available on the website.

References

ActionAid (2005). *Contradicting commitments: How the achievement of education for all is being undermined by the International Monetary Fund.* Johannesburg.
ActionAid (2006). *Girl power: The impact of girls' education on HIV and sexual behaviour.* Johannesburg.
Boler, T., and A. Jellema (2005). *Deadly inertia: A cross-country study of educational response to HIV/AIDS.* Johannesburg: Global Campaign for Education.
Center for Global Development (2007). *Does the IMF constrain health spending in poor countries?* Washington DC.
DfID (Department for International Development)/Treasury (2005). From commitment to action. www.dfid.gov.uk/pubs/files/g8-outcomes-overview.pdf.
Education International (2005). *Brain drain: Rich country seeks poor teachers.* Brussels.
Fedelino, A., et al. (2006). *Aid scaling up: Do wage bill ceilings stand in the way?* IMF working paper WP/06/106. www.imf.org/external/pubs/ft/wp/2006/wp06106.pdf.
FTI Secretariat (2006). *Education for all: Fast-track initiative status report.* Paper prepared for the Partnership meeting, Cairo, November.
GCE (Global Campaign for Education) (2007). *Not up to scratch.* School report assessing rich countries' progress towards the EFA goals. Johannesburg.
Hargreaves, J., and T. Boler (2006). *Girl power: The impact of girls' education on HIV and sexual behaviour.* Johannesburg: ActionAid.
HRW (Human Rights Watch) (2005). *The less they know, the better:* Abstinence-only HIV/AIDS programs in Uganda. New York.
Mehrotra, S., and R. Jolly (1997). *Development with a human face: Experiences in social achievement and economic growth.* Oxford: Clarendon Press.
Migwi, W. (2007). Small change: Free sanitary towels keeping Kenyan girls in school. *Equals* 19, January–April. London: Beyond Access: Gender, Education and Development.
Oxfam (2006). *In the public interest: Health, education, water and sanitation for all.* Oxford.
Oxfam (2007). *Paying for People.* Oxford.
PSI (Public Services International) Research Unit (2005). *Focus on public services.* London.
Rose, P. (2003). Community participation in school policy and practice in Malawi: Balancing local knowledge, national policies and international agency priorities. *Compare* 33(1), January: 47–64.
Save the Children (2006). *Rewrite the future: Education for children in conflict affected countries.* London.
Save the Children (2007). *Last in line, last in school: How donors are failing children in conflict-affected fragile states.* London.
Tomasevski, K. (2006). *The state of the right to education worldwide. Free or fee: 2006 Global Report.* Copenhagen. www.katarinatomasevski.com/images/Global_Report.pdf.

Tooley, J. (2001). Serving the needs of the poor: The private education sector in developing countries. In C. Hepburn, *Can the market save our schools?* Vancouver: Fraser Institute.

UNESCO (United Nations Educational, Scientific and Cultural Organization) (2006). *Education for all: Global monitoring report.* Paris.

UNESCO (2007). *Education for all: Global monitoring report.* Paris.

UNESCO Institute for Statistics (2006). *Teachers and educational quality: Monitoring global needs for 2015.* Paris.

D I . I   The global health landscape

The last few years have been good for 'global health'. Everyone talks about it. Large amounts are spent on it. Many universities have created departments of global health. The prominence of health indicators among the Millennium Development Goals also shows the ascendancy of 'global health' in international affairs. Even Hollywood celebrities fly the 'global health' flag.

The need to 'govern' health at a global level is important for several reasons. For a start, health care itself has become 'globalised'. Health workers are imported and exported from one country to another. Tele-medicine, medical tourism and the number and size of multinational medical enterprises are expanding. The Severe Acute Respiratory Syndrome (SARS) epidemic, multi-drug-resistant tuberculosis and the threat of a lethal global flu pandemic have further focused attention on global health governance and the need for laws, guidelines and standards to optimise disease control across national borders. Finally, many of the underlying determinants of poor health are global in nature. The effects of the globalised economic system on poverty and nutrition, as well as climate change, all point to the need for strong and effective global health leadership.

Meanwhile, a raft of new organisations, institutes, funds, alliances and centres with a 'global health' remit have mushroomed, radically transforming the 'global health landscape', raising questions about the accountability, effectiveness and efficiency of global health governance.

Development assistance for health and global health partnerships

Development assistance for health (DAH) has increased dramatically. According to the World Bank it rose from US$2.5 billion in 1990 to almost US$14 billion in 2005 (World Bank 2007). Most of this increase has come from official donor country aid. But new sources of global health financing, in particular the Gates Foundation, have been significant. Private funding now accounts for about a quarter of all development aid for health (Bloom 2007). In sub-Saharan Africa, external health sector funding accounts for 15 per cent of all health spending on average, and a much higher proportion of public health financing (World Bank 2007).

There are three main sets of sources of DAH (see Figure D1.1). The first is official government aid, mainly from member countries of the Development Assistance Committee (DAC) of the OECD. In 2006, DAC countries collectively disbursed $10.6 billion for health assistance, of which the United States contributed approximately half. The US proportion of aid increased in 2007. The amount of non-DAC aid for health to low- and middle-income countries is not known because of a lack of available data. For example, China, which has increased its development assistance budget in recent years, provides few data on where and what this money is spent on.

The second set comprises private foundations, and in particular the Gates Foundation. In 2006, the Gates Foundation awarded 195 global health grants totalling US$2.25 billion. Finally, funding is also provided by individuals, typically through donations to international humanitarian and health-related organisations and charities, as well as by businesses, often through what are called 'corporate social responsibility' programmes.

The recipients of DAH can be broadly grouped into four sets of actors. The first group consists of recipient-country governments. The second consists of a variety of non-state actors involved in providing health services at country level, including non-governmental organisations (NGOs), faith-based organisations and a variety of health research organisations. The third group consists of UN agencies such as the World Health Organization (WHO), the United Nations Children's Fund (UNICEF) and the Joint United Nations Programme on HIV/AIDS (UNAIDS). And the final group consists of what are called global health partnerships (GHPs), many of which are relatively new.

Some DAH is channelled directly from donor to recipient. For example, donor governments may channel their funding to recipient governments or NGOs directly through bilateral programmes of aid; the Gates Foundation makes many grants directly to NGOs and research organisations. Some DAH, however, is channelled through multilateral agencies or new global health financing agencies such as the Global Fund to Fight AIDS, TB and Malaria (GF) and the GAVI Alliance.

Figure D1.1.1 illustrates a summarised version of the complex and convoluted global health aid architecture. However, each box listed in the contains a much bigger number of separate actors and institutions.

FIGURE DI.I.I   **Overview of global funding in health in 2006**

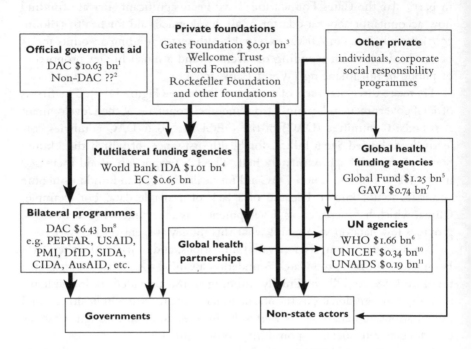

Notes

1. Current bilateral and multilateral disbursements (gross) for health and population programmes by DAC countries in 2006. The commitment of US$1.01 billion to the World Bank has been added to this figure. The total current commitments (gross) for 2006 are $13.64 billion.
2. A figure for 2006 is not available. However, for comparison, non-DAC countries total ODA (net) for 2005 was $3.23 billion. Note that health-sector spending will be a small fraction of this figure. The list of non-DAC countries does not include China (see the World Bank Development Indicators 2007 for more details: http://siteresources.worldbank.org/datastatistics/Resources/table6_11.pdf).
3. Grants paid for global health in 2006. The commitments made in 2006 are much larger at $2.25 billion (www.gatesfoundation.org/GlobalHealth/Grants/default.htm?showYear=2006).
4. Current commitments (gross) for health and population programmes by Development Assistance Committee (DAC) countries via the World Bank in 2006. Data for disbursements in the health sector alone were unavailable.
5. Current disbursements (gross) for health and population programmes by DAC countries via the Global Fund to Fight AIDS, Tuberculosis and Malaria in 2006. The current commitments (gross) for 2006 are $1.73 billion.
6. Current disbursements (gross) for health and population programmes by DAC countries via the European Commission in 2006. The current commitments (gross) for 2006 are $0.51 billion.
7. Cash received by the Global Alliance for Vaccines and Immunisation in 2006. Annual disbursements were unavailable.
8. Current bilateral disbursements by DAC countries in 2006. The cash received by GAVI from DAC countries of $0.74 billion has been deducted for the purposes of the overview – it is included in the OECD figures as 'bilateral assistance'.
9. Half of the WHO proposed programme budget for 2006 and 2007.
10. Current disbursements (gross) for health and population programmes by DAC countries via UNICEF in 2006.
11. Current disbursements (gross) for health and population programmes by DAC countries via UNAIDS in 2006.

Sources: OECD 2008; Gates 2006; GAVI 2008; WHO 2006.

According to the UK government, global health assistance is now 'over-complex', and includes 40 bilateral donors, 26 UN agencies, 20 global and regional funds and 90 global health initiatives (DFID 2007). In addition, international NGOs such as Médecins Sans Frontières, Oxfam, Save the Children, International Planned Parenthood Federation, Care International and CAFOD have become bigger, more numerous and more important to health-care delivery in low-income countries (LICs).

At the global level, the new actors have caused a crisis of identity for many of the more established actors such as the WHO, UNICEF and the World Bank and the bilateral donor agencies. The adoption of narrow results-based performance measures have also led some global health initiatives to pursue their objectives without enough consideration of the impacts of their activities on the wider health system or the wider aid system. The chase for funding, success and public attention undermines efforts to ensure a more organised system of mutual accountability, coordination and cooperation (Buse and Harmer 2007).

The competitive and uncoordinated global environment results in expensive transaction costs for ministries of health having to deal with so many partners and having to manage fragmented health provision and competing for the limited numbers of trained staff. Zambia, for example, has major support from fifteen donor agencies, all of which demand separate reports, meetings and time from government officials. Bilateral donor channels often run outside Zambia's efforts to coordinate a sector-wide approach to health systems development.

According to the World Bank, 'never before has so much attention – or money – been devoted to improving the health of the world's poor'; but it warns that 'unless deficiencies in the global aid architecture are corrected and major reforms occur at the country level, the international community and countries themselves face a good chance of squandering this opportunity' (World Bank 2007).

The ninety or so global health initiatives come in different shapes and sizes. Some have been established as global health financing agencies (e.g. the Global Fund and the GAVI Alliance); some have been established to provide coordination around efforts related to a particular disease or health issue (e.g. the Partnership for Maternal, Newborn and Child Health; Stop TB; Roll Back Malaria; the Global Health Workforce Alliance); while many others have been established to improve the availability of medicines, vaccines and other health technologies (e.g. the Medicines for Malaria Venture; the Alliance for Microbicide Development; the International AIDS Vaccine Initiative). Sixteen of these GHPs have been described in brief in Table D.1.1.1 to illustrate the different types of GPP and their complex configurations.

TABLE DI.I.I   **Summary of selected GHPs**

GHP	Major partners	Purpose of partnership	Main funders
Alliance for Microbicide Development	American Foundation for AIDS Research, AIDS Vaccine Advocacy Coalition, Family Health International, Gay Men's Health Crisis, Global Campaign for Microbicides, Global Microbicide Project, International Family Health, International Partnership for Microbicides, National Organizations Responding to AIDS, WHO	Advocate for and support microbicide development	International Partnership for Microbicides, Rockefeller Foundation, Gates Foundation, other foundations, ODA
Aeras Global TB Vaccine Foundation	More than fifty IGOs, universities, biotech and pharmaceuticals companies, vaccine manufacturers, foundations, advocates and governments	Develop new vaccines against TB and ensure availability to all who need them	Gates Foundation, ODA
Global Alliance for the Elimination of Lymphatic Filariasis	More than forty IGOs, universities, biotech and pharmaceuticals companies, vaccine manufacturers, foundations, advocates and governments	Advocate for and fund the development and provision of technologies and services to treat and prevent lymphatic filiarisis	Gates Foundation, ODA
Global Alliance for Improved Nutrition	Tetra Pak, World Food Programme, Danone, UNICEF, Cargill, WHO, Helen Keller International, Micronutrient Initiative, National Fortification Alliance, Unilever, World Bank Institute	Reduce malnutrition through food fortification and other strategies to improve nutritional health of at-risk populations	Gates Foundation, ODA
Global Alliance for TB Drug Development	GlaxoSmithKline, Bayer, RTI International, Stop TB partnership	To develop and ensure the availability of affordable and better TB drugs	Gates Foundation, Rockefeller Foundation, bilateral donors, DFID
Global Alliance for Vaccines and Immunisations	UNICEF, WHO, World Bank, civil society organisations, public health institutes, donor and implementing country governments, Gates Foundation	Promote the development of new vaccines and expanded coverage of existing vaccines	International Finance Facility, Gates Foundation, ODA

GHP	Major partners	Purpose of partnership	Main funders
Global Fund to Fight AIDS, Tuberculosis and Malaria	UNAIDS, WHO, World Bank, Stop TB, Roll Back Malaria, bilateral donors, recipient governments, Gates Foundation, CSOs and business sector	Finance HIV/AIDS, TGB and Malaria programmes in low- and middle-income countries	Gates Foundation, ODA
International AIDS Vaccine Initiative	Over twenty partners from different sectors	Develop an HIV/AIDS vaccine	Gates Foundation, New York Community Trust, Rockefeller Foundation, World Bank, corporate donors, other foundations and charities
International Trachoma Initiative	Over thirty partners from different sectors including universities, foundations, governments, advocates and IGOs	Support the treatment and prevention of trachoma worldwide	Gates Foundation, pharmaceuticals corporations, Rockefeller Foundation, ODA
Mectizan Donation Programme	African Programme for Onchocerciasis Control; the Carter Center River Blindness Program; CDC; Helen Keller International, International Eye Foundation; Merck, Pan American Health and Education Foundation, pharmaceuticals corporations, SightSavers International, UNICEF, World Bank, WHO	Provide administrative oversight of the donation of Mectizan by Merck for the treatment of onchocerciasis	Merck, GlaxoSmithKline
Medicines for Malaria Venture	Africa Matters Ltd, Hospital Clinic Universitat de Barcelona, GlaxoWellcome, Program for Appropriate Technology in Health, Medicines for Malaria Venture, European and Developing Countries Clinical Trials Partnership, Oswaldo Cruz Foundation, Gates Foundation, Tsukuba Research Institute, Global Forum for Health Research	Develop new malaria treatments	Gates Foundation, Rockefeller Foundation, ODA, pharmaceuticals corporations, IGOs, US National Institutes of Health, Wellcome Trust

GHP	Major partners	Purpose of partnership	Main funders
Pediatric Dengue Vaccine Initiative	WHO, UNICEF, UNDP, US Army and Navy, CDC, NIH, Mahidol University in Bangkok, Pedro Kouri Tropical Medicine Institute in Havana, Ministry of Public Health in Thailand, Taiwan CDC, and other ministries of health in Southeast Asia and the Americas, Sanofi Pasteur, GlaxoSmithKline, Hawaii Biotech	Develop dengue vaccines and diagnostics	Gates Foundation, Rockefeller Foundation
Roll Back Malaria	UNICEF, UNDP, WHO, World Bank, ExxonMobil, GSK, Alternate, Novartis, BASF, Gates Foundation, UN Foundation	Enable sustained delivery and use of effective programmes through coordination, evaluation and advocacy on behalf of partners	World Bank, GFATM, BGMF, ODA
Stop TB	WHO is the main partner. Another seven hundred partners including IGOs, universities, biotech and pharmaceuticals companies, vaccine manufacturers, foundations, advocates and governments	Eliminate tuberculosis as a public health problem through coordination in prevention, treatment and advocacy	WHO, ODA
Global Health Workforce Alliance	WHO plus a hundred partners including IGOs, universities, foundations, advocates and governments	Identify and implement solutions to the health workforce crisis.	WHO
Partnership for Maternal, Newborn and Child Health	WHO, World Bank Group, UNICEF, ODA plus over 240 partners including IGOs, universities, foundations, advocates and governments	Provide a forum coordinating action to address the major conditions that affect children's health	WHO

While the new global health initiatives have raised the profile of certain diseases, and helped develop new technologies for many neglected diseases (often through effective brand-building exercises, good public relations and the allocation of resources to advocacy and communications), the recognition that there has been too much poor coordination, duplication and fragmentation has led to a number of initiatives aimed at improving harmonisation and supporting country-led development. These include the 2005 Paris Declaration on Aid Effectiveness; the Three Ones Agreement (to encourage all agencies addressing HIV/AIDS to work through one action framework, one national coordinating authority and one monitoring and evaluation system); and the International Health Partnership (IHP) initiative launched by the UK government in 2007 to improve coordination around country-driven processes of health-sector development.

Since July 2007, eight international organisations have also been meeting to develop a framework for coordination and to define more clearly their respective roles and responsibilities (UNICEF 2007). The group, known as the 'Health 8', comprise the WHO, Global Fund, Global Alliance for Vaccines and Immunisation, United Nations Population Fund, World Bank, UNAIDS, UNICEF and the Gates Foundation. While these initiatives are welcome, the problems of poor coordination by donors and external agencies have been present for many years, and the prospect that these new initiatives will be successful is poor for three reasons.

First, there are simply too many global health actors and initiatives – better coordination and a truly country-driven approach to health improvement will require a radical rationalisation and shrinkage of the global health architecture. Second, consensus on a coherent health systems development agenda is missing. Third, there is inadequate monitoring of the policies and actions of donors and GHPs – they are largely immune from scrutiny or censure.

The lack of a shared understanding or vision for health systems strengthening (HSS) is discussed in greater detail in Chapter B1. The point to stress in this chapter is that health systems have actually been weakened by the way in which global health programmes and policies are organised and orientated. There is some recognition of this to the extent that most global health institutions are now stressing the importance of 'health systems strengthening'. However, behind the rhetoric are a lack of clarity and even contradictions within and between global health institutions about what constitutes 'health systems strengthening'.

It is, for example, unclear where organisations and GHPs stand on the role of public institutions and markets within the health sector. There is no clear or shared view on the circumstances under which for-profit and not-for-profit providers should be encouraged or discouraged, nor any policy guidance on how countries should respond to the problems associated with health-care commercialisation. Long-term strategies to strengthen the administrative and stewardship capacities of ministries of health remain either absent, under-resourced or undervalued. Without a detailed analysis of how vertically organised selective health programmes will support across-the-board (horizontal) HSS plans, the glib and opaque notion of 'diagonalisation' has been promoted.

Furthermore, the lack of leadership and policy coherence around a HSS agenda among the big global health actors operating out of Geneva, Washington, London and Seattle is only a little better than the prospect of bad leadership and policy. As discussed in the chapter on the World Bank, there is a worry that the same neoliberal thinking that helped to decimate health systems in many countries in the 1980s will prevail into the future.

Finally, what is also glaring is the lack of meaningful debate on two critical policy tensions. The first is between strategies needed to respond immediately and urgently to preventable and treatable adult and child deaths in poor countries and the longer-term strategies required to strengthen health systems. The second is between a predominantly clinical and technicist approach to disease and illness and a more developmental and holistic approach to health improvement.

Accountability and inappropriate partnerships

A major feature of the changing global health landscape has been the promotion of the 'public–private partnership paradigm' since the 1990s, based on the argument that international cooperation in today's globalised world can no longer be based primarily on the multilateralism of nation-states. Partnerships involving business organisations and civil society are required to achieve what governments and the UN cannot manage alone (Martens 2007).

Although this new approach coincided with a period of zero real growth and real budget cuts to the UN, which was forced to seek supplementary funding from the private sector and fulfil its mandate through partnerships with other organisations, the theory was that public–private partnerships occupy a middle ground between markets and states, permitting 'more nuanced and potentially more effective policymaking' (Kaul 2006). Although reference is often made to partnerships with civil society, the main focus of attention has been on partnerships between intergovernmental organisations (IGOs) and business/industry.

Within the health sector Gro Harlem Brundtland strongly encouraged public–private partnerships during her tenure as director-general of the WHO. The Rockefeller and Gates foundations were also instrumental (Widdus 2003). The Rockefeller Foundation, for example, helped establish the Initiative on Public Private Partnerships for Health (IPPH), which promotes international public–private partnerships in the health sector. And many global health partnerships (GHPs) rely almost entirely on the Gates Foundation for funding, or list it as a major donor.

In addition to the issues raised earlier of coordinated and more effective DAH, the new global health landscape raises political issues about the accountability of global health actors and global health governance.

While partnerships are good in principle, there must be an appropriate framework of principles guiding their development and ensuring that the integrity, authority and capacity of public bodies to carry out their public functions are maintained (or developed where necessary). Partnerships must reflect an appropriate spread of power, roles and responsibilities across the public, private and civic sectors.

Presently, the balance of power between public institutions, business and civil society appears skewed in favour of the corporate sector. Globalisation, economic liberalisation and the growth in wealth of multinational corporations require the existence of global public health institutions that are able to ensure appropriate regulation of commercial behaviour to protect health.

One concern is that the public–private paradigm has diminished global public responsibility and allowed businesses to wield undue influence (Buse 2004). Civil society organisations (CSOs) have pointed out fundamental conflicts between commercial goals and public health goals, and a lack of stringent guidelines to govern public interaction with the commercial sector. According to Wemos, 'industry partnerships and industry sponsorship without strong, enforceable, accountable and transparent guidelines for these relationships will undermine and destroy the WHO's role and responsibility' (Wemos 2005).

The imbalance of power is exemplified by an analysis conducted by Buse and Harmer of the composition of the boards of twenty-three selected GHPs (see Figure D1.1.2). Out of a total of 298 board seats, the private (corporate) sector occupied 23 per cent; academic and NGO representatives occupied 23 per cent and 5 per cent respectively; and international and government representatives occupied 20 per cent. The WHO was found to be significantly under-represented at the board level of the most important partnerships (Buse and Harmer 2007). Overall, low- and middle-income countries account for 17 per cent of all seats.

FIGURE DI.I.2   **GHP board analysis**

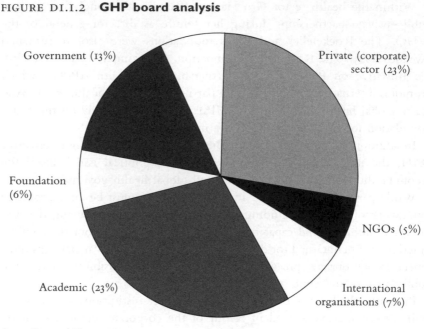

Government (13%)

Private (corporate)
sector (23%)

Foundation
(6%)

NGOs (5%)

Academic (23%)

International
organisations (7%)

Source: Buse and Harmer 2007.

A notable imbalance not represented in the figure above is the huge influence wielded by the Gates Foundation. It is on the board of all the major GHPs as well as being a major funder. But, unlike the WHO, it is free of any form of democratic or political accountability.

These findings raise a number of questions. Why is the private (corporate) sector so well represented, especially when its financial contribution is so modest? Why are publicly mandated institutions, such as the WHO, under-represented? On this evidence, the WHO is clearly underpowered to hold its private partners to account where it matters most – at the decision-making level. Why is NGO representation limited? And while global public–private initiatives (GPPIs) give the impression of equal rights for stakeholders and broad representation, in practice it is the wealthy actors from the North that dominate, whether they are governments, corporations or private foundations (Martens 2007).

In theory, GHPs concerned with health in LICs should be accountable to the governments and people of low-income countries. In practice, the under-representation of Southern stakeholders in governance arrangements, coupled with the Northern location of most GHP secretariats, is reminiscent of imperial approaches to public health. While the broken health systems of many poor countries lie in a state of disrepair, a vast global health industry operating a loosely connected portfolio of initiatives and programmes exists to help the poor. But the poor themselves and the public institutions of the South are mostly invisible as real partners.

In addition, many governments lack the skills or inclination to provide effective stewardship over their countries' health systems. Universities, NGOs and the local media may also be underdeveloped and unable to perform an effective watchdog role over both the government and the international aid industry.

If one steps back to take a panoramic view of the global health landscape, one might even conclude that, while purporting to do good for the world's poor, the global health apparatus not only helps to excuse a global political economy that perpetuates poverty and widens disparities, but also benefits the corporate and rich world through 'bluewashing' (the lending of credibility by the UN) and the opportunity for companies to establish new markets in medical products with minimal commercial risk, while improving access to public and academic expertise and to governments. Bull and McNeill's (2007) investigation into GHPs concluded that 'there are some examples of behaviour by the big pharmaceutical companies which appear to be altruistic, but also many cases in which the companies have enjoyed the benefits of an expanded market without contributing to bringing the prices down.'

Final comments

Many of the radical changes to the global health aid architecture remain inadequately described and evaluated. More work is needed to understand the changes taking place and to enable a more informed and critical discussion. While this chapter deals specifically with 'health', it also reflects on global governance more generally, and on the role of the United Nations, the corporate sector and others in managing the challenges of social and economic development worldwide. The chapter draws out three suggestions for action by civil society.

The first concerns the need for effective and accountable global health leadership. It is possibly a good thing that the 'Health 8' has been formed – hopefully it will lead to a clearer delineation of roles and functions and better coordination. But it is unclear who is ultimately responsible for bringing order to the chaotic environment and how the key actors will be effectively held to account.

Better leadership should also produce a more rational system of development assistance for health. The current system is too fragmented, competitive and top-down. It does not place a premium on country-based plans and strategies. The principle of the International Health Partnerships is sound and must be supported, but this will require strategies to develop the capacity of ministries of health to provide effective stewardship and improved systems for holding both external agencies and governments to account.

There are also particular implications for the WHO, the World Bank and the Gates Foundation. In theory, the WHO has the mandate and legitimacy to provide the much-needed global health leadership. In practice, its funding arrangements and its reluctance to assume more leadership prevent it from doing this. The challenge facing civil society and the WHO in ensuring more effective public and accountable leadership in global health is discussed in Chapter D1.2. The World Bank, no longer the dominant player on the field, has an important role to play as a bank. But its democratic deficiencies, neoliberal instincts and record of poor and biased research do not make it an appropriate institution for global health leadership. The Gates Foundation is arguably the dominant player currently. But it lacks transparency and accountability, and, as described in Chapter D1.3, it has become an over-dominant influence.

There is no simple solution to the challenge of knitting together the approaches, ideologies and agendas of the different actors. But civil society organisations need to generate more debate and discussion about global health leadership and accountability.

The second issue, related to the first, is the need for a coherent health systems development agenda. This must include the strengthening of public health systems and their absorptive capacities. There is a special need to examine and challenge the ongoing promotion of market-based solutions to health systems failures. Independent and critical assessments of the major global health initiatives and their impact on health systems within low-income countries are badly needed. Health systems policies that are consistent with the principles and logic of the 1978 Alma Ata Declaration need to replace the top-down, disease-based and neoliberal policies that are currently prevalent.

Low-income countries already struggle with a narrow policy space due to globalisation and dependence on external donors. Their policy space is shrinking even further as aspects of health that are characterised as 'global public goods' come to be increasingly 'managed' from the outside by global institutions. The lack of coordination among global health actors currently undermines efforts to ensure effective national health stewardship. However, externally supported health programmes have the potential to support the double aim of improving access to health care *and* contributing to the social, political and systems-wide changes that are required to sustain health improvements.

The third issue concerns the public–private paradigm. There are good reasons for thinking that the present distribution of risk and benefit across the public and private sectors are skewed in favour of the private sector, and that the current partnership models are inefficient. The UN should conduct a comprehensive review of the entire public–private paradigm. Specifically, the WHO needs to monitor and set up transparent regulatory mechanisms of GHPs.

References

Bloom, D.E. (2007). Governing global health. *Finance and Development* 44(4), December.

Bull, B., and D. McNeill (2007). *Development issues in global governance: Public–private partnerships and market multilateralism*. Abingdon: Routledge.

Buse, K. (2004). Governing public–private infectious disease partnerships. *Brown Journal of World Affairs* 10(2), Winter/Spring. London School of Hygiene and Tropical Medicine.

Buse, K., and A. Harmer (2007). 'Seven habits of highly effective public–private health partnerships: Practice and potential'. *Social Science and Medicine* 64: 259–71.

DFID (Department for International Development) (2007). The international health partnership launched today. 5 September. www.dfid.gov.uk/news/files/ihp/default.asp.

Gates Foundation (2006). *Annual Report 2006*. www.gatesfoundation.org/nr/public/media/annualreports/annualreport06/assets/GatesFoundationAnnualReport2006.pdf.

GAVI (2008). Cash received 2000 to 2007. www.gavialliance.org/resources/Contribution_actuals_2000_2007_updated_14_Jan08.xls.

Kaul, I. (2006). Exploring the policy space between markets and states: Global public–private partnerships. In I. Kaul and P. Conceição (eds), *The new public finance: Responding to global challenges*. New York: Oxford University Press.

Martens, J. (2007). Multistakeholder partnerships: Future models of multilateralism? *Dialogue on Globalization*, Occasional Papers, Berlin.

OECD (2008). DAC–CRS Database. http://stats.oecd.org/WBOS/Default.aspx?DatasetCode=CRSNEW.

UNICEF (United Nations Children's Fund) (2007). Informal meeting of global health leaders, 19 July. www.unicef.org/health/files/Meeting_of_Global_Health_Leaders_-_Final_Summary.pdf.

Wemos (2005). Risky remedies for the health of the poor, Amsterdam: Wemos Foundation. http://wemos2004.ddg22.tamtam.nl/Documents/executive per cent20summary per cent20klein per cent20bestand.pdf.

WHO (2006). Proposed programme budget 2006–7. www.who.int/gb/ebwha/pdf_files/PB2006/P1-en.pdf.

Widdus, R. (2003). Public–private partnerships for health require thoughtful evaluation. *Bulletin of the World Health Organization* 81(4): 235. Geneva: World Health Organization. www.who.int/bulletin/volumes/81/4/Editorial1.pdf.

World Bank (2007). *Healthy development: The World Bank strategy for health, nutrition, and population results*. Washington DC: World Bank.

DI.2 The World Health Organization and the Commission on the Social Determinants of Health

This chapter is written in the belief that it is worth aspiring to an accountable and effective multilateral global health agency, driven by a desire to promote health with the understanding that the distribution of health and health care is a core marker of social justice.

For many, the World Health Organization (WHO) is emblematic of an organisation designed to enable international cooperation in pursuit of a common public good. Its constitution, written in a different era, needs to be updated to reflect current realities, but it remains a good reminder of the aspirations that have been invested in it. Among the principles governing the WHO's constitution are:

- The enjoyment of the highest attainable standard of health is one of the fundamental rights of every human being.
- The health of all peoples is fundamental to the attainment of peace and security and is dependent upon the fullest cooperation of individuals and states.
- Unequal development in different countries in the promotion of health and control of disease, especially communicable disease, is a common danger.
- The extension to all peoples of the benefits of medical, psychological and related knowledge is essential to the fullest attainment of health.

The actual state of global health indicates a reality that is more brutal, cynical and unforgiving than the WHO's constitution suggests. But for many, the hopes and ideals reflected in the constitution are worth fighting for.

As an intergovernmental organisation, the WHO is also important because it has the mandate and opportunity to establish or influence laws, regulations and guidelines that set the foundations for international and national health policy. It is the closest thing we have to a ministry of health at the global level. Given the degree and extent of globalisation, this calls for greater public interest in and scrutiny of the WHO. Support for the WHO also reflects support for the United Nations (UN) system. For all its often-reported structural and operational failings, the UN (including the WHO) does much good and is ultimately irreplaceable and vital to human security.

Since publication of the first *GHW*, there have been significant changes at the WHO, including the election of a new director-general following the sudden death of Director-General Dr Lee Jong-wook in May 2006. Regrettably, many of the challenges facing the WHO that were identified in the first *Global Health Watch* remain, and in some cases have become more acute. The WHO is still pushed and pulled by the tidal forces of international politics; it remains underfunded, and over-reliant on so-called 'public–private partnerships'; it faces a crowded global health arena; and internally, low morale among staff and the sclerotic nature of WHO bureaucracy are still problematic.

This chapter is not a comprehensive review of the WHO over the past three years. Rather it describes a selection of issues to illustrate the challenges facing the WHO. These include:

- the WHO's funding and budget for 2008/09;
- the highly contentious boundary between trade and health policy;
- international developments in global preparedness for a potential avian flu pandemic;
- progress made by the Commission on the Social Determinants of Health.

Underfunded, donor-driven and compromised?

Most of the WHO's funding comes from its member states. 'Assessed contributions' provided by member states (usually through ministries of health) form the basis for the WHO's regular budget funds (RBFs). The relative contribution of each state is calculated using a UN funding formula based on a country's population and size of economy. This results in a small number of countries providing most of the WHO's core budget. For example, the United States' assessed contribution is currently 22 per cent (it used to be 25 per cent but this was reduced following US requests). In contrast, Tuvalu contributes 0.001 per cent (WHO 2007a).

In addition to the assessed contributions, the WHO receives extra-budgetary funds (EBFs), in the form of grants or gifts. These are contributed

FIGURE DI.2.I   **Assessed and voluntary contributions from WHO member states in 2006**

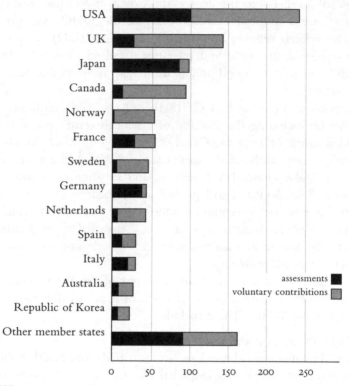

Source: WHO 2007c.

by member states (usually from their ODA budgets), other parts of the United Nations, foundations, non-governmental organisations (NGOs), charities and private companies.

The relative contribution of RBFs and EBFs has changed over time. In 1970, EBFs accounted for 20 per cent of total WHO expenditure, with over half these funds coming from other UN organisations (Lee 2008). EBFs exceeded RBFs for the first time in the 1990/91 biennium. Today, EBFs account for about three-quarters of the WHO's expenditure, most of which is sourced from member states (WHO 2007b). Unlike the RBFs, most of the voluntary contributions made to the WHO are tied to specific projects determined by the donors, although some donors provide EBFs that are not tied to specific projects.

The US was the largest contributor in terms of both assessed and voluntary contributions in 2006, followed by the UK, Japan, Canada, Norway,

FIGURE DI.2.2   **Allocation of 2008/09 budget by region**

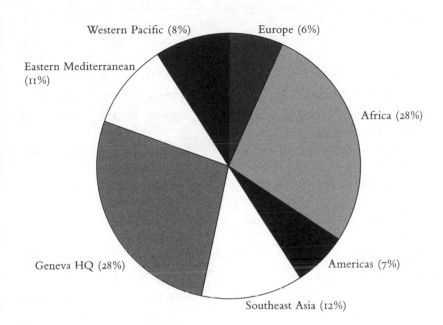

Source: WHO 2007d.

France, Sweden, Germany and the Netherlands. The Gates Foundation provided voluntary contributions of $99.4 million in 2006, which made it the third equal (with Japan) largest contributor of funding to the WHO (see Figure DI.2.1) (WHO 2007c).

The much greater reliance on EBFs reflects the preference of donors towards having greater control over the use of their money. In addition, it reflects a period of financial austerity imposed upon the UN as a whole. First, major donors introduced a policy of zero real growth in 1980 to the RBFs of all UN organisations. In part, this was a reaction to the perceived 'politicisation' of UN organisations, in particular UNESCO and the International Labour Organisation (ILO), but also to the WHO's campaigns against irrational prescribing of medicines and breastmilk substitutes (Lee 2008). Then in 1993, a policy of zero nominal growth was introduced, reducing the WHO's RBFs in real terms.

The WHO (and other UN organisations) have also had to contend with late or non-payment by member states. Non-payment by the United States has been particularly problematic. By 2001, the US had become the largest debtor to the UN, owing it US$2 billion. Arrears to the WHO rose from around US$20 million in 1996 to US$35 million in 1999 (Lee 2008).

TABLE DI.2.I   **Budget for WHO strategic objectives, 2008/09**

Strategic aim	Budget		RBF	EBF
	(US$ m)	(%)	(%)	(%)
1. Communicable diseases	894.043	21.1	9.5	90.5
2. HIV/AIDS, malaria and tuberculosis	706.932	16.7	6.9	93.1
3. Non-communicable disease, mental health, injuries and violence	158.104	3.7	28.6	71.4
4. Maternal and child health, sexual and reproductive health and healthy ageing	359.833	8.5	15.5	84.5
5. Emergencies, disasters and conflicts	218.413	5.2	8.1	91.9
6. Risk factors to health: alcohol, tobacco, other drugs, unhealthy diet, physical inactivity and unsafe sex	162.057	3.8	24.1	75.9
7. Social and economic determinants of health	65.905	1.6	21.9	78.1
8. Environmental health	130.456	3.1	25.1	74.9
9. Nutrition, food safety and food security	126.934	3.0	18.2	81.8
10. Health services	514.054	12.2	27.2	72.8
11. Medical products and technologies	134.033	3.2	23.3	76.7
12. Global health leadership	214.344	5.1	65.1	34.9
13. Organizational improvement of WHO	542.372	12.8	52.8	47.2
Total working budget	4,227.480	100.0	22.7	77.3

Source: WHO 2007e.

The problems associated with a heavy reliance on EBFs are fairly apparent. They include unhealthy competition among departments within the WHO and with NGOs and other organisations chasing donor funding, as well as limitations on the WHO's ability to plan, budget and implement its strategic aims coherently. Even projects authorised by World Health Assembly (WHA) resolutions are reliant on a chase for funding.

In theory, budget allocations are determined by the WHA and WHO Regional Committee meetings. In practice, they are set by the WHO Secretariat under the influence of donors and powerful member states. It is difficult to determine what conditions donors place on their funds and what impact this has on budget-setting by the secretariat.

The WHO's budget for the 2008/09 biennium, made up of both RBFs and EBFs, is US$4.2 billion (WHO 2007d). This is an increase of 15 per cent on its previous biennium. The Geneva headquarters is allocated $1.18 billion (27.8 per cent), with the rest shared across the six regions. The Africa region receives the biggest proportion of regional funding – $1.19 billion (see Figure D1.2.2) (WHO 2007d). Although the Western Pacific is the second largest region by population, its relatively small budget is related to the WHO's lack of presence in China.

The budget for 2008/09 is also subdivided into thirteen strategic objectives (see Table D1.2.1). What is striking about the budget is the reliance on EBFs and the high allocations to communicable diseases relative to food and nutrition; non-communicable disease; social and economic determinants of health; and environmental health.

Putting health first

With its dependence on EBFs, the WHO is particularly vulnerable to donor influence. Margaret Chan, director-general of the WHO, said that she will 'speak the truth to power', and certainly the WHO has resisted pressure from powerful interests in the past (quoted in Schuchman 2007). It did so, to some extent, when it helped establish the Framework Convention on Tobacco Control and the International Code on the marketing of breastmilk substitutes. On both occasions, civil society organisations and member state representatives also played a vital role in protecting the WHO from being bullied.

But on other occasions it has buckled under pressure. When the WHO recommended the lower consumption of free sugars and sugar-sweetened drinks, the sugar industry lashed out with a barrage of threatening letters, and appeals to the US government to intervene (which it did) (Simon 2005). By the time the WHO finalised its Global Strategy on Diet, Physical Activity and Health, it had been heavily watered down (Cannon 2004). As one WHO official noted: 'During discussions on the Global Strategy on diet, US representatives never made a mystery of the fact that they would not let WHO go beyond a sanitary, education-focused strategy' (quoted in Benkimoun 2006). Ongoing challenges to the public health responsibility and independence of the WHO are often played out in the arena of trade, as illustrated by the following recent stories.

Our man in Bangkok

Few people will have heard of William Aldis, but for a short period he was the WHO's top health adviser in Thailand. In January 2006, he published an article in the *Bangkok Post*, criticising a bilateral trade agreement that was being negotiated between the US and Thailand. Aldis was concerned that the treaty would have negative consequences for Thailand's generic drug industry and on the cost of second and third-line HIV drugs (Aldis 2006). The US was furious. Its ambassador to the UN visited the then head of the WHO, Dr Lee, and followed this up with a letter. According to a staff member who read the letter, Lee was reminded of the need for the WHO to remain 'neutral and objective' over matters of trade (quoted in Williams 2006).

Aldis quickly found himself transferred to the WHO's New Delhi office. Although the WHO strongly denied that the decision was due to pressure from Washington, *The Lancet* was in no doubt about the real significance of Aldis's transfer: 'This action was a clear signal of US influence on WHO' (Benkimoun 2006).

The anecdote involving Aldis is part of a longer-running story of pressure from the US to prevent the WHO from taking a proactive, health–protecting stance with regard to trade negotiations and trade policy, even though the agreement on Trade-Related Aspects of Intellectual Property Rights (TRIPS) and the General Agreement on Trade in Services (GATS) have extensive and profound implications for health care across the world.

The WHO does have a unit dealing with trade and health. But it is small and underfunded. In 2006, the WHA passed Resolution 59.26 on international trade and health.[1] Although welcome at one level, the resolution was weak, vague and half-hearted.

Tripping up over TRIPS

Controversy followed the WHO back to Thailand in February 2007 when Margaret Chan visited the National Health Security Office in Bangkok. Much to the dismay of many, Chan praised the pharmaceuticals industry, promoted drug donation as a solution to the problem of poor access to medicines and suggested that the Thai government's recent issuing of three compulsory licences to import and/or produce locally generic copies of patented drugs for HIV/AIDS and heart disease was counterproductive. Chan is alleged to have said: 'I'd like to underline that we have to find a right balance for compulsory licensing. We can't be naive about this. There is no perfect solution for accessing drugs in both quality and quantity' (quoted in Third World Network 2007).

NGOs and Thai health officials were appalled. The president of AIDS Access Foundation summed up the general feeling: 'It's disappointing. The [WHO] should have supported drug access and promoted the study of quality and inexpensive drugs for the sake of the global population rather than supporting pharmaceutical giants' (Treerutkuarkul 2007). A worldwide petition followed. Chan later wrote to the Thai minister of public health stating her deep regret that her comments had been 'misrepresented' in the Thai press, and for any embarrassment that this may have caused.

Censorship and the even more slippery slope of self-censorship

Conflicts between public health and commerce are nothing new. But it is important that such conflicts are played out in the open, particularly when they involve the WHO. In 2006, acting head of WHO Anders Nordstrom should have informed senior WHO staff of US opposition to a report co-written by a member of WHO staff and jointly published with the South Centre. He didn't. The report was shelved, and senior staff only found out about US complaints from a leaked memo. The publication, *The Use of Flexibilities in TRIPS by Developing Countries: Can They Promote Access to Medicines?*, had been critical of US interpretation of the WTO's TRIPS agreement. The perception was that the top brass at the WHO had bowed to US pressure (IPW 2006).

The US subsequently demanded a full review of the WHO's publication policy. At the January 2008 Executive Board meeting, it was proposed that all publications by the WHO should be subject to review and clearance by a Guidelines Review Committee and that sensitive publications should be cleared by the director-general herself. When several developing-country delegations raised concerns that the proposals were too 'centralised' and could result in external censorship, Margaret Chan gave the following reassurance: 'in no situation during my tenure will I compromise editorial independence ... . don't worry I can stand the political pressure – it is our duty to guard publications based on science and that are peer reviewed' (Tayob 2008).

Partnerships or the privatisation of international health policy?

During the leadership of Director-General Brundtland, partnerships with the private sector became a prominent feature of the WHO. According to David Nabarro, Brundtland's senior adviser,

> We certainly needed private financing. For the past decades, governments' financial contributions have dwindled. The main sources of funding are the private sector and the financial markets. And since the American economy is the world's richest, we must make the WHO attractive to the United States and the financial markets. (quoted in Motchane 2002)

The argument goes that if a financially dependent public institution such as the WHO enters into a partnership with a wealthy partner such as a major multinational, the latter will set the agenda and the former will become its stooge. The WHO is particularly sensitive to this charge. If the

WHO is perceived to have been hijacked by the private corporate sector, it will lose its authority as an impartial norm-setter on global health issues.

Has the WHO compromised itself through its partnership with the private sector? It is hard to say. But there are certainly reasons for concern. In June 2006, the WHO became embroiled in controversy again when its director of mental health and substance abuse, Benedetto Saraceno, suggested to the head of the European Parkinson's Disease Association (EPDA) that EPDA accept a donation of $100,000 from GlaxoSmithKline on WHO's behalf (Day 2007). In an email, Saraceno wrote:

> WHO cannot receive funds from the pharmaceuticals industry. Our legal office will reject the donation. WHO can only receive funds from government agencies, NGOs, foundations and scientific institutions or professional organisations. Therefore, I suggest that this money should be given to EPDA, and eventually EPDA can send the funds to WHO which will give an invoice (and acknowledge contribution) to EPDA, but not to GSK. (quoted in Day 2007)

Although Saraceno explained that his email had been 'clumsily worded', the incident demonstrates a likely side effect of the WHO's funding arrangements and the need to clarify the WHO's protocol for engaging in relationships with the private sector. There has not been a comprehensive review of WHO–private sector relations since the publication of the WHO's *Guidelines on Interaction with Commercial Enterprises to Achieve Health Outcomes* seven years ago. A report (Richter 2004) on the WHO and the private sector, which called for a public review and debate on the benefits, risks and costs of public–private interactions in health when compared to alternatives, fell on deaf ears. Half a decade on, civil society should renew pressure on the WHO to take a fresh look at WHO–corporate relationships.

The avian flu vaccine controversy

The prospect of a global flu pandemic is the subject of intense discussion and fear. World attention was further focused when the Indonesian Health Ministry announced in early 2007 that it would no longer provide avian flu viral material to the WHO's 'Global Influenza Surveillance Network' (GISN) for the purposes of assisting with surveillance and vaccine development.

The GISN is made up of the WHO, four Collaborating Centres (WHO CCs) based in Australia, Japan, the United Kingdom and the United States, and about nine WHO H5 Reference Laboratories.[2] GISN's work and outputs rely on viruses being submitted every year by various country-based National Influenza Centres (NICs).

The Indonesian government discovered that avian flu viral material that it had voluntarily submitted to the GISN ended up in the hands of pharmaceuticals companies for vaccine development, without its permission. This was contrary to WHO guidelines, which state that any further distribution of viruses beyond the WHO reference laboratories must require the permission of the originating country (WHO 2005, 2006).

When the WHO was taken to task about the breach of its own guidelines, the guidelines were removed from the WHO website. The WHO then proposed a new document[3] describing best practices for sharing influenza viruses and viral sequence data. This latest offering contradicted the Convention of Biological Diversity (CBD) principle, which holds that countries have national sovereignty over their biological resources and should derive a fair share of the benefits arising from the use of them.

There has been a dramatic increase in the number of patent applications covering the influenza virus (or parts of it), as well as for actual vaccines, treatments and diagnostics, in recent years (Hammond 2007). The discovery that patents had been sought on modified versions of other viral material (and its use in vaccines) shared through GISN without the consent of the supplying countries reinforced the perception that the GISN is part of a system that begins with the free sharing of viral material, which goes through the WHO, then through public laboratories, and finally ends up with private pharmaceuticals companies having a monopoly over the end product.

The system results in a clear set of winners and losers. Commercial vaccine developers have already obtained many millions of dollars' worth of contracts from developed countries to supply vaccines, in addition to grants and subsidies for their R&D activities. Populations in developed countries have a better chance of being protected from a flu pandemic, although the taxpayer is probably paying an extremely high premium to keep the commercial companies well in profit.

Developing countries, particularly those most likely to be badly affected, face potentially astronomical bills for the purchase of vaccines and other medical supplies. As drug companies can produce only a limited amount of vaccines in a given year, many developed countries have made advance purchase orders for vaccines, limiting even further the prospects of countries like Indonesia benefiting from vaccine development (Fedson 2003).

These and related issues were raised by Indonesia, together with the support of more than twenty other developing countries, at the 2007 WHA, culminating in a resolution that sets out a series of proposals to achieve both 'the timely sharing of viruses and specimens' and the promotion of 'transparent, fair and equitable sharing of the benefits arising from the generation of information, diagnostics, medicines, vaccines and other technologies' (WHA 2007f). The resolution also recognises the sovereign right of states over their biological resources and the right to fair and equitable sharing of benefits arising from the use of the viruses.

At the intergovernmental meeting convened in November 2007, tensions resurfaced. Indonesia reiterated the need for developing countries to have trust in a multilateral system that did not undermine their sovereign rights over biological resources (based on the CBD), nor disadvantage the health of people living in poor countries. Developed countries in turn argued that the stance taken by Indonesia was jeopardising global health security and violated the WHO's International Health Regulations (IHR), which was designed to ensure international compliance with a set of public health standards and practices aimed at preventing and mitigating global health risks. Presently, the IHR does not expressly require the sharing of biological samples (Fidler 2007). It has been suggested that even though Indonesia is not in contravention of the letter of the law, its stance is in violation of the spirit of the IHR. However, the primary sticking point is the lack of a mechanism to ensure equitable access to vaccines and technologies in preparation and in the event of a global flu pandemic.

This incident succinctly illustrates the fundamental conflict between a patent-based system of commercial vaccine production and the WHO's mission to promote and protect health worldwide. Having failed to manage properly the practices of actors within the GISN, the WHO now has the opportunity to demonstrate its value and worth both as a technical agency and as a moral arbiter on international health policymaking.

The Commission on the Social Determinants of Health

When the WHO's Commission on Macroeconomics and Health (CMH) reported in 2001, many public health activists criticised the way that health care had been portrayed in a purely instrumental way as a requirement for economic development. The notion of health as a human right and the economic and political determinants of poor health and under-resourced health systems were largely ignored.

Thus when the WHO launched the Commission on the Social Determinants of Health (the Commission) in May 2005, many people hoped this would mark the beginning of a new programme of work that would engage with the fundamental economic, political and social determinants of health, complementing the WHO's existing focus on diseases and health services.

Michael Marmot, a British epidemiologist known for studying health inequalities, chairs the Commission. There are eighteen other commissioners, including the Nobel prizewinning economist Amartya Sen. Nine Commissioners come from rich countries, but twelve live in them. Four come from Africa, two from Asia, and one from Latin America. As a group, the commissioners represent a broad spectrum of views, ranging from a former senior US administration official with impeccable Republican credentials, to individuals with progressive credentials such as Pascoal Mocumbi (former prime minister of Mozambique), Giovanni Berlinguer (Italian member of the European Parliament), Monique Begin (former Canadian minister of health) and Fran Baum (People's Health Movement).

The Commission consists of five workstreams (Irwin et al. 2006):

1. Nine *knowledge networks* (KNs) to inform policy proposals and action on the following topics: early childhood development; globalisation; health systems; urban settings; women and gender equity; social exclusion; employment conditions; priority public health conditions; measurement and evidence.
2. *Country-based workstreams*, involving more than ten countries at the time of writing.
3. Engagement with *civil society*, involving the inclusion of civil society representatives on the Commission and formal consultations with civil society groups.
4. Engagement with *key global actors and initiatives*.
5. *Institutional change* at WHO to advance the work of the Commission after it ends. This has mainly involved the creation of a separate KN and engagement with the regional WHO offices, of which only the Pan American Health Organization (PAHO) seems to be taking the Commission's work seriously. As for institutional change in Geneva, several hurdles appear in the way of overcoming the disproportionate influence of clinically oriented disease-based programmes that do not readily view health through a broader social and political lens.

The conceptual framework for the Commission's work is based on an understanding that ill-health and unequal health outcomes are produced through a chain of causation that starts from the underlying social stratification of societies and that interventions can be aimed at: decreasing stratification by, for example, redistributing wealth; decreasing exposure to factors that threaten health; reducing the vulnerability of people to health-damaging conditions; strengthening the community and individual level factors which promote resilience; and providing accessible, equitable and effective health care.

Representatives of civil society have attended all but one Commission meeting and made presentations to the commissioners. They have participated in the KNs and fed into the thinking of the Commission. Civil society groups have been contracted to conduct consultations in each region of the world although there have been questions about the extent to which this engagement is real or token, and about the lack of administrative support and funding to support this work.

At this stage it is only possible to provide an interim and partial assessment of the Commission's work. In July 2007, the Commission released an Interim Statement. Among other things, it explicitly promoted health as a human right and with intrinsic value. It stressed the importance of fairness and equity, gender, and the value of social movements in achieving change. And it provided strong support for the principles of the Comprehensive Primary Health Care (PHC) Approach, calling for 'a global movement for change to improve global health and reduce health inequity'.

Compared to many recent WHO reports, the Interim Statement is much more strongly committed to equity. It doesn't explicitly criticise neoliberalism, but provides a strong voice for action to reduce inequities and goes beyond poverty reduction to consider issues of trade imbalance and net outflows from poor to rich countries. However, it was disappointing that the Interim Statement failed to draw lessons that have contemporary significance from historical analyses of population health improvement in Europe that identify, for example, the role of wealth accumulation through colonial exploitation and the agricultural and industrial revolutions, and later social reforms enacted by the state following bitter struggles by the urban poor. The final report of the CSDH, launched in August 2008 (CSDH 2008), will be important as it sets out an agenda for action on the social determinants of health and establishes the pursuit of health equity as a crucial matter of social justice.

Prospects for the future

The Commission has an opportunity to make a significant and lasting impact on the future performance of the WHO, as well as upon the broader health policy landscape. But to do this, it must resist the pressures to produce a weak, consensus report that is acceptable to all players. It must stay true to its intellectual idealism and challenge the climate of cynicism about what multilateral institutions can achieve.

Thus far, the Commission appears not powerful enough to have much influence on the major players in global health, especially given the neo-liberal perspectives of some actors, and the widespread support for vertical, top-down, disease-based programmes by other actors. Pressure from civil society will be required to ensure that the progressive aspects of the Interim Statement are retained in the final report.

A crucial determinant of the Commission's impact will be whether its central messages are adopted, supported and championed by the WHO.

Dr Chan will be pivotal. She must give full support to the Commission's report through her personal endorsement and the commitment of resources to enable implementation of the recommendations. At the time of writing, the WHO seems to be adopting a wait-and-see approach. Global Health Watch must monitor the extent to which the WHO takes up the strong social justice message of the report and whether it puts bold action on the social determinants of health equity at the centre of its operations.

However, there was considerable anger at the failure of Dr Chan to support and budget for ongoing work at the 2007 World Health Assembly. Thailand's senior health official Dr Suwit Wibulpolprasert insisted that a reference to social determinants be reinserted into the WHO's budget document to indicate that the Organization will take the goals of the CSDH seriously.[4] The Commission will now report to the World Health Assembly in May 2009.

Conclusions

This chapter has placed the WHO under the spotlight. It is intended to make uncomfortable reading.

The WHO's funding situation is unacceptable. Instead of being funded as a democratic UN agency, it is in danger of becoming an instrument to serve donor interests and yield 'quick gains' even if this may not serve the WHO's overall strategic goals. The imbalance between EBFs and RBFs must be corrected. Civil society organisations, thus far, have failed to take this up as an issue. But in the meantime, the WHO should exert stronger independence, resist the influence of donors, and demand greater support for its own strategic plan and programmes.

While the need for 'better funding' is obvious, does the WHO need 'more funding'? By common consensus, it does. The increase in the WHO's 2008/09 budget is therefore cause for optimism. But the WHO needs to do more to improve its administrative and management performance, and a good place to start would be for its regional offices – particularly in Africa – to demonstrate their value more than they currently do.

The WHO also needs to reappraise its purpose, roles, responsibilities, budget allocations and workplan, especially in light of the changing global health landscape. The emergence over the last twenty years of other actors, notably the World Bank, the Gates Foundation, GAVI and the Global Fund, as well as the public–private partnerships paradigm, has left the WHO often following an agenda, rather than setting it.

The WHO must 'speak the truth to power', as its director-general promises it will. But that means standing up to powerful industries and being more prepared to speak out against its most powerful member state. Critically, the WHO must define a stronger role for itself in the trade arena, particularly in the face of worldwide economic liberalisation and growing corporate power. Too often, social aims and objectives are treated as secondary concerns when it comes to the way the global political economy is shaped and governed. Often, the needs and priorities of the poor are neglected in favour of those of the rich. The application of basic public health principles at the global level provides some form of protection against these trends. But the WHO needs to assert itself as the guardian of international public health. But in doing so, it must not be forced into a limited role of monitoring and controlling communicable diseases within a narrowly defined health security agenda.

Some will say that as a multilateral organisation, governed by its member states, the WHO will always be held hostage to international politics. This is true. But it is equally true that significant improvements in global health and a concurrent reduction in the gross disparities in health and access to care will only be achieved through political negotiation and international diplomacy. This should place the WHO at the centre of the stage, not as a peripheral player.

Change is possible. But for this to happen, civil society organisations must also come together around a coordinated plan to strengthen the ability of the WHO to fulfil its mandate and to act as an organisation of the people as well as of governments.

Notes

1. See www.who.int/gb/ebwha/pdf_files/WHA59–REC1/e/Resolutions-en.pdf.
2. See www.who.int/csr/disease/influenza/surveillance/en/and www.who.int/csr/disease/avian_influenza/guidelines/referencelabs/en/.
3. A60/INF.DOC./1 dated 22 March 2007.
4. See www.twnside.org.sg/title2/avian.flu/news.stories/afns.008.htm.

References

Aldis, W. (2006). Opinion: It could be a matter of life or death. *Bangkok Post*, 9 January. Available at: www.bilaterals.org/article.php3?id_article=5072.
Benkimoun, P. (2006). How Lee Jong-wook changed WHO. *The Lancet* 367: 1806–8.
Cannon, G. (2004). Why the Bush administration and the global sugar industry are determined to demolish the 2004 WHO global strategy on diet, physical activity and health. *Pub Health Nutr* 7: 369–80.
CSDH (Commission on the Social Determinants of Health) (2008) *Closing the gap in a generation: Health equity through action on the social determinants of health.* Geneva: WHO.
Day, M. (2007). Who's funding WHO? *British Medical Journal* 334: 338–40.

Fedson, D.S. (2003). Pandemic influenza and the global vaccine supply. *Clin Infect Dis* 36: 1552–61.

Fidler, D. (2007). Influenza virus samples: International law, and global health diplomacy. *Emerging Infectious Diseases* 14(1): 88–94.

Hammond, E. (2007). 'Some intellectual property issues related to H5N1 influenza viruses, research and vaccines. www.twnside.org.sg/avian.flu_papers.htm.

Intellectual Property Watch (IPW) (2006). Internal memo suggests shift in WHO handling of US criticism. 10 November.

Irwin, A., et al. (2006). The Commission on Social Determinants of Health: Tackling the social roots of health inequities. *PLoS Med* 3(6). http://medicine.plosjournals. org/perlserv/?request=get-document&doi=10%2E1371%2Fjournal%2Epmed%2E0030 106&ct=1.

Lee, K. (2008). *The World Health Organization*. London: Routledge.

Motchane, J.L. (2002). Health for all or riches for some: WHO's responsible? *Le Monde Diplomatique*, July.

Richter, J. (2004). Public–private partnerships and health for all: How can WHO safeguard public interests? GASPP Policy Brief. http://gaspp.stakes.fi/NR/rdonlyres/8F169CDC-9A01-4C20-B9B6-4FDF272F00E7/0/policybrief5.pdf.

Schuchman, M. (2007). Improving Global Health – Margaret Chan at the WHO. *New England Journal of Medicine* 356(7): 653–6.

Simon, M. (2005). Bush supersizes effort to weaken the World Health Organization. *International Journal of Health Services* 35(2): 405–7.

Tayob, R. (2008). WHO publications will come under committee review. SUNS 6402, 29 January. Geneva. www.twnside.org.sg/title2/intellectual_property/info. service/2008/twn.ipr.info.080103.htm.

Treerutkuarkul, A. (2007). WHO raps Compulsory Licence plan: Government urged to seek talks with drug firms. *Bangkok Post*, 2 February.

TWN (Third World Network) (2007). 'WHO DG's shocking views on compulsory licensing criticised by health movements', 13 February. www.twnside.org.sg/title2/intellectual_property/info.service/twn.ipr.info.020706.htm.

WHO (2005). Guidance for the timely sharing of influenza viruses/specimens with potential to cause human influenza pandemics. Geneva. www.sdnpbd.org/sdi/issues/health/birdflue/other/timelysharing.pdf.

WHO (2006). Procedures for obtaining release of H5N1 sequences to the public domain. Geneva. www.who.int/csr/disease/avian_influenza/guidelines/h5n1sequences2006_08_23/en/print.html.

WHO (2007a). Scale of assessments 2008–2009. WHA60.5. Geneva.

WHO (2007b). *Working for health: An introduction to the World Health Organization*. Geneva. www.who.int/about/brochure_en.pdf.

WHO (2007c). Unaudited interim financial report for the year 2006. Annex: extra-budgetary resources for programme activities A60/30 Add.1. Geneva.

WHO (2007d). *Proposed programme budget 2008–2009*. Geneva. www.who. int/gb/ebwha/pdf_files/MTSP-PPB/en_mtsp_p5.pdf.

WHO (2007e). Appropriation resolution for the financial period 2008–2009. WHA60.12. Geneva. www.who.int/gb/ebwha/pdf_files/WHA60/A60_R12-en.pdf.

WHO (2007f). WHA Resolution 60.28 'Pandemic Influenza Preparedness: Sharing of influenza viruses and access to vaccines and other benefits'. Geneva. 23 May. www.who.int/gb/ebwha/pdf_files/WHA60/A60_R28-en.pdf.

D I . 3   The Gates Foundation

> We expect the rich to be generous with their wealth, and criticize them when
> they are not; but when they make benefactions, we question their motives, deplore
> the methods by which they obtained their abundance, and wonder whether their
> gifts will do more harm than good. (Bremner 1988)

So wrote Robert Bremner in *American Philanthropy*. Clearly a full and
informed understanding of philanthropy requires not just an assessment of
what it does and who it benefits, but also where the money has come from
and how it is managed and used.

The Gates Foundation is a major player in the health sector, spending
billions of dollars on health across the world. Most published literature
and media coverage have focused on the positive impact of the Gates
Foundation. The purpose of this chapter is to stimulate a more critical
discussion about this important global health actor and about philanthropy
in general. It is based on information from peer-reviewed publications,
magazines and newspapers, websites, and some unpublished information.
It also draws on interviews with twenty-one global health experts from
around the world in academia, non-governmental organisations, the World
Health Organization (WHO) and government, all of whom requested
anonymity or indicated a preference to speak off the record. Several
who recounted specific incidents or experiences asked that these not be
described so as to protect their identity. Some journalists who specialise
in global health were interviewed on the record. The Gates Foundation
also contributed by replying to a set of written questions drafted by
the GHW. Finally, an analysis of all global health grants issued by the
Foundation was conducted.

Background

The Bill and Melinda Gates Foundation was formed in January 2000 following the merger of the Gates Learning Foundation and the William H. Gates Foundation. By 2005, it had become the biggest charity in the world with an endowment of $29 billion. To put this in perspective, the second and third biggest international benefactors – the UK's Wellcome Trust and the Ford Foundation – have endowments of about $19 billion and $11 billion respectively (Foundation Centre 2008). The donation of $31 billion from US investor Warren Buffett in June 2006 made the Gates Foundation even bigger (Economist 2006a). Its annual spend will increase to over $3 billion in 2008.

On the Foundation's website, a set of fifteen guiding principles reflect the Gates family's views on philanthropy and the impact they want the Foundation to have:

- This is a family foundation driven by the interests and passions of the Gates family.
- Philanthropy plays an important but limited role.
- Science and technology have great potential to improve lives around the world.
- We are funders and shapers – we rely on others to act and implement.
- Our focus is clear and limited – and prioritizes some of the most neglected issues.
- We identify a specific point of intervention and apply our efforts against a theory of change.
- We take risks, make big bets, and move with urgency. We are in it for the long haul.
- We advocate – vigorously but responsibly – in our areas of focus.
- We must be humble and mindful of our actions and words. We seek and heed the counsel of outside voices.
- We treat our grantees as valued partners, and we treat the ultimate beneficiaries of our work with respect.
- Delivering results with the resources we have been given is of utmost importance – and we seek and share information about these results.
- We demand ethical behaviour of ourselves.
- We treat each other as valued colleagues.
- Meeting our mission – to increase opportunity and equity for those most in need – requires great stewardship of the money we have available.
- We leave room for growth and change.

Operationally, the Foundation is organised into three programmes: Global Health, Global Development and the US Program. The Global Health Program, which is the focus of this chapter, commands the biggest slice of the Foundation's spending.

Philanthropy: more than business, less than charity?

Chambers Dictionary defines philanthropy as 'a charitable regard for one's fellow human beings, especially in the form of benevolence to those in need, usually characterized by contributing money, time, etc. to various causes' (Chambers 2008). The origin of the word is Greek: *philia*, love; and *anthropos*, man.

The tradition of philanthropy has strong American roots from a hundred years ago when multimillionaire industrialists created foundations through which to channel their wealth. The first was the Russell Sage Foundation set up in 1907, followed by Rockefeller in 1910 and Carnegie in 1911 (Smith 1999). By the early 1960s, foundations were growing at a rate of 1,200 per year. Today, US foundations have assets of $500 billion and spend around $33.6 billion annually (Gunderson 2006). The Gates Foundation is, by far, the biggest of the big American foundations.[1]

The growth of private philanthropy mirrors the growth of private wealth in the US and other parts of the world, especially Europe. The global wealth boom and the collapse of the Soviet state have also created billionaires in countries like Russia, India, Mexico and Turkey, some of whom have initiated philanthropic initiatives in their own countries. As of 2007, there were 946 billionaires (nearly half of whom were US residents) with a combined net worth of about $3.5 trillion (Forbes 2007). The number is growing. *Forbes* magazine calculated a 23 per cent increase in the number of billionaires between 2006 and 2007.

But an equally astounding fact is that over 2.5 billion people live on less than $2 a day – more than ever before (Chen and Revallion 2007). Andre Damon (2007) describes this paradox as 'a by-product of the staggering growth of social inequality, the vast accumulation of personal wealth by a financial oligarchy at the expense of the rest of humanity'. This line of thinking implies that the origins of philanthropic wealth matters. To most people it matters if philanthropic spending is based on wealth that has been accumulated unethically, especially if it has involved either the direct or indirect exploitation or oppression of people.

Bill Gates made his money from technological innovation, business acumen and a favourable patents regime which enabled him to control large segments of a lucrative market. For some, Microsoft is one of the great success stories of modern-day business and Bill Gates's subsequent philanthropy an exemplar of generosity and humanity.

But there is a need to look at philanthropy more critically. The lack of examination of how wealth is created can perpetuate the myth that scarcity, rather than inequality, is at the root of much persisting social and

TABLE DI.3.I   **Forbes top twenty billionaires in 2008**

	Name	Citizenship	Net worth ($ bn)	Residence
1	Warren Buffett	US	62	US
2	Carlos Slim Helu and family	Mexico	60	Mexico
3	William Gates III	US	58	US
4	Lakshmi Mittal	India	45	UK
5	Mukesh Ambani	India	43	India
6	Anil Ambani	India	42	India
7	Ingvar Kamprad and family	Sweden	31	Switzerland
8	K.P. Singh	India	30	India
9	Oleg Deripaska	Russia	28	Russia
10	Karl Albrecht	Germany	27	Germany
11	Li Ka-shing	Hong Kong	27	Hong Kong
12	Sheldon Adelson	US	26	US
13	Bernard Arnault	France	26	France
14	Lawrence Ellison	US	25	US
15	Roman Abramovich	Russia	24	Russia
16	Theo Albrecht	Germany	23	Germany
17	Liliane Bettencourt	France	23	France
18	Alexei Mordashov	Russia	21	Russia
19	Prince Alwaleed Bin Talal Alsaud	Saudi Arabia	21	Saudi Arabia
20	Mikhail Fridman	Russia	21	Russia

Source: Forbes 2007.

economic problems and nurtures a culture of *noblesse oblige* for the wealthy and privileged to help the less fortunate. Neither does it help address the implications of conceding such power to the wealthy.

Furthermore, in many countries, philanthropy is a way for the rich to avoid paying tax. In the US, it is estimated that 45 per cent of the $500 billion that foundations hold actually 'belongs to the American public' in the sense that this is money forgone by the state through tax exemptions (Dowie 2002). Similarly, corporate social responsibility programmes can distract public attention away from the lowering of corporate tax rates across the world and the avoidance of tax by the rich.

It should also be noted that philanthropy is not always philanthropic. As *The Economist* suggests: 'The urge to give can have many different guises', including at times nothing more than 'a vain hope of immortality, secured by your name on a university chair or hospital wing' (Economist 2006b).

Many foundations also give to 'causes' that benefit the wealthy through, for example, the funding of museums, the arts and other cultural interests, or of hospitals, universities and research (for example, cancer research). Funds are also spent on plush offices, generous salaries to foundation employees and large stipends to trustees. Unsurprisingly, US foundations are seen by some as an extension of America's banks, brokerage houses, law firms, businesses and elitist universities.

None of this is to suggest that philanthropy doesn't have a good side. Some great things have been achieved through private acts of charity and good. But it is vital in today's world of immense wealth and enduring poverty to question the mainstream portrayal of philanthropy as being entirely benign.

In 1916, the US Commission on Industrial Relations warned that foundations were a danger because they concentrated wealth and power in the service of an ideology which supported the interests of their capitalist benefactors (Howe 1980). In the US, some benefactors play an important role in supporting think-tanks that advocate cuts in public services for the poor while advancing the agenda of 'corporate welfare' and privatisation (Covington 1997). There have also been examples of philanthropy being used covertly to support and further US political, economic and corporate interests abroad (Smith 1999; Karl and Karl 1999; Colby and Dennett 1995).

Even foundations with an explicit social and liberal agenda often support actions and programmes that are conservative in nature and fail to serve the long-term interests of the poor. In some instances, foundations have acted to steer labour or social movements towards more conservative positions by, for example, paying the leaders of social movements to attend 'leadership training programmes' or enticing them into well-paid jobs within professionalised non-governmental organisations (Allen 2007; Hawk 2007).

By premissing social change and development upon charity and the benevolence of the wealthy, the energy required to mobilise political action to tackle the root, structural injustices within society is dampened (Ahn 2007). Instead of campaigning for land reform and land rights, for example, NGOs and charities are harnessed to ameliorate the living conditions of slum dwellers whose land has been appropriated. Philanthropy can be a potent instrument for 'managing' the poor rather than empowering them. Few grants go to civil rights and social movements. Even fewer are given to programmes calling for a redistribution of wealth and land.

Robert Arnove (1980) charged that foundations can have

> a corrosive influence on a democratic society; they represent relatively unregulated and unaccountable concentrations of power and wealth which buy talent, promote causes, and in effect, establish an agenda of what merits society's attention. They serve as 'cooling-out' agencies, delaying and preventing more radical, structural change. They help maintain an economic and political order, international in scope, which benefits the ruling-class interests of philanthropists.

The need for professionalised NGOs to compete for funding also promotes division and competition within civil society, while increasing the power of patronage of private funders.

So far as the Gates Foundation is concerned, most people believe that humanitarianism lies at the core of its work in global health. It is fundamentally a charitable organisation. But whether its work is based on a true commitment to equity and social justice is open to question.

Its motivations were called into question following two articles published in January 2007 in the *LA Times* on the investments of the Gates Foundation (Piller et al. 2007). The articles described how investments worth at least $8.7 billion (excluding US and foreign government securities) were in companies whose activities were contrary to the Foundation's charitable goals.

Initially the Foundation reacted by saying that it was rethinking its investment policy (Heim 2007). However, it subsequently announced that there would be no changes to the Foundation's investment policy because it would have little impact on the problems identified by the *LA Times* (Gates Foundation 2008). The Foundation told GHW that it 'can do the most good for the most people through its grant-making, rather than through the investment of its endowment'. On its website,[2] the Foundation also notes that Bill and Melinda Gates have chosen not to 'rank' companies because 'there are dozens of factors that could be considered, almost all of which are outside the Foundation's areas of expertise'. The two exceptions to this rule are that the Foundation will not invest in tobacco, or in companies that represent a conflict of interest for Bill or Melinda.

Many people find the 'passive investor' stance of the Gates Foundation disappointing. Many other foundations (e.g. the Wellcome Trust), charities and individuals practise ethical and socially responsible investment and some even pursue a policy of active shareholder involvement. Why not the Gates Foundation?

TABLE DI.3.2   **Twenty largest individual grants awarded by the Gates Foundation, 1999–2007**

Grantee	Year	Total ($ m)	Length (months)	Purpose
GAVI Alliance	1999	750	60	Purchase new vaccines
GAVI Alliance	2005	750	120	General operating support
Global Fund	2006	500	43	Support the Global Fund in its efforts to address HIV/AIDS, tuberculosis and malaria in low- and middle-income countries
Medicines for Malaria Venture	2005	137	60	Further develop and accelerate antimalarial discovery and development
PATH	2005	108	72	Clinical development of the RTSS malaria vaccine
University of Washington	2007	105	120	Create the Health Metrics Institute at the University of Washington
Global Alliance for TB Drug Development	2006	104	60	Decrease tuberculosis mortality by developing new anti-TB treatments
International AIDS Vaccine Initiative (IAVI)	2001	100	60	Accelerate the global effort to create and distribute AIDS vaccine via vaccine design studies, clinical infrastructure and non-human primate studies
Global Fund	2002	100	120	General operating support
PATH	2004	100	48	Support the continuation and expansion of the work of the Malaria Vaccine Initiative from 2004 through 2007
Aeras Global TB Vaccine Foundation	2004	82	60	Develop and license improved TB vaccine for use in high burden countries
PATH	2006	75	60	Support a portfolio of pneumococcal vaccine projects
PATH	2001	70	120	Support the elimination of epidemic meningitis in sub-Saharan Africa
University of Washington Foundation	2007	61	72	Conduct a placebo-controlled proof-of-concept Phase III trial of the safety and efficacy of TDF and FTC/TDF in reducing HIV acquisition among HIV-negative partners within heterosexual HIV-discordant couples

Grantee	Year	Total ($ m)	Length (months)	Purpose
International Partnership for Microbicides	2003	60	60	Strengthen capacity in microbicide development
Save the Children Federation	2005	60	72	Test and evaluate newborn health care tools and technologies
University of Washington Foundation	2003	60	48	Facilitate multi-site study in Africa to assess the efficacy of acyclovir treatment on the transmission of HIV
Columbia University	2004	57	60	Reduce maternal deaths in developing countries by improving access to life-saving treatment for serious obstetric complications
Americans for UNFPA	2000	57	60	Reduce HIV/AIDS, STIs and unintended pregnancies by designing and implementing comprehensive, sustainable adolescent reproductive health programmes in Botswana, Ghana, Tanzania and Uganda
International Vaccine Institute	2002	55	72	Fund effective and affordable dengue vaccines for children in dengue-endemic areas

Source: Data from Gates Foundation website.

Overview of the Gates Foundation's global health grants

According to the Foundation's website, the majority of funding is provided for research in the areas of malaria, HIV/AIDS, immunisation, reproductive and maternal health, and other infectious diseases. The breakdown of funds (as published on the website) provided between late 1998 and March 2007 are as follows:

HIV, TB, and reproductive health	$1,854,811,111
Infectious diseases	$1,869,151,983
Global health strategies	$2,874,141,716
Global heath technologies	$466,671,428
Research, advocacy and policy	$766,612,229

Based on data collated from its website, we calculated that the Foundation had awarded 977 grants for global health from January 1999 to December 2007. The cumulative total of these grants was US$ 8.1 billion. Individual grant amounts vary considerably in size, ranging from $3,500 to $750 million. The twenty largest grants are shown in Table D1.3.2.

Grants are awarded for varying lengths of time, with some lasting for periods of less than a year, whilst others cover periods of up to eleven years. When grants are examined in terms of amounts per month, there is slight variation in the top ten grantees (see Table D1.3.3).

TABLE D1.3.3   **Top ten grantees in terms of amount/month**

Grantee	Year	$/month	Purpose
GAVI Alliance	1999	12,500,000	Purchase new vaccines
Global Fund	2006	11,627,907	Support the Global Fund in its efforts to address HIV/AIDS, tuberculosis and malaria in low- and middle-income countries
GAVI Alliance	2005	6,250,000	General operating support
World Health Organization (WHO)	2006	3,314,493	Support the Global Polio Eradication Initiative in accelerating polio eradication in Nigeria and preventing international spread of wild poliovirus across west and central Africa
Medicines for Malaria Venture	2005	2,283,333	Further develop and accelerate antimalarial discovery and development projects
PATH	2004	2,083,333	Support the continuation and expansion of the work of the Malaria Vaccine Initiative 2004–07
WHO	2005	2,083,333	Support the initiative to eradicate the polio virus
Elizabeth Glaser Pediatrics AIDS Foundation	2007	1,944,201	Accelerate the development of a global paediatric HIV/AIDS vaccine through basic research and Phase I clinical trials
Global Alliance for TB Drug Development	2006	1,740,064	Decrease tuberculosis mortality by developing new anti-TB treatments
International AIDS Vaccine Initiative (IAVI)	2001	1,666,667	Accelerate the global effort to create and distribute AIDS vaccine via vaccine design studies, clinical infrastructure and non-human primate studies

Source: Data from Gates Foundation website.

TABLE DI.3.4 **Top ten favoured grantees based on cumulative total of grants, 1999–2007**

Grantee	Cumulative amount awarded
World Bank Group	134,486,883
Institute for One World Health	144,825,148
University of Washington	151,973,070
IAVI	153,780,244
Johns Hopkins University	192,320,238
Medicines for Malaria Venture	202,000,000
World Health Organization	336,877,670
Global Fund	651,047,850
PATH	824,092,352
GAVI	1,512,838,000

Source: Data from Gates Foundation website.

A number of grantees are strongly supported by the Gates Foundation. Table D1.3.4 lists the top ten grantees in terms of the cumulative amount received from the Gates Foundation.

Accountability, influence and domination

The Gates Foundation is governed by the Gates family. There is no board of trustees; nor any formal parliamentary or legislative scrutiny. There is no answerability to the governments of low-income countries, nor to the WHO. Little more than the court of public opinion exists to hold it accountable.

The experts interviewed by the GHW cited the lack of accountability and transparency as a major concern. According to one, 'They dominate the global health agenda and there is a lack of accountability because they do not have to implement all the checks and balances of other organisations or the bilaterals.' Another described how the Foundation operates like an agency of a government, but without the accountability.

In addition to the fundamental lack of democratic or public accountability, there was little in the way of accountability to global public health institutions or to other actors in the health field. The fact that the Gates Foundation is a funder *and* board member of the various new Global Health

Initiatives (e.g. the Global Fund; GAVI, Stop TB Partnership; and Roll Back Malaria) means that other global health actors are accountable to the Gates Foundation, but not the other way round.

When these concerns were put to the Foundation, their reply focused on programmatic transparency accountability: 'We take accountability very seriously, and one of our top priorities is to effectively monitor the impact of our grant-making. We require grantees to report on their progress against agreed-upon milestones, and we often support third-party evaluations of our grants.' They continue, 'We are working to improve and expand the information we make available to the public, which already includes a detailed overview of grant-making priorities, information on all grants to date, annual reports, third-party evaluations, and case studies of what we're learning.' They also explain that by funding groups such as the Health Metrics Network and the Institute for Health Metrics and Evaluation, the effectiveness of investments in global health, including their own, would become easier to measure.

The Gates Foundation website states: 'Once we've made a grant, we expect the grantee to measure the results. We require our grantees to carefully track and report on their work in the field. ... We seek to share evaluations in various forums, including by circulating them to our partners and posting them on our site.'

In reality, there is surprisingly little written about the pattern and effectiveness of grant-making by the Gates Foundation. Limited information is available on the Foundation's website. A Global Health Programme Fact Sheet and a Global Health Grantee Progress document provide minimal information about specific diseases and conditions, and identify some of the grantees who receive recurring funding for ongoing work. Annual reports with more detailed financial information are also available. But none of these documents provides comprehensive information, or any data or analysis about the outcome of completed grants and projects.

Several interviewees also felt that the way grant proposals are solicited, reviewed and funded is opaque. Many grants appear to be made on the basis of personal contacts and informal networking. While the Foundation has advisory committees consisting of external experts, there has been no critical evaluation of how they are constituted, to what extent they are free from the patronage of the Foundation, nor whether they represent an appropriate mix of views and expertise.

The absence of robust systems of accountability becomes particularly pertinent in light of the Foundation's extensive influence. As mentioned above, it has power over most of the major global health partnerships, as well as over the WHO, of which it is the third-equal biggest single funder.

Many global health research institutions and international health opinion-formers are recipients of Gates money. Through this system of patronage, the Foundation has become the dominant actor in setting the frames of reference for international health policy. It also funds media-related projects to encourage reporting on global health events.

According to one of our interviewees, a senior health policy officer from a large international NGO, the sphere of influence even encompasses bilateral donors:

> You can't cough, scratch your head or sneeze in health without coming to the Gates Foundation. And the people at WHO seem to have gone crazy. It's 'yes sir', 'yes sir', to Gates on everything. I have been shocked at the way the bilateral donors have not questioned the involvement and influence of the Gates in the health sector.

The Foundation also funds and supports NGOs to lobby US and European governments to increase aid and support for global health initiatives, creating yet another lever of power and channel of influence with respect to governments. Recently, it announced a Ministerial Leadership Initiative aimed at funding technical assistance to developing-country ministries of health.

The extensive financial influence of the Foundation across such a wide spectrum of global health stakeholders would not necessarily be a problem if the Foundation was a passive funder. But it is not. It is an active funder. Very active and very involved, according to many people.

Not only is the Foundation a dominant actor within the global health landscape; it is said to be 'domineering' and 'controlling'. According to one interviewee, 'they monopolise agendas. And it is a vicious circle. The more they spend, the more people look to them for money and the more they dominate.' Interviewees also drew attention to similarities between Microsoft's tactics in the IT sector and the Foundation 'seeking to dominate' the health sector. In the words of one interviewee: 'They work on the premiss of divide and conquer. They negotiate separately with all of them.' Another interviewee warned of their 'stealth-like monopolisation of communications and advocacy'.

According to another interviewee, the Foundation has generated not just a technical approach, but also one that is elitist. Another interviewee described the Foundation as 'a bull in a china shop and not always aware of what has gone before – they have more to learn about learning'.

In February 2008, a senior official from a public agency broke cover. Arata Kochi, the head of the WHO's malaria programme, released a memorandum that he had written to his boss in 2007. According to the *New York Times*, which broke the story, Kochi complained that the growing dominance of malaria research by the Gates Foundation was running the risk of stifling diversity of views among scientists and of wiping out the WHO's policymaking function (McNeil 2008).

While recognising the importance of the Foundation's money, Kochi argued that many of the world's leading malaria scientists are now 'locked up in a "cartel" with their own research funding being linked to those of others within the group'. According to Kochi, the Foundation's decision-making is 'a closed internal process, and as far as can be seen, accountable to none other than itself'. Others have also been critical of the 'group think' mentality among scientists and researchers that has been induced by the Foundation.

The concerns raised by Kochi's letter were felt by many others in October 2007 when, apparently without consultation with the WHO or any other international bodies or so-called partners, at a conference in Seattle, the Foundation launched a new campaign to eradicate malaria. Apart from the lack of consultation, what was astonishing about the announcement was that it took everyone, including the WHO and the Roll Back Malaria Initiative, completely by surprise. For many people, this was another example of the Foundation setting the global health agenda and making the international health community follow.

The Gates Foundation in the health sector

Venture philanthropy

Partnership with industry is an explicit and prominent part of the Gates Foundation's global health strategy. Many of its senior employees also come from the corporate world. Chief Executive Patty Stonesifer is former senior vice president at Microsoft. The head of the Global Health Programme, Tadataka Yamada, came from GlaxoSmithKline.

The Gates Foundation also appears to be favourably disposed to actors like the McKinsey consulting group, which are consequently carving out a more prominent role for themselves in international health and development. According to one interviewee, private-sector players like the Foundation instinctively turn to their own kind to produce research on health.

Unsurprisingly, the Foundation's approach to global health is business-oriented and industrial in its approach. Such an approach is in keeping with what has been called 'venture philanthropy', the charitable equivalent of venture capitalism whereby 'social investors' search for innovative charitable projects to fund (Economist 2006c). As with venture capitalists, there is a demand for a high 'return', but in the form of attributable and measurable social or health outcomes (Economist 2006d).

The Foundation's corporate background and its demand for demonstrable returns on its investment appear to have resulted in a bias towards bio-medical and technological solutions. In the words of one interviewee: 'The Gates Foundation is only interested in magic bullets – they came straight out and said this to me.' One analysis of the Foundation's research grants linked to child mortality in developing countries found a disproportionate allocation of funding towards the development of new technologies rather than to overcoming the barriers to the delivery and utilisation of existing technologies (Leroy et al. 2007). Another example of the Foundation's technological orientation is its 'Grand Challenges in Global Health' – an initiative designed to stimulate scientific researchers to develop new tech-nological solutions for major health problems.

In a critique of the 'Grand Challenges', Birn (2005) argued that 'it is easy to be seduced by technical solutions and far harder to fathom the political and power structure changes needed to redistribute economic and social resources within and between societies and foster equitable distribution of integrated health-care services.' According to her, 'The longer we isolate public health's technical aspects from its political and social aspects, the longer technical inventions will squeeze out one side of the mortality balloon, only to find it inflated elsewhere.'

Health systems

Criticisms of the Foundation's technological and clinical focus would be tempered if more attention were paid to strengthening health systems, capacitating ministries of health to provide more effective stewardship and management, and tackling the market failures that are so prevalent in the mainly commercialised health systems of low-income countries.

However, going on past performance the Gates Foundation has not been interested in health systems strengthening and has rather competed with existing health services. One interviewee explains that the business model approach to health improvement is seen as distinct from 'development', which is the remit of official development assistance. Another said: 'the Gates Foundation did not want to hear about systems strengthening, they said that was for governments.'

Because results are more easily delivered through vertical and selective programmes, and more so through NGOs that can bypass national bureau-cracies and integrated planning systems, the Foundation has been a signifi-cant reason for the proliferation of global public–private initiatives (GPPIs) and single-issue, disease-based vertical programmes, which has fragmented health systems and diverted resources away from the public sector.

Neither has there been great interest in health systems research. In the words of one interviewee: 'They are not yet ready to accept that health systems etc. are researchable questions. They do not see the importance of research in this area.' Another recounted: 'The issues we presented to the Gates Foundation were around health-system strengthening, demand and access. We had no magic bullets, but a lot of priorities around operational research – i.e. not technological research. The Gates Foundation said that we were not thinking big enough.'

However, there are signs that the Foundation is turning its attention to health systems strengthening. According to one interviewee, a senior health policy adviser at the Foundation confirmed that 'health systems' was a new area of work they want to expand into. Another sign is that the Foundation is a signatory of the International Health Partnership, which is designed to improve aid effectiveness in the health sector and help strengthen health systems through a country-driven process.

But what would the Foundation's interest in health systems mean in practice? How will it marry 'venture philanthropy' with health systems strengthening? Where does the Foundation stand on the issue of the balance between markets and plans, and between the public and the private? Will it allow itself to be subjected to more bottom-up priority-setting? Will it shift away from short-term results towards long-term development?

When GHW asked the Gates Foundation if it would ever consider helping to fund the recurrent salary costs of public-sector health workers, it avoided answering the question directly: 'This is an important issue and we are strongly committed to ensuring that trained health workers are in place in developing countries. We are exploring ways the Foundation can contribute to efforts to address this issue.' And when asked if it would put funds into budget support or a country-wide SWAp (sector-wide approach), the reply was similarly evasive: 'We're open to many approaches to improving global health. For example, the Malaria Control and Evaluation Partnership in Africa (MACEPA), a Foundation grantee that supports Zambia's national malaria control program, is integrated into that country's sector-wide approach to health care.'

However, it appears that the corporate, market-oriented instincts of the Foundation will be extended to the health sector. Various remarks made in private and public by Gates Foundation employees indicate a wish to expand the role of the private sector in delivering health care in low-income countries (for example, see Cerell 2007). Recently, the Foundation funded and worked with the International Finance Corporation (an arm of the World Bank) to explore ways to invest more in the private health sector in Africa (IFC 2007).

Too close to Pharma?

The ties between the Foundation and the pharmaceuticals industry, as well as its emphasis on medical technology, have led some health activists to question if the Foundation is converting global health problems into business opportunities. Others worry about the Foundation's position with regard to intellectual property (IP) rights and the effect this has on the price of essential medicines.

Microsoft played an important role in pushing through the TRIPS agreement, and, together with other corporations, it is still lobbying to strengthen IP rights even further. At the 2007 G8 meeting in Germany, for example, a joint letter from various corporations, including Microsoft, helped push through an agreement that higher levels of IP protection should be demanded in emerging economies, especially regarding the issuing of compulsory licences for the manufacture of medicines. Many NGOs were dismayed. Oxfam suggested this would 'worsen the health crisis in developing countries'; MSF said the decision would 'have a major negative impact on access to essential medicines in all developing countries and fails to promote health innovation where it is most needed' (MSF 2007).

When GHW questioned the Gates Foundation on the issue of IP, it replied that it was working to overcome market barriers to vital drugs and vaccines in the developing world, but in a manner that was consistent with international trade agreements and local laws. This is similar to the position of Big Pharma, which is either to leave alone or to strengthen IP rights, while encouraging a greater reliance on corporate social responsibility and public–private 'partnerships' to overcome market failures.

But it is not clear where the Gates Foundation stands on the TRIPS flexibilities designed to enable poor countries to avoid the barriers created by patents and monopolies. For example, when Tadataka Yamada was reported in *The Economist* as saying that compulsory licensing could prove 'lethal' for the pharmaceuticals industry, one would be forgiven for wondering if he was speaking as a former employee of GlaxoSmithKline (Economist 2007e). However, in September 2007, he appeared to endorse the use of compulsory licences and even criticised his former employers by saying: 'Pharma was an industry in which it was almost too easy to be successful. It was a license to print money. In a way, that is how it lost its way' (Bowe 2007).

When asked about the patents on medicines, vaccines or diagnostic tools that the Gates Foundation itself has helped to develop, the Foundation said: 'We work with our grantees to put in place Global Access Plans designed to ensure that any tool developed with Foundation funding be made accessible at a reasonable cost in developing countries. We're employing a variety of approaches to help achieve that access, including innovative IP and licensing agreements.' However, whether Gates philanthropy will improve access to knowledge and technology, or buttress the trend towards the increasing privatisation of knowledge and technology, remains to be seen.

Final word

If 'global health' ten years ago was a moribund patient, the Gates Foundation today could be described as a transfusion of fresh blood that has helped revive the patient. The Gates Foundation has raised the profile of global health. It has helped prime the pipelines for new vaccines and medicines for neglected diseases. It is offering the prospect of the development of heat-stable vaccines for common childhood infections.

Bill Gates could have spent his money on art museums or vanity projects. He could have spent his money on cancer research, or on the development of space technology. He chose instead to tackle the diseases of the poor. He chose to go to Africa with much of his money.

The Foundation has also resisted the evangelical excesses of the Bush administration by, for example, supporting comprehensive sexual and re-productive health programmes. It has cajoled the pharmaceuticals corporate sector to become more responsible global actors. It has encouraged civic activism around the right to life-saving treatment. It has supported NGOs to pressure donor governments to live up to their aid commitments.

The Foundation has done much, and it will be doing even more as its level of spending sets to increase. But there are problems with what is happening. The Foundation is too dominant. It is unaccountable. It is not transparent. It is dangerously powerful and influential.

There are problems with the way global health problems are being framed. Technocratic solutions are important, but when divorced from the political economy of health they are dangerous. Public–private partnerships are potentially important, but unless the mandate, effectiveness and resource base of public institutions are strengthened, and unless there is much stronger regulation of the private sector (especially the giant multinationals), they can be harmful. Charity and philanthropy are good, but, unless combined with a fairer distribution of power and wealth, they can hinder what is just and right.

Similarly, the development of new technologies and commodities is positive but less so if the Foundation is not more supportive of the implementation by low- and middle-income countries of legitimate TRIPS flexibilities, such as compulsory licences.

The ability of individuals to amass so much private wealth should not be celebrated as a mark of brilliant business acumen, but seen as a failure of society to manage the economy fairly. Nothing is as disappointing as the Gates Foundation's insistence on continuing to act as a 'passive investor'. The reasons for *not* adopting an ethical investment strategy are unconvincing and reveal a double standard.

It is natural for he who pays the piper to call the tune. But other actors in the global landscape appear unable or unwilling to provide an adequate counterbalance to the influence of the Foundation. There is a profound degree of self-censorship. People appear scared to contradict the Foundation, even on technical, public health issues. This is not healthy. Joel Fleishman, author of *The Foundation*, argues that rather than accountability being a voluntary trait, foundations should be obliged to be accountable to the public (Fleishman 2007).

The Gates Foundation needs to consider its relationships with other actors. While it should preserve its catalytic, innovative and bold approach to global health, it needs to learn to know when it should follow and not lead. At the global level, the mandate and responsibility of organisations like the WHO must be strengthened, not weakened and undermined. And at the country level, while many low-income-country governments suffer from a real lack of capacity, the institution of government must be respected and strengthened.

There are concerns about the Foundation's rose-tinted perspective of the market and the simplistic translation of management practices from the commercial sector into the social and public sector of population health. For this reason, it could be argued that the Foundation should stay out of the business of strengthening health systems. It has neither the expertise nor the mandate to participate in this field of public policy. On the other hand, because the Foundation has a massive impact on health systems through its financing of GPPIs and its contribution to the dominance of a top-down, vertical approach to health-care delivery across the world, it should be involved. But it would then need to adopt a clearer, more evidence-based and responsible role towards national health systems.

One way forward suggested by several GHW interviewees was for the Foundation to support more people with experience of working in under-resourced health-care settings or with the understanding that health improvement is as much about facilitating appropriate social, institutional and political *processes* as it is about applying technocratic solutions.

Another way forward was for civil society to demand a comprehensive and independent evaluation of all its grantees and grants. In the absence of rigorous public debate and challenge from international health agencies and public health experts, it may be necessary for civil society to take the lead in making demands for improved performance and more accountability from the Gates Foundation.

Notes

1. See www.foundationcenter.org.
2. See www.gatesfoundation.org/AboutUs/Announcements/Announce-070109.htm.

References

Ahn, C. (2007). Democratising American philanthropy: In the shadow of the shadow state. In INCITE! Women of Color Against Violence (ed.), *The revolution will not be funded: The rise of the non-profit industrial complex*. Cambridge MA: South End Press.

Allen, R. (2007). Black awakening in capitalist America. In INCITE! Women of Color Against Violence (ed.), *The revolution will not be funded: The rise of the non-profit industrial complex*. Cambridge MA: South End Press.

Arnove, R. (1980). *Philanthropy and cultural imperialism*. Boston: GK Hall.

Birn, A.-E. (2005). Gates's grandest challenge: Transcending technology as public health ideology. *The Lancet* 366: 514–19. www.thelancet.com/journals/lancet/article/PIIS 0140673605664793/fulltext.

Bowe, C. (2007). New direction urged for pharma industry. *Financial Times*, 27 September.

Bremner, R. (1988). *American philanthropy*. Chicago: University of Chicago Press.

Cannon, G. (2004). Why the Bush administration and the global sugar industry are determined to demolish the 2004 WHO global strategy on diet, physical activity and health. *Pub Health Nutr* 7: 369–80.

Cerrell, J. (2007). Making markets work. *Finance and Development*, 44(4): 36–7. www.imf.org/external/pubs/ft/fandd/2007/12/pdf/point.pdf.

Chambers Reference Online (2008). www.chambersharrap.co.uk/chambers/chref.py/main?query=philanthropy&title=21st.

Chen, S., and M. Ravallion (2007). *Absolute poverty measures for the developing world, 1981–2004*. Working Paper WPS4211. Washington DC: World Bank.

Colby, G., and C. Dennett (1995). *Thy will be done*. New York: HarperCollins.

Covington, S. (1997). *Moving a public policy agenda: The strategic philanthropy of conservative foundations*. Washington DC: NCRP.

Damon, A. (2007). The Gates Foundation and the rise of 'free market' philanthropy. 22 January. www.wsws.org/articles/2007/jan2007/gate-j22.shtml.

Dowie, M. (2002). *American foundations: An investigative history*. Cambridge MA: MIT Press.

Economist (2006a). Bilanthropy. *The Economist*, 29 June. www.economist.com/opinion/displaystory.cfm?story_id=E1_STTQPJG.

Economist (2006b). Give and make. *The Economist*, 22 June. www.economist.com/opinion/displaystory.cfm?story_id=7086794.

Economist (2006c). Virtue's intermediaries. *The Economist*, 23 February. www.economist.com/surveys/displaystory.cfm?story_id=E1_VVTSSTN.

Economist (2006d). The birth of philanthrocapitalism. *The Economist*, 23 February. www.economist.com/surveys/displaystory.cfm?story_id=E1_VVTSGVG.

Economist (2007e). A Gathering storm. *The Economist*, 7 June. www.economist.com/business/displaystory.cfm?story_id=9302864.

Fleishman, J. (2007). *The foundation: A great American secret*. New York: PublicAffairs.

Forbes Magazine (2007). *The World's Billionaires.* www.forbes.com/2007/03/07/billionaires-worlds-richest_07billionaires_cz_lk_af_0308billie_land.html.

Foundation Centre (2008). Top 100 U.S. foundations by asset size. http://foundationcenter.org/findfunders/topfunders/top100assets.html.

Gates Foundation (2008). *Our investment philosophy.* www.gatesfoundation.org/AboutUs/Announcements/Announce-070109.htm.

Gunderson, S. (2006). Foundations: Architects of social change. *EJournal USA,* http://usinfo.state.gov/journals/itsv/0506/ijse/gunderson.htm.

Hawk, M.T. (2007). Native organising before the non profit industrial complex. In INCITE! Women of Color Against Violence (ed.), *The revolution will not be funded: The rise of the non-profit industrial complex.* Cambridge MA: South End Press.

Heim, K. (2007). Gates Foundation to review investments. http://archives.seattletimes.nwsource.com/cgi-bin/texis.cgi/web/vortex/display?slug=gatesinvest10&date=2007 0110&query=Heim+.

Howe, B. (1980). The emergency of scientific philanthropy, 1900–20: Origins, issues and outcomes. In R. Arnove (ed.), *Philanthropy and cultural imperialism.* Boston: GK Hall.

Karl, B., and A. Karl (1999). Foundations and the government: A tale of conflict and consensus. In C. Clotfelter and T. Erlich (eds), *Philanthropy and the non-profit sector in a changing America.* Bloomington: University of Indiana Press.

Leroy, J.L., et al. (2007). Current priorities in health research funding and lack of impact on the number of child deaths per year. *Am J Public Health* 97: 219–23.

McNeil, D. (2008). Gates Foundation's influence criticized, *New York Times,* 16 February. www.nytimes.com/2008/02/16/science/16malaria.html.

MSF (2007). G8 Declaration on innovation and intellectual property will directly harm access to medicines across the developing world. Press release, 7 June. www.msf.org.za/PR/PR_G8_070607.html.

Piller, C., F. Sanders and R. Dixon (2007). Dark clouds over the good works of the Gates Foundation. *LA Times,* 7 January. www.latimes.com/news/nationworld/nation/la-na-gatesx07jan07,0,6827615.story?coll=la-home-headlines.

Smith, J.A. (1999). The evolving role of American Foundations. In C. Clotfelter and T. Erlich (eds), *Philanthropy and the non-profit sector in a changing America.* Bloomington: University of Indiana Press.

The Global Fund to Fight AIDS, Tuberculosis and Malaria

One of the most prominent new actors within the global health landscape is the Global Fund to Fight AIDS, Tuberculosis and Malaria (GF), a private foundation based in Switzerland. As of June 2007, GF-supported programmes are said to have extended antiretroviral treatment (ART) to 1.1 million people; provided TB treatment to 2.8 million people; and distributed 30 million insecticide-treated bednets (ITNs).

However, there is a need for a more critical assessment. It is one thing to claim improvements in coverage or the distribution of medical outputs, it is another to demonstrate their impact and cost-effectiveness. Given its focus on three diseases, it is also necessary for the GF to avoid collateral damage to other essential health services.

Generally speaking, the GF's work in funding and catalysing responses to HIV/AIDS, TB and malaria has been successful. Many people have benefited. However, it is not possible to say whether these benefits are sustainable, or have been cost-effective and equitably distributed, without better data and more detailed country-by-country analysis.

History, functions and modus operandi

The beginnings

The GF first took shape at the G8 summit in July 2000 when a commitment was made to address the harms caused by HIV/AIDS, TB and malaria (G8 Communique 2000). At a 2001 Organisation of African Unity (OAU) Summit, Kofi Annan called for a 'war chest' of $10 billion per year to fight HIV/AIDS and other infectious diseases (Annan 2001). The UN Special Session on HIV/AIDS subsequently established a working group to delineate

IMAGE DI.4.I
**HIV activists in
South Africa**

the functions and structure of the GF. The GF approved the first round of grants in April 2002 – three months after the first meeting of its board.

Throughout this period, treatment activists in civil society played a critical role in creating the political momentum required to create the GF, whilst helping to drive down the cost of medicines and winning the argument that ART was feasible in even the poorest countries. Their use of moral persuasion, legal tactics and calculated acts of civil disobedience were critical aspects of their challenge to both governments and pharmaceuticals companies. By shaping the structure and policies of the GF, civil society organisations (CSOs) thus demonstrated their ability to influence global health governance (GF 2007a).

Functions

From the beginning, the GF was set up as a financial instrument, not an implementing agency. Its aim and purpose were to leverage additional financial resources for health. It would operate transparently, demonstrate accountability and employ a simple and rapid grant-making process. It would support country-led plans and priorities, and there was a particular emphasis on developing civil society, private-sector and government part-nerships, and supporting communities and people living with the diseases. It would adopt a performance-based approach to disbursing grants.

Organisational structure

The GF is headed by an executive director and has approximately 240 staff located in Geneva. As it is a non-implementing agency, there are no staff based in recipient countries.

It is governed by a 24-member Board of Directors, of whom 20 are voting members. The voting members consist of: 7 representatives from developing countries (one from each of the six WHO regions and an additional representative from Africa); 8 from donor countries; 3 from civil society; 1 from 'the private sector'; and a Gates Foundation representative. The four non-voting members are representatives of UNAIDS (the Joint United Nations Programme on HIV/AIDS), the World Health Organization (WHO), the World Bank, along with a Swiss citizen to comply with the legal status of the GF. The three civil society seats are designated for: one 'developed country non-governmental organisation (NGO) representative'; one 'developing country NGO representative'; and one person who represents 'communities affected by the diseases'.

Grant-making

The GF responds to proposals received from countries. These are reviewed by a Technical Review Panel (TRP), consisting of various appointed experts. Grants are awarded through specified 'rounds' of funding. Since its inception, there have been seven rounds of grant-making. As of December 2007, the GF had approved a total of US$10 billion to 524 grants in 136 countries, with US$4.8 billion having actually been disbursed to recipients in 132 countries (GF 2008a). Proposals take the form of five-year plans – grants are initially approved for two years (Phase 1) and then renewed for up to three additional years (Phase 2). Because the earlier grants have come to the end of their five-year lifespan, there has been much discussion about what should happen next.

As part of its 2007–2010 strategy, the GF has announced the introduction of a Rolling Continuation Channel (RCC). This will allow the continued funding of high-performing grants for up to a further six years. It is said that this will help improve performance in the last years of life of a grant; facilitate the expansion of successful programmes; reduce the risk of gaps in funding; and remove the costs associated with countries having to submit a new proposal.

Allocation of funds

Between 2002 and 2007, 55 per cent of grant funds were disbursed to sub-Saharan Africa countries. When stratified by income, 64 per cent, 28 per cent and 8 per cent of disbursements went to low-, lower-middle- and upper-middle-income countries respectively (Grubb 2007). During this period, 57 per cent, 15 per cent and 27 per cent of grant funds were allocated to HIV/AIDS, TB and malaria programmes respectively. The Fund estimates that it provides two-thirds of all global donor funding for malaria,

TABLE DI.4.I   **Allocation of funding across the spectrum of health
interventions** (%)

	Treatment	Prevention	Care and support	Other
HIV/AIDS ($315 million)	32	30	14	24
Tuberculosis ($223 million)	25	15	6	54
Malaria ($202 million)	40	35	–	25

Source: Global Fund 2007d.

45 per cent of all global donor funding for TB, and about 20 per cent of
funding for HIV/AIDS (CGD 2006). Relatively more funding has been
allocated to treatment than to prevention (see Table DI.4.I).

The lion's share of funding is spent on commodities, products and medicines (Figure DI.4.I). The second largest item of expenditure is 'human
resources', mostly in the form of training interventions.

FIGURE DI.4.I   **Resources by budget item after Round 6**

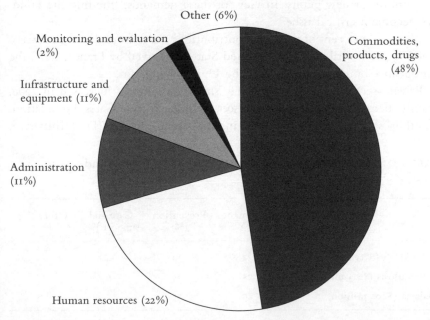

Source: Global Fund 2008b.

FIGURE DI.4.2   **The rising financial commitments of the Global Fund**
(actual and projected commitments and disbursements, cumulative totals,
US$ billion)[1]

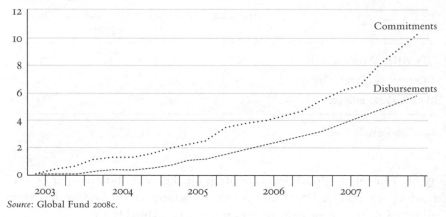

Source: Global Fund 2008c.

Funding the Fund

As expected, the annual expenditure and projected commitments of the GF
have steadily and rapidly increased (see Figure DI.4.2). In March 2007, the
GF presented a three-year funding projection for 2008–10 which amounted
to US$5 billion for existing commitments, and an additional US$7.2 billion
per annum for new grants. In view of these demands, 'funding the Fund'
has become a critical issue.

About 96 per cent of the GF's contributions come from donor countries.
The biggest contributor is the United States, followed by France, Italy, the
European Commission (EC) and the United Kingdom.

Private-sector funding is relatively small, although it increased in 2006,
mainly because of a pledge of $500 million by the Gates Foundation.
Another source of private financing has been the (RED)™ Initiative,

TABLE DI.4.2   **Funding disbursements of the Global Fund**
(as of 1 October 2007)

	Treatment (%)	Prevention (%)	Care and support (%)	Other (%)
HIV/AIDS ($315 million)	32	30	14	24
Tuberculosis ($223 million)	25	15	6	54
Malaria ($202 million)	40	35	–	25

Source: Global Fund 2008d.

BOX DI.4.I   **Trends from the 2007 replenishment meeting**

- The four countries that pledged (or are projected to pledge) the most for 2008–10 were the US ($2,172 million), France ($1,274 million), Germany ($849 million) and the UK ($729 million).
- The three countries that pledged the largest percentage of their gross national income (GNI) were Norway (0.087 per cent), Ireland (0.076 per cent) and Sweden (0.075 per cent).
- The three developed countries that pledged the smallest percentage of their GNI were Japan, Finland and Switzerland.
- The three countries whose pledges grew the most since the previous three years were Russia (increased 8.7 times), Saudi Arabia (3.6 times) and Spain (3.4 times).
- The Gates Foundation pledged $300 million, an increase of 50 per cent from the 2005–07 period.

Source: GFO 2007a.

---

through which participating companies contribute a percentage of their sales to the Fund. As of March 2008, the Initiative has contributed $61 million. So far, the GF has discouraged private-sector contributions in the form of earmarked donations or non-financial contributions (GF 2008d).

'Replenishment meetings' take place every two years to discuss the funding of the GF. At the meeting in September 2007 (see Box DI.4.I), the GF was pledged *at least* $6.3 billion for the period 2008–10 by twenty-six governments and the Gates Foundation (GFO 2007a). With projections that other donors will give a further $3.4 billion, the Fund has secured a total of $9.7 billion. This is enough for it to continue operations at its current level for at least another three years, but less than the $12–18 billion that it predicted it would need for 2008–10.

How the GF works within countries

A general requirement of the GF is the establishment of a Country Co-ordinating Mechanism (CCM) consisting of representatives from government; multilateral or bilateral agencies (e.g. UNAIDS, WHO); NGOs; academic institutions; private businesses; and people living with the diseases. The CCM is expected to oversee the submission of proposals to the GF as well as grant implementation.

In most countries, the CCM is chaired by a representative of government. In order to ensure adequate multi-stakeholder involvement, the GF has a set of criteria for CCM composition which are supposedly used to determine eligibility of grant proposals (GF 2005). These include the requirement for non-governmental CCM members to be selected through clear and transparent processes, and the inclusion of people living with and/or affected by the diseases. In addition, GF priorities for the future are said to include strengthening 'community systems', increasing the representation of vulnerable groups, and providing more support for CCM administration (GF 2007b).

The actual awards of grants are made to a named principal recipient (PR). Government agencies are the PR for about two-thirds of all grants. Nonprofit development organisations and multilateral organisations also act as PRs. In some countries a dual- or multiple-track model is used – where a grant is split across more than one recipient. As part of a set of strategic innovations for the next four years, the GF intends to promote the routine use of 'dual-track financing' (GF 2007b).

Government institutions are the main implementing agencies in about 59 per cent of grants, while NGOs represent 30 per cent of implementing agencies. Government agencies make up a higher proportion of implementing agencies in sub-Saharan Africa than in Asia.

Because there is no GF presence in recipient countries, Local Fund Agents (LFAs) are hired to monitor grant implementation, and to rate performance. LFAs may also be used to review budgets and work plans prior to the signing of a new grant agreement. There is normally one LFA per country. Most LFAs come from two of the big private consultancy firms (see Box D1.4.2).

Grant recipient and LFA reports are then used by the relevant GF portfolio manager to score the progress and achievements of the projects. Grant disbursement and renewal ratings are posted onto the GF website to encourage CCMs and other stakeholders to track progress. Countries deemed to be performing poorly can have further disbursements of funding withheld, or the grant cancelled or handed over to another principal recipient.

BOX D1.4.2   **List of LFAs and number of countries served**

- PricewaterhouseCoopers (69)
- KPMG (28)
- Emerging Markets Group (8)
- Swiss Tropical Institute (8)
- UNOPS (7)
- Crown Agents (1)
- World Bank (1)

Discussion

A model of good global health governance?

A frequent comment about the GF is that civil society and developing-country representatives are prominent in its governance structures. With a board of twenty-four that includes five representatives from low-income countries and three from civil society, this may be true relative to other global institutions. However, numerically, the board is still dominated by donor representatives. And while there are only two representatives of the private sector, one of them is currently chair of the board and the other is the Gates Foundation. In addition, the Gates Foundation funds the McKinsey firm to perform a range of secretariat functions on behalf of the GF.

However, the GF appears to live up to its reputation for transparency. Financial information is readily available, as are details about the approval of proposals and the disbursement of funding. An electronic library houses both internal and external evaluations of the Fund. Transparency has also been enhanced by the regular publication of the *Global Fund Observer* (GFO), a newsletter produced by an independent NGO called Aidspan. It reports on the financing of the Fund; monitors progress and comments on the approval, disbursement and implementation of grants; provides guidance for stakeholders within applicant countries; reports and comments on board meetings. Altogether it provides a useful information service and performs an important 'watchdog' role (GFO 2008).

The GFO reflects the extensive engagement of CSOs with the GF, which arises in part from the existence of a large, well-resourced and well-organised network of disease-based NGOs that feel a degree of ownership over the GF. Not only do they effectively engage with the GF, they have established mechanisms for influencing the policies of other stakeholders, in particular donors, vis-à-vis the GF.

Indeed a form of interdependency exists. Many CSOs which were formed to address HIV/AIDS, TB and malaria view the GF as an important ally. At the same time, the GF understands the importance of CSOs to its own survival and growth. There is a dedicated Civil Society Team within the GF's External Relations Unit, as well as various forums through which CSOs are encouraged to influence GF policies and practices (for example, the biannual Partnership Forum). The GF has even helped create and support a number of 'Friends of the GF' organisations designed to advocate on its behalf.

The GF and its constellation of associated actors thus present a number of features which have broader relevance. For example, there is much about the GF's provision of information that can and should be replicated by other global health initiatives, and the GFO is an exemplary model of civil society monitoring that should be applied to other institutions.

When it comes to CS engagement, the model may be less transferable. The degree of transparency and 'democratic space' that exists in relation to the GF may have been tolerated because the GF embodies a relatively shared set of aims across a wide range of stakeholders. Northern governments, including the US; developing-country governments; the medical profession; health activists; pharmaceuticals companies; venture philanthropists; and the 'celebrity' spokespersons of the West's conscience – all share an interest in seeing action taken against 'the big three' diseases. It is hard to see how synergy across such diverse constituencies could be replicated in organisations like the WTO or the World Bank, for example. Nonetheless, the GF may provide a useful benchmark for comparison.

National governance

As global institutions become more numerous and prominent, important questions arise about their effect on governance at the national level. National governance is especially pertinent to the GF because an effective and equitable response to HIV/AIDS, TB and malaria ultimately requires the protection of human rights, social development, peace and effective health-sector stewardship, which in turn requires governments to work and democracy to flourish.

Together with its civil society partners, the GF can claim some credit for having enhanced participatory approaches to health policymaking in many countries. A key instrument has been the CCM. While its primary purpose is to help plan and oversee the implementation of GF grants, it is also intended to enhance public accountability and enable the entry of vulnerable and marginalised groups into health policymaking spaces. Some CCMs have been criticised for being tokenistic and lacking representation of rural groups, for example, but in several countries they have become arenas within which relationships between government, civil society and NGOs are being contested and redefined.

The GF has also influenced governance processes by acting on allegations of corruption and financial mismanagement. In 2005, it suspended grants to Uganda following reports of mismanagement and irregularities in procurement and subcontracting (Bass 2005). In 2006 it suspended two grants to Chad and phased out its grants to Myanmar for similar reasons.

It appears therefore that the potential for 'public health' to catalyse positive change within countries is being demonstrated by the GF. However, it should be noted that in some countries CCMs have sometimes been viewed as an inappropriate, unnecessary and inefficient imposition from outside and a reminder of the need for the GF and health activists to be better informed about the historical, political and social context of governance within countries and to reject the temptation of a one-size-fits-all approach to 'good governance'.

Health-sector governance

The GF impacts on health-sector governance by boosting health budgets and by placing considerable expectations on countries to deliver on various HIV/AIDS, TB and malaria targets. Its influence on health budgets is shown in Table D1.4.3, which lists the five countries where GF grants made up the biggest proportion of total health expenditure between 2003 and 2005. In Burundi, GF grants amounted to more than the entire public budget for health, including direct funding of public services by other donors. GF grants were also a significant proportion of total health expenditure in Burundi (32 per cent), Liberia (17 per cent) and the DRC (15 per cent) respectively.

Concerns have been raised about the ability of countries to absorb such large injections of funding. Initially there was an assumption that capacity within countries would either be sufficient or that technical assistance (TA) would be provided by other agencies to help ensure effective use of GF grants. This did not turn out to be the case. According to one analysis, 'the international community dramatically underestimated TA requirements' and had not anticipated constraints in human resources, basic management and health systems infrastructure (CGD 2006). In addition, the expectation that other agencies would support capacity development caused irritation

TABLE D1.4.3   **The contribution of the GF to national expenditure on health, May 2003**[2]

	GF disbursements (US$ million)	GF disbursements as % of total health expenditure	GF disbursements as % of public health expenditure
Burundi	21.8	31.8	118.2
Liberia	14.2	17.6	28.0
Dem. Rep. Congo	48.3	15.3	31.1
Rwanda	53.1	12.6	22.4
Gambia	10.4	12.4	46.0

Sources: Global Fund 2008c; WHO 2007b.

and led to other agencies complaining that supporting GF programmes was an 'unfunded mandate'.

Such experiences raise the issue of donor and agency coordination. As discussed in Chapter D1.1, there is now greater explicit recognition of the need for external agencies to cooperate and harmonise their activities. One manifestation of this recognition is the 2004 Three Ones Agreement, which was designed to encourage all agencies to work together on HIV/AIDS through one action framework, one national coordinating authority, and one monitoring and evaluation system.[3] However, thus far, even the modest goals of this agreement, dealing with only one disease area, have not been met.

While the lack of coordination among donors and global health initiatives isn't the fault of the GF alone, it should take on the challenge of ensuring maximum harmonisation with the US government's Presidents Emergency Plan for AIDS Relief (PEPFAR) and the World Bank's Multi-Country AIDS Programme (MAP). One promising development has been the decision by the GF to invite National Strategy Applications from recipient countries, the purpose of which is to help eliminate parallel planning efforts and improve harmonisation among donors and other relevant health programmes (GF 2007b).

Strengthening health systems

The intense global focus on three diseases has led to concerns about other health priorities being undermined. The expansion of NGO-run projects has further fragmented already disorganised health systems. There is now recognition that general health systems weaknesses are constraining the scale-up of dedicated HIV/AIDS, TB and malaria programmes. So what is the GF doing to prevent the displacement of resources from other essential health services and to avoid undermining the longer-term agenda of health systems development?

At one point the GF had a stand-alone grant application process for 'health systems strengthening' (HSS). However, this was stopped due to views (mainly among external stakeholders) that the GF did not have the mandate or 'comparative advantage' to fund HSS.

Presently, the GF encourages applicants to budget for HSS activities within disease-specific grant proposals, but states that these activities must be 'essential to reducing the impact and spread of the disease(s)' (GF 2007c). The board has also decided that grants can be used to strengthen public, private or community health systems, but only if it helps to combat the three diseases (GFO 2007b). Examples of HSS actions given by the GF consist of activities that one would expect in any disease-based plan (e.g. training health workers, purchasing and maintaining diagnostic equipment).

On paper, therefore, the GF does not support the argument that because of the extraordinary money and public attention that have been captured by the 'big three' diseases, the GF should help strengthen the health system *as a whole* and for the benefit of other health needs.

However, the GF maintains a view that its grants naturally strengthen health systems by pointing, for example, to the huge investments in training health workers. In fact only a quarter of GF expenditure has been on 'human resource' line items, most of which has been training-related, with more than 80 per cent focused on clinical training targeted at the three diseases. By contrast, little has been directed at human resource (HR) recruitment or remuneration, or strengthening systems-wide HR management and administrative capacity. There has also been little analysis of the impact of GF spending on the 'internal brain drain' within countries.

The GF has also had the opportunity to support and strengthen procurement, logistics and supply systems within countries. But in many low-income countries, separate stand-alone systems for HIV/AIDS, TB and malaria supplies remain in place. While this makes sense from the perspective of disease-specific targets, it is also costly and inefficient and can ultimately delay the development of effective and efficient integrated systems.

On a positive note, a WHO report identified seven countries where GF grants were strengthening health systems (WHO 2007a). Most notable was a Round 5 Grant to Malawi, which was used to support a six-year, sector-wide HR programme. Other examples listed were Afghanistan's Round 2 proposal, which included interventions to build managerial and administrative capacity in the Ministry of Public Health; Rwanda's Round 5 grant, which helped expand community-based health insurance schemes, electrify health centres and support generic management training; Kenya's Round 6 proposal, which included plans to renovate a third of all public dispensaries, recruit 155 staff, strengthen district-level planning and management, and train laboratory technicians to provide an essential laboratory package; Ethiopia's Round 1 proposal for TB, which focused on improving drug supply management across the health system.

However, the effect of these grants on strengthening health systems cannot be assumed. For example, although the GF contributed to Malawi's sector-wide HR Programme, it is not known to what extent this has expanded HR capacity as a whole, or mainly expanded capacity for HIV/AIDS, TB and malaria services. The question of whether the privileged funding of these services has strengthened or weakened health systems overall has provoked fierce debates within the international health community. The answer, however, is likely to vary from country to country.

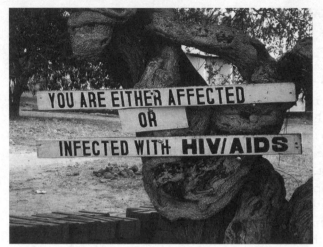

IMAGE DI.4.2
**Sign on tree
in rural village**

Conclusion

This chapter has provided a broad-brush sketch of the Global Fund, placing it in the context of global health governance more generally, and of weak and fragmented health systems in low-income countries. Any recommendations about the GF have to take into account the many other actors within the global health environment, as well as the particular priorities and health systems requirements at the country level.

The GF has recently completed a strategic planning exercise which has resulted in a number of future plans (GF 2007b). First, the GF intends to grow over the next few years in terms of both the number of grants and its annual expenditure. It is projected that by 2010 the GF will be spending US$8–10 billion per year, triple the level in 2006. Resource mobilisation efforts will become ever more important. At present it is unclear where this requirement for additional funding will come from.

But as the GF embarks upon Round 8, one is struck by the lack of debate about the optimum and appropriate size of the GF. Just how big should it become? Can it get too big? What should its size be relative to that of other agencies? What will be the opportunity costs associated with the tripling of expenditure from 2006 to 2010? Can it have too many grants spread across too many countries? There are currently 517 grants spread across 136 countries – why so many countries? Would it be prudent to focus attention on a smaller number of 'struggling' countries or on high-burden countries? Should its remit be extended to include a broader set of diseases? Should it become a global fund for health systems in general?

Another issue for the GF (together with other initiatives) is its impact on health systems, particularly in relation to five interconnected issues:

- ensuring appropriate, coordinated, country-led and sector-wide health planning and management;
- fixing the current Balkanisation of health systems by bringing order to the disjointed and vertical projects and programmes;
- harnessing the large and unregulated commercial sector to serve the public good;
- reducing the inequity between urban and rural populations, between rich and poor, and between privileged and unprivileged diseases and illnesses;
- guarding against an inappropriate overconcentration on medical technologies and products at the expense of health promotion and tackling the social determinants of ill health.

The GF can and should play a more responsible HSS role in many more countries, especially where it accounts for a significant proportion of public health expenditure. In these countries, the GF should explicitly encourage HSS activities that will improve services for HIV/AIDS, TB and malaria, but only in a way that simultaneously strengthens the whole health system.

Even the Fund's Technical Review Panel (TRP) noted that of the $2,762 million approved for Round 7 grants, only 13.1 per cent was targeted towards HSS actions, and that there was an opportunity to do more in this area (GFO 2007c). It also felt that many of the proposed HSS actions were focused on the immediate obstacles to health-care delivery, and not enough on planning, financing and other more upstream actions. The TRP therefore recommended that the GF provide intensive technical support on HSS for Round 8 and add health systems indicators to the monitoring and evaluation framework (GFO 2007c).

The GF must avoid creating perverse incentives through its target-driven approach. Coverage targets must not be set in a way that overemphasises numbers 'treated' or 'reached' at the expense of measures of quality, equity or sustainability. The short and quick route to expanding coverage is not always the best route to take in the long term. While it is best to 'raise all boats' rather than to pull back on services for HIV/AIDS, TB and malaria, there must be stronger guarantees that other priority health services are not being harmed.

The GF can help by encouraging better monitoring and research. The difficulties of having to make choices between the three diseases and the health system as a whole, or between short-term/emergency demands and long-term development needs, will be eased with better data. The GF can also insist on proposals being demonstrably aligned to sector-wide plans or health systems policy. In the long run, the GF should also consider what proportion of its grants should be pooled into sector-wide budgets and set itself some targets accordingly.

In late 2008, a Five Year Evaluation of the Fund is due to be published. In spite of the evaluation being one of the biggest ever commissioned, there are two limitations. First, it is largely reliant on retrospective study methods. Second, it does not address the specific question of the GF's impact on the wider health system.

Interestingly, national debates on the relative priorities of treatment versus prevention have subsided. Although there is consensus that both treatment and prevention are important, and furthermore are interlinked, it is not clear whether the optimum balance between different treatment and prevention strategies has been achieved within countries. The GF's expenditure pattern appears to reflect an emphasis on treatment over prevention. Although there are methodological difficulties in generating the data to determine if this is true or not, it is important to keep asking the question, if only to ensure that careful thought and consideration continue to go into the process of priority-setting.

When all Round 1 to 6 grants are taken into account, 48 per cent of the GF's budget is allocated to drugs, commodities and other products. Most of the 22 per cent of expenditure on human resources is used to train existing health workers to use these drugs, commodities and products. A further 11 per cent is allocated to infrastructure and equipment. Such facts, particularly in light of the heavy involvement of the private sector, must raise further questions about the broader orientation of the GF response to HIV/AIDS, TB and malaria. Is it overly biomedical? Does it reflect the lessons learnt about achieving 'good health at low cost' from countries and settings such as Sri Lanka, Costa Rica and Kerala?

It would not be appropriate to make a list of concrete recommendations to the GF given the need to bring greater coherence and order to the broader global health landscape. However, this chapter aims to provide a good description of a new actor on the global scene and raise some useful questions, in the hope that the relevant actors will seek out the correct answers.

Notes

1. This figure makes a number of assumptions about grant approvals, renewal and disbursement rates and other variables. But it shows the general trend of an increasingly steep rise in both commitments and disbursements.
2. Total health expenditure refers to all spending on health, including by private individuals. Public Health Expenditure refers to spending by public bodies only,

such as the Ministry of Health. However, some funding may have originated from external donors. For example, Burundi spent $18 million through the Ministry of Health between 2003 and 2005, $14 million of which was sourced from the GF (the GF spent $7 million elsewhere in the health economy through private organisations in this time).

3. www.who.int/3by5/newsitem9/en/.

References

Annan, K. (2001). Remarks available online at www.un.org/News/Press/docs/2001/SGSM7779R1.doc.htm.

Bass, E. (2005). Uganda is learning from its Global Fund grant suspension. *The Lancet* 366: 1839–40.

CGD (Center for Global Development) (2006). Challenges and opportunities for the new executive director of the Global Fund: Seven Essential Tasks. Washington DC.

G8 Communique Okinawa (2000). www.g7.utoronto.ca/summit/2000okinawa/finalcom.htm.

GF (Global Fund) (2005). Revised guidelines on the purpose, structure and composition of country coordinating mechanisms and requirements for grant eligibility. Global Fund to Fight AIDS, Tuberculosis and Malaria. 10th board meeting, Geneva.

GF (2007a). *An evolving partnership: The Global Fund and civil society in the fight against AIDS, tuberculosis and malaria.* Geneva: GFATM. www.theglobalfund.org/en/media_center/publications/evolvingpartnership/.

GF (2007b). *A strategy for the Global Fund: Accelerating the effort to save lives.* www.theglobalfund.org/en/files/publications/strategy/Strategy_Document_HI.pdf.

GF (2007c). Guidelines for proposals, Round 7. www.theglobalfund.org/en/files/apply/call/seven/Guidelines_for_Proposals_R7_en.pdf.

GF (2007d). *Partners in impact: Results report 2007.* Geneva: GFATM. www.theglobalfund.org/en/files/about/replenishment/oslo/ProgressReport2007_low.pdf.

GF (2008a). Monthly progress update. www.theglobalfund.org/en/files/publications/basics/progress_update/progressupdate.pdf.

GF (2008b). Distribution of funding after 6 rounds. www.theglobalfund.org/en/funds_raised /distribution/.

GF (2008c). Current grant commitments and disbursements. www.theglobalfund.org/en/funds_raised/commitments/.

GF (2008d). Pledges and contributions. www.theglobalfund.org/en/funds_raised /pledges/.

GFO (Global Fund Observer) (2007a). *Global Fund Observer* 77, September. www.aidspan.org/index.php?page=gfobackissues.

GFO (2007b). *Global Fund Observer* 80, November. www.aidspan.org/index.php?page=gfobackissues.

GFO (2007c). *Global Fund Observer* 82, December. www.aidspan.org/index.php?page=gfobackissues.

GFO (2008). An evaluation of GF grants. www.aidspan.org/index.php?page=gfgrants.

Grubb, I. (2007). Presentation to the Action for Global Health meeting in London, 13 September.

WHO (2007a). *The Global Fund strategic approach to health systems strengthening.* Report from WHO to the Global Fund Secretariat. Geneva.

WHO (2007b). *Country information: National health accounts.* www.who.int/nha/country/en/.

D I . 5 The World Bank

The World Bank is emerging from a period of intense controversy in the wake of the presidency of Paul Wolfowitz, who stepped down as a consequence of a favouritism scandal in June 2007. Under the new leadership of Robert Zoellick, the institution is once more being backed by donors, and it has launched a high-profile new health strategy.

This chapter looks at the way the Bank's funding, structure and internal incentives shape its behaviour. It describes the history of the Bank's involvement in the field of health and raises serious questions about the central planks of its new strategy for the sector.

Overview of the Bank

History and structure

The World Bank Group comprises five parts, all set up at different times and with different roles:

- The *International Bank for Reconstruction and Development* (IBRD) is the oldest arm, established at the founding of the Bank in 1944. It was set up to finance the reconstruction and development of the war-ravaged European economies, but it gradually moved into financing large infrastructure projects in newly independent developing countries from the 1950s onwards. The IBRD lends money to governments at market interest rates. Its financial resources come from its initial endowment from its shareholders, from money raised on the financial markets and from interest payments made on its loans.
- The second major arm is the *International Development Association* (IDA), which was established in 1960 to provide grants and soft loans (i.e. with

low interest rates and long repayment periods) to developing countries. The IDA's budget is replenished by donor countries every three years.

These two core components of the World Bank Group are supplemented by three affiliates:

- The *International Finance Corporation* (IFC), which was established in 1956 to allow lending directly to the private sector. The IFC has its own staff, budget and building and is somewhat smaller than the rest of the Bank. Its aim is to facilitate private-sector investment and development in low- and middle-income countries.
- The *International Centre for Settlement of Investment Disputes* (ICSID), which was set up in 1966 to arbitrate on international investment disputes.
- The *Multilateral Investment Guarantee Agency* (MIGA), which was established in 1985 to provide financial guarantees to foreign investors wishing to invest in developing countries.

Governance

On its website, the Bank describes itself as a co-operative. There is some truth in this statement, in so far that it has 185 country members who are shareholders in the Bank. However, this comforting formulation of the Bank's identity belies the reality of an institution that mirrors global inequality. For a start, the Bank's shareholders do not have equal power. Votes are weighted according to a country's financial contributions.

The Bank's five most powerful shareholders – the United States, Japan, Germany, United Kingdom and France – control 37.24 per cent of votes in the IBRD, and 39.78 per cent of votes in the IDA (Weaver 2007). The Bank's primary clients, low- and middle-income countries (LMICs), have little say. Even larger developing countries such as Brazil, Russia, India and China struggle to influence Bank decisions. The recent call made by African finance ministers meeting in Maputo for improvements in Africa's decision-making position at both the World Bank and the International Monetary Fund (IMF) shows that this is a key issue, but their demands appear to have been left unanswered (Agencia de Informacao de Mocambique 2007).

The most powerful donor state is the US, which controls 16.4 per cent of the votes on the IBRD's board (Weaver 2007) and 14.7 per cent on the IDA board. With an 85 per cent 'super-majority' required to change the Bank's constitution, the dominance of the US is considerable. Furthermore, the Bank president is, by tradition, an American chosen by the US president in consultation with the US Treasury. Many of its staff are American or have been educated in American institutions and its working language is

English (Weaver 2007). All these factors give weight to the accusation that the Bank operates in the interest of its major shareholder.

Because the IDA is dependent on aid financing from donor countries, the three-yearly rounds of IDA replenishments are often accompanied by government lobbying, in particular by the US. For example, in 2002 the US used the IDA replenishment meetings to lobby for an 'increased role for the private sector in health care, education and water' (Weaver 2007).

However, it is important to note that the Bank has a degree of independence. Much of the Bank's resources are raised independently of governments on the capital markets. The president, senior managers and its staff are also important in setting the Bank's agenda.

When the US appointed Paul Wolfowitz, a key neoconservative in the Bush administration and an architect of the war on Iraq, as president of the Bank in 2005, there was widespread protest both in diplomatic circles and by World Bank staff themselves. His appointment was felt to exemplify US government contempt for multilateral institutions. Once in post, he brought in a team of lieutenants who 'set about administering the Bank in a brutal and highly ideological way'. They showed 'undisguised contempt for senior managers' (Wade 2007), causing widespread dissatisfaction among staff. When he was finally caught up in a favouritism scandal, the lack of support from staff contributed to him eventually losing his job.

Since then, Robert Zoellick, a former US deputy secretary of state and lead trade representative, has become the Bank's latest president. NGO reactions were unfavourable. Zoellick has close ties to the private sector, coming immediately from a stint at US investment bank Goldman Sachs and previously serving on the advisory board of US energy giant Enron.

What is the Bank?

The structure of the World Bank, with its five arms, reflects its complex nature and multiple personalities. For its first few decades, the Bank mainly invested in large infrastructure projects which could generate high rates of return. It was believed that this kind of investment would drive economic growth and development. Finance for 'human capital' was seen as wasteful, or at least money which would not generate much visible return. It was only towards the end of the 1960s that investment in people's skills began to be understood as necessary for economic growth. Subsequently, the Bank's education programmes began to grow.

The idea of development also soon came to be seen as being more than about just generating wealth — fighting poverty mattered too. It was Bank president Robert McNamara who, in the 1970s, took the Bank into the fields of poverty eradication, agriculture, social projects, as well as urban development and public administration (Vetterlein 2007). Over time, the Bank extended its activities to the health sector.

With the establishment and growth of the IDA, the Bank began to transform into a donor agency, offering grants or soft loans. In doing so, it transformed further, by developing in-house research and policy analysis capacity as an adjunct to its lending and grant-making activities. This aspect of the Bank's work was given explicit attention during the presidency of James Wolfensohn when he sought to identify the Bank as a 'knowledge bank' for the world.

The Bank is therefore an institution with many forms of power. It has the power to raise capital for development projects. It has the power to act as a donor. It has the power to generate knowledge and frame policy development. It is therefore important that this influence is used benevolently.

But many people believe that it has not been used benevolently or wisely. For some, the Bank has been a key player in driving forward the set of neoliberal policies known as the 'Washington Consensus' which has facilitated a form of capitalism that has increased disparities, deepened poverty and enriched multinationals.

Others are critical of an internal intellectual climate rooted in and dominated by an economic rationality that leads to unnecessarily narrow policy advice (Rao and Woodcock 2007). Weaver also notes how this climate pushes staff to adopt a blueprint approach rather than a country-by-country approach. While the Bank's rhetoric consists of 'putting countries in the driver's seat', reality may be closer to what some have styled the taxi-cab approach in which 'the country is in the driver's seat, but no-one is going anywhere until the Bank climbs in, gives the destination and pays the fare' (Pincus and Winters 2002, cited in Weaver and Park 2007).

A recent high-profile peer review of the World Bank's research output also noted the use of research 'to proselytize on behalf of Bank policy, often without taking a balanced view of the evidence, and without expressing appropriate scepticism. Internal research that was favourable to Bank positions was given great prominence, and unfavourable research ignored' (Banerjee et al. 2006). This dominance of particular, 'accepted' points of view is reinforced by a low tolerance of public dissent or criticism by staff. As Wade puts it: 'the Bank's legitimacy depends upon the authority of its views; like the Vatican, and for similar reasons, it cannot afford to admit fallibility' (Wade 1996, cited in Weaver 2007).

The Bank has come under tremendous criticism from many directions for a string of failures, especially related to its structural adjustment programmes (SAPs). The scandal and damage caused by Wolfowitz, coupled with the fact that lending to middle-income countries from the IBRD is small and declining as a percentage of total flows to these nations, suggested at one point that the Bank's influence was diminishing. However, from another perspective the Bank is in good health: the IDA was recently pledged a record $41.6 billion for the period 2008 to 2011, 30 per cent more than in the prior three years. IFC investments have also been rising and totalled $8 billion in 2007.

The World Bank in health

History

The Bank's first significant venture into the health sector was the On-chocerciasis Control Programme (regarded as one of its most successful initiatives). This was followed in 1975 by the formulation of a health policy paper which focused on basic care, the urban bias in health services and community workers. A key message that signalled a different perspective from the prevailing health policy discourse at the time was the Bank's interest in discouraging unnecessary health care and 'charging for services at their real cost' (Brunet-Jailly 1999).

But the Bank did not really invest in the health sector until a second health policy paper in 1980 set out guidelines for health-sector lending. Money would be funnelled towards 'basic health infrastructures, the training of community health workers and para-professional staff, the strengthening of logistics and the supply of essential drugs, maternal and child health care, improved family planning and disease control' (Brunet-Jailly 1999).

When the health systems of low-income countries were hit by the worldwide recession and debt crises of the late 1970s and 1980s, and at a time when its own SAPs were forcing cuts in public expenditure on health, Bank lending in the health sector grew enormously (Figure D1.5.1). This was partly the Bank following the general rise in international attention towards human development. In addition, it was reacting to the negative effects of structural adjustment. Health lending was a way of shoring up public budgets in the midst of economic crisis and adjustment (Brunet-Jailly 1999).

The World Bank soon became the world's leading external financier of health in low-income countries. With the World Health Organization (WHO) in decline, it also became prominent in developing international health policy and strategy. The 1993 *World Development Report, Investing in Health,* called for more funding for health, but linked this to a cost-effectiveness agenda and a call on governments to prioritise a 'basic package' of services. It argued that by focusing on a basic package of services,

FIGURE DI.5.1   **Cumulative growth in HNP lending and projects**
(1996 US$ billion)

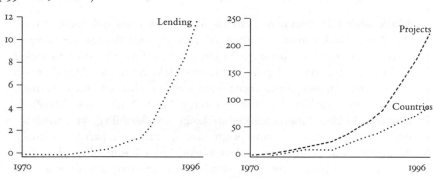

Source: World Bank 1997.

governments could ensure that more public resources were spent on the poor and priority population health measures such as immunisation programmes. Other services could be purchased by patients through insurance and out-of-pocket payments. The report argued that public-sector provision could be deeply inefficient and rarely reached the poor. Governments were encouraged to boost the role of the private sector.

These ideas fitted the broader neoliberal orientation of the Bank. In contrast to the integrated, participatory and comprehensive vision of the primary health care (PHC) approach, the Bank's reforms limited the role of the public sector and encouraged the privatisation and segmentation of the health system. The multi-sectoral and public health emphasis of the PHC approach was replaced with an emphasis on technologies that were amenable to the cost-effectiveness analyses of the Bank's economists.

The expanding Bank portfolio and the criticism it was attracting led the Bank to publish a formal Health, Nutrition and Population (HNP) Strategy in 1997. Now the Bank argued against private financing of health care and promoted the need for risk-pooling, but continued to encourage the growth of the private sector's role in health-care provision.

At the turn of the century, calls began to be made on the Bank to step up its funding to combat the HIV crisis and other priority diseases. The Bank responded with the high-profile Multi-Country AIDS Programme. However, the programme has conflicted with its systems approach to health-sector policy, and been plagued by monitoring, evaluation and ownership weaknesses common in other parts of its work (See Box D.1.5.1).

282 Holding to account

BOX DI.5.I **The Multi-Country AIDS Programme**

While adult HIV prevalence rates soared in the 1980s and 1990s, it took the World Bank's management until 1997 to acknowledge the severity of the crisis and 2000 before it began a robust funding effort to tackle it. In 1999, the Bank declared that the HIV crisis was Africa's main development challenge and committed itself to what it termed 'business unusual' by launching its Multi-Country AIDS Programme (MAP). It described MAP as 'unprecedented in design and flexibility' with emphasis on 'speed, scaling-up existing programmes, building capacity, "learning by doing", and continuous project rework'. It committed nearly US$1 billion to twenty-four countries to what was generally acknowledged as a bold and innovative approach to the pandemic (World Bank 2000).

Evaluations undertaken by the Bank's Operations Evaluation Department (OED) have shown that the Bank made substantial progress in persuading governments to increase political commitment to tackle HIV, improve the efficiency of national AIDS programmes, create and strengthen national AIDS institutions and build NGO capacity (World Bank 2005). However, these same evaluations also showed that a cluster of institutional weaknesses that severely reduced the relevance and effectiveness of the Bank's first generation of HIV interventions (1986–97) and efforts to tackle other priority diseases (World Bank 1999) continued into the new millennium and persist today.

These weakness seemed to have their roots in the fact that the Bank was an institution whose 'core business processes and incentives remained focused on lending money rather than achieving impact' (World Bank 1999). The interim review of MAP (World Bank 2001) found that although it was anticipated that the Bank would allocate 5–10 per cent of programme funds for monitoring and evaluation (M&E), it 'contributed almost no financial resources to provide M&E technical and implementation support to task teams and clients' (World Bank 2001).

In places like sub-Saharan Africa where there is 'a dearth of information at the country level and local levels on the epidemic' (World Bank 2005), the Bank resorted to blueprint models of programming, not tailored to local needs. OED found that the Bank needs to 'improve the local evidence base for decision-making and should create incentives to ensure that the design and management of country-level aids assistance is guided by relevant and timely locally produced evidence and rigorous analytical work' (World Bank 2005). A formulaic approach obviously undermines ownership, relevance and effectiveness.

Since 2000, the Bank's dominance in health has arguably shrunk. Its lending to the health sector has fallen by nearly one-third. Middle-income countries are borrowing less from the Bank to fund their health-sector investments. The number of staff working in the HNP sector has also fallen by 15 per cent from 243 to 206. And the arrival of new actors such as the Global Fund, GAVI and the Gates Foundation have crowded out some of the Bank's policy and programmatic space.

The shrinking health portfolio has not been matched by any increase in effectiveness. In fact, the implementation quality of HNP projects is now the lowest out of all nineteen sectors in the Bank (World Bank 2007). Monitoring and evaluation data on impact are 'scarcely available', despite the recognition of this problem in the 1997 strategy (World Bank 2007).

The Bank has become more sensitive to the charge that its policies have been harmful to the poor. The pro-poor rhetoric has strengthened and it has rowed back on its advocacy of user charges. But policy contradictions remain, particularly on the central issue of commercialisation. Influence from the US, as well as internal ideological predispositions, have meant that the financing and providing role of the private sector remains high on the agenda.

The new World Bank health strategy

The Bank's latest health-sector strategy was developed in 2007, and sets out to steer the Bank into five key areas (World Bank 2007).

1   *Renew Bank focus on results*

The lack of a 'results focus' was noted in the 1997 Health Sector Strategy and criticised in the 1999 OED evaluation of the Bank's activities. Donors have been putting pressure on the Bank to focus on results within IDA. Little appears to have improved.

As the new Strategy notes, monitoring and attributing blame or praise for outcomes are difficult in the health sector. All donors face dilemmas in how to report their impact. More demands for measurement of results, if pushed too far, can have adverse affects such as focusing only on what is visible, popular and measurable, while neglecting interventions that may be unfashionable or hard to measure such as strengthening public administration, improving management systems or enhancing health worker performance. Creating the social, economic and political changes needed for health reform is also a slow process not amenable to donor demands for swift change.

A results strategy can also damage the goal of putting countries in the driving seat. Too often, results are set by the donors, measured by the donors, and their success evaluated by the donors (Eyben 2006). Not only does this weaken government capacity and undermine autonomy and sovereignty in policymaking; it also does nothing to enhance the fragile links of accountability between governments and their people.

Whilst there is a clear need for a massive improvement in monitoring and evaluation, this should not be linked to blueprint approaches to aid disbursement and more conditions on client countries. Instead, the Bank should focus resources (as the Strategy suggests) on building up country-led health surveillance systems, to enable informed debate about health priorities and policies at the country level, which Bank funding should then respond to.

2   *Strengthen well-organised and sustainable health systems*

A strong feature of the Bank's Strategy is its claim to have a comparative advantage in health system strengthening (even though the Strategy noted that the Bank itself requires 'significant strengthening' in this area). The intention of the Bank is to establish itself as the lead global technical agency for health systems policy. This intention is exemplified by its earlier role in influencing the decision to close down the Global Fund's health system strengthening 'window', and in a comment in the 2007 Strategy which suggested that the WHO's comparative advantage was not in health systems but in technical aspects of disease control and health facility management.

When it comes to health systems policy in the 2007 Strategy, the attitude taken towards commercialisation and the public sector remains largely unchanged from previous positions. A notable bias remains, with the public sector frequently described as being inefficient and anti-poor, while the potential of the private sector to deliver health care to the poor is highlighted.

The Strategy notes that private providers 'deliver most ambulatory health services in most low-income countries' (World Bank 2007). This is true. However, the Strategy fails to say anything about the importance of the public sector in the provision of in-patient services. Hospital care is nothing like as commercialised as primary level care, with most in-patient services in low-income countries taking place in the public sector. In many countries, public-sector hospitals arguably place a floor under the lack of quality and high costs that patients, especially the poorest ones, face in market-driven systems (Mackintosh and Koivusalo 2005). The health-sector strategy could have addressed this reality and proposed more support to public hospitals in poor countries.

The Bank also shows how better-off groups in society tend to capture more of the benefits of public spending on health than poorer ones. While true, this again shows only part of the picture. Public spending may be unequally distributed, but it is generally not as unequally distributed as market incomes. In fact public spending on health frequently narrows these inequalities. Chu et al. (2004) show that in sub-Saharan Africa 'all thirty available studies find government health spending to be progressive' in that the poor benefit more relative to their private income or expenditure than the better-off. But building on these redistributive effects – maintained in desperately poor circumstances – is not, it appears, a priority for the Bank.

User fees are downplayed much more than in the Bank's past, but there is still an emphasis on strengthening demand-side interventions through financial incentives, to be mediated by insurance schemes of various sorts. There is little in the Strategy about strengthening public-sector management and service provision, encouraging non-financial incentives for health workers, or building effective public accountability and community empowerment mechanisms. In overall terms, the Strategy suggests a continued inclination towards pro-private, market-oriented policies and segmented health systems, with a public sector charged mainly with the responsibility for financing a basic package for the poor.

3 Ensure synergy between health system strengthening and priority disease interventions

Buried in the appendices of the HNP Strategy are two shocking figures: whilst aid devoted to HIV/AIDS more than doubled between 2000 and 2004, the share devoted to primary care dropped by almost half; at the same time only about 20 per cent of all health aid goes to support the government programme (as general budget or sector-specific support), whilst about half of health aid is off-budget (World Bank 2007).

The Bank acknowledges the problems caused by vertical disease programmes but maintains that health system strengthening can be achieved whilst concentrating new resources on priority diseases (World Bank 2007). But, as discussed in other chapters, the claims that this will be done lack the credibility that would come from a concrete description of how it will happen.

4 Strengthen inter-sectoral action

The Bank is an immense creature with many different parts. The potential for the Bank to join up different sectors to promote health is highlighted in the 2007 Strategy. However, the Bank itself admits that intersectorality is difficult to realise 'due to both Bank and client constraints' (World Bank

2007). Hall (2007) explains that one reason for this is that there are few incentives for cross-departmental collaboration within the Bank. In fact, 'a department's kudos is judged by the size of its own managed portfolio rather than by its participation in cross-sector collaboration.' This leads to competition over project ownership and under-recognition of cross-sectoral activities. This tendency is reinforced by the fact that staff promotion is based on project portfolio size and financial turnover, which creates further inter-departmental competition. The Strategy is silent on how these constraints will be overcome.

5   Increase selectivity and improve engagement with global partners on division of labour

The HNP Strategy sensibly proposes a better division of labour to prevent duplication of effort and reduce the number of institutions to engage with. It suggests that the Bank should work with others that share its comparative advantages in 'health system finance, intersectorality, governance and demand-side interventions' (World Bank 2007), and also collaborate to develop policy and knowledge; it will increasingly concentrate its advocacy strength on health systems rather than global partnerships.

But the strategy paper goes further to implicitly marginalise the role of agencies such as the WHO and United Nations Children's Fund (UNICEF), which are already involved in health system policy at the global level. There is no systematic comparison of strengths and weaknesses between these agencies and the Bank, so there is some uncertainty as to why the Bank feels it has a comparative advantage.

Private-sector development, the IFC and health

As mentioned earlier, the IFC has grown in size recently. The health sector is not currently a prominent part of the IFC. Of its US$8.2 billion budget for 2007/08, health and education together accounted for 2 per cent (US$164 million) (Warner 2008). The recent independent evaluation of IFC projects noted that the health and education sector on average performed the worst of all the IFC's investments (World Bank IEG 2007). There are also no clear criteria for determining when and whether it is appropriate to support private-sector growth in the health sector. Nevertheless following an upbeat study of the Bank's potential role in private-sector development undertaken by McKinsey's and financed by the Bill and Melinda Gates Foundation, the IFC announced that it would coordinate some $1 billion in equity investments and loans to finance private-sector health provision in sub-Saharan Africa.

Conclusion

The World Bank remains an institution that promises much but that still delivers poorly. It remains unduly influenced by the rich countries of the world, and by the same economic orthodoxy that has largely failed the planet over the past few decades. Civil society organisations should call for:

• An independent panel to review the Bank's role in health and the comparative advantages of the Bank and the other leading global health institutions. This should include an assessment of the depth of these different organisations' accountability to developing countries. It is unclear how far an organisation with the skewed accountability of the World Bank should be involved in setting global health priorities and policy guidelines.

• Country-level debate about the Bank's vision of greater private-sector involvement in the health sector.

• More country-level analysis of the health impact of the World Bank's projects and policies.

References

Agencia de Informaçao de Mocambique (2007). Calls for change to Bretton Woods voting structure. http://allafrica.com/stories/200707301209.html.

Banerjee, A., et al. (2006). *An evaluation of World Bank research 1998–2005*. Washington DC: World Bank. http://siteresources.worldbank.org/DEC/Resources/84797-1109 362238001/726454–1164121166494/research-evaluation-2006–Main-Report.pdf.

Bretton Woods Project (2007). The International Finance Corporation (IFC): Behind the rhetoric. *Bretton Woods Project Update* 58. www.brettonwoodsproject.org/art-558877.

Brunet-Jailly, J. (1999). Has the World Bank a strategy on health? *International Social Science Journal* 51(161): 347–61.

Chu, K.-Y., H. Davoodi and S. Gupta (2004). Income distribution and tax and government spending policies in developing countries. In G.A. Cornia (ed.), *Inequality, growth and poverty in an era of liberalisation and structural adjustment*. Oxford: Oxford University Press.

Eyben, R. (2006). Making relationships matter for aid bureaucracies. In R. Eyben (ed.), *Relationships for Aid*. London: Earthscan.

Hall, A. (2007). Social policies in the World Bank: Paradigms and challenges. *Global Social Policy* 7(2): 151–75.

Mackintosh, M., and M. Koivusalo (eds) (2005). *Commercialization of health care: Global and local dynamics and policy responses*. London: Palgrave Macmillan.

Pincus, J., and J. Winters (eds) (2002). *Reinventing the World Bank*. Ithaca: Cornell University Press.

Rao, V., and M. Woolcock (2007). The disciplinary monopoly in development research at the World Bank. *Global Governance* 13(4): 479–84.

Vetterlein, A. (2007). Economic growth, poverty reduction, and the role of social policies: The evolution of the World Bank's social development approach. *Global Governance* 13: 513–33.

Wade, R. (1996). Japan, the World Bank, and the art of paradigm maintenance: The East Asian miracle in political perspective. *New Left Review* 1(217), May–June: 3–36.

Wade, R. (2007). The world's World Bank problem. *Open Democracy*, 10 July. www.opendemocracy.net/globalisation/institutions_government/world_bank_problem.

Warner, M. (2008). What should be the role of the Bank's private sector arms – the IFC and MIGA? Presentation made to meeting in London, 13 February.

Weaver, C. (2007). The World's Bank and the Bank's world. *Global Governance* 13(4): 493–512.

Weaver, C., and S. Park (2007). The role of the World Bank in poverty alleviation and human development in the twenty-first century: An introduction. *Global Governance* 13(4): 461–4.

World Bank (1987). Financing health services in developing countries: An agenda for reform. Washington DC.

World Bank (1993). *World Development Report 1993: Investing in health.* Washington DC. www-wds.worldbank.org/external/default/main?pagePK=64193027&piPK=6418793 7&theSitePK=523679&menuPK=64187510&searchMenuPK=64187283&siteName=W DS&entityID=000009265_3970716142319.

World Bank (1997). Health nutrition and population sector strategy. Washington DC. http://web.worldbank.org/wbsite/external/topics/exthealthnutritionand population/ 0,,contentMDK:20133760~pagePK:210058~piPK:210062~theSitePK:282511, 00.html.

World Bank (OED) (1999). *Investing in health: Development effectiveness in health nutrition and population sector.* Washington DC: World Bank Operations Evaluation Department.

World Bank (2000). *Multi-country HIV/AIDS program.* Washington DC. www.worldbank. org/afr/aids/map.htm.

World Bank (OED) (2001). The US$500 million multi-country HIV/AIDS program (MAP for Africa, Progress Review Mission, FY01). Washington DC.

World Bank (OED) (2005). Committing to results: Improving the effectiveness of HIV/AIDS Assistance. Washington DC.

World Bank (2007). Healthy development: The World Bank strategy for health, nutrition, and population results. Washington DC. http://web.worldbank.org/wbsite/external/ topics/exthealthnutritionandpopulation/0,,contentMDK:21010634~ menuPK:282527~ pagePK:210058~piPK:210062~theSitePK:282511,00.html.

World Bank IEG (Independent Evaluation Group) (2007). Independent evaluation of IFC's development results 2007. Washington DC.

D2 Government aid

No one really knows if the entire 'aid industry' is a good or bad thing. Most people working in the aid industry probably feel strongly that aid is good, or at least that it can do much good. Certainly they are able to point to the translation of aid money into lives saved, clinics built and medicines dispensed. Others argue that aid deflects attention from the structural economic and political inequalities between rich and poor countries that perpetuate poverty. It has also been suggested that aid is used to further the foreign policy and economic objectives of donor countries and that it creates dependency and enables corruption.

In this subsection of *Global Health Watch 2*, we discuss the foreign assistance programme of the world's biggest donor: the United States. This is followed by a chapter that discusses aspects of the aid programmes of two smaller donor countries: Canada and Australia. It then ends with a chapter describing the linkage between 'security' and 'health' which has been strongly promoted by the powerful donor countries, in particular the US.

Have the rich countries delivered on their commitments?

Commitments to reach the UN target of 0.7 per cent have generally been poor. Major donor countries have provided a mere 0.26 per cent of their gross national income (GNI) to official development assistance (ODA) in 2004. Indeed since the Millennium Summit in 2000, based on Reality of Aid (ROA)[1] calculations, deducting new aid resources due to aid to Afghanistan and Iraq, debt cancellation, and support for refugees in donor countries, only 25 per cent (or $6.9 billion) of the $27 billion in new aid resources from 2000 to 2004 were available for poverty reduction or Millennium Development Goals (MDG) programmes.

Even the Development Assistance Committee (DAC) secretariat of the Organization for Economic Cooperation and Development (OECD) registered caution about the will of donors to meet their own targets. They noted that the recent 'aid boom' in 2005–06 was primarily due to debt relief for Iraq and Nigeria, and emergency aid to countries hit by the Indian Ocean tsunami in December 2004.

Aid effectiveness

According to ROA, aid 'is hobbled not only by the severe shortfalls in committed aid outlined above but also by the myriad problems in aid relationships that stray from the principles of equality and mutuality in development cooperation'. It lists three aspects of aid effectiveness:

- The political economic relationships surrounding aid partnerships. This refers to issues of selectivity of aid partners and the use of aid to leverage political, economic, military and other concessions from the recipient country; the economic underpinnings of aid relationships such as debt, export credit agencies and tied aid; and policy conditionalities.
- Administrative issues regarding lack of harmonisation of donors, alignment to country priorities and systems, management for development results and accountability mechanisms.
- Issues of aid delivery and implementation.

Does aid go to countries that most need it?

According to ROA, 'instead of allocating their aid based on where it is most needed, rich countries often favour recipients that are of direct political or economic interest to them.' As a result, 'the most impoverished people of the planet actually receive less aid than people living in middle-income countries.'

What about tied aid?

Tied aid mandates developing countries to buy products only from donor countries as a condition for development assistance. According to ROA 2006, the US, Germany, Japan and France insist that a major proportion of their aid is used to buy products originating only in their countries.

What about conditionalities?

Many have argued that conditionalities imposed by the World Bank and the International Monetary Fund (IMF) on developing countries have harmed development in some of the poorest countries. ROA suggests that there is a growing body of evidence that conditionality has failed:

- aggregate World Bank and IMF economic policy conditions rose on average from 48 to 67 per loan between 2002 and 2005;
- the World Bank and IMF continue to put conditions on privatisation and liberalisation despite the acknowledged frequent failures of these policies in the past;
- IMF macroeconomic conditions impair much needed spending on social and economic development.

Note

1. ROA is a North–South international non-governmental initiative focusing on analysis and lobbying of the international aid regime. It produces a two-yearly report on aid effectiveness for poverty reduction.

D2.1 US foreign assistance and health

The unparalleled military, economic and cultural power of the United States gives it the capacity to impact hugely on global health, both negatively and positively. Many people feel that the balance sheet is negative despite the large amounts of aid the US has given to the developing world. They cite, among other things, US influence over the design of a global political economy that has widened inequalities and obstructed poverty alleviation; multiple examples of US foreign policy undermining democracy and fuelling conflict; the use of military force and other means to secure control of strategic natural resources; the hindering of efforts to tackle climate change; and opposition to the International Criminal Court.

This view of the US is at odds with its image of itself and the role it projects onto the global landscape – that of the leader of the free and democratic world; benevolent and principled; and the largest contributor of official development assistance. This chapter provides a contribution to this discussion by looking at various aspects of US foreign assistance, as well as US policy in certain priority global health challenges. A longer and more detailed version of this chapter is available from the GHW website.

An introduction to US foreign assistance

The organisation of foreign assistance

A number of definitions are used to describe and measure aid. The term *official development assistance* (ODA) refers to the definition used by the Organization for Economic Cooperation and Development's (OECD) Development Assistance Committee (DAC), which counts only non-military grants and low-interest loans to low- and middle-income countries. The term *foreign assistance* refers to the full range of programmes funded by the US Foreign Operations Bill (also known as the Foreign Assistance Bill), including military assistance and aid to high-income countries. As a result of these differing definitions, the figures for the US's contribution to development often appear contradictory.

Foreign assistance appropriated by the Foreign Operations Bill is commonly divided into four subcategories. These are:

- *Development assistance*, which includes support for health, education and other development programmes. Until recently, Child Survival and Health used to be the primary health account of US foreign assistance, but there are new initiatives now for HIV/AIDS through the President's Emergency Plan for AIDS Relief (PEPFAR) and malaria. Development assistance funds are also split between bilateral assistance to countries and multilateral assistance that is channelled through organisations like the World Bank and the World Health Organization (WHO). The Treasury manages the bulk of multilateral aid, whilst most of the bilateral assistance is administered by USAID, the State Department, PEPFAR, the Millennium Challenge Corporation (MCC), and other smaller agencies such as the Peace Corps.
- *Humanitarian assistance*, which consists of responses to humanitarian emergencies, is mainly administered through USAID's Office of Foreign Disaster Assistance (OFDA) and Office of Transition Initiatives. A proportion is also administered by the State Department's Bureau of Population, Refugees and Migration.
- *Political and security assistance*, which is designed explicitly to support the economic, political or security interests of the United States and its allies, and includes finance to help countries economically, as well as programmes to address terrorism, narcotics and weapons proliferation. The most prominent instrument for administering these programmes is the State Department's Economic Support Fund.
- *Military assistance*, which refers to the provision of equipment, training and other defence-related services by grant, credit or cash sales. Most of this is administered by the Department of Defense (DoD).

Foreign Assistance funding is allocated to a number of accounts that are administered through a convoluted system involving multiple agencies (see Figure D2.1.1). At the last count, 26 different agencies were conducting aid programmes, although the majority of US foreign assistance is managed by USAID, the Department of Defense (DoD), the Department of State and the Department of Agriculture (which administers the US food aid budget). See Figure D2.1.2.

FIGURE D2.1.1   **The structure of US foreign assistance**

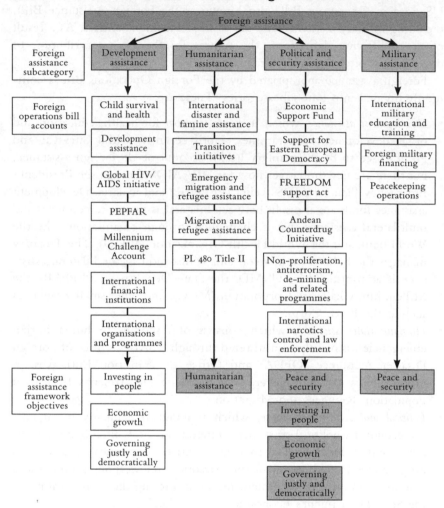

The key agencies

Historically, USAID has been the main agency for implementing US programmes in health, education, humanitarian relief, economic development, family planning and agriculture. It currently operates in about ninety countries, but its share of foreign aid is declining: from 50.2 per cent of total ODA in 2002 to 39 per cent in 2005 (OECD 2006a). One cause of this decline has been the increase in foreign assistance disbursements to the DoD, up from 5.6 per cent of the ODA budget in 2002 to 21.7 per cent in 2005 (OECD 2006a).

FIGURE D2.1.2 **Management of US ODA by agency, 2005**

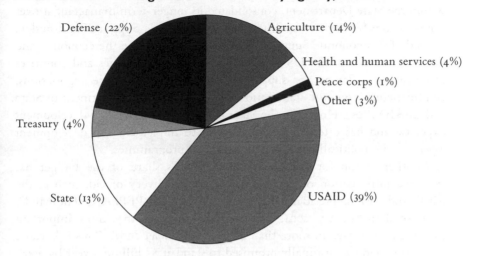

Source: OECD 2006b.

The arrival of the DoD in the development arena has been one of the most conspicuous policy events of recent years, representing vividly the extent to which the US government is blurring the boundaries between defence, diplomacy and development. The DoD now accounts for nearly 22 per cent of United States' ODA but also works in the provision of non-ODA assistance, including training and equipping of foreign military forces in fragile states.

A large proportion of DoD funding and activities is accounted for by massive reconstruction efforts in Afghanistan and Iraq and humanitarian relief after the Indian Ocean tsunami (OECD 2006b). However, it has also expanded its remit to include activities that might be better suited to USAID or other civilian actors. This includes being a contractor to PEPFAR in Nigeria, work in HIV/AIDS vaccine research, and the building of schools and hospitals in Tanzania and Kenya. These activities and the announcement of a US military command for Africa, AFRICOM, 'raise concerns that US foreign and development policies may become subordinated to a narrow, short-term security agenda at the expense of broader, longer-term diplomatic goals and institution-building efforts in the developing world' (Patrick and Brown 2007).

The role of the State Department, the US equivalent of a Ministry of Foreign Affairs, in development and humanitarian relief is also a cause for controversy. The State Department is traditionally and increasingly accorded a higher status than USAID. Under the Bush administration, it has acquired a lead role in HIV/AIDS interventions through the location of PEPFAR within the State Department, consolidated its longer-term management over funds for the UN system and has seen its Economic Support Fund budget expand. The Economic Support Fund is used to promote the economic and political interests of the US by providing assistance to allies and countries in transition to democracy, supporting the Middle East peace negotiations, and financing economic stabilisation programmes (US Department of State and USAID 2005). However, the State Department has limited development expertise and has often relied on USAID to implement the development aspects of its politically negotiated assistance programmes.

Another reason for the decline in USAID's share of the budget has been the introduction of new agencies in the delivery of aid, such as the MCC and various presidential initiatives, including PEPFAR. The MCC, established in January 2004, has been described as the 'most important foreign aid initiative in more than 40 years' (Radelet 2003). This is because of its large budget (originally promised to stand at $5 billion a year by 2006, although it is currently falling far short of this) and its unique approach to foreign assistance, namely that it only awards assistance to countries that have met minimum standards in relation to three aspects of development: ruling justly, investing in people and encouraging economic freedom.

The indicators that have been established to assess country eligibility include measures of civil liberties, political rights, control of corruption and rule of law; indicators of health and education coverage; and various indicators of trade, commercial regulation and fiscal policy. Although it is the closest the US comes to giving budget support to developing-country governments, there are concerns that the criteria and standards used by the MCC to determine eligibility are designed to push through a set of reforms that will maximise US corporate and foreign policy benefits. In addition, the MCC's lack of consultation with other donors, overemphasis on measurable results and short-term horizons (the MCC limits countries to one five-year Compact) are likely to be prejudicial towards aid harmonisation and sustainable development.

The other big new agency is PEPFAR. First announced by Bush in his 2003 State of the Union address, the five-year $15 billion prevention, care and treatment initiative for AIDS relief started in early 2004. Its management is independent from USAID, with lines of reporting that go to the secretary of state, but in-country implementation is often carried out in conjunction with USAID. PEPFAR's budget is now considerably larger than the Child Survival and Health account of USAID. In the fiscal year (FY) 2007, the PEPFAR budget was US$3.14 billion while the Child Survival and Health budget was US$1.59 billion (US Department of State 2007).

Finally, reforms to the architecture of US foreign assistance also appear to involve USAID being increasingly drawn into the orbit of the Department of State (Patrick 2006). It is believed that this will ensure that USAID's traditional focus on development will come under the greater influence of the Department of State's focus on foreign policy. The head of USAID (who is appointed by the president) now also acts as director of foreign assistance (DFA), an office that carries some responsibility for the coordination of State Department foreign aid programmes. The post is at the level of deputy secretary of state and marks another sign of the growing strategic importance of foreign aid.

Expenditure

The United States aid programme is the largest in the world. In 2005, it contributed almost twice as much ODA as Japan, the next largest donor. Contrary to expectation, the Bush administration increased spending on foreign assistance. Much of this can be attributed to expenditure in Iraq and Afghanistan, and debt relief (particularly to the Democratic Republic of Congo and Nigeria). Aid to sub-Saharan Africa (SSA), particularly for HIV/AIDS, also accounts for some of the increase.

The exact amount of foreign assistance spent on health is difficult to calculate because of the convoluted system of accounts and agencies. However, the Child Survival and Health and Global HIV/AIDS accounts

FIGURE D2.1.3 **US net ODA disbursement**
(at constant 2004 US$ billion and as share of GNI, 1989–2005)

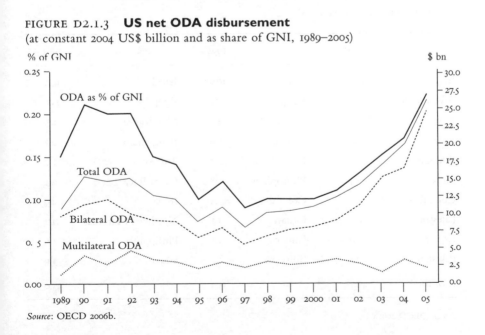

Source: OECD 2006b.

take up the bulk of health funding. Overall, US spending on health has increased from about US$1.6 billion in 2001 to just over US$4 billion in 2006, giving the US's foreign aid health programme a considerably larger budget than that of the WHO. Compared with other DAC members, the US also allocated a higher percentage of its total ODA to health – 18 per cent compared with a DAC member average of 13 per cent in 2002–04 (OECD 2005).

However, whilst it donates large amounts in absolute terms, the US has one of the lowest rates of aid as a percentage of gross national income (GNI), a mere 0.22 per cent in 2005. Although this is its highest level since 1986, it is well below the DAC average of 0.47 per cent of GNI, and the US has failed to set a timetable for reaching the 0.7 per cent target of the UN.

Who gets US foreign assistance?

It has long been the case that aid recipients are often selected on the basis of their strategic value to the US. However, several of these countries are also in need of assistance. For example, Sudan and Ethiopia are important for geopolitical reasons but are also desperately poor. It is also noteworthy

TABLE D2.1.1   **Top ten recipients of US foreign assistance**
(as % of total ODA 1984–2005)

	2005		1994		1984
Iraq	25.1	Israel	10.9	Israel	14.1
Afghanistan	3.8	Egypt	7.1	Egypt	13.0
Egypt	2.7	El Salvador	4.1	El Salvador	2.5
Sudan	2.1	Somalia	3.6	Bangladesh	2.3
Ethiopia	2.0	Haiti	2.7	Turkey	2.2
Jordan	1.3	Philippines	1.8	Costa Rica	2.1
Colombia	1.3	Colombia	1.4	India	1.9
Palestine	0.8	Jordan	1.3	Northern Marianas	1.7
Uganda	0.8	Jamaica	1.3	Philippines	1.6
Pakistan	0.8	Bolivia	1.2	Sudan	1.6
% of total	40.7		35.4		43.0

Source: OECD 2006a.

FIGURE D2.1.4 **Recipients of US foreign assistance by region**

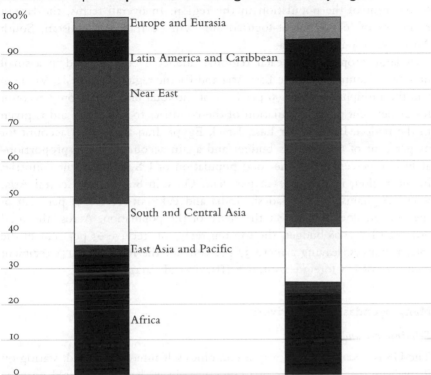

Source: US Department of State 2007.

that Israel and Egypt are receiving less ODA than previously. Furthermore, only three of the 1994 top ten appear in the 2005 top ten, and only four of the 1984 top ten appear in the 1994 top ten.

In 2005, the United States directed 29 per cent of its ODA to low-income countries and 70 per cent to middle-income countries, in contrast to the DAC member average of 53 per cent and 47 per cent respectively (OECD 2006a). When the Foreign Operations budget request for FY 2008 (which includes 'military assistance' and aid to high-income countries) is analysed, more than 15 per cent of the funds are earmarked for high-income countries such as the United Arab Emirates, Qatar, Singapore and Israel.

Under the new Foreign Operations FY 2008 budget request, Africa experiences the biggest increase in funding – up 54 per cent on FY 2006. Over 75 per cent of the resources for Africa will be focused on development programmes, mainly to do with HIV/AIDS. The largest recipients in Africa are Sudan, South Africa, Kenya, Nigeria and Ethiopia, followed by Liberia, the Democratic Republic of the Congo and Somalia. These eight countries claim over 56 per cent of the budget for Africa, but account for 65 per cent of the population in the region. In overall terms, the largest recipients of 'development-focused aid' will be Iraq, Afghanistan, South Africa, Kenya and Nigeria.

A large proportion of each regional budget is concentrated in a small number of countries. In the East Asia and Pacific region, Indonesia, Vietnam and the Philippines claim 79 per cent of the total budget but only account for 21 per cent of the population of the countries to which US aid is given in the region. In the Near East, Israel, Egypt, Iraq and Jordan account for 93 per cent of the region's budget and again account for a disproportionately low percentage of the total population of US aid-recipient countries in the region, in this case 40 per cent. Only in South and Central Asia, where Afghanistan, Bangladesh, India and Pakistan receive 93 per cent of the budget, does this reflect the share of the population. Across the total proposed FY 2008 budget, the top ten recipients receive 63 per cent of the total resources, leaving a mere 37 per cent for the remaining 143 recipient countries of US foreign assistance (Bazzi et al. 2007).

Many agendas, many drivers

Self-interest and aid

The US is open about the way it combines self-interest with aid, stating on its website that 'US foreign assistance has always had the twofold purpose of furthering America's foreign policy interests ... while improving the lives of the citizens of the developing world.' These two aims do not have to be in conflict with each other, but often are. The election of George W. Bush and the ascendancy of a reactionary, neoconservative administration, combined with the events of 9/11, have resulted in self-interest and the security of the US becoming paramount within its foreign assistance programmes. The 2002 National Security Strategy also formally added 'development assistance' to the two traditional bastions of foreign policy: 'defence' and 'diplomacy'.

Not only is aid being increasingly used to achieve geopolitical objectives, but underdevelopment and ill-health are being framed as security threats. For example, during Bush's first election campaign, no new initiative to deal with the HIV/AIDS crisis was announced and the efforts of Clinton were actually disparaged. After 9/11, AIDS became an issue of relevance and the groundwork for establishing PEPFAR was laid by identifying the need to secure public health as part of the Global War on Terror. The increased coupling of 'aid' and 'global health', driven largely by the US, is discussed in greater detail in Chapter D2.3.

TABLE D2.1.2 **The foreign assistance framework**

Five objectives of foreign assistance framework	Categorisation of countries
1. Advancing peace and security	1. Rebuilding
2. Promoting just and democratic governance	2. Developing
3. Encouraging investments in people	3. Transforming
4. Promoting economic growth	4. Sustaining partnership
5. Providing humanitarian assistance	5. Restrictive

A new US Foreign Assistance Framework crystallises the aim of building and sustaining 'democratic, well-governed states' into five new objectives and five different categories of countries (see Table D2.1.2). Funding for objectives 2, 3 and 4 are described collectively as 'development-focused aid'.

Two other observations about the new framework are worth noting. One is the conspicuous lack of focus on poverty reduction. Unlike other donors, the US has no international poverty reduction policy. In fact the framework contains only one mention of poverty reduction and even this had been absent in earlier versions. Second, the categorisation of countries is perplexing – what, for example, makes Tanzania a 'transforming state' but its more developed neighbour Kenya a 'developing state'?

From the American people?

According to the USAID logo, American foreign assistance is a gift 'from the American people'. The administration believes that this logo has a positive impact on the minds of people overseas and helps fulfil public diplomacy goals. But do the American people see US foreign assistance as their gift to the developing world?

In reality, US public support for foreign assistance is weak and always has been, in part due to the low levels of knowledge and understanding about the root causes of poverty, global inequity, as well as the positive and negative dimensions of the aid industry. Findings from poll after poll reveal that most people have an incorrect and overinflated perception about the generosity of the United States, thereby leading to opposition to requests for increased aid budgets. Attitudes to aid are also complicated by the common perception that much US aid is wasted by recipient countries and fails to reach the poor. Unsurprisingly, in one poll, 64 per cent of Americans support helping poor countries as a measure to combat international terrorism, whilst aid for poverty reduction is less popular (Chicago Council on Foreign Relations 2004).

Congress

In the US system of government, Congress exerts considerable influence over foreign assistance. It can review and block proposed policy; attach earmarks and directives to accounts; and request oversight investigations and policy reviews. The influence of Congress opens up foreign assistance plans to the influence of myriad special interest groups. The scope and specificity of these influences have increased so much over the years that the Foreign Assistance Act has been likened to a 'Christmas tree' of different whims and special interests (Raymond 1992).

The ability of Congress to specify precisely how much money USAID and other agencies can spend on any programme area in the upcoming year means that USAID missions and other programmes abroad find it very difficult to adjust and adapt their activities according to changing circumstances and local conditions.

NGOs: abroad and at home

The delivery of aid through non-governmental organisations (NGOs), of which private voluntary organisations (PVOs) are a component, is a prominent feature of the US approach to international development.[1] During the 1990s, USAID's overseas presence shrunk as part of efforts to streamline government. This had the consequence of further changing the character of USAID from being an implementing agency to being a contracting agency.

By 1996, 34 per cent of USAID's assistance was channelled through PVOs and NGOs (OECD 2006b). Today the figure is almost certainly much higher, with USAID reporting channelling $2.4 billion through PVOs in FY 2007 (USAID 2007). Globally this trend is reflected by the percentage of ODA being channelled through NGOs increasing from 0.18 per cent in 1980 to 6 per cent in 2002, according to the OECD (2005).

Currently, USAID works with more than 200 national PVOs and around 30 international PVOs as primary grantees or contractors (USAID 2007). However, the relationship is tightly controlled and includes having to comply with complicated grant agreements and contracts, including 'branding and marking' guidelines. For example, during the 2004 tsunami aftermath, some NGOs were reprimanded by USAID for not sufficiently publicising its contribution. PEPFAR also has requirements regarding the branding of its HIV/AIDS programmes, even if this might accentuate the stigmatisation of the recipients of support.

Within the US, a striking feature about the PVO community is its greater reliance on government funding compared with European NGOs' relationship with their national governments. This reliance is reflected in a more muted and uncritical interaction between PVOs and the US government. Although a few PVOs play a courageous role in questioning the US's role in holding decision-makers to account, many pursue a more 'pragmatic' line of self-censorship and avoid the role of campaigning for a more just and fair US impact on global development and health.

Stafano Prato, of the Society for International Development, notes that donors are increasingly engaging NGOs as implementing agents of government agendas. As a result of a growing financial dependency, NGOs are being co-opted into governmental policies and limiting their capacity to be more active and freely expressive in important political spaces (Prato 2006).

In contrast to Europe, there is reduced effort on the part of civil society organisations to inform the public about the purposes or achievements of aid or to act as a watchdog of their government's policies. Worryingly, the constant invocation of patriotism, 'Anti-Terrorist Financing Guidelines', the prosecution of several Muslim charities, and restrictions placed on the freedom of speech of PVOs operating in Iraq represent concerted attempts by the administration to further close down the space for civil society debate and dissent. In a newspaper article, a UK parliamentarian described this as part of the new American imperium: 'you not only invade countries, but also charities' (quoted in Maguire 2003).

Making a profit from poverty

The aid industry is good business for many American companies. The reconstruction effort in Iraq is a prime example of the murky way in which foreign assistance budgets have been channelled into the bank accounts of corporations with close connections to the Bush administration. US food aid is another example of business interests trumping development (see Box D.2.1.1). Specifically, business has been a persuasive lobby for the 'tying' of aid to the purchase of US goods and services. According to a former USAID administrator, 'foreign assistance is far from charity. It is an investment in American jobs, American business' (quoted in Bate 2006).

BOX D2.1.1   **US food aid**

The US accounted for 59 per cent of international food aid between 1995 and 2003 (Congressional Research Service 2005). In FY 2006 it delivered food aid to over fifty countries (US Government Accountability Office 2007). However, complaints are made about US food aid:

- A large proportion is channelled bilaterally rather than through the coordinated and multilateral system of the World Food Program (WFP).
- US law specifies that 75 per cent of all food aid transported must be handled by shipping companies carrying the US flag, which has the effect of inflating costs.
- Very little of the US contributions to the WFP is as cash, which would give the WFP more opportunity to purchase food from sources that are closer to where the need is.
- The dumping of US food aid distorts local markets, undermines local agriculture, contributes to long-term food insecurity and increases delivery costs.
- Food spoilage is common due to poor management.

At the root of these problems is the use of food aid to subsidise US agribusiness (e.g. Cargill, Louis Dreyfus, ADM/Farmland, and Kalama Export Company) and open up markets for their expansion. Unfortunately, the 2007 Farm Bill, which proposed that a quarter of emergency food aid should consist of crops purchased from other countries, was blocked by the agriculture and shipping business sectors and charities dependent on selling US food aid for their income.

Source: Oxfam 2005.

According to the OECD, only 3 per cent of total US bilateral ODA to least developed countries was untied (OECD 2006a), despite the negative impact of tied aid (OECD 2001). The OECD (2001) estimates that by excluding non-US firms from contracts, tied aid raises the costs of goods and services by between 15 and 30 per cent (OECD 2001). Untying American aid could have added an extra $4.37 billion to the aid effort in 2005, a sum of money that could have been used to provide health care for nearly 135 million people a year in developing countries. Tied aid also results in projects that are capital-intensive or that require US-based technological expertise rather than in projects that are based on local priorities and needs assessments.

Onward Christian soldiers

America is a nation that has experienced a steady erosion of the boundary between the seats of public office and the pulpits of Christian churches. The influence of evangelical Christian groups has not left foreign assistance programmes untouched. Kent Hill, a well-known conservative evangelical with no formal qualifications in medicine or health, is USAID's head of Global Health. In 2001, President Bush launched the Faith-Based Initiative as an embodiment of his philosophy of 'compassionate conservatism'. This entailed advocating the role of Christian organisations in delivering health, education and welfare services in the US and overseas. Whilst this was another embodiment of Bush's hostility towards public institutions, it was also a reward to the Christian groups for their part in his election victory.

According to the *Boston Globe*, between FY 2001 and FY 2005 more than $1.7 billion was allocated to 159 faith-based organisations (FBOs) (Stockman et al. 2006). FBOs accounted for 10.5 per cent of all USAID dollars to NGOs in 2001 and 19.9 per cent in 2005. This growth in FBO grantees has not only increased the undue influence of religious doctrine on sexual and reproductive health programmes, but has also incorporated inexperienced and unqualified agents into the health sector, some of whom seem more interested in the use of government money for proselytisation.

Forget the UN

US foreign assistance is also characterised by a long history of mistrust and hostility towards the UN and multilateralism. This has manifested itself in a decline in the share of America's ODA to multilateral organisations from almost 26 per cent in 2002 to 8 per cent in 2005 (OECD 2006b).

The Bush administration's relationship with the United Nations Population Fund (UNFPA) is emblematic of its lack of enthusiasm for multilateral organisations and the imposition of national values on to the international stage. In July 2002, US funding to UNFPA was cut off because its presence in China was said to imply tacit support for China's family-planning policies, which include coercive abortion and involuntary sterilisation. Four separate investigative teams, including one sent by the US Department of State, concluded that UNFPA was in fact working to end coercive population control. However, the US continues to withhold funding.

According to Ilona Kickbusch, unilateralism has not only changed US policy but has also influenced the way health advocates frame the global health agenda: 'The subtle but definite shift in orientation and language is very evident, and indeed many international documents read as if they have been written for members of Congress rather than for the broader global health community. This is clearly an expression of American hegemony' (Kickbusch 2002).

The United States in global health

Notwithstanding the self-serving agendas of US foreign aid, the US is the largest international donor of global health assistance and its spending on health has increased since 2000. Health care reaching millions of people is sustained by US aid. But it is questionable whether this funding is used in a way that maximises benefit, efficiency and equity.

The primary agents of US global health

The two primary agents of US foreign assistance for health are USAID and PEPFAR. Within USAID, its Bureau for Global Health plays the biggest role with an annual budget of around $1.6 billion and presence in USAID Missions in approximately sixty countries. A substantial amount of funding for health in disaster and emergency situations ($79 million in FY 2006) is also provided through USAID's Office of Foreign Disaster Assistance (OFDA).

USAID also has inter-agency arrangements with the National Institutes of Health (NIH), the US Department of Health and Human Services (DHHS) and the Centers for Diseases Control (CDC). These agencies possess specialist skills in epidemiology, disease surveillance and biomedical research and have seen large increases in funding since 2002. In 2005, USAID was also handed responsibility for administering the President's Malaria Initiative (PMI).

The five-year PMI was launched in 2005 to reduce malaria deaths by 50 per cent in fifteen focus countries with a budget of $300 million in FY 2008, which will grow to $500 million in 2010. In recipient countries the PMI is led by USAID in collaboration with the US Department of Health and Human Services and CDC. It implements activities in four areas: indoor spraying of homes with insecticides, provision of insecticide-treated mosquito nets, provision of anti-malarial drugs, and treatment to prevent malaria in pregnant women.

Whilst the PMI's profile has been low compared with that of PEPFAR, it has won praise for its measured approach and desire to learn from past mistakes. However, critics counter that the same initiatives could have been incorporated into existing institutions such as the Global Fund and the Roll Back Malaria Campaign, and that the insistence upon setting up a parallel programme has reduced the overall potential impact. There have also been criticisms of specific aspects of PMI's programme, such as the overly complicated voucher systems used to distribute insecticidal nets and the use of DDT pesticide in indoor spraying.

PEPFAR was set up as a separate administration to USAID. It received a five-year $15 billion budget for HIV/AIDS prevention, care and treatment in 2004. As of March 2007, PEPFAR reports having supported antiretroviral treatment for approximately 1.1 million in its fifteen focus countries. Figures from 2006 show that up to 2 million orphans and vulnerable children and another 2.4 million people living with AIDS were provided care services from PEPFAR.

However, PEPFAR has garnered much criticism for its undue and ineffective emphasis on abstinence programming; restrictive policies surrounding the distribution of condoms and the purchase and use of generic medicines; ineffectual procurement and distribution mechanisms; lack of investment in health systems strengthening; excessive focus on targets, which have turned health projects into a 'numbers game'; burdensome application and reporting requirements; and lack of harmonisation with other actors working in the sector.

Finally, PEPFAR is severely limited by a requirement for it to spend not less than 55 per cent of its funds on treatment activities, of which at least 75 per cent should be spent on the purchase and distribution of antiretroviral pharmaceuticals. Only 20 per cent of budgets can be spent on prevention, of which one-third must be used to promote abstinence; 15 per cent is earmarked for palliative care of individuals with HIV/AIDS; and only 10 per cent for assistance to orphans and vulnerable children. Such an arbitrary and top-down allocation of funds, with a clear bias towards treatment and pharmaceuticals purchasing, fails to meet even the most basic requirements of needs and evidence-based public health planning.

Harmonisation and country support

Although the US endorsed the Paris Declaration on Aid Effectiveness in 2005, it has made limited progress towards its goals, particularly in the areas of aid harmonisation and predictability. In many countries, there is even poor coordination between the various US agencies operating in-country, let alone with other donors.

One of the major deficiencies of US assistance for health stems from its annual appropriation cycles, which constrain the potential for long-term planning. A strong emphasis on measurable results and the potential for financial penalisation if results are not achieved can also have negative effects on sustainability and the setting of appropriate targets. For example, at a 2007 PMI conference in Tanzania, it was made clear to implementing partners that it would be difficult to convince Congress to authorise the following year's budget if they could not present strong results for this year, even though it was recognised that many of the required interventions would take longer than a year to show effect.

The US also provides little support for general budget support (GBS) and sector-wide approaches (SWAps) because of its preference for earmarking resources, attributing results to US funding and operating through NGOs. Often the result is a portfolio of project-based activities that run in parallel to on-budget activities supported by recipient governments and other donors through a more harmonised approach.

The absence of support for government processes also limits the United States' ability to support crucial aspects of health systems development, such as the recurring costs of personnel. Although US-funded health programmes employ many local people in their projects, there is a need to distinguish short-term workforce expenditure from longer-term investment in human capacity development that can only be done effectively through harmonised and predictable aid modalities.

Health priorities

Given its strong unilateralism, the US has a particular responsibility for ensuring that its health spending matches the needs and requirements of the people in recipient countries. However, there has been limited evaluation of the appropriateness of US development assistance for health.

The rapid increase in the funding of PEPFAR and PMI has also encroached upon the budgets of more traditional conduits of health assistance and concentrated aid in a smaller number of 'focus' countries. It also appears to have contributed to a decline in spending on maternal and child health, which is 22 per cent less than it was ten years ago (Daulaire 2007).

Others have also questioned the appropriateness of the way HIV/AIDS and malaria have dominated the United States' development assistance for health (Mathers et al. 2006; Global Health Council 2006; MacKellar 2005). Shiffman (2006) argues that research into different diseases is also prioritised according to the potential profit for pharmaceuticals companies.

Health systems

The United States' record on health systems strengthening (HSS) is poor. During the 1980s and 1990s, USAID supported many of the neoliberal reforms that contributed to the dysfunctionality of many health systems (Ruderman 1990). Non-participation in SWAps, the disproportionate funding of NGOs, short-term financing and support for vertical disease-based initiatives continue ultimately to hinder comprehensive and coherent health systems development.

USAID does have some HSS projects, including a $125 million five-year flagship programme called Health Systems 20/20 and the Quality Assurance/Workforce Development (QA/WD) Project. The Agency is also promoting community-based health financing in a number of countries. However, a closer analysis reveals several shortcomings. For example, 'Health Systems 20/20', which only works in eleven countries, includes a focus on HIV/AIDS in three countries and consists of a portfolio of work that is piecemeal and lacking in any substantial commitment to HSS.

Finally, USAID's leaning towards market-based health systems and privatisation remains evident. For example, a recently published manual for conducting a comprehensive 'health systems assessment' emphasises the benefits of expanding private-sector delivery without any mention of the potential disadvantages. When regulation is discussed, it is in relation to creating an environment that promotes private-sector development, rather than in relation to regulation that will curtail harmful private-sector practices.

Intellectual property and generic production

Under the current international intellectual property rights regime, the supply of affordable medicines is hindered by pharmaceuticals oligopolies. It was hoped that the 2001 'Doha Declaration on the TRIPS Agreement and Public Health' would allow poor countries easier access to generic medicines. These safeguards centre upon the use of compulsory licensing agreements; parallel importing; and permitting manufacturers to conduct regulatory tests before a patent has expired to speed the entry of generic drugs into the market.

However, the US in particular has put pressure on developing countries not to utilise the safeguards provided in the Doha Declaration. Furthermore, the US has enforced even stronger standards of intellectual property protection through bilateral and regional trade agreements. The Peruvian Ministry of Health has calculated that under the terms of its free-trade agreement with the US, Peru will incur additional medicine expenses of $199.3 million within ten years (Oxfam 2006).

When Bush acknowledged in his 2003 State of the Union Address that lower-cost antiretrovirals could 'do so much for so many', it was hoped that the US stance towards generic drugs would be softened, at least for PEPFAR programmes. Instead, a burdensome and inefficient system limits access to medicines (Health Gap 2005). This includes:

- the establishment of a parallel approval system for generic AIDS drugs that duplicates the WHO pre-qualification programme and undermines national policies and protocols;

- the approval of only a small number of generic AIDS drugs for procurement;
- a reliance on single-source suppliers that has led to shortages and stock-outs of essential medicines.

The US also imposes strict procurement rules and regulations on non-PEPFAR grants and contracts with USAID. Prior approval must be obtained for the procurement of pharmaceuticals and must be restricted to the list of US-approved products. Waivers to these regulations can be awarded but many PVOs avoid providing pharmaceuticals as part of their USAID-funded programmes because of the complicated rules and regulations associated with their procurement.

Human resources for health

The global health crisis is fuelled by a well-documented shortage of health workers in many countries. Much of this crisis stems historically from the structural adjustment programmes implemented by the World Bank and the IMF, and supported by USAID. Caps on salary levels, ceilings on the number of public-sector health workers, and limits to investment in higher education and training were all advocated (Ruderman 1990).

Today, the US does little to support the development of a public workforce of health providers in poor countries. Instead, the US actively encourages the recruitment of foreign-trained health personnel and international medical graduates. In 2002, more than 23 per cent of doctors practising in the US had come from abroad, the majority from low- or lower-middle-income countries (Hagopian et al. 2004), while the share of nurses from low-income countries grew from 11 per cent in 1990 to 20.7 per cent in 2000 (Polsky et al. 2007).

US-based training programmes for foreign health workers have been presented as a form of human capacity development for low-income countries. However, the benefits of this form of aid are undermined by the fact that few of the trainees return to their home countries (Mick et al. 1999). A more effective approach is USAID's American Schools and Hospitals Abroad (ASHA) programme, which provides grants to private, non-profit universities and secondary schools, libraries and medical centres abroad.

Finally, the HR crisis in poor countries is aggravated by the strong US support for stand-alone disease-based initiatives and preferred use of NGOs, which has resulted in an internal brain drain of public workers into the private sector. In Tanzania, for example, a focus country for PEPFAR and PMI, competition for skilled health workers is intense and has resulted in the movement of doctors from clinical practice into NGO programme management. A local health programme manager working for an NGO on a PEPFAR or PMI-funded project gets paid around $30,000 a year, compared to around $8,000 a year as a general practice doctor.

Sexual and reproductive health policies

Sexual and reproductive health policies are among the most controversial issues in US foreign assistance. Since 1973, the US approach to abortion, contraception and sexual health promotion has become increasingly conservative and ideological.

One of the most polarising policies is the 'Global Gag Rule', which restricts foreign NGOs that receive US family-planning assistance from advocating for or providing abortion-related services, even with their own resources and even if abortion is permitted by local laws. Organisations that provide information about abortion services forfeit all family-planning assistance from USAID and the Department of State.

In an amendment to the original 1984 policy, Bush's 2001 legislation does not prohibit the use of population funds for post-abortion care. It also permits referrals for abortions or abortion services that are performed with the NGO's own funds in order to save the life (but not the health) of the mother and if the mother was made pregnant by rape or incest. Nonetheless, there is evidence that the Rule leads to an overall loss of life. The International Planned Parenthood Federation (2006) estimates that of 19 million women who had an unsafe abortion in 2006, approximately 70,000 died as a result.

The Global Gag Rule also impacts on comprehensive reproductive health services by either forcing clinics to stop providing access to abortion or to cut back on their services when they forfeit US funding. For fear of falling foul of the Rule, many organisations have been discouraged from activities that are actually permissible, such as providing post-abortion family planning or conducting research on the consequences of illegal abortion. It can thus deny women access to contraception, counselling, referrals and accurate health information, causing more unwanted pregnancies and more unsafe abortions.

The common misconception that US agencies are prohibited from purchasing, distributing or promoting condoms and other contraceptives is not true. The US government is the largest distributor of condoms in the world and provides more than a third of total donor support for contraceptive commodities (UNFPA 2005).

However, the mark of social conservatives can be seen through the increasing credence given to views that condoms are ineffective and encourage immoral behaviour. USAID has diluted its advice on the effectiveness of condoms in preventing HIV transmission, and the CDC has edited its fact sheets to remove instruction on how to use condoms and how to compare the effectiveness of different kinds of condom. The Bush administration has also tried to restrict sex education in schools on the false understanding that it would promote underage sex.

PEPFAR's relationship with condoms also illustrates the influence of the Christian right lobby. Where PEPFAR supports condom promotion, there are restrictions aimed at limiting condom provision to high-risk populations, ignoring the interaction between high-risk populations and the general public.[2]

The 'Anti-Prostitution Pledge' prohibits PEPFAR funds from being spent on activities that 'promote or advocate the legalisation or practice of prostitution and sex trafficking'; and from being used by any group or organisation that does not explicitly oppose prostitution and sex trafficking. However, because the pledge does not clearly define what it means to 'oppose' prostitution, many organisations have avoided all health activity related to commercial sex in order to avoid any difficulty.

Many experts argue that the best way to reduce the negative health impacts of the sex industry is to decriminalise sex work and enable better access for clinical and public health services. The moralising approach of the current administration, however, does the opposite by reducing access for health workers and stigmatising the very individuals who need to be reached with health care.

Despite implicit opposition to the Anti-Prostitution Pledge, most NGOs have adopted the 'pragmatic' approach of altering their programmes to protect their funding. However, three courageous US-based organisations (DKT International, the Alliance for Open Society, and Pathfinder International) have filed two separate lawsuits against USAID arguing that the Pledge violates rights to free speech and is unconstitutional.[3]

Conclusion and recommendations

The US tendency to favour unilateralism, short-term gain and commercial interests, and to assuage the immediate demands of the country's security complex, make elusive the longer-term approaches necessary for lasting change for the world's poorest and most vulnerable. In the words of the former head of the Division of Global Health at Yale University School of Medicine, these approaches

> indicate the close interplay between the global-health debate and the wider political and economic context within which the United States defines its role. American unilateralism weakens international organisations and mechanisms,

and its hegemonic power defines strategies proposed in the global forum. The global-health challenge is increasingly defined in economic and managerial terms rather than as a commitment to equity, justice, democracy, and rule of law. (Kickbusch 2002)

In response to this assessment of United States aid, the following recommendations are made to health advocates:

- *Lobby for greater US aid effectiveness* The United States should fully adopt and adhere to the standards set out in the Paris Declaration on Aid Effectiveness. This would contribute to making American aid more transparent, predictable and effective. It incorporates re-engaging with the multilateral system and promoting better coordination with other donors; untying aid and disentangling the nation's foreign assistance from the bottom lines of powerful US business interests; providing more long-term and predictable aid; and streamlining the bureaucratic architecture responsible for the appropriation and management of foreign aid.
- *Reclaim poverty reduction as the primary goal of aid* It is vital that the US targets its development and humanitarian assistance where the need is greatest, rather than according to the US's own national security concerns. The US should reorient its aid agenda to have a more explicit poverty focus and emphasis on the attainment of the Millennium Development Goals.
- *Insist that the large vertical disease-based health initiatives do not eclipse other US technical assistance and funding to the health sector* The tendency towards vertical programming and the lack of support given to the overall development and sustenance of health systems, human resources and training are detrimental to the efficacy and long-term impact of initiatives such as PEPFAR and the PMI.
- *Question whether the agents and agencies of US aid are suitable and effective* The move towards securitising and politicising aid and the concomitant marginalisation of USAID vis-à-vis new initiatives and actors in development such as the MCC, PEFPAR and the Department of Defense must be closely monitored. USAID is not an agency without flaws but it, and other development-focused agencies, should be strengthened rather than abandoned. The movement towards a much greater role for the Department of Defense in US humanitarian and development work is undesirable.
- *Assess the appropriateness of domestic agendas for international policies* Policies that are motivated by parochial or localised concerns should not be allowed to translate into international policies affecting the lives of

millions of people around the world. Inappropriate religious and moral agendas should not be pursued. The United States' own health-care-worker demands should not outweigh those of developing countries; and US business interests should not dictate the terms of aid at the expense of the right of all people to health.

*   *Encourage greater levels of knowledge and engagement about development among the American public*   Currently, the voices of single-issue or ideologically charged interest groups are disproportionately heard whilst the majority of the American public remains uninformed and disengaged from the foreign aid and development debate. Greater efforts are required to make foreign assistance an accessible issue for the broader US public, ensuring that the tyranny of the minority ceases to define US aid policy.

These are ambitious aims for a more humane and poverty-focused agenda for American foreign assistance. NGOs and international bodies are beginning to engage more vocally with these debates. In today's politicised and securitised environment it is inevitable that they will come up against considerable opposition from the vested interests who profit, either in soft or hard financial and power terms, from the current structures of US foreign assistance. But it is important that these issues are understood, discussed and debated. It is only with knowledge that civil society and global health advocates around the world will be able to stand up and demand from the United States and other donors the reforms and policies that will make the right to health and the right to the conditions necessary for health a reality for all people.

Notes

1. USAID defines a PVO as a tax-exempt, non-profit organisation working in, or intending to become engaged in, international development activities. These organisations receive some of their annual revenue from the private sector (demonstrating their private nature) as well as contributions from the public (demonstrating their voluntary nature). Non-governmental organisations include any entity that is independent of national or local government. These include for-profit firms, academic institutions, foundations and PVOs. The US uses the term 'NGO' for local and partner-country NGOs only.
2. For details of the activities permissible under PEPFAR funding, see *PEPFAR Guidelines for Implementing the ABC Approach, 2006* at: www.pepfar.gov/guidance/c19545. htm
3. See the Brennan Center for Justice at New York University for details of *Alliance for Open Society* vs. *USAID* and the legal case that applies to both cases. www.brennan-center.org/stack_detail.asp?key=102&subkey=8348 www.soros.org/initiatives/health/focus/sharp/articles_publications/publications/pledge_20070612/antipledge_20070612. pdf.

References

Bate, R. (2006). The trouble with USAID, *American Interest* 1(4): 113–21.

Bazzi, S., S. Herring and S. Patrick (2007). *Billions for war, pennies for the poor: Moving the president's FY2008 budget from hard power to smart power*, Washington DC: Center for Global Development.

Chicago Council on Foreign Relations (2004). *American public opinion and foreign policy*. Chicago.

Congressional Research Service (2005). *International food aid: US and other donor contributions*. Library of Congress. Washington DC: CRS Report for Congress.

Daulaire, N. (2007). Testimony of Nils Daulaire, President of the Global Health Council, *Senate subcommittee on state and foreign operations regarding bilateral funding for maternal and child health and family planning programs*. Washington DC, 18 April.

Global Health Council (2006). Overcoming neglected tropical diseases with cost-effective, integrated programs, Policy brief. Washington DC.

Hagopian, A., et al. (2004). The migration of physicians from sub-Saharan Africa to the United States of America: Measures of the African brain drain. *Human Resources for Health* 2(17). www.human-resources-health.com/content/pdf/1478-4491-2-17.pdf.

Health Gap (2005). *Medicine procurement of ARVs and other essential medicines in the US global AIDS program*. Washington DC: PEPFAR Watch.

International Planned Parenthood Federation (2006). *Death and denial: Unsafe abortion and poverty*. www.ippfwhr.org/atf/cf/{4FA48DD8-CE54-4CD3-B335-553F8BE1C230}/death_denial_en.pdf.

Kickbusch, I. (2002). Influence and opportunity: Reflections on the US role in global public health. *Health Affairs* 21(6): 131–41.

Mackellar, L. (2005). Priorities in global assistance for health, AIDS and population. *Population and Development Review* 31(2): 293–312.

Maguire, K. (2003). Charity faced US pressure on Gaza: New Anglo-American row revealed at Save the Children, *Guardian*, 29 November.

Mathers, C.D., A.D. Lopez and C.J.L. Murray (2006). Global burden of disease and risk factors. In A.D. Lopez, C.D. Mathers, M. Ezzati, D.T. Jamison and C.J.L. Murray (eds), *Global Burden of Disease and Risk Factors*. Washington DC: World Bank and Oxford University Press.

Mick, S., D. Goodman and C. Chang (1999). Medical migration: Seasonal or secular? 4th International Conference on the Medical Workforce, San Francisco.

OECD (2001). Untying aid to the least developed countries. *OECD Observer*, July.

OECD (2005). *Recent trends in official development assistance to health*. Paris.

OECD (2006a). *Implementing the 2001 DAC Recommendations on Untying Official Development Assistance to the Least Developed Countries*. Development Assistance Committee, DAC High Level Meeting, 4–5 April, Paris.

OECD (2006b). *United States: DAC peer review*. Paris.

Oxfam (2005). *Food aid or hidden dumping? Separating wheat from chaff*. Oxfam Briefing Paper 71. Oxford.

Oxfam (2006). *Patents versus patients: Five years after the Doha Declaration*. Oxfam Briefing Paper 95. Oxford.

Patrick, S. (2006). *US foreign aid reform: Will it fix what is broken?* Washington DC: Center for Global Development.

Patrick, S., and K. Brown (2007). *The Pentagon and global development: Making sense of the DoD's expanding role*. Working Paper Number 131. Washington DC: Center for Global Development.

PMI (2007). *Fast Facts*. www.fightingmalaria.gov/resources/pmi_fastfacts.pdf.

Polsky, D., et al. (2007). Trends in characteristics and country of origin among foreign-trained nurses in the United States, 1990 and 2000. *American Journal of Public Health* 97(5): 895–8.

Prato, S. (2006). Funding NGOs: Making good the democratic deficit. Interview with Stefano Prato. *Development* 49(2): 11–14.

Radelet, S. (2003). *Challenging foreign aid: A policymaker's guide to the millennium challenge account.* Washington DC: Center for Global Development.

Raymond, S, (1992). Foreign assistance legislation. In S. Raymond (ed.), *The United States and development assistance.* New York: Carnegie Commission on Science, Technology and Government.

Ruderman, A.P. (1990). Economic adjustment and the future of health services in the third world. *Journal of Public Health Policy* 11(4): 481–90.

Shiffman, J. (2006). Donor funding priorities for communicable disease control for the developing world. *Health and Policy Planning* 21(6): 411–20.

Stockman, F., et al. (2006). Bush brings faith to foreign aid. *Boston Globe,* 8 October.

UNFPA (2005). *Donor support for contraceptives and condoms for STI/HIV prevention 2004.* www.unfpa.org/upload/lib_pub_file/590_filename_dsr-2004.pdf.

USAID (2007). *2007 VolAg: Report of voluntary agencies.* Washington DC.

US Department of State and USAID (2005). *US foreign assistance reference guide.* Washington DC.

US Department of State (2007). *FY 2008 congressional budget justification for foreign operations.* Washington DC.

US Government Accountability Office (2007), *Various challenges impede the efficiency and effectiveness of U.S. food aid.* Report to the Committee on Agriculture, Nutrition, and Forestry, US Senate. April.

D2.2 Canadian and Australian health aid

Official development assistance (ODA) is becoming an increasing feature of the public health landscape in low- and middle-income countries (LMICs). However, questions about the appropriateness and efficacy of such aid has been raised with some commentators suggesting that ODA reflects the strategic interests of the donor country rather than the developmental needs of countries that receive the aid. This chapter reviews some of the structures, policies and programmes of Canadian and Australian ODA. It reflects on the recent trends that have emerged from these countries' giving patterns, analyses the impact that the respective ODA has had in recipient countries, and then provides a snapshot of the Cuban approach to development assistance in juxtaposition to the Canadian and Australian systems. A more detailed version of this chapter can be found on the GHW website.

Canadian aid

Canada is a high-income country whose role in the world is often portrayed as that of a middle power. In 1976, Canada joined with the world's most powerful economies to form the Group of Seven (now the G8 with the addition of Russia), positioning itself to play a leadership role in promoting development. This built on the favourable international image Canada had established in the 1950s by championing peacekeeping, diplomacy and multilateral cooperation. In spite of this legacy and despite Canada being among the wealthiest countries in the world, the country's actual delivery of ODA tells a story that undermines its benevolent reputation.

Overview of players and policies

Canada's lead agency for development assistance is the Canadian International Development Agency (CIDA). Among its stated objectives are to 'support sustainable development in developing countries in order to reduce poverty and contribute to a more secure, equitable, and prosperous world; to support democratic development and economic liberalization ... and to support international efforts to reduce threats to international and Canadian security' (CIDA 2006). Its humanitarian goals are thus intermixed with Canadian commercial, political and security objectives, with conflicting results for health programming. For example, Canada continues to export asbestos, a known carcinogen banned domestically, to LMICs in order to support Canadian commercial interests.

Health has always been part of CIDA's mandate, although a specific 'Strategy for Health' was only published in 1996. CIDA has also recently expressed commitments to increase support for HIV/AIDS and health systems strengthening. Its focus on HIV/AIDS, in particular, may be seen as a response to public pressure. In addition to its own bilateral and targeted programmes, CIDA channels funds through multilateral efforts, such as the Global Fund to Fight AIDS, Tuberculosis and Malaria.

Nevertheless, Stephen Lewis, the former UN special envoy for HIV/AIDS in Africa and a respected Canadian, has observed that the government 'seems to have all the time in the world for conflict and very little time for the human condition' (quoted in Collier 2007). When the government published its International Policy Statement (IPS) in 2005, it stopped short of any dramatic reorientation towards the needs of vulnerable population groups, an issue that had been raised during the extensive consultation period prior to the release of the IPS. Health is limited to the development sector of the document and is not mentioned in relation to diplomacy, defence or commerce. The 2006 election of Conservative prime minister Stephen Harper appears to have further reduced the chances of a more substantive focus on health in Canadian foreign policy, with anti-terrorism and the promotion of Canadian business interests being primary preoccupations for the government.

Official expression of Canadian health aid priorities tends to focus on globally defined objectives such as the Millennium Development Goals (MDGs). However, CIDA's 2002 strategic statement also stresses a comprehensive approach to development cooperation based on a set of principles, including local ownership of strategic initiatives, improved donor coordination, and greater coherence between aid and non-aid policies.

While this statement represents an important step away from the critical weaknesses of traditional vertical, narrowly focused, non-sustainable

FIGURE D2.2.I   **Net ODA as a percentage of GNI, 2005**

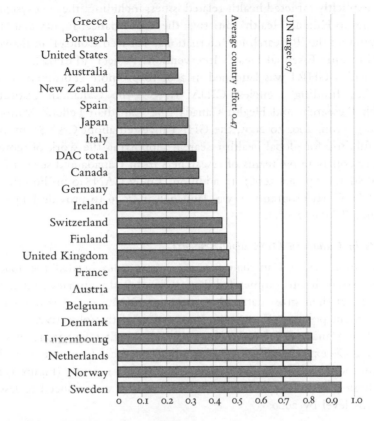

Source: Adapted from *OECD Factbook 2007* (OECD 2007).

donor projects, CIDA is still criticised for its high degree of dependency on IMF and World Bank conditionalities, and the limited participation of civil society actors representing the poor and marginalised (Tomlinson and Foster 2004).

One positive dimension of Canada's international development effort in the health sector is its support of research for and with partners in LMICs. The drivers for this effort are the International Development Research Centre (IDRC) and the Global Health Research Initiative (GHRI).

IDRC was established in 1970 to 'initiate, encourage, support, and conduct research into the problems of the developing regions of the world and into the means for applying and adapting scientific, technical, and other knowledge to the economic and social advancement of those regions'.[1] It provides assistance almost exclusively to researchers and institutions based in LMICs. While health has not been a primary focus, several initiatives have explicitly targeted health-related issues, including: the 'Ecosystem Approaches to Human Health' initiative; the 'Governance, Equity and Health' programme; the 'Research for International Tobacco Control' initiative; and the 'Tanzania Essential Health Interventions Project' (TEHIP).

Canada's GHRI was launched in 2001 to promote coordination among four key funding agencies: CIDA, IDRC, the Canadian Institutes of Health Research, and Health Canada (the Canadian Federal Ministry of Health). From 2002 to 2005, the GHRI invested about CAN$8 million in new funding for global health research, supporting the work of more than seventy collaborative teams of researchers from Canada and several LMICs (Neufeld and Spiegel 2006). In addition, a new CAN$10 million fund, the Teasdale–Corti programme, was launched in 2006 to provide longer-term funding (IDRC 2007a).

Trends in Canadian ODA disbursements

Although it was a Canadian prime minister who headed the 1969 UN Commission that recommended that all developed countries contribute 0.7 per cent of their gross national products to ODA, there has never been a government policy to ensure implementation of this objective.

While Canadian ODA grew steadily in the first few years of CIDA's and IDRC's existence, the overall funding trend has been one of declining commitments, which has been reversed only very recently (Figure D2.2.2). The high point of 0.53 per cent of GNI in 1976 was reduced to less than half this level by 2000.

FIGURE D2.2.2   **Net Canadian ODA as a percentage of GNI, 1976–2005**

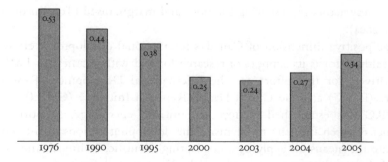

Source: OECD ODA Statistics 2004–05 (OECD 2006).

FIGURE D2.2.3 **Proportion of CIDA expenditure by region,**
FY 2005–06 (total expenditure CAN$2.782 billion)

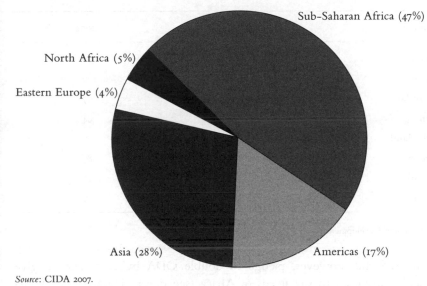

Sub-Saharan Africa (47%)

North Africa (5%)

Eastern Europe (4%)

Asia (28%)

Americas (17%)

Source: CIDA 2007.

TABLE D2.2.1 **Top ten recipients of gross ODA, 2004–05**

Rank	Country	Amount (US$ million)
1	Iraq	229
2	Afghanistan	73
3	Ethiopia	62
4	Haiti	60
5	Indonesia	56
6	Ghana	50
7	Bangladesh	50
8	Mozambique	42
9	Mali	40
10	Cameroon	39

Source: OECD ODA Statistics 2004–05 (OECD 2006).

TABLE D2.2.2   **Untied aid as a percentage of total ODA, 1990/91–2004**

Country	1990–91	2004
Norway	61	100
Ireland	–	100
Switzerland	78	97
Japan	89	94
Netherlands	56	87
Sweden	87	87
Australia	33	77
Canada	47	57

Source: Human Development Report 2006 (OECD 2006).

The IPS did, however, pledge to double ODA by 2010, and to give particular attention to the needs of Africa (see Figure D2.2.3). The Conservative government elected in 2006 reasserted this pledge and in 2007 the Canadian parliament passed an all-party Better Aid Bill. Nevertheless, the implications of this for ODA remains to be seen – policy statements in 2007 have notably indicated a move away from the targeting of increased aid to Africa (Riley 2007).

In recent years, there has also been a heightened commitment to military involvement in Afghanistan, and the portion of ODA associated with security-related issues has grown substantially, with Iraq and Afghanistan now being the largest recipient countries (Table D2.2.1).

Furthermore, in spite of being a signatory of the *Paris Declaration on Aid Effectiveness*, a very significant percentage of Canada's ODA is still tied (i.e. restricted to the procurement of goods and/or services from mainly Canada, or some other specific countries).

Health-sector aid

Strengths and weaknesses of the Canadian approach to health-related ODA are illustrated in the example of the Tanzania Essential Health Interventions Project (TEHIP), funded by IDRC in the 1990s. TEHIP was praised for its degree of local community involvement, systematic application of health information to guide interventions and, ultimately, its impact on improving health outcomes (IDRC 2007b). Despite the widely acclaimed success of TEHIP, there have been delays in the 'roll-out' of this project. Indeed, under the auspices of CIDA's African Health Systems Initiative (AHSI), the expansion of TEHIP is barely in progress.

AHSI aims to improve access to basic health care by providing assistance to train, equip and deploy existing and new African health-care workers. As with the majority of CIDA's health-sector work, these aims are undermined by tacit acceptance of delivery models and privatisation policies drawn from international financial institutions. The extent of private-sector involvement in CIDA health-care reform projects is unclear, but CIDA does have a general mandate to target private-sector development in its work (CIDA 2003), a possible source of tension in the case of health-related ODA.

AHSI is also a useful starting point to stress another contradiction. While it sets out to strengthen health-care systems and support human resources in health, several Canadian provinces are simultaneously recruiting physicians and nurses from the very same countries and regions, compromising efforts to build health systems, and contributing to large financial losses incurred by the source countries. Some of the authors of this chapter have witnessed, in various forums, an inexcusable lack of communication between Canadian ODA officials and provincial health officials on this issue.

Another dimension along which Canadian ODA can be assessed is its humanitarian disaster relief interventions. In the mid-1990s, Canada established the Disaster Assistance Response Team (DART), a military organisation designed to deploy rapidly anywhere in the world to help in crises ranging from natural disasters to complex humanitarian emergencies. This programme has produced mixed results.

Following the October 2005 earthquake in Pakistan that killed 73,000 people and displaced an additional 3 million, Canada's official response came through DART at a cost of over CAN$15 million. Conceived to provide immediate support *for up to forty days*, until more permanent aid takes over, DART became fully operational in Pakistan fourteen days after the earthquake. While the Department of National Defense viewed the operation as 'an unconditional success', DART's own members (Agrell 2005), as well as independent observers (Valler 2005), questioned the actual value of the operation. It was especially criticised for the excessive emphasis given to technological solutions, contrasting greatly with the approach of Cuba (discussed in Box D2.2.1 later in the chapter). This type of criticism has been expressed at least as early as Canada's 1985 relief operation following the earthquake in Mexico City (Montoya 1987). It also followed DART's deployment for the 2004 Asia–Pacific tsunami disaster (CBC 2005). As in the case of Pakistan, it was suggested that a more effective response would have included the rapid deployment of human resources able to venture out and reach victims in the shortest possible time.

Australian aid

Most of Australia's aid (about 90 per cent) is absorbed by the Asia–Pacific region (AusAID 2005). Table D2.2.3 shows the top ten recipients of Australia's bilateral aid budget for 2007–08 by partner country or region. Africa receives limited aid from Australia; and more of the 2007–08 budget is allocated to Afghanistan than to the whole of Africa (see Table D2.2.3). Note that this excludes aid allocated to regional efforts and multilateral organisations.

When it comes to generosity, Australia's record is poor. It has not reached the UN's target of allocating 0.7 per cent of GNI to aid. The general trend has been a decline from a high of 0.5 per cent in 1974–75, which has only been partially reversed in recent years (see Figure D2.2.4). Although the 2007–08 Australian federal aid budget represents a AU$209 million increase over the previous year's budget, aid still only accounts for 0.3 per cent of GNI. However, the newly elected federal Labor government has pledged to raise Australia's official aid to 0.5 per cent of GNI by 2015–16, with a vague commitment to work towards the UN goal of 0.7 per cent (Rudd 2007).

Most of Australia's aid budget is managed by AusAID, an agency within the Department of Foreign Affairs and Trade. However, a notable feature

TABLE D2.2.3   **Top ten recipients of the 2007–08 Australian aid budget**

Country/region	Budget estimate (AU$ million)	% of total budget
Indonesia	458.8	14.5
Papua New Guinea	355.9	11.3
Solomon Islands	223.9	7.1
Philippines	100.6	3.2
Afghanistan	99.6	3.2
Africa	94.4	3.0
Vietnam	90.8	2.9
Timor-Leste	72.8	2.3
Cambodia	54.0	1.7
Bangladesh	47.6	1.5

Source: Australian Government 2007.

of Australia's aid is that as much as a quarter of it is delivered by 'other government departments' including the Australian Centre for International Agricultural Research, the Treasury and the Australian Federal Police (Duxfield, Flint and Wheen 2007) – a trend that increased under the Howard government (see Figure D2.2.5).

FIGURE D2.2.4 **Australian aid levels compared with the average effort of OECD countries**

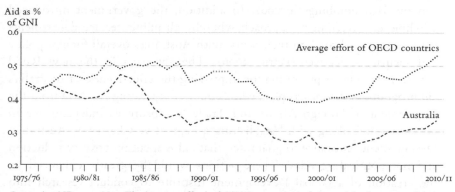

Source: AusAID 2005. *Note*: The 'average effort' of OECD countries is the unweighted average of their ODA/GNI ratios.

FIGURE D2.2.5 **Proportion of Australian aid administered by AusAID and other agencies**

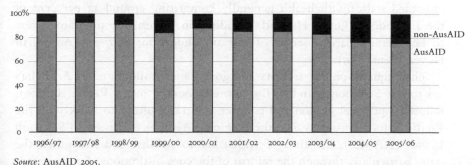

Source: AusAID 2005.

Overview of players and policies

As with other donors, Australia is explicit about the use of aid to further its own strategic interests. Development assistance is expected to be 'in line with Australia's national interest' (AusAID 2007). By helping to reduce poverty and promote development, 'the aid program is an integral part of Australia's foreign policy and security agenda' (Australian Government 2006).

The priorities and approaches laid down during the Howard government's term of office from 1996 to 2007 have been criticised for accentuating the use of aid to serve Australian security, foreign policy and economic interests, particularly following the terrorist attacks on the US in 2001 and the Bali bombings in 2002. In addition, the government introduced a 'whole of government' approach whereby all public service departments were encouraged to align their work with Australia's overall foreign policy and security objectives (Pettitt 2006). The approach of the new Rudd government appears promising for improving the effectiveness of Australia's aid programme. Labor has pledged to consider separating AusAID from the Department of Foreign Affairs and Trade 'to ensure its independence in policymaking', along with 'establishing a Legislative Charter on Australian Development Assistance to guarantee that aid is spent on poverty reduction and not political agendas'. These actions would be greatly enhanced by the creation of a Global Development Institute to conduct research into 'creative responses to aid delivery', which Labor says it will also consider. NGOs therefore need to keep pressuring the government to deliver on these commendable pledges.

One of the ways in which aid has been used to promote Australia's foreign policy interests is through the funding of 'good governance' programmes. Figure D2.2.6 reveals that much of the increase in the Australian aid budget in recent years has comprised funding for 'governance' and 'security' issues, while allocations to health, education and agriculture have remained static (with health generally comprising around 12 per cent of the aid budget). Under Howard, spending on 'governance programs' grew to become the largest sector of the aid budget for 2007–08 (Australian Government 2007).

The emphasis on law, security and governance is illustrated by Australia's aid to the Solomon Islands – the poorest country in the Pacific. In 2003, following political tension and conflict, Australia agreed to work with the Pacific Islands Forum to field the Regional Assistance Mission to Solomon Islands (RAMSI), the aims of which are to stabilise and strengthen the state, particularly through the reform of the core institutions of government

FIGURE D2.2.6   **Australian aid budget, 2000–2007**

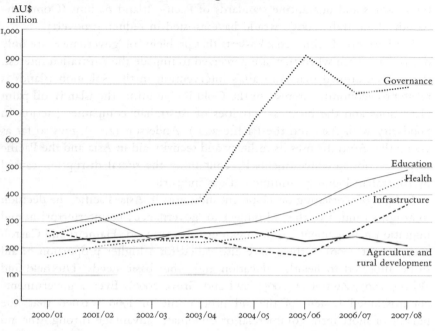

Source: AusAID 2007.

(Baser 2007). Australia's four-year contribution to RAMSI includes the provision of 235 Australian Federal Police and 130 technical advisers. Of the $95.4 million of aid budgeted for the Solomon Islands in 2007–08, over 70 per cent will be directed through RAMSI.

Justification for channelling so much aid through RAMSI was based on the long-standing view within the Australian Department of Defence that the island nations to the north and east (referred to as the 'arc of instability') pose a security threat to Australia (Ayson 2007; Hameiri and Carroll 2007; Pettitt 2006). By 2005 the view that neighbouring countries had the potential to become breeding grounds and refuges for transnational criminal groups and terrorists had become so entrenched within AusAID that an OECD Development Assistance Committee (DAC) review concluded that Australia's development programme was at risk of being 'dominated by an Australian-driven law and order agenda rather than a broader development agenda with strengthening local ownership' (OECD 2005). The increased concern with regional and national security has been criticised and questioned by other commentators (e.g. Davis 2006).

It is also difficult to see how the allocation of AU$160 million for detaining asylum-seekers in offshore detention centres and sending others home

(Nicholson 2007), as well as the allocation of AU$2.5 million for improving the customs and quarantine standards of Pacific Island nations (Commonwealth of Australia 2005), would have assisted in reducing poverty.

Furthermore, Cirillo (2006) asserts that problems of 'governance' are only described as such when they are perceived to impede the Australian interest. It has been argued that Australia's intervention in the Solomon Islands is related to economic interests in the Gold Ridge mine, the islands' oil palm plantations and the business activities of Australian companies (Action in Solidarity with Asia and the Pacific 2003). Anderson (2006) goes so far as saying that Australia uses its military and security aid in Asia and the Pacific to protect foreign investments by containing the social disruption caused by Australian logging, mining and gas industries.

In light of worsening development indicators in Asia–Pacific, the decision to assign so much of the aid budget to 'governance', counterterrorism and migration management has been extensively critiqued (Hameiri and Carroll 2007; Pettitt 2006). Others have also called for a higher proportion of aid to be allocated to health, education and other basic needs (Duxfield and Wheen 2007; Zwi et al. 2005; Zwi and Grove 2006). Even a government-commissioned review of the aid programme in 1996 warned that 'the pursuit of short-term commercial or diplomatic advantage through the aid program can seriously compromise its effectiveness and should play no part in determining project and program priorities' (Simons Committee 1997)

Kilby (2007) asserts that AusAID's preference for dealing with absolute poverty rather than inequality may have actually exacerbated poverty among some groups, and increased the rural–urban divide. He sees part of the problem as a product of poverty analyses which 'provide an overview of where the poor are, but not much about who the poor are or why they are poor'. Without a deeper analysis of the drivers of poverty in each country, merely alluding to poverty reduction does not guarantee poverty-reduction outcomes.

Hopefully, with a commitment by the new Rudd government to use the MDGs as the basis for the aid programme's strategy (which the former government was unwilling to do), and Labor's emphasis on human rights and respect for indigenous rights and culture, Australia's aid programme will become more effective in bringing about long-term health and development gains in the Asia–Pacific region – where two-thirds of the world's poor live.

Health-sector aid

The characteristics of global development assistance for health described in Chapter D1.1 apply as much to the Asia–Pacific region as elsewhere: vertical disease-based programmes and a tendency to fund lots of small and often short-term projects through Australian NGOs and contracting agencies. The extensive use of technical cooperation provided by firms based in Australia (AusAID 1997) has come at the expense of high transaction costs and the failure to develop capacity in recipient countries.

Another area of controversy is AusAID's policy prohibiting the use of funds for 'activities that involve abortion training or services, or research trials or activities, which directly involve abortion drugs'. The United Nations Association of Australia stated that Australia's aid programme 'denies funds for activities that educate about safe abortion and denies assistance until a woman seeks post abortion care, assuming she survives the unsafe procedure' and that the guidelines 'have the effect of driving women down the path to unsafe abortion with the associated shame, disability, and often, death' (United Nations Association of Australia 2007). According to Christina Richards, former CEO of the Australian Reproductive Health Alliance, AusAID restrictions are 'more restrictive than domestic policies, and seek to influence practice and values in recipient countries in ways that contravene international human rights' (Richards 2007).

Despite the Howard government formally untying all aid in 2006, Australia's development assistance has been termed 'boomerang aid' because one-third of official aid never leaves Australia and up to 90 per cent of contracts are won by Australian-based companies (Duxfield and Wheen 2007).

In fact AU$88.5 million of official aid budgeted for 2007–08 has been earmarked for government departments other than AusAID without being earmarked for any particular region or country. Some of this funding will reach the shores of Australia's developing-country partners, but much will not. For example, a significant portion of Australian aid is effectively used to support Australia's tertiary education sector – one of Australia's largest export industries – through the provision of scholarships for students from the Asia–Pacific region to study at Australian universities. This is arguably designed to subsidise Australian universities, which have suffered from public funding cuts (Anderson 2006).

Conclusion

This chapter shows that ODA is often informed by self-interest and in general has failed to provide catalytic support for health systems development. There is a strong need for ODA to support health systems rather than discrete health services and vertical programmes. Civil society organisations have a role to play in ensuring that their governments move away from a

---

BOX D2.2.I   **Cuba's approach to foreign aid for health**

In August 2005, following the disaster of Hurricane Katrina in the US, Cuba offered to send a medical brigade of 1,586 health professionals along with 36 tons of supplies to the affected region. The brigade was assembled and ready for deployment within days of the hurricane. While Washington refused the offer, the brigade eventually applied its services a few months later, following the devastating Pakistan earthquake. By the time Canada's foreign affairs team arrived in Pakistan, Cuba already had 300 health professionals in the affected region. By the time the first Canadian doctors landed in Pakistan, the Cuban brigade had 600 health professionals on the ground, had constructed several field hospitals, and was already journeying to outlying regions, on foot, to treat victims in their home communities.

Altogether, 1,481 Cuban physicians and 900 Cuban paramedics served in Pakistan (Gorry 2005). The brigade managed to treat 103,000 patients over a three-month period (Granma International 2006). Upon leaving Pakistan, Cuba offered 1,000 medical scholarships for young Pakistanis to receive free medical training so that they could carry on the work the Cuban brigade had begun.

Cuban medical internationalism is a long-standing cornerstone of its foreign policy, dating back to assistance given to Chile after an earthquake levelled Santiago in 1960. Cuba has provided medical assistance to over 100 countries worldwide, including ideologically hostile nations, such as Nicaragua, following the 1973 earthquake that struck during the reign of the Somoza dictatorship.

For a poor country that has struggled with interminable economic shortcomings, Cuba has provided widespread health-care services to some of the poorest regions in the world. In response to Hurricane Mitch in 1998, Cuba sent medical brigades to Honduras, El Salvador, Guatemala and Nicaragua, countries that still receive Cuban assistance. As of 2007, Cuba had 31,000 health-care professionals working in 71 countries (CubaCoopera 2007).

Unlike many ODA interventions in times of disaster, Cuba, more often than not, remains on site well after other countries have pulled out. In East Timor, Cuban physicians remained for a year following earthquakes and landslides that left the country in peril (Gorry 2006). Cuba's approach involves strong investment in human resources – more so than material resources – to achieve long-term stability rather than short-term relief. Since 1999, Cuba has trained over 11,000 medical students from twenty-nine different countries, including the US (Huish and Kirk 2007). Aid is not a short-term endeavour but is seen as long-standing cooperation, knowing that achieving impact in communities takes as much time as it takes effort.

'donor interest' model of ODA to a 'recipient need' model, and must call for comprehensive and detailed evaluations of their countries' ODA and for the pledge of countries committing 0.7 per cent of its gross national income to aid to be realised.

The case study in Box D2.2.1 provides an alternate model of international aid and offers some salutary lessons for countries wanting to examine their own aid programmes.

Note

1. For more information, see www.idrc.ca.

References

ABS (Australian Bureau of Statistics) (2007). 1301.0 Year Book Australia. Canberra: Commonwealth of Australia. www.abs.gov.au/ausstats/abs@.nsf/Productsby Catalogue/E1FEB51066DDDDF5CA2572350083D310?opendocument.

Action in Solidarity with Asia and the Pacific (2003). Australia in the Solomons: Security in whose interests? Background briefing paper. 8 July.

Agrell, S. (2005). DART parents. 'Why aren't you there yet?' National Post, 19 October.

Anderson, T. (2006). The Howard government, Australian aid and the consequences. Symposium: A decade of Howard government. Australian Review of Public Affairs, 23 February.

AusAID (Australian Agency for International Development) (1997). Better aid for a better future: Seventh Annual Report to Parliament on Australia's Development Cooperation Program and the government's response to the Committee of Review of Australia's Overseas Aid Program. Canberra: Commonwealth of Australia.

AusAID (2005). Core group recommendations report for a White Paper on Australia's aid program. Canberra: Australian Government.

AusAID (2007). Strategic Framework for Australia's Aid Program. Commonwealth of Australia. www.ausaid.gov.au/makediff/strategy.cfm.

Australian Government (2006). Australia's overseas aid program 2006–07. Canberra: Commonwealth of Australia.

Australian Government (2007). Australia's overseas aid program 2007–08. Canberra: Commonwealth of Australia. www.ato.gov.au/budget/2007-08/ministerial/html/ausaid-03.htm.

Ayson, R. (2007). The 'arc of instability' and Australia's strategic policy. Australian Journal of International Affairs 61: 215–31.

Baser, H. (2007). Provision of technical assistance personnel in the Solomon Islands. What can we learn from the RAMSI experience? ECDPM Discussion Paper 76. Maastricht: ECDPM.

CIDA (Canadian International Development Agency) (1996). Strategy for health. Ottawa.

CIDA (2002). Canada making a difference in the world: A policy statement on strengthening aid effectiveness. Ottawa.

CIDA (2003). CIDA's policy on private sector development. July. Quebec. www.acdi-cida. gc.ca/inet/images.nsf/vluimages/pdf/$file/psd.pdf.

CIDA (2006). Departmental performance report 2005–2006. www.tbs-sct.gc.ca/dpr-rmr/0506/ CIDA-ACDI/cida-acdi01-eng.asp.

CBC (2005). Canada's tsunami response 'amateur,' CARE chief says. CBC News. Canadian Broadcasting Corporation.

CIDA (2007). CIDA in Brief. www.acdi-cida.gc.ca/CIDAWEB/acdicida.nsf/En/4533 A7AA3E24F02185257116006C9B64?OpenDocument.

Cirillo, S. (2006). Australia's governance aid: Evaluating evolving norms and objectives. Canberra: Australian National University.

Collier, R. (2007). 'Canada is going in reverse' on AIDS fight. *Ottawa Citizen*, 11 August.

Commonwealth of Australia (2005). A global partnership for development: Australia's contribution to achieving the Millennium Development Goals. 2005 Progress Report. Canberra: AusAID.

CubaCoopera (2007). Cooperación Internacional del Gobierno de Cuba en materia de salud. www.cubacoop.com/CubaCoop/inicio.html.

Davis, T. (2006). 'Does Australia have an international development assistance policy? National interest and foreign aid policymaking. Refereed paper presented to the Second Oceanic Conference on International Studies, University of Melbourne, 5–7 July.

Duxfield, F.M., and K. Wheen (2007). 'Fighting poverty or fantasy figures? The reality of Australian aid. Aid Watch. www.aidwatch.org.au/assets/aw01084/Fantasy%20Figures%20Final.pdf.

Granma International (2006). Cuban medical brigade returns from helping Indonesia. *Granma International*.

Gorry, C. (2005). Cuban disaster doctors in Guatemala, Pakistan. *MEDICC Review* 7(5), November/December. www.medicc.org/publications/medicc_review/0905/international-cooperation-report.html.

Gorry, C. (2006). Medical education cooperation with East Timor expanded. *MEDICC Review* 8(1), March/April. www.medicc.org/publications/medicc_review/0406/headlines-in-cuban-health.html#3.

Hameiri, S., and T. Carroll (2007). The Pacific: New policies for the Pacific. *Australian Policy Online*, 16 January.

Huish, R., and J.M. Kirk (2007). Cuban medical internationalism and the development of the Latin American School of Medicine. *Latin American Perspectives* 34(6): 77–92.

IDRC (International Development Research Centre) (2007a). *Social and economic policy. Teasdale-Corti.* www.idrc.ca/en/ev-94787-201-1-DO_TOPIC.html.

IDRC (2007b). *Social and economic policy. Tanzania Essential Health Interventions Project.* Ottawa.

Kilby, P. (2007). The Australian aid program: Dealing with poverty? *Australian Journal of International Affairs* 61: 114–29.

Montoya, D. (1987). Responding to disaster: Canada and the Mexico City earthquake. *Canadian Medical Association Journal* 137: 68–70.

Neufeld, V., and J.M. Spiegel (2006). Canada and global health research: 2005 update. *Canadian Journal of Public Health* 97(1): 39–41.

Nicholson, B. (2007). 'Creative' figures skew aid picture. *The Age* (Melbourne), 5 February.

OECD (Organisation for Economic Co-operation and Development) (2005). DAC peer review: Australia. Paris: OECD Development Assistance Committee.

OECD (2006). *National accounts of OECD countries.* Paris.

OECD (2007). *Factbook 2007: Economic, environmental and social statistics.* http://lysander.sourceoecd.org/vl=6035414/cl=55/nw=1/rpsv/fact2007/10-02-05-g01.htm.

Pettitt, B. (2006). Poverty, security, and the Australian aid program: From the Simons Review to the White Paper. Proceedings of the Anti-Poverty Academic Conference with International Participation, Institute for Sustainability and Technology Policy, Murdoch University, Perth.

Richards, C. (2007). Comment on Draft International Health Strategy – AusAID. Canberra: Australian Reproductive Health Alliance.

Riley, S. (2007). Fiddling with foreign aid. *Ottawa Citizen*, 26 October.

Rudd, K. (2007). Speech to the Lowy Institute, Sydney, 5 July.

Simons Committee (1997). *One clear objective: Poverty reduction through sustainable development*. Report of the committee of review on the Australian overseas aid program. Commonwealth of Australia, Canberra.

Tomlinson, B., and P. Foster (2004). *At the table or in the kitchen? CIDA's new aid strategies, developing country ownership, and donor conditionality*. Halifax Initiative Briefing Paper. Ottawa: Canadian Council for International Cooperation.

United Nations Association of Australia (2007). *Australia and the United Nations*. Canberra.

Valler, R. (2005). In Pakistan's earthquake zone global relief has failed its test. *British Medical Journal* 331: 1151.

Zwi, A.B., N.J. Grove and M.-T. Ho (2005). Keeping track to keep Australia's overseas aid on track (editorial). *Medical Journal of Australia* 183: 119–20.

Zwi, A., and N.J. Grove (2006). Australia's role in promoting achievement of the Millennium Development Goals. *Medical Journal of Australia* 184: 103–4.

D2.3   **Security and health**

A recent development in global health has been the way in which health issues are being framed in terms of security. This section describes the origins of this development and raises questions that civil society should be grappling with.[1]

One of the drivers for this development is the awareness of the potential for fast-moving epidemics to deliver shocks to the global economy. The threat of a lethal influenza pandemic has further accentuated the process of framing disease as a security issue. In 2005 the World Health Assembly (WHA) adopted a revised version of the International Health Regulations, which establishes a set of obligations and standards for countries to respond to 'public health emergencies of international concern'. In 2007 the World Health Organization (WHO) devoted its annual *World Health Report* to 'Global Public Health Security in the 21st Century'.

Bioterrorism has been another focus of attention, especially following anthrax attacks in the US, which led to increased international collaboration via the Global Health Security Initiative (GHSI).[2] However, while there are some synergies between preparedness for bioterrorist events and other health risks, the overall nature of the bioterrorism preparedness agenda and the disproportionate allocation of scarce resources, particularly within the US, have been questioned (Tucker 2004).

Since the Cold War, and especially after the 9/11 terrorist attacks on the United States, issues such as poverty, climate change and HIV/AIDS have also become framed as security threats by virtue of their negative impact on economic and political stability, both within countries and across borders. A range of US government agencies, including the Departments of State and Defense and the Central Intelligence Agency (CIA), began working on HIV–security links during the mid-1990s. A resulting US Strategy on HIV/AIDS argued that the pandemic needed to be seen not only in terms of human health or international development, but also as a threat to 'international security' and to the security of the US (USDS 1995).

It noted that 'as the HIV/AIDS pandemic erodes economic and security bases of affected countries, it may be a 'war-starter' or 'war-outcome-determinant'. It also described how 'HIV directly impacts military readiness and manpower, causing loss of trained soldiers and military leaders', and how 'worldwide peacekeeping operations will become increasingly controversial as militaries with high infection rates find it difficult to supply healthy contingents.'

This view subsequently gained ground within Washington. In 2000, the US National Intelligence Council (NIC) issued a report on the threat of global infections to the US (NIC 2000). In the same year, the Clinton administration declared that HIV/AIDS represented a threat to US national security interests. This led to a US-backed UN Security Council resolution identifying HIV/AIDS as a threat to international peace and security (UNSC 2000).

The National Intelligence Council returned to the subject in 2002, issuing a report on five countries (Nigeria, Ethiopia, Russia, China and India) strategically important to the United States that identified links between disease, political instability and the threat to socioeconomic development and military effectiveness (NIC 2002). By 2005 the Global Business Coalition on HIV/AIDS was making links between AIDS, economic decline and potential terrorist threats, including speculating on how a steady stream of orphans might be exploited and used for terrorist activities (Neilson 2005).

At one level, the linkage of health to security can be viewed positively in the sense that it can highlight the concept of *human security*, which can help move the focus in security thinking away from state security and more towards people and their basic rights and needs.

At another level, there are risks associated with extending the scope of security into the health and development spheres. Importantly, the framing of health in terms of security has emerged from global power centres. As the foreign policy and intelligence agencies of the most powerful states are drawn into the domain of health within low- and middle-income countries, health policies and programmes may be co-opted into serving economic and political projects, especially in the post 9/11 landscape in which counter-terrorism has emerged as an overriding policy priority, and which has made the space for health and human rights harder to maintain.

While the interest of security actors in selected aspects of public health has increased markedly, parts of the public health and medical communities have also adopted the language of security, seeing opportunities to advance broader public health goals. By accentuating the destabilising effects of HIV/AIDS and poverty, civil society groups have helped gain much-needed attention and resources for the long neglected health concerns of poorer countries.

Yet the linking of health with security is not necessarily a win–win situation. Crucially, those seeking to use security arguments to boost health up the political agenda may not be able to control where the logic of security takes them. While the linking of health and security may generate more attention and resources for health, the use of health as an instrument of foreign policy, or as a bridge for securing better control over strategic resources in other countries, is also evident. For example, the 2002 NIC report on HIV/AIDS stated in relation to Nigeria that HIV/AIDS could contribute to the deterioration of state capacity in a country important to US energy security and US counterterrorism strategies (CSIS 2005).

This forms part of the context for the massive increases in US aid for Nigeria. Indeed, through 2007 PEPFAR allocated some US$578 million for Nigeria, far outstripping other donors. As part of this, PEPFAR is creating a total HIV surveillance system for the Nigerian military; conducting prevention initiatives; creating more reliable supply chains; and organising treatment for military personnel and dependants who are living with HIV.[3]

To an extent this might be welcomed. HIV/AIDS is a multidimensional problem affecting all sectors of society, including the military. The HIV/AIDS–security link has also drawn attention to the spread of HIV via military and security forces in conflict or peacekeeping situations. But questions might be asked as to whether targeting such sectors in HIV/AIDS relief risks privileging certain parts of society because of their relevance to US strategic goals (Elbe 2005).

There is now concern that political and economic elites will be able to insulate themselves from the worst effects of HIV/AIDS while exploiting scaled-up AIDS relief to entrench their positions (de Waal 2006). While saving lives in the short term, HIV/AIDS relief could perpetuate a closed political loop that is detrimental to wider human security and fails to address the deeper-rooted social determinants of health. It is also noteworthy that the hypothesis that high-prevalence HIV/AIDS epidemics would destabilise national and regional security has not been substantiated, raising the question of whether HIV/AIDS has been used opportunistically by the security apparatus (Whiteside et al. 2006; Barnett and Prins 2006).

The trade-offs associated with the linking of security to health is illustrated also with the prevention and control of acute infectious disease outbreaks. Some authors argue that global health security has helped to normalise the intrusive and extensive use of external surveillance and the suspension of sovereignty across a range of policy areas (Hooker 2006). Whilst protecting the health security of populations is a good thing, it is necessary to ask who is being secured, from what, how, and at whose cost?

The surveillance of public health threats requires a major upgrading of data capture and information systems. While efforts have been made by the WHO and other agencies to ensure that data are managed and used for politically neutral and scientific purposes, some researchers have identified links between public health surveillance networks and intelligence communities, calling its supposed neutrality into question (Weir and Mykhalovskiy 2006). It also places demands on poorer countries to develop surveillance and response strategies that can help protect the global community. However, it is unclear whether such demands are affordable or appropriate to their health priorities (Lee and Fidler 2007). The focus on cross-border infectious disease control may mask structural problems in global public health, leading to solutions which benefit the rich more than the poor.

The linking of health and security therefore creates a complex political space that requires discussion and research, particularly in relation to three issues (Lee and McInnes 2004).

First is the process of determining what is and isn't a security issue. The same powerful actors who determine what constitutes a security issue also tend to be responsible for shaping international responses to those threats. Placing health issues in national security strategies or on the agenda of bodies like the UN Security Council, or defining the WHO's role in terms of global security, creates a space where particular ideas of security and associated interests that are promoted must be questioned and reframed if necessary.

Second is the danger that efforts to address health problems deemed important through a security lens, rather than more objective measures of need, will distort health priorities. How is the conceptualisation of health as a poverty, justice or human rights issue to be reconciled, for example, with strategic objectives linked to 'fragile states', 'failed states' or 'rogue states'? What are the consequences of health being used as an instrument of foreign policy?

Third, a concern with security may reinforce problematic aspects of health policy. For example, the desire to enhance security may lead donors to prioritise bilateral funding mechanisms at the expense of multilateral channels. A 'control and containment' focus on infectious disease outbreaks may detract from more effective and sustainable approaches to health promotion. Vertical, disease-control policies and programmes, with their emphasis on disease prevention, may flourish at the expense of comprehensive primary health-care programmes and emphasise an authoritarianism within the health sector that runs against principles of decentralisation and community empowerment, or could lead to certain communities being demonised as 'security threats' (Elbe 2006).

Final comments

The recently created links between health and security will help raise the profile of certain health issues, but they may also reframe them to the advantage of the more powerful. The key question is whether this shift represents a welcome advance in ideas of security, or the co-option of health by vested interests, raising the risk that security will simply lead to new forms of selectivity and inequality in the landscape of global health and the global political economy. Public health advocates need to examine and debate the issue in four ways:

• Monitor the links being made between health and security in a wide range of settings.
• Contribute to the evidence base on how health–security links are affecting global health initiatives in practice. More detailed case studies from a wider range of places are required.
• Encourage critical debate and discussion about different conceptions of security, whilst constantly advancing perspectives grounded in human rights and ethics.
• Support networks of enquiry and discussion for groups from different disciplines and regions to develop more comprehensive understandings of links between health and security, whilst building the capacity to react to unwanted developments in the field.

Notes

1. A longer version of this chapter is available at www.ghwatch.org.
2. The members of the GHSI are Canada, France, Germany, Italy, Japan, Mexico, the UK, the US and the EU. See www.ghsi.ca/english/index.asp.
3. Information on PEPFAR in Nigeria via www.pepfar.gov/.

References

Barnett, A., and Prins, G. (2006). *HIV/AIDS and security: Fact, fiction and evidence. A report to UNAIDS.* London: LSEAIDS.

CSIS (2005). *HIV/AIDS in Nigeria: Toward sustainable US engagement.* Washington DC. www.csis.org/media/csis/pubs/0508_hivaids_nigeria.pdf.

Elbe, S. (2005). AIDS, security, biopolitics. *International Relations* 19(4): 403–19.

Elbe, S. (2006). Should HIV/AIDS be securitized? The ethical dilemmas of linking HIV/AIDS and security. *International Studies Quarterly* 50(1): 119–44.

de Waal, A. (2006). *AIDS and power: Why there is no crisis, yet.* London: Zed Books.

Hooker, C. (2006). Drawing the lines: Danger and risk in the age of SARS. In A. Bashford (ed.), *Medicine at the border: Disease, globalization and security, 1850 to the present* London: Palgrave Macmillan.

Lee, K., and D. Fidler (2007). Avian and pandemic influenza: progress and problems with global health governance. *Global Public Health* 2(3) 215–34.

Lee, K., and C. McInnes (2004). A conceptual framework for research and policy. In A. Ingram (ed.), *Health, foreign policy and security: Towards a conceptual framework for research and policy.* London: Nuffield Trust. www.nuffieldtrust.org.uk/publications/detail. asp?id=0&prID=21.

Neilson, T. (2005). *AIDS, economics and terrorism.* New York: Global Business Coalition on HIV/AIDS.

NIC (National Intelligence Council) (2000). *National intelligence estimate: The global infectious disease threat and its implications for the United States.* NIE 99–17D. Washington DC.

NIC (2002). *Intelligence community assessment: The next wave of HIV/AIDS: Nigeria, Ethiopia, Russia, India, and China.* ICA 2002–04D. Washington DC.

Tucker, B. (2004). Biological threat assessment: Is the cure worse than the disease? *Arms Control Today.* www.armscontrol.org/act/2004_10/Tucker.asp.

UNSC (UN Security Council) (2000). United Nations Security Council Resolution 1308. S/RES/1308. New York.

USDS (US Department of State) (1995). *US international strategy on HIV/AIDS*, Appendix D. http://dosfan.lib.uic.edu/ERC/environment/releases/9507.html.

Weir, L., and E. Mykhalovskiy (2006). The geopolitics of global public health surveillance in the twenty-first century. In A. Bashford (ed), *Medicine at the border: Disease, globalization and security, 1850 to the present.* London: Palgrave Macmillan.

Whiteside, A., A. de Waal and T. Gebre-Tensae (2006). AIDS, security and the military in Africa: A sober appraisal. *African Affairs* 105(419): 201–18. Also in A. Barnett and G. Prins (eds), *HIV/AIDS and security: Fact, fiction and evidence: A report to UNAIDS.* London: LSEAIDS.

WHO (World Health Organization) (2007). *World health report 2007: A safer future. Global public health security in the 21st century.* Geneva.

D3.1 **Protecting breastfeeding**

Today nearly all governments and health-care institutions recognise breast-feeding as a health priority. Yet global breastfeeding rates remain well below acceptable levels – according to the United Nations Children's Fund (UNICEF), 'more than half the world's children are not as yet being optimally breastfed', and many children suffer from malnutrition and chronic morbidity as a consequence of sub-optimal breastfeeding. Improved breast-feeding practices could save some 1.5 million children's lives per year (WHO 2001; UNICEF 2008). One of the causes of the problem is the persistent marketing of infant formula products by commercial companies. According to UNICEF (1997): 'Marketing practices that undermine breastfeeding are potentially hazardous wherever they are pursued: in the developing world, WHO estimates that some 1.5 million children die each year because they are not adequately breastfed. These facts are not in dispute.'

Formula companies give the impression that promoting breast-milk substitutes is like any other type of advertising. However, artificial feeding products are not like other consumer or even food products. The object of artificial feeding is the replacement of a fundamental reproductive activity that destroys the natural sequence of birthing to feeding. Artificial feeding is inferior to breastfeeding, costly and, in many parts of the world, tragically harmful.

While no one would suggest a complete ban on infant feeding formula, it is imperative that women are not misled by spurious or misleading information about artificial feeding, and that health-care systems do not deliberately or inadvertently support inappropriate artificial feeding or diminish the importance of natural feeding.

The evolution of the problem

The establishment of bottle-feeding cultures is embedded in the history of the development and promotion of industrial 'replacement' products. Since the late nineteenth century, Nestlé, the world's largest producer of infant formulas, has undermined women's confidence in their ability to breastfeed and, through clever social marketing, created a benign acceptance of its products.

Initially, a lack of knowledge about the sub-optimal nutritional value of artificial milk and the important protective immunological properties of breastmilk helped create a more accepting environment for artificial feeding, especially among mothers who had to work outside the home. Marketing included the association of artificial feeding with being a good (even angelic) mother, and persuaded communities that formula milk is nutritionally better, as well as more fashionable and modern than breast-milk. Special promotions and the liberal provision of free samples drew women into the practice of artificial feeding in many parts of Asia, Africa and Latin America. By the 1970s it was estimated that only 20 per cent of Kenyan babies and 6 per cent of Malaysian babies were predominantly breastfed (WABA 2006).

Health-care workers have also been complicit. The industry has success-fully established subtle and overt advertising through the health system by providing health workers with free 'gifts' that carry the logos of companies and products, publishing 'health education' materials and sponsoring health conferences. All this helps companies and their products to be identified with those who promote and protect health.

Once seduced into using artificial milk, mothers can become trapped by their decision. In poor economic situations, they can soon find themselves diluting formula milk or turning to cheap replacements to calm a hungry baby. The desperation of mothers of young babies dependent upon formula foods in New Orleans after the Hurricane Katrina disaster demonstrates that similar problems can occur in developed countries as well. Responses to humanitarian emergencies and natural disasters still often result in inappropriate donations of formula foods from governments, the public and milk companies; there have also been allegations of 'dumping' formula that is close to expiry.

The developing world, where the majority of the world's babies are born, is seen as a lucrative market for infant-food industries. The threat of undermining normal infant and young child feeding has expanded to include commercial food products to address nutrition needs of the 6- to 24-month age group. Follow-on milks were developed by companies as a strategy to get around the restrictions of the International Code of Marketing Breastmilk Substitutes. The aggressive promotion of these milks, which are supposedly for older babies, is very confusing and health professionals all over the world have long noted how these milks inevitably end up being used as breastmilk substitutes for very young babies.

In an attempt to circumvent the strong condemnation they receive from the global health community, many companies have formed 'partnerships' with UN agencies ostensibly to combat malnutrition. No doubt these industries see good business sense in linking their brands with the humanitarian image of UN agencies in order to benefit from the billions in aid funds pouring into these agencies from donor governments. Global Alliance for Improved Nutrition (GAIN) global health partnership opens its website with the message, 'Improving nutrition can also seriously benefit your business by creating growth in new and existing markets.'

The health effects of the problem

Breastmilk is vital for mother and child health, regardless of socioeconomic setting. Although the health and development consequences of less than optimal breastfeeding are significantly worse for mothers and infants in low-income countries, research on the risks of formula feeding finds an increased risk of gastric and respiratory infectious diseases, higher levels of non-communicable diseases such as diabetes, and lower IQ capacity and visual acuity (Malcove et al. 2005; Weyerman et al. 2006; Cesar et al. 1999). Studies have demonstrated mortality rates up to 25 per cent higher for artificially fed compared to breastfed children (Victora et al. 1989; WHO 1981).

Over the past few years, milk companies have also exploited the dangers and concerns associated with HIV transmission through breastmilk (Iliff et al. 2005). Evidence, however, shows that exclusive breastfeeding for the first months of life reduces both mortality and the risk of transmission (Guise et al. 2005).

During early 2006, Botswana was battered by a diarrhoeal outbreak serious enough to require outside intervention from the Center for Disease Control (CDC) and UNICEF. Most of those affected were infants under eighteen months old. Abnormally heavy rains in the first months of 2006 resulted in flooding and dirty puddles of standing water, which combined with poor sanitation to spread the disease, killing 470 children between January and April. According to UNICEF, infant formula played a significant role in the outbreak and the CDC reports that formula-fed babies were disproportionately affected by the disease – one village, for example, lost 30 per cent of formula-fed babies. According to a report by the National

AIDS Map organisation, not having been breastfed was the most significant risk factor associated with children being hospitalised during the period of the outbreak.

The International Code of Marketing Breastmilk Substitute

When it became recognised that artificial feeding was both harmful and being promoted in ways that were unethical, a civil society campaign led by the International Baby Food Action Network (IBFAN) successfully enabled the World Health Organization (WHO) and UNICEF to establish the International Code of Marketing of Breastmilk Substitutes (the International

---

BOX D3.1.1 **Summary of the International Code**

1. No advertising or promotion of breastmilk substitutes to the public.
2. No free samples or gifts to mothers.
3. No promotion of products covered by the Code through any part of the health-care system.
4. No company-paid nurses or company representatives posing as nurses to advise mothers.
5. No gifts of personal samples to health workers.
6. No words or images, such as nutrition and health claims, idealising artificial feeding or discouraging breastfeeding, including pictures of infants on product labels.
7. Only scientific and factual information may be given to health workers regarding the product.
8. Information explaining the benefits of breastfeeding and the costs and hazards associated with artificial feeding must be included in any information on the product, including the labels.
9. No promotion of unsuitable products, such as sweetened condensed milk.
10. Warnings to parents and health workers that powdered infant formula may contain pathogenic microorganisms and must be prepared and used appropriately, and that this information is conveyed through an explicit warning on packaging.
11. Governments must provide objective information on infant and young child feeding, avoiding conflicts of interest in funding infant feeding programmes.
12. No financial support for professionals working in infant and young child health that creates conflicts of interest.

Source: IBFAN 2007.

Code) (IBFAN 2007). This was adopted by the World Health Assembly (WHA) in 1981 as a *minimum* requirement for all member states, which are required to implement it in its entirety in their national guidelines and legislation on the marketing of infant feeding formulas, bottles and artificial nipples (see Box 3.1.1).

Subsequently a number of additional resolutions have been adopted. These resolutions have equal status to the International Code and close many of the loopholes exploited by the baby food industry. Some of the resolutions include stopping the practice of free or low-priced breastmilk substitutes being given to health facilities (1992); ensuring that complementary foods are not marketed for or used in ways that undermine exclusive

---

BOX D3.1.2   **The International Baby Food Action Network**

IBFAN is a global network with a presence in over 100 countries. It has been successfully working since 1979 to protect health and reduce infant and young child deaths and malnutrition. Some of its priority activities include:

- Supporting national implementation of the Global Strategy for Infant and Young Child Feeding, adopted at the World Health Assembly (WHA) by a resolution in 2002.
- Monitoring compliance to the International Code of Marketing of Breastmilk Substitutes as well as subsequent relevant WHA resolutions at the country level.
- Raising awareness of and support for the human right to the highest attainable standard of nutrition and health for women and children.
- Protecting all parents' and carers' rights to sound, objective and evidence-based information.
- Informing the public of the risks of artificial feeding and commercial feeding products.
- Working to improve the quality and safety of products and protecting optimal, safe infant feeding practices through the Codex Alimentarius product standard-setting process.
- Promoting maternity protection legislation for mothers returning to work.
- Promoting sustainable complementary feeding and household food security recommending the widest possible use of indigenous nutrient-rich foods.
- Supporting and providing health worker training for the implementation of the UNICEF/WHO Baby Friendly Hospital Initiative.

and sustained breastfeeding (1996); recognising exclusive breastfeeding for six months as a global public health recommendation and declaring that there should be no infant-food industry involvement in infant nutrition programme implementation (2002).

IBFAN monitors the implementation of the Code, and their 2006 report notes that to date some 32 countries have incorporated the full Code into law; 44 countries have partially incorporated the Code into law; 21 have established the Code as voluntary guidelines (IBFAN 2006). The US and Canada have taken no action at all.

Case studies

I   *Commercial pressure: the case of the Nestlé boycott*

Nestlé is the largest baby food manufacturer in the world. For decades, as industry leader, it has led the way in aggressively marketing its products. Saleswomen were dressed in nurses' uniforms and sent into the maternity wards of hospitals throughout many parts of the world. Mothers faced a constant barrage of formula advertisements on billboards, television and radio. Aggressive marketing by Nestlé and its competitors under-mined breastfeeding, contributing to a dramatic drop in rates in many countries.

In 1977, a public interest group based in Minneapolis, INFACT USA, launched a campaign to boycott the company's products. Campaigners urged the public not to buy Nestlé brands until it changed its marketing policies. By 1981, the boycott was international and the momentum it gathered contributed to the creation of the International Code. Nestlé's public image was at an all-time low. By 1984, with the boycott in effect in ten countries, Nestlé promised to halt its aggressive promotion and adhere to the International Code and the boycott was suspended. However, the IBFAN groups continued to monitor and the hollowness of Nestlé's promises soon became apparent – while some of the most obvious viola-tions, such as sales staff dressed as nurses and babies' pictures on formula labels, had been stopped, the company had no intention of abiding by all the provisions of the International Code, particularly now the boycott had been suspended. The boycott was reinstated in 1989.

While the boycott has compelled Nestlé to change some policies, such as the age of introduction of complementary foods, and stops specific cases of malpractice if these gain sufficient exposure, Nestlé continues systematically to violate the International Code. It remains the target of the world's largest international consumer boycott, which, in this second round, has been launched by groups in twenty countries. An independent survey by GMI found in 2005 that Nestlé is one of the four most boycotted companies on the planet (GMI Poll 2005).

Official statements from Nestlé claim that the company abides by the International Code, but only in 'developing nations'. This itself is a violation of the International Code, because, as the name suggests, it is a *global* standard and companies are called on to ensure their practices comply in every country, not just those of Nestlé's choosing.

Nestlé has also fought hard to prevent countries enshrining the International Code in legislation. For instance in 1995, the company filed a Writ Petition with the government of India that challenged the validity of proposed laws implementing the International Code. Nestlé claimed that a law implementing the International Code would restrict its marketing rights and would be unconstitutional. Nestlé battled hard in the courts to stop the Code's legislation in India, but fortunately failed to do so, and India has since passed exemplary laws, which enshrine the Code in national legislation.

2   *Commercial pressure: the case of the Philippines*

Despite the incorporation of almost all of the provisions of the International Code into domestic law in 1981, formula advertising has run rampant in the Philippines over the past two and a half decades. Advertisements on Filipino television claim that formula makes babies smarter and happier and company representatives are sent into the country's poorest slums to promote formula directly to mothers. As a result of these aggressive marketing tactics, the Philippines has some of the lowest recorded breastfeeding rates in the world. Only 16 per cent of Filipino children are breastfed exclusively at four to five months of age, and each year it's estimated that 16,000 infants die from inappropriate feeding practices (Jones et al. 2003). The Department of Health estimates that at least $500 million is spent annually on imported formula milk and over $100 million is spent promoting these products (Nielsen 2006) – more than half the total annual Department of Health budget – and where 40 per cent of the population live on less than $2 a day. To combat this national health disaster, in May 2006 the Department of Health (DOH) drafted the Revised Implementing Rules and Regulations (RIRR), which updated the 1981 law and sought to ban formula advertising altogether.

Almost immediately the formula industry fought back, using the powerful US-based Chamber of Commerce, claiming that the RIRR would illegally restrict their right to do business. In 2006, the Pharmaceutical and Health Care Association of the Philippines (PHAP), representing three US formula companies (Abbott Ross, Mead Johnson and Wyeth), Gerber (now owned by Swiss Novartis) and other international pharmaceuticals giants, took the Filipino government to court. In July 2006, the Supreme Court declined PHAP's application for a temporary restraining order to stop the RIRR from coming into effect.

Three weeks later, in a leaked letter dated 11 August 2006, the president of the US Chamber of Commerce, Mr Thomas Donohue, warned President Arroyo of 'the risk to the reputation of the Philippines as a stable and viable destination for investment' if she did not re-examine her decision to place marketing restrictions on pharmaceuticals and formula companies and restrict the promotion of infant foods. Within a month, on 15 August, four days after the letter from the American Chamber of Commerce was received, the Supreme Court overturned its own decision by granting a temporary restraining order in favour of PHAP.

However, following an international support campaign coordinated by IBFAN and the Save Babies Coalition, in October 2007 the Supreme Court lifted the restraining order and upheld the following provisions and principles:

- The scope of the laws should cover products for older children, not just infants up twelve months.
- The right of the Department of Health to issue regulations governing formula advertising.
- The need for formula labels to carry a statement affirming there is no sub-stitute for breastmilk, and for powdered formula labels to carry a warning indicating the product may contain pathogenic microorganisms.
- Company information targeting mothers may not to be distributed through the health-care system.
- The necessity for the independence of infant feeding research from baby milk companies.
- Companies cannot be involved in formulating health policy.
- A prohibition on donations (of covered products) and the requirement of a permit from the DOH for donations of non-covered products from companies.

The Court also ruled that the marketing of formula must be

objective and should not equate or make the product appear to be as good or equal to ... or undermine breastmilk or breastfeeding. The 'total effect' should not directly or indirectly suggest that buying their product would produce better individuals, or result in greater love, intelligence, ability, harmony or in any manner bring better health to the baby or other such exaggerated and unsubstantiated claim. (Supreme Court of the Philippines 2007)

While the Court decided not to uphold the outright ban on advertising called for by the health advocates, the committee overseeing the advertising is empowered to curtail the vast majority of it, and the enormous publicity generated by the case has hopefully helped to promote breastfeeding among Filipino mothers.

The campaign now moves to the next stage to close a loophole in the primary legislation to ban advertising completely.

3 *India's legislation on infant-milk substitutes*

The history of the battle against bottle feeding in India dates back to the 1970s when multinational companies promoted infant foods through advertisements and aggressive marketing.

In 1981, Indian prime minister Indira Gandhi made a stirring speech at the WHA in support of the International Code. Many member states agreed to invigorate a suitable national legal framework for implementation of the Code. In 1983, the Indian government launched the 'Indian National Code for Protection and Promotion of Breastfeeding'. Meanwhile several individuals and organisations like Voluntary Health Association of India (VHAI) led national advocacy initiatives with parliamentarians to enact legislation for the protection of breastfeeding.

However, due to the lobbying of baby-food companies, it took eleven years for comprehensive legislation on infant-milk substitutes to be formulated. The Infant-milk substitutes, Feeding Bottles and Infant Foods (IMS) Act came into force in August 1993. With this, India became the tenth country to pass such legislation.

However, having passed this law, India found that it was not fully equipped to implement it and curb the unlawful marketing of the milk companies. In addition there were some ambiguities in the law about the difference in the terms 'infant-milk substitutes' and 'infant food'. There were also some gaps relating to the exemption of doctors and medical researchers from the prohibition of 'financial inducements' to health workers.

The Breastfeeding Promotion Network of India (BPNI) and Association for Consumer Action on Safety and Health (ACASH) have been instrumental in exposing the unlawful practices of baby-food manufacturing companies and in pointing out loopholes that existed in the national legislation. In 1994 and 1995 the Government of India issued a notification in the *Gazette of India* to authorise BPNI and ACASH and two other national semi-government organisations to monitor the compliance with the IMS Act and empowered them to initiate legal action. For nearly eight years, effective implementation of the IMS Act has been poor, with infant-food advertisements appearing on soap wrappers, tins of talcum powder and other unrelated products. 'I love you Cerelac' posters were widely displayed in the streets and markets; mandatory warnings were not being printed; feeding bottles were given as 'free gifts'; and government-led media also aired commercials of 'Cerelac' and nearly all television channels broadcast commercials for baby foods. The hold of the baby-food manufacturers on the health system grew. Free samples of baby food were given to doctors for 'testing'. Nestlé offered international fellowships to paediatricians and sponsored meetings and seminars. Likewise, Heinz announced sponsorship for research in nutrition.

In 1994, ACASH took Nestlé to court for advertising the use of formula *during* the 'fourth' month when the IMS Act stated that infant foods could only be introduced *after* the fourth month. In 1995, the court took cognisance of offence and admitted the case against Nestlé to face trial, saying that there is sufficient matter on record to proceed with criminal proceedings for violating the IMS Act. Nestlé has been trying since then to find some means to challenge the basic allegation. However, no higher court has so far granted an injunction.

Nestlé has since challenged the validity of the IMS Act in a petition filed in the High Court. Final decisions on this case are still awaited. Apart from Nestlé, two other companies were also taken to court for violating the IMS Act. Johnson & Johnson was the first, which faced two cases for selling feeding bottles on discount, and for the advertising of feeding bottles and promotion of a 'colic-free nipple' (teat). The company has since voluntarily agreed to withdraw completely from the feeding bottle market in India and stopped its manufacturing in late 1996, finally withdrawing completely in March 1997.

Wockhardt, an Indian manufacturer of pharmaceuticals and infant formula, was also taken to court by ACASH due to violations of the labelling requirements similar to those committed by Nestlé. Wockhardt apologised through an affidavit in the Magistrate's Court, undertook to follow the rules, and volunteered to stop using the name of its formula for other paediatric products, such as vitamin drops, which were being used for surrogate advertising of formula.

Acting on BPNI's advice, the Information and Broadcasting Ministry amended the Cable Television Networks Regulation Amendment Act 2000 and its Rules that banned direct or indirect promotion of infant-milk substitutes, feeding bottles and infant foods. Overnight, advertisements on baby food and infant-milk substitutes disappeared from Indian television channels. The action taken by this ministry was a significant victory for breastfeeding advocates and a lesson that other countries could draw on.

Based on their earlier experience, the continued violations by baby-food manufacturers, and the new World Health Assembly (WHA) resolutions, in 1994, BPNI and ACASH approached the government to amend the IMS Act in order to improve the regulation of the marketing of baby foods. The Ministry of Human Resource Development constituted a national task force consisting of experts from various ministries and departments of government as well as voluntary agencies to look into this and suggest amendments. Many meetings of this task force took place.

Workshops to sensitise the media and political leaders were organised. Finally, in 1998, the task force recommended amendments to the 1992 law. However, multinationals succeeded in ensuring that the process was stalled. With the continued efforts of the civil society groups, in March 2002 the bill was taken back to the lower house of parliament before finally being passed in both houses of parliament in May 2003 – some fourteen months after the process began.

The new law now prohibits the following:

- Promotion of all kinds of foods for babies under the age of 2 years.
- Promotion of infant-milk substitutes, infant foods or feeding bottles in any manner including advertising, distribution of samples, donations, using educational material and offering any kind of benefits to any person.
- All forms of advertising including electronic transmission by audio or visual transmission for infant-milk substitutes, infant foods or feeding bottles.
- Promotion of infant-milk substitutes, infant foods or feeding bottles by a pharmacy, drug store or chemist shop.
- Use of pictures of infants or mothers on the labels of infant-milk substitutes or infant foods.
- Funding of 'health workers' or an association' of health workers for seminars, meetings, conferences, educational courses, contests, fellowships, research work or sponsorship.

Despite legislative provisions, Nestlé and other companies have not been thwarted. Under the guise of its Nestlé Nutrition Services, Nestlé continues to sponsor doctors' meetings, and many new strategies are being used to push the company's products.

In 2005, the IMS Act as amended in 2003 was under threat. A campaign to save the Act involving both governmental and civil society organisations, with support from the media, was successful.

The Indian experience demonstrates how the sustained advocacy and action by civil society groups can influence public opinion and decision-makers. Forging links and working with people's representatives in political parties in order to focus their attention on issues that affect their constituencies is also crucial. Campaigns and activist initiatives are doomed to fail if the political will to address a situation does not exist.

India has yet to see the impact of the IMS Act on child malnutrition. However, merely a change in legislation is insufficient. Efforts must now focus on increasing breastfeeding rates in the country.

References

Cesar, J.A., et al. (1999). Impact of breastfeeding on admission for pneumonia during postneonatal period in Brazil: Nested case-controlled study. *BMJ* 318: 1316–20.

Estavillo, M. (2006). Pharmaceutical firms protest looming ban on infant milk ads. *Business World*, 14 July.

GMI Poll (2005). More than a third of all consumers boycott at least one brand. Press release, 29 August. www.gmi-mr.com/gmipoll/release.php?p=20050829.

Guise, J.M., et al. (2005). Review of case-controlled studies related to breastfeeding and reduced risk of childhood leukemia. *Paediatrics* 116: 724–31.

IBFAN (International Baby Food Action Network) (2006). State of the code by country. Penang.

IBFAN (2007). Breaking the rules, stretching the rules. International Code Documentation Centre. Penang.

Iliff, P.J., et al. (2005). Early exclusive breastfeeding reduces the risk of postnatal HIV-1 transmission and increases IV-free survival. *AIDS* 19: 699–708.

Jones, G., et al (2003). How many child deaths can we prevent this year? *The Lancet* 362, 5 July: 65–71.

Malcove, H., et al. (2005). Absence of breast-feeding is associated with the risk of type 1 diabetes: A case-control study in a population with rapidly increasing incidence. *Eur J Pediatr* 165: 114–19.

Supreme Court of the Philippines (2007). *Pharmaceutical and Health Care Association of the Philippines* vs *Health Secretary Franciso Duque III*. Supreme Court decision, 9 October.

UNICEF (1997). Baby milk action. Press release, 14 January. www.babymilkaction.org/resources/yqsanswered/yqacode.html.

UNICEF (2008). Breastfeeding and complementary feeding. www.childinfo.org/eddb/brfeed/index.htm.

Victora, C.G., et al. (1989). Infant feeding and deaths due to diarrhea: A case-controlled study. *Amer J Epidemiol* 129: 1032–41.

WABA (World Alliance for Breastfeeding Action) (2006). Gender, child survival and HIV/AIDS: From evidence to policy. Joint Statement from the conference at York University, Toronto. www.waba.org.my/hiv/conference2006.html.

Weyerman, M., et al. (2006). Duration of breastfeeding and risk of overweight in childhood: A prospective birth cohort study from Germany. *Int J Obes*, 28 February.

WHO (1981). International code of marketing of breastmilk substitutes. Geneva.

WHO (2001). WHA Resolution 54.2: Infant and young child nutrition. May. Geneva. http://ftp.who.int/gb/archive/pdf_files/WHA54/ea54r2.pdf.

D 3.2 **Tobacco control: moving governments from inaction to action**

The ability of the tobacco industry to stay healthy while its customers get sick is one of the more amazing feats of the last century. In the fifty years since it was first established that cigarette smoking causes lung cancer, worldwide tobacco use has increased. Addiction, corporate power, government indifference and poorly informed consumers are among the factors responsible for the spread of the tobacco epidemic.

Every effort to regulate the industry has been met with an equal or greater effort to evade regulation. The industry has delayed, diluted or derailed tobacco control efforts in country after country. Rival companies have coordinated their efforts in opposing legislation, so that the same tactics, arguments and hired consultants have appeared in places as far flung as Canada, Hong Kong, South Africa and Sri Lanka (Saloojee and Dagli 2002).

The global strategy of the tobacco industry has elicited a global public health response. In May 2003, the World Health Assembly (WHA) adopted its first ever treaty – the World Health Organization (WHO) Framework Convention on Tobacco Control (FCTC). The Convention reflects agreement among WHO member states on a set of international minimum standards for the regulation of tobacco use and the tobacco trade. Its basic aim is to stimulate governments worldwide to adopt effective national tobacco control policies. Another aim is to promote collective action in dealing with cross-border issues like the illicit trade in tobacco, Internet sales and advertising.

The WHO sees the Convention as a major weapon in its counterattack against a problem that, if left unchecked, will kill 450 million people in the next fifty years. With 70 per cent of future deaths likely to occur in lower-income countries, the treaty is particularly important for these nations.

TABLE D3.2.1 **An outline of tobacco industry tactics**

Tactic	Goal
Intelligence gathering	Monitor opponents and social trends to anticipate future challenges.
Public relations	To mould public opinion using the media to promote pro-industry positions.
Political funding	Use campaign contributions to win votes and legislative favours from politicians.
Lobbying	Cut deals and influence political process.
Consultancy programme	To produce 'independent' experts critical of tobacco control measures.
Smokers' rights groups	Create impression of spontaneous, grassroots public support.
Creating alliances	Mobilise farmers, retailers and advertising agencies to influence legislation.
Intimidation	Use legal and economic power to harrass and frighten opponents.
Philanthropy	Buy friends and social respectability – from arts, sports and cultural groups.
Litigation	Challenge laws.
Bribery	Corrupt political systems; allow industry to bypass laws.
Smuggling	Undermine tobacco excise tax policies and increase profits.
International treaties	Use trade agreements to force entry into closed markets.

The WHO FCTC has become one of the most widely embraced treaties in the history of the United Nations. By January 2008, 152 parties had ratified the Convention, representing more than 80 per cent of the world's population. This chapter looks at the background to the treaty and its potential role in halting and reversing the tobacco epidemic.

Non-mandatory WHA resolutions

The WHO has long tried to get states to control tobacco. Since 1970, the WHA has adopted twenty resolutions on tobacco and repeatedly called upon member states to take action, but outcomes have been far from optimal. By 2000, about ninety-five countries had legislation regulating tobacco but most states had weak laws. Bans on sales to minors, vague health warnings on tobacco packs, or restrictions on smoking in health facilities are measures commonly adopted. For the most part, such laws are inconsequential, neither seriously threatening the market for, nor affectng the profitability of, tobacco. On the other hand, a handful of countries with comprehensive policies did succeed in reducing tobacco consumption rapidly and significantly.

It is against this background that the WHO changed tack in 1996 by electing to use its treaty-making powers to regulate tobacco. International conventions to reduce marine pollution or to protect the ozone layer had helped states overcome powerful, organised industry resistance to regulation. Such successful environmental pacts served as precedents for the FCTC (Taylor and Roemer 1996).

The negotiations

Formal negotiations on the FCTC commenced in October 2000. The talks were arduous and highly political. An effective treaty could have quickly and readily emerged, if the talks were simply guided by the scientific evidence. Instead, it was clear early on that WHO member states had conflicting interests and obtaining agreement would be difficult. Countries that were host to the major tobacco transnationals argued for optional rather than mandatory obligations, which would significantly weaken the treaty (Assunta and Chapman 2006). As the treaty was to be finalised by consensus, the challenge for health advocates was to find the highest common denominator – to devise a treaty with meaningful policy measures that would also win wide support.

African, Southeast Asian, Caribbean and Pacific Island countries emerged as the champions of a robust treaty that incorporated international best practice. It is these countries that will bear the future brunt of the epidemic and thus it is appropriate that the FCTC reflect their needs.

Some of the keenest debates were on issues like a tobacco advertising ban and on trade. The United States, Germany and Japan opposed a total ban on tobacco advertising and promotion, arguing that it would not be permitted by their respective constitutions. Early drafts of the treaty only prohibited advertising aimed at youth. The majority of countries rejected this proposal as unworkable and ineffective.

This issue was resolved in the final hours of the negotiations, when a compromise championed by the NGO community was accepted. Tobacco advertising and promotion were banned but with a narrow exemption for countries with constitutional constraints. These states were required to take the strongest measures available, short of a total ban.

The final treaty contains significant recommendations on demand, supply and harm-reduction strategies. Among its many measures, the treaty requires countries to increase tobacco taxes; establish clean indoor air controls; impose restrictions on tobacco advertising, sponsorship and promotion; establish new packaging and labelling rules for tobacco products; and strengthen legislation to clamp down on tobacco smuggling (WHO 2003). Mechanisms for scientific and technical cooperation, the exchange of information and reporting were also included.

Making the FCTC work

Experience with other treaties demonstrates that the dynamics of negotiation, peer pressure, creating a commonality of purpose, global standard setting and establishing institutional mechanisms all contribute to effective implementation of treaties.

The FCTC negotiations raised the profile of tobacco control among governments to a level never seen before. States that had previously ignored the issue were exposed to the scientific evidence on the health and economics of tobacco control, other countries' experiences and counter-arguments to the industry's positions on core issues. They actively debated options and agreed the content of the treaty. This generated new understandings, greater political commitment and shifts in behaviour.

The negotiations also galvanised non-governmental organisations (NGOs). Truly global NGO coalitions – the Framework Convention Alliance and the Network for Accountability of Tobacco Transnationals – emerged incorporating health, consumer, environmental and legal groups from North and South. The NGOs provided technical support, supplied detailed analyses of the draft texts and advocated key policy positions. They also played a watchdog role, by naming and shaming, or praising delegations.

To ensure that the momentum is maintained, an intergovernmental body, the Conference of the Parties (COP), is responsible for overseeing the Convention. The COP will take decisions in technical, procedural and financial matters relating to the implementation of the treaty, such as the funding and financial support and monitoring and reporting on implementation progress, and the possible elaboration of protocols, among others.

The impact of the FCTC

In international law, states are the most important actors. It is they who have to translate a treaty into national laws and develop enforcement mechanisms. International treaties provide blueprints for action, but it is not until lawmakers get busy putting decisions into practice at home that lives will be saved.

Public monitoring of compliance with the treaty can provide a powerful incentive for countries to act. As President Mbeki of South Africa noted: 'No head of state will go to the UN and say he or she is for global warming or against the landmine treaty. However, upon returning home from New York or Geneva, under the everyday pressures of government they are likely to forget their treaty commitments.' President Mbeki suggested that it was the task of NGOs to hold governments accountable for their international obligations, so as to make a treaty a reality on the ground.

Already, several states have used the Convention as an umbrella either to introduce new legislation or to revise current laws to bring them into line with the treaty. In 2004, Ireland made history as the first country to implement a total smoking ban in indoor workplaces, including restaurants and pubs. The policy has been remarkably successful, and started a global rush to introduce comprehensive bans on indoor smoking by, among others: England, Estonia, France, Iran, Italy, Montenegro, the Netherlands, New Zealand, Norway, Scotland, Spain, Sweden and Venezuela.

In 2000, Canada became the first country to require picture-based health warnings on tobacco packaging. Countries that have since developed picture-based warnings include: Australia, Belgium, Brazil, Chile, Canada, Hong Kong, India, Jordan, New Zealand, Romania, Singapore, Switzerland, Thailand, the United Kingdom, Uruguay and Venezuela.

Other examples of legislative action in various countries include:

- In 2004, Bhutan banned the sale of tobacco products throughout the Himalayan kingdom. The predominantly Buddhist nation is the first country in the world to impose such a ban.
- Brazil has introduced anti-smuggling measures, including a mechanism for 'tracking and tracing' tobacco products.
- In Cuba, smoking was banned on public transport, in shops and other closed spaces from 7 February 2005. Cuban leader Fidel Castro kicked the habit in 1986 for health reasons.
- France raised the price of cigarettes by 20 per cent in October 2003, provoking a tobacconists' strike.
- India has banned direct and indirect advertising of tobacco products and the sale of cigarettes to children. The law originally included a ban on smoking in Bollywood films.
- In Kenya, a new Tobacco Act was passed in 2007. Among its provisions are a tax increase on tobacco and a ban on smoking in churches, schools, bars, restaurants and sports stadiums.

- South Africa is set to become the first country in the world to have a national ban on smoking in cars when children are present. The country is also set to join New York State and Canada in introducing self-extinguishing cigarettes to reduce the fire risks from tobacco smoking.
- In July 2003, Tanzania banned the selling of tobacco to under 18s and advertising on radio and television and in newspapers. Public transport, schools and hospitals were declared smoke-free zones.

A major challenge in implementing the Convention is that nations will interpret the treaty in different ways. The treaty establishes a set of minimum standards, while encouraging countries to go beyond these. Further, some treaty articles are mandatory and others are discretionary. There is therefore a danger that not all countries will adopt comprehensive tobacco control laws based on best practice, but that a diversity of laws will emerge providing uneven protection for the citizens of different countries and creating potential loopholes that the industry can exploit.

Recognising this problem, the COP will provide guidelines to support countries in drafting more stringent laws. The second meeting of the COP, held in Bangkok in July 2007, adopted guidelines for development of smoke-free legislation. The guidelines recommend the complete elimination of smoking in all indoor public places and workplaces within five years In addition agreement was also reached to:

- begin work on a protocol to address tobacco smuggling;
- develop guidelines for eliminating tobacco advertising and sponsorship or, where this is not constitutionally permissible, regulating advertising;
- develop guidelines for cigarette warning labels;
- begin work towards guidelines on monitoring the tobacco industry, public education, and helping tobacco users quit;
- to continue initial work on tobacco product testing standards and economically viable alternatives to tobacco growing.

To help countries comply with their legal obligations the Convention includes mechanisms to share information, technology, training, technical advice and assistance. Many lower-income countries had hoped for a global fund to support them in implementing the FCTC, but after intense negotiations the donor countries resisted this idea and instead opted for a bilateral approach to funding. This is less than satisfactory from a developing-country perspective. The European Union (EU), for instance, will fund tobacco control as part of development aid. However, few lower-income countries consider tobacco to be a developmental problem, and not a single country has asked the EU to support its tobacco control programmes as part of its development agenda. Unless donors specifically earmark funds for tobacco control activities, the latter will remain a poor cousin of other developmental aid programmes.

Conclusion

Tobacco control involves both politics and science, and until recently science has taken a back seat to politics. The FCTC promotes evidence-based measures to control tobacco. Massive challenges still lie ahead in delivering on the promise of the FCTC, but it is safe to assume that business will not get any easier for the tobacco industry.

References

Assunta, M., and S. Chapman (2006). Health treaty dilution: A case study of Japan's influence on the language of the WHO Framework Convention on Tobacco Control. *J Epidemiol Community Health* 60: 751–6.

Saloojee, Y., and E. Dagli (2002). Tobacco industry tactics for resisting public policy on health. *Bulletin of the World Health Organization* 80: 902–10.

Taylor, A.L., and R. Roemer (1996). An international strategy for global tobacco control. WHO Doc. PSA/96.6. Geneva: WHO.

WHO (2003). WHO framework convention on tobacco control. A56/8. Geneva. www.who.int/gb/EB_WHA/PDF/WHA56/ea568.pdf.

E Postscript: resistance

The earlier chapters in this book highlight inequities and injustice lying at the root of much ill-health, human suffering and premature death. The exploitation of many by a few is illustrated by an increase in poverty during a period of unprecedented wealth generation. While medical advances result in ever increasing longevity among the rich, an average in excess of 26,500 children die every day (almost ten times the death toll of the 11 September 2001 World Trade Center attack) from causes that are preventable and treatable.

This book has argued for changes of policy; more research; better systems of accountability; bigger amounts of aid; the proper regulation of markets; and appropriate intervention when markets fail. However, since many of the causes of global public health problems arise from imbalances in power that permit exploitation and subjugation, our moral obligation to address the political determinants of health is inescapable. As the German physician and scientist Virchow reminded his colleagues in the nineteenth century, 'Medicine is a social science, and politics is nothing but medicine on a large scale.'

In tackling the root political and economic causes of ill-health and injustice, it's useful to be reminded of one fundamental point. Those who currently suffer the brunt of the consequences of injustice are not passive. There is resistance, courage, inspiration and hope to be found in the actions of ordinary individuals who stand up to the abuse of power. This final chapter describes three people's movements that have done exactly that.

To begin with, I ask you not to confuse resistance with political opposition. Opposition does not oppose itself to power but to a government, and its fully-formed shape is that of an opposition party; resistance, on the other hand, cannot be a party, by definition: it is not made in order to govern but ... to resist. (Segovia 1996)

The People's Health Movement Right to Health campaign

The People's Health Movement (PHM) has grown from the fundamental premiss that health care is not a commodity but a human right. The PHM arose from the first People's Health Assembly in 2000 in Savar, Bangladesh. Approximately 1,500 people from 75 countries met for five days to share, discuss and develop strategies to put health care back into the hands of the people. The meeting unanimously resolved to establish a People's Health Movement.[1] The foundations include various health groups campaigning against growing disparities in access to health care; the expansion of user fees; and the abandonment by the WHO of the principles of the 1978 Alma Ata Declaration. It grew from a need to analyse the state of global health through a political lens.

At the core of the PHM is the commitment to give a voice to those who are being excluded and violated by the system. By supporting people affected or excluded by the system to speak out in public forums, there is a building of solidarity that is deeply empowering. In identifying violations, these forums have sometimes led to confrontation with those responsible and to the regaining of health rights.

The PHM's vision of health care is based on the primary health-care approach that includes preventive, curative and rehabilitative health services,

IMAGE E1   **People's Health Movement: launch of Right to Health campaign in South Africa**

as well as health promotion through public provision of adequate and safe food, sufficient clean drinking water and sanitation and adequate housing, as well as other social goods. Whilst the PHM has a special focus on health systems, other determinants of health are actively promoted by the PHM and engaged with at various levels, including campaigns on the right to water, education, housing and food. The PHM recognises the fundamental role of oppressive power structures and encourages resistance against the injustices of the neoliberal system.

> Illness and death every day anger us. Not because there are people who get sick or because there are people who die. We are angry because many illnesses and deaths have their roots in the economic and social policies that are imposed on us. (voice from the People's Health Assembly, Cuenca, Ecuador)

In India, the health system has been in a state of crisis for some time. The intensification of privatisation and the grossly inadequate levels of public funding have led to a deterioration of health services and high rates of denial of care, maltreatment and household impoverishment.

The 'Jan Swasthya Abhiyan' (JSA) (or PHM India) emerged in 2000 out of the growing activism for health.[2] In 2003, the twenty-fifth anniversary of the Alma Ata 'Health for All' declaration, the JSA launched the 'Right to Health Care Campaign'. The first phase of the campaign involved documenting individual instances of denial of health services and recording of structural denial of health care. A national public consultation was organised in Mumbai and attended by hundreds of delegates from sixteen

IMAGE E2 **Right to Health Campaign march, South Africa, 2007**

states across India. At the consultation, over sixty cases of 'denial of health care' were presented. Testimonies included the deaths of children from common illnesses and of women due to botched sterilisations in badly equipped camps. The chairperson of the National Human Rights Commission (NHRC) acknowledged the frequent accounts of human rights violations and promised action.

Subsequently 'Jan Sunwais' (People's Health Tribunals) were held in some states: these were public hearings at which people were supported to make public testimonies concerning their experience of being denied health care in front of impartial adjudicators and government health officials. This strategy of holding hearings in front of large audiences publicised health rights violations, put pressure on health systems to become accountable, and raised awareness of health rights among the masses.

In 2004, the JSA, in collaboration with the NHRC, organised Public Hearings on the Right to Health Care in all regions of India. Each hearing was attended by hundreds of delegates from various districts and states, along with key public health officials. The hearings were widely advertised in regional newspapers and many people came forward to present their testimonies. This opportunity to share was hugely empowering and the movement began to take on its own momentum.

These hearings culminated in a National Public Hearing on the Right to Health Care that was attended by the central health minister, senior health officials from twenty-two states across the country and the NHRC chairperson and officials. Over a hundred JSA delegates from over twenty states presented numerous health-rights violations, and nine sessions on key areas of health rights were held, including on women's and children's health rights, mental health rights, and health rights in the context of the private medical sector. The hearing concluded with the declaration of a national action plan to operationalise the Right to Health – jointly drafted by the NHRC and JSA.

Prior to the 2004 elections, discussions took place between JSA panellists and representatives of several political parties on the need to strengthen public health services. In 2005, the newly elected government launched the National Rural Health Mission (NRHM), expressing a renewed commitment to strengthen public health systems. The Mission envisages a substantial increase in the national health budget, a woman community health worker in each village of the eighteen focus states, provision of united funds and strengthening of public health facilities at various levels, and decentralised planning of public health services. However, being a programme for 'health system reform in the era of globalisation–privatisation', it is a mix of policy elements, making provision for semi-privatisation and privatisation of health services. JSA members continued to fight to strengthen the core public health rights in the Mission and introduced a number of monitoring mechanisms to counter the negative provisions leading towards privatisation. In direct response to the NRHM, JSA launched a 'People's Rural Health Watch' in eight northern states, through which communities actively monitor the quality of care and are enabled to propose suggestions and alternative strategies for the improvement of health.

As a follow-up to the public hearings, JSA represented civil society during national review meetings on health rights organised by NHRC in 2006 and 2007. JSA representatives testified on the state of implementation of the national action plan and on the status of public health services. The idea of developing People's Health Plans has also emerged in discussions in JSA. The Plans were seen as a necessary component in the process of making public health systems work effectively and in a responsive manner. This kind of local, appropriate people's control and planning could pose one of the most definitive challenges to hegemonic globalisation. JSA continues to provide a platform for collaboration among various streams of the health movement dealing with the health rights of various groups with special health needs, taking an overall health system perspective.

There is now a global 'Right to Health and Health Care Campaign' (RTHHCC) and groups in other countries have embarked on a similar process to that undertaken in India. There are currently about twenty countries with active committees signed up to the RTHHCC, some of which have begun implementing campaign activities, including Guatemala, Brazil, Uruguay, Paraguay, Ecuador, South Africa, Benin, Congo, Democratic Republic of the Congo, Cameroon, Gabon, Egypt, Morocco, Burkina Faso, Bangladesh, the US and India. A further seventeen countries have groups that have expressed interest in initiating a campaign in their country, but have not yet started activities.

But the struggle for health is more than a struggle to ensure responsive and effective health care. It is also a struggle against an economic and political system that keeps millions of people oppressed and impoverished. Millions of people experience life as a series of economic and political assaults upon their dignity and livelihoods and this inevitably undermines their health.

Resistance in Mexico

The Zapatistas are a people's movement in Mexico fighting for freedom, democracy and justice. The Zapatistas, the majority of whom are indigenous, fight for the rights of vulnerable and indigenous people in Mexico and affiliate themselves with subjugated groups globally. While resistance to oppression and exploitation has existed for decades, a more focused and explicit form of resistance began in 1994 when the Zapatista National Liberation Army (ZNLA) occupied four areas of significance in Chiapas. The date was chosen to coincide with the launch of the North American Free Trade Agreement (NAFTA) in Mexico – an agreement that is already threatening the survival of poor and indigenous communities. The military responded to the ZNLA by forcefully trying to recapture the towns. Chiapas, the ancestral land of the Mayas and Zoques, has a wealth of natural resources. Extraction and exploitation, however, have made it the poorest state in Mexico.

As campaigns for the 2006 national elections began in Mexico, the ZNLA launched 'The Other Campaign'. This was to campaign for an end to privatisation of public resources and autonomy for indigenous communities; and to raise consciousness and open space for dialogue.

The state of Oaxaca, ancestral land of the Mixtecs and Zapotec people, is also rich in natural resources and has the greatest biodiversity in Mexico. It is home to a third of the country's indigenous population. It is also the second poorest state in the country, with three-quarters of the population living in extreme poverty. Education provisions are severely neglected and health care is minimal. The state's resources and residents are heavily exploited and corruption is common.

In 2006, Oaxaca city and much of the state of Oaxaca became a government-free autonomous zone. In today's world of heightened control of populations, this was, and continues to be, an incredible display of strength and resistance. It began in May 2006 when teachers held a peaceful strike and protested against their poor working conditions. In June, the governor, Ulises Ruiz Ortiz, responded to the protests by sending state and municipal police on a raid against 15,000 encamped protesters. The encampment was set aflame and protesters and their families were assaulted and fired upon. The protesters fought back and later regrouped en masse – between 300,000 to 500,000 people marched to express outrage at their treatment.

The injustice and violence of the state's attack transformed a peaceful protest into resistance that has drawn widespread national and international support. Social organisations, co-operatives, unions and civilians organised to form the 'The Popular Assembly of the Peoples of Oaxaca' (APPO in its Spanish initials). APPO organised protests and demanded the resignation of Governor Ortiz on the grounds of abuse of power and corruption. Barricades were also erected to prevent the police from re-entering the city.

University students set up 'Radio Universidad', creating a crucial space for discussion, analysis, information exchange, education and solidarity. A group of Oaxacan women marched to the government-owned television station, 'Canal 9', indignant at the biased portrayal of the uprising. When they were refused airtime, they took over the station and began broadcasting the causes of the uprising. Throughout, they emphasised the need for non-violence. At this time, the governor went into hiding.

Over the next months, the uprising built momentum and a series of 'mega-marches' were held. In a state of three and a half million people, an estimated one and a half million people were actively resisting. Meanwhile, paramilitary activity increased and state repression worsened. Many APPO members were tortured and imprisoned and some 'disappeared'. In October, thousands of state troops were sent to bring an end to the uprising. As the battle continued, the repression deepened and many people were forced to go into hiding. Unsurprisingly, the mainstream media distorted coverage of the events in favour of the government.

The resistance persists today. State and federal police continue to use force, but the spirit of the uprising has not diminished. Demonstrations and strikes continue and the people are demanding the release of hundreds of political prisoners. Oaxaca is now labelled 'ungovernable' by the state.

People's opposition to building dams in India

According to archaeologists, the Narmada Valley is the only valley in India that contains an uninterrupted record of human occupation from the Old Stone Age. The Narmada river winds its way through beautiful forest and some of the most fertile land in India before joining the Arabian Sea. The valley is home to 25 million people, mostly Adivasi (indigenous) and low-caste Dalit farmers, who live almost completely autonomously, in a symbiotic relationship with the delicate ecosystem.

The Narmada has been targeted for 'water resource development'; this means the building of 3,200 dams along the 1,300 kilometre river. Whilst big dams have become obsolete in rich countries due to the harm they cause, India has become the third largest dam builder in the world. In 1985, the World Bank offered a loan of $450 million to fund the Sardar Sarovar mega-dam in Narmada, before any studies had been done and before the project had been cleared for human and environmental impact.

In her essay 'The Greater Common Good', Arundhati Roy exposes the disturbing facts of dam construction. Although the government has no records of the number of people displaced by dams, the conservative estimate is a staggering 50 million (Saxena 1999) (more than double the population of Australia). The Narmada Valley Project will submerge and destroy 4,000 square kilometres of natural deciduous forest along with the homes, lives and histories of those who live on the riverbanks. People are being moved, with court orders or forced by policemen and government-controlled militias, into camps. In these substandard resettlement colonies, people are cut off from their means of subsistence, and with no prospect of earning an income their health deteriorates and poverty increases.

Large dams are sold under the slogan of 'People's Dams'; in fact, they take from the people and provide for the powerful. The government claims that the Sardar Sarovar will produce 1,450 megawatts of power. In fact, the dam will consume more than it produces. It is claimed that the immense reservoirs will provide water to millions. In reality it will be providing for sugar mills, golf courses, five-star hotels, water parks, water-intensive cash crops and urban centres. While 85 per cent of Gujarat state's irrigation budget goes on the Sardar Sarovar project, smaller and more appropriate local water projects have been neglected. In the words of Arundhati Roy:

> Big dams are to a Nation's 'Development' what nuclear Bombs are to its Military Arsenal. They're both weapons of mass destruction ... both twentieth century emblems that mark a point in time when human intelligence has outstripped its own instinct for survival. (Roy 1999)

When construction of the Sardar Sarovar began in 1988, a community worker, Medha Patkar, started speaking to people to ascertain whether the resettlement plans for those who were being displaced by the water were adequate and fair. She found them to be completely inadequate and unjust. As the true horror of the dam's impact became clear, various peoples' organisations grouped together and the Narmada Bachao Andolan (NBA) was established. In 1988, the NBA called for all work on the Narmada Valley to cease.

People declared that they would not move from their homes, even if that meant drowning. The NBA was joined by other resistance movements, and in 1989, 50,000 people gathered in the valley to resist. The state responded by turning the site into a police camp and barricading people in. The people pledged to drown rather than move. As international pressure from activist groups developed, the repression intensified. Protesters were repeatedly lifted from the rising waters, arrested and beaten.

In 1990, 6,000 men and women walked over 100 kilometres accompanying a seven-member sacrificial group who had decided to lay down their lives for the river. Police stopped the protesters, whose hands were tied as a statement of non-violence. They were beaten, arrested, and some were killed. The protesters returned and continued their march. In 1991 the sacrificial group went on an indefinite hunger strike.

Resistance to the building of the dam continued, and as national and international media interest increased the World Bank announced that it would set up an independent review of the Sardar Sarovar Dam. The resulting *Morse Report* criticised the Indian authorities and the World Bank and recommended that work on the dam cease immediately (Morse and Berger 1992).

The Indian government, as an emerging superpower, is reluctant to give up the 'nation-building' dams despite the widespread devastation they cause. However, the World Bank withdrew from the Narmada Valley project. They are now more cautious in selecting the countries where they finance projects that involve mass displacement. In China, Malaysia, Guatemala and Paraguay, signs of revolt against dam building have been swiftly crushed.

The stories from Mexico and India describe those under attack – the poor, the indigenous, the landless, those deemed 'lower class' and exploitable by society. However, the vulnerable are affected around the world by a political and corporate complex that concentrates wealth in a few and places profit ahead of lives. As John Berger writes, 'Anybody ... who does not consume, and who has no money to put into a bank, is redundant. So, the emigrants, the landless, the homeless are treated as the waste matter of the system: to be eliminated' (2001).

In April 2008, the Johannesburg High Court in South Africa handed down a historical judgment which declared the city's forcible installation of prepaid water meters in Phiri (part of the huge Soweto township) both unlawful and unconstitutional. The City of Johannesburg has also been instructed to supply residents with 50 litres of free water per day instead of the current 25 litres. Residents must also be given the option to have an ordinary credit metered water supply installed. Currently, residents are only able to either use a standpipe or prepaid water meters. The residents of Phiri and other townships have resisted the installation of prepaid meters and have been fighting for accessible, affordable and sufficient water supply. Although this judgment may be appealed against, residents are confident the decision will be upheld. Other examples of the struggle for clean, affordable water can be found in Chapter C5.

In 2003, an estimated 30 million people in approximately 800 cities around the world protested against the US-led invasion of Iraq. This unprecedented, powerful act of solidarity was the largest demonstration in history. Although this demonstration was significant in size, its overall effects have been minimal at best. The occupation and the injustices it has caused continue. Despite this, the sense that 'another world is possible' has progressively become more tangible. Coordinated global demonstrations continue across a range of struggles against exploitation and injustice.

Ultimately, all these diverse struggles are connected, and each in its own way is a struggle for health.

> I believe in people. People's health is safest in people's hands. The objective is to empower individuals and communities with the knowledge and skills necessary to achieve health for themselves. (Dr John Oommen, Orissa, India, 2003)

Notes

1. See www.phmovement.org.
2. http://phm-india.org/.

References

Berger, J. (2001). Against the great defeat of the world. In *In the Shape of a Pocket*. London: Bloomsbury,

India's greatest planned environmental disaster: The Narmada Valley dam projects. www.umich.edu/~snre492/Jones/narmada.html.

Lendman, S. (2006). Courage and resistance in Oaxaca and Mexico City. www.zmag.org/znet/viewArticle/3296.

Morse, B., et al. (1992). *The report of the independent review*. Ottawa: Resource Futures International.

Roy, A. (1999). The greater common good. In *The Cost of Living*. New York: Random House.

Saxena, N.C. (1999). Secretary to the Planning Commission, private lecture organised by the Union Ministry of Rural Areas and Employment, New Delhi, 21 January.

Segovia, T. (1996). *Alegatorio*. Mexico: Ediciones Sin Nombre.

Contributors

Managing editors

David McCoy.
Antoinette Ntuli.
David Sanders.

Contributors and reviewers

Edlyne Anugwom, University of Lagos.
Nurul Izzah binti Anwar Ibrahim, People's Justice Party.
Yolanda Augustin.
Peter Barron, Health Systems Trust.
Francoise Barten, Radboud University Nijmegen, UMCN, International Health and
    People's Health Movement.
Sonja Bartsch, German Institute of Global and Area Studies.
Fran Baum, People's Health Movement Australia and Department of Public Health,
    Flinders University, Adelaide.
Sara Bennett, Alliance for Health Policy and Systems Research.
Martine Berger, Council on Health Research for Development (COHRED).
Valentina Bertotti, Flinders University, Adelaide.
Marion Birch, Medact.
Martin Birley.
Patrick Bond, University of KwaZulu–Natal, Centre for Civil Society.
Mike Brady, Baby Milk Action.
Ruairi Brugha, Royal College of Surgeons in Ireland.
Alice Burt, Centre of International Studies, University of Cambridge.
Elias Byaruhanga, Psychiatry Department, Mbarara Regional Referral Hospital,
    Uganda.
Belinda Calaguas, Director of Policy and Campaigns, ActionAid UK.
Cynthia Callard, Physicians for a Smoke-Free Canada.
Sudeep Chand, University College London, Centre for International Health and
    Development.
Chan Chee Khoon, Universiti Sains Malaysia.

Dhianaraj Chetty, ActionAid International.
Mickey Chopra Health Systems Research Unit, Medical Research Council, South Africa.
John Christensen, Tax Justice Network International Secretariat, London.
Jeff Conant, Hesperian Foundation.
Andrea Cortinois, University of Toronto.
Leonie Cox, Queensland University of Technology.
Kerry Cullinan, Health-e News Service.
Sylvia de Haan, Council on Health Research for Development (COHRED).
Michael Devlin, Council on Health Research for Development (COHRED).
Klaudia Dmitrienko, Department of Public Health Sciences, University of Toronto.
Bob Douglas, Australian National University.
Kristie Ebi, ESS, LLC.
Lucia Fry, Global Campaign for Education.
Kizzy Gandy, Australian National University.
Jane Gilbert, Disaster and Development Centre, Northumbria University, Newcastle upon Tyne.
Cynthia Golembeski, University of Wisconsin.
Spring Gombe, Knowledge Ecology International.
Susan Greenblatt, People's Health Movement.
Amit Sen Gupta, Peoples Health Movement – India.
Arun Gupta, International Baby Food Action Network (IBFAN) Asia.
May Haddad.
Emily Hansson, Global Health Watch and People's Health Movement.
Sophie Harman, University of Warwick and City University, London.
Andrew Harmer, London School of Hygiene & Tropical Medicine.
Shawn Hattingh, International Labour Research and Information Group.
Corinna Hawkes, Centre for Food Policy, City University, London.
Dan Henderson, Flinders Health and Human Rights Group, Adelaide.
Robert Huish, Simon Fraser University, Trudeau Foundation Scholar, Chercheur postdoctorant, Université de Montréal.
Terry Hull, Australian Demographic and Social Research Institute, Australian National University.
Carel Ijsselmuiden, Council on Health Research for Development (COHRED).
Alan Ingram, Department of Geography, University College London.
Ghassan Issa, Arab Resources Collective, Lebanon.
Surinder Jaswal, Tata Institute of Social Sciences, India.
Janaka Jayawickrama, Northumbria University, Newcastle upon Tyne.
Afamia Kaddour, Harvard School of Public Health, Department of Population and International Health.
Maija Kagis, Canadian Society for International Health.
Gayatri Kembhavi, Centre for International Health and Development.
Andrew Kennedy, Council on Health Research for Development (COHRED).
Kate Kenny.
Alex Kent, Global Campaign for Education.
George Kent, University of Hawaii.
Ron Labonte, Institute of Population Health, University of Ottawa.
Kelley Lee, London School of Hygiene & Tropical Medicine.
David Legge, International People's Health University, La Trobe University, Melbourne.
Bridget Lloyd, Global Health Watch and People's Health Movement.
Rhona MacDonald.

Farai Madzimbamuto, Zimbabwe Association of Doctors for Human Rights (ZADHR).
Chris Manz, Duke University, Durham NC.
Jihad Mashal, Palestinian Medical Relief Society.
Kaaren Mathias, Community Health Action Initiative, India.
Karen McColl.
David McCoy, University College London.
David McDonald, Queens University, Kingston ON.
Martin McKee, London School of Hygiene & Tropical Medicine.
Philip McMichael, Cornell University, Ithaca NY.
Diana Mitlin, International Institute for Environment and Development and University of Manchester.
Ravi Narayan, Centre for Health and Equity, Bangalore, and People's Health Movement.
Thelma Narayan, Centre for Health and Equity, Bangalore, and People's Health Movement.
Stephanie Nixon, University of Toronto Department of Physical Therapy, Canada, and Health Economics and HIV/AIDS Research Division (HEARD), South Africa.
Amy North, Institute of Education, University of London.
Henry Northover, WaterAid.
Antoinette Ntuli, Global Equity Gauge Alliance (GEGA) and Health Systems Trust.
Colleen O'Manique, Trent University, Peterborough, ON.
Ashnie Padarath, Health Systems Trust.
Kristin Peterson, University of California, Irvine.
Ben Phillips, Oxfam.
Jack Piachaud, Medact, London.
Jeff Powell, Bretton Woods Project.
Zyde Raad, Harvard School of Public Health.
Martin Rall, Mvula Trust.
Kumanan Rasanathan, University of Auckland.
Sunanda Ray, Zimbabwe Association of Doctors for Human Rights (ZADHR).
Louis Reynolds, People's Health Movement, and School of Child and Adolescent Health, University of Cape Town.
Jon Rhode, James P. Grant School of Public Health, BRAC University, Dhaka.
Michael Rowson, Centre for International Health and Development, UCL Institute of Child Health, London.
Leonard Rubenstein, Physicians for Human Rights.
Patti Rundell, Baby Milk Action.
Simon Rushton, Centre for Health and International Relations, Aberystwyth University.
Peter Ryan, IRC International Water and Sanitation Centre.
Yusef Saloojee, National Council Against Smoking.
Jane Salvage.
David Sanders, School of Public Health, University of the Western Cape and People's Health Movement.
Helen Schneider, Centre for Health Policy, School of Public Health, University of Witwatersrand.
Claudio Schuftan, People's Health Movement.
Andrew Seal, Centre for International Health and Development Institute of Child Health, University College London.
Sangeeta Shashikant, Third World Network.
Abhay Shukla, SATHI-CEHAT.

Victor Sidel, Distinguished University Professor of Social Medicine, Montefiore
   Medical Center, Albert Einstein College of Medicine, Bronx, NY.
Chris Simms, School of Health Services Administration, Dalhousie University, Halifax
   NS.
Anthony So, Duke University, Durham NC.
Jerry Spiegel, Liu Institute for Global Issues, University of British Columbia.
Devi Sridhar, University of Oxford.
Elisabeth Sterken, Infant Feeding Action Coalition Canada and International Baby
   Food Action Network.
Ruth Stern, School of Public Health, University of the Western Cape.
Barbara Stilwell, Capacity Project.
Robin Stott, Medact, London.
Derek Summerfield, Institute of Psychiatry, King's College, University of London.
Riaz Tayob, Third World Network.
Liz Thomas, Medical Research Council and Centre for Health Policy, School of
   Public Health, WITS University.
David Traynor, University of New South Wales.
Laura Turiano, People's Health Movement.
Jose Urtero, Médicos del Mundo España.
Timeyin Uwejamomere, WaterAid.
Ton van Naerssen, Faculty of Management Sciences, Radboud University, Nijmegen.
Michael Watts, Center for African Studies, University of California at Berkeley.
Edmundo Werna, International Labour Organization.
Michael Windfuhr, Human Rights Director, Bread for the World, Germany.
David Woodward.
Mariam Yunusa, UN–Habitat.
Anthony Zwi, School of Public Health and Community Medicine, University of New
   South Wales.

Organizations

ActionAid International.
Alliance for Health Policy and Systems Research.
Arab Resources Collective, Lebanon.
Australian Demographic and Social Research Institute, Australian National University.
Baby Milk Action.
Bretton Woods Project.
Capacity Project.
Centre for Food Policy, City University, London.
Centre for Health and Equity, Bangalore.
Centre for Health and International Relations, Aberystwyth University.
Centre for International Health and Development, University College London
   Institute of Child Health.
Centre of International Studies, University of Cambridge.
Community Health Action Initiative, India.
Cornell University.
Council on Health Research for Development (COHRED).
Department of Geography, University College London.
Department of Public Health, Flinders University, Adelaide.
Department of Public Health Sciences, University of Toronto.
Disaster and Development Centre, Northumbria University, Newcastle upon Tyne.

Duke University, Durham NC.
Flinders Health and Human Rights Group, Adelaide.
German Institute of Global and Area Studies.
Global Campaign for Education.
Harvard School of Public Health, Department of Population and International Health.
Health Systems Trust.
Hesperian Foundation.
Infant Feeding Action Coalition, Canada.
Institute of Education, University of London.
Institute of Population Health, University of Ottawa.
Institute of Psychiatry, King's College, University of London.
Institute of Social Sciences, India.
International Baby Food Action Network (IBFAN).
International Labour Organization.
International Labour Research and Information Group.
International People's Health University, La Trobe University, Melbourne.
IRC International Water and Sanitation Centre.
James P. Grant School of Public Health BRAC University, Dhaka.
Knowledge Ecology International.
Liu Institute for Global Issues, University of British Columbia.
London School of Hygiene and Tropical Medicine.
Mbarara Regional Referral Hospital, Uganda.
Medact.
Médicos del Mundo España.
Mvula Trust.
National Council Against Smoking.
Northumbria University, Newcastle upon Tyne.
Oxfam.
Palestinian Medical Relief Society.
People's Health Movement.
People's Justice Party.
Physicians for a Smoke-Free Canada.
Physicians for Human Rights.
Queens University, Kingston, ON.
Queensland University of Technology.
Royal College of Surgeons in Ireland.
SATHI-CEHAT.
School of Child and Adolescent Health at the University of Cape Town.
School of Health Services Administration, Dalhousie University, Halifax NS.
School of Public Health and Community Medicine, University of New South Wales.
School of Public Health, University of the Western Cape.
Simon Fraser University.
Tax Justice Network, London.
Third World Network.
Trent University, Peterborough, ON.
UN–Habitat.
Université de Montréal.
Universiti Sains Malaysia.
University of Auckland.
University of California, Irvine.
University of Hawaii.
University of Lagos.

University of KwaZulu–Natal, Centre for Civil Society.
University of Oxford.
University of Warwick and City University, London.
University of Wisconsin.
WaterAid.
Zimbabwe Association of Doctors for Human Rights (ZADHR).

Photographers

Image A1 © Ed Kashi, courtesy of Michael Watts.
Image B1.1 © Asem Ansari/ICDDRB, 1979, courtesy of Photoshare.
Image B1.2 © Janaka Jayawickrama.
Image B2.1 © Victor Caivano/PictureNet.
Image B3.1 © Andrew Aitchison.
Image B4.1 © Joao Silva/PictureNet.
Image B5.1 © CCP, courtesy of Photoshare.
Image C1.1 © Emily Hansson.
Image C1.2 © Bridget Lloyd.
Image C3.1 © P. Virot/WHO.
Image C4.1 © Fran Baum.
Image C5.1 © P. Virot/WHO.
Image C5.2 © Curt Carnemark, World Bank.
Image C6.1 © Ed Kashi, courtesy of Michael Watts.
Image C6.2 © Ed Kashi, courtesy of Michael Watts.
Image C6.3 © Ed Kashi, courtesy of Michael Watts.
Image C7.1 © Bridget Lloyd.
Image C8.1 © Alex Kent.
Image C8.2 © Janaka Jayawickrama.
Image D1.4.1 © Louis Reynolds.
Image D1.4.2 Courtesy of Every Stock Photo, http://creativecommons.org/licenses/
    by/2.5/.
Image E1 © Bridget Lloyd.
Image E2 © Bridget Lloyd.

Index

abortion, 329, 341: coercive, 315; 'Global Gag Rule', 311; unsafe, 143, 329
Abt Associates, humanitarian contract, 194
Abu Ghraib prison, 81
Abuja target, health, 40
accountability, 221; official development, 164
Action on Antibiotic Resistance (reAct), 87, 99, 111
ActionAid, 191, 204
Advanced Market Commitments (AMCs), 90
advertising: tobacco, 356–7; Nestlé, 345, 368
'affluenza', 49
Afghanistan: Australian aid, 324; Canadian aid, 322; debt relief, 289, 297; detainee mistreatment, 118; GF Round 2 proposal, 271; reconstruction monies, 295; refugees from, 63; Rustaq earthquake, 187–8; torture victims, 80; US aid, 300
Africa: Canary Islands crossing, 64; history of psychiatry, 51; oil boom, 170–71; refugees in, 63; US military command (AFRICOM), 295; WHO funding, 229; see also sub-Saharan Africa
aggregate incomes, deceptive measure, 12
Agreement on Agriculture, 1994, 128
agriculture: colonial patterns, 142; export subsidies, 23; inputs subsidy removal, 128; Northern subsidies, 127
aid: bilateral, 5; 'boomerang', 329; discretionary nature, 21; EU commitments, 29; tied, 290, 304; untied, 322; water and sanitation, 164
AIDS Access Foundation, 230

Aidspan, 267
air ticket 'solidarity alliance', 41
Aldis, William, 229–30
Algeria, 170–71
Allende, Salvador, 115
Alliance for Open Society, 312
Alma Ata Declaration 1978, 222, 360–61
Al-Mustansiriya University, Iraq, 119
Amin, Samir, 25–6
Amnesty International, 80–81, 83, 174
Angola, 170–71
antibiotic overuse/resistance, 3, 92–9
antimicrobials, R&D, 93
Application of Sanitary and Phytosanitary Measures, 128
Arbenz, Jacob, coup against, 116
Archer Daniels Midland (ADM), 131, 135
Argentina, 25; vegetable oils, 135; Venezuelan loans, 28
Arnove, Robert, 245
Arroyo, Gloria, 347
ASEAN (Association of Southeast Asian Nations), 25
asylum-seekers: definition, 63; detention centres, 68; health-care access, 65; PTSD, 70; US detention centres, 69
AusAID, 324, 326; abortion services prohibition, 329; national security agenda, 327; poverty exacerbation, 328
Australia: aid programme, 289; regional aid spending, 324
Australian Centre for International Agricultural Research, 325
Australian Federal Police, aid delivery, 325, 327